general editor John M. MacKenzie

When the 'Studies in Imperialism' series was founded more than twenty-five years ago, emphasis was laid upon the conviction that 'imperialism as a cultural phenomenon had as significant an effect on the dominant as on the subordinate societies'. With more than ninety books published, this remains the prime concern of the series. Cross-disciplinary work has indeed appeared covering the full spectrum of cultural phenomena, as well as examining aspects of gender and sex, frontiers and law, science and the environment, language and literature, migration and patriotic societies, and much else. Moreover, the series has always wished to present comparative work on European and American imperialism, and particularly welcomes the submission of books in these areas. The fascination with imperialism, in all its aspects, shows no sign of abating, and this series will continue to lead the way in encouraging the widest possible range of studies in the field. 'Studies in Imperialism' is fully organic in its development, always seeking to be at the cutting edge, responding to the latest interests of scholars and the needs of this ever-expanding area of scholarship.

Genteel women

SELECTED TITLES AVAILABLE IN THE SERIES

Race and empire: Eugenics in colonial Kenya
Chloe Campbell

*Labour and the politics of Empire: Britain and Australia
1900 to the present*
Neville Kirk

Gender and imperialism
ed. Clare Midgley

*Gender, crime and empire: Convicts, settlers and the state
in early colonial Australia*
Kirsty Reid

*Child, nation, race and empire: Child rescue discourse,
England, Canada and Australia, 1850–1915*
Shurlee Swain and Margot Hillel

Genteel women

EMPIRE AND DOMESTIC MATERIAL CULTURE, 1840–1910

Dianne Lawrence

MANCHESTER
UNIVERSITY PRESS

Copyright © Dianne Lawrence 2012

The right of Dianne Lawrence to be identified as the author of this work has been asserted by her in accordance with the Copyright, Designs and Patents Act 1988.

Published by Manchester University Press
Altrincham Street, Manchester M1 7JA, UK
www.manchesteruniversitypress.co.uk

British Library Cataloguing-in-Publication Data is available

Library of Congress Cataloging-in-Publication Data is available

ISBN 978 0 7190 9736 2 *paperback*

First published by Manchester University Press in hardback 2012

This paperback edition first published 2015

The publisher has no responsibility for the persistence or accuracy of URLs for any external or third-party internet websites referred to in this book, and does not guarantee that any content on such websites is, or will remain, accurate or appropriate.

Printed by Lightning Source

For Marco and Tom, and in memory of Alf and Mary

CONTENTS

List of illustrations—viii
General editor's introduction—xiii
Acknowledgements—xvi

1	Introduction: gentility and the performance of self	1
2	'Dress indicates mind': the art and practice of appearance management	12
3	'The arrangement requires much taste and judgement': creating critical space, the living room	73
4	'No-one can over-estimate the pleasure of tending flowers': tasteful gardening and growing attachment	135
5	'The guests being seated at the dinner table, the lady serves the soup': food and household management	186
6	Conclusion: the work of migrancy	233

Select bibliography—239
Index—257

LIST OF ILLUSTRATIONS

Figures

2.1 Three women in garden, Queensland, c.1904–9, Photo ID 00901. Photograph reproduced by kind permission of James Cook University Library, Frederick Charles Hall Collection, North Queensland Historic Photographic Collection.   21

2.2 Mrs Spencer Hopkins on verandah at back of the house 'Devanah', Queensland, c.1908, Photo ID 16785. Photograph reproduced by kind permission of James Cook University Library, Hollis Hopkins Family Collection, North Queensland Historic Photographic Collection.   22

2.3 Taking tea on the verandah of 'Rosebank', home of solicitor Russell Young, Hobart, Tasmania, c.1890s, Ref.: Q1999.29.10.8. Collection: Tasmanian Museum and Art Gallery.   23

2.4 Group taking tea on verandah, Queensland, c.1907–9, Photo ID 00576. Photograph reproduced by kind permission of James Cook University Library, Frederick Charles Hall Collection, North Queensland Historic Photographic Collection.   24

2.5 Lady's silk and lace blouse, c.1900, Local History Collection, Townsville Library Service, Townsville City Council. Photograph: D. Lawrence. Reproduced by kind permission of Townsville Library Service.   33

2.6 Purple and black taffeta dress, aniline dyed, c.1875, Costume Collection, Album Notes, Bicentennial Exhibition. Photograph: D. Lawrence. Reproduced by kind permission of Narryna Heritage Museum, Hobart.   40

2.7 Mrs Alphen's dressmaking store, Charters Towers, Queensland, Photo ID 15941. Photograph reproduced by kind permission of James Cook University Library, Hawton/De Castres Collection, North Queensland Historic Photographic Collection.   42

2.8 *Carte-de-visite*, woman in checked dress, c.1850s, Hobart, Tasmania. Private Collection.   59

2.9 *Carte-de-visite*, woman wearing dress with bustle, c.1870s, card printed 'Froup, American Glace Photo

LIST OF ILLUSTRATIONS

	Studio, Maryborough'. Local History Collection, Townsville Library Service, Townsville City Council. Reproduced by kind permission of Townsville Library Service.	60
2.10	*Carte-de-visite*, woman wearing frilled dress, early 1890s, card printed 'H. G. Livesey, Photographer', probably Townsville. Local History Collection, Townsville Library Service, Townsville City Council. Reproduced by kind permission of Townsville Library Service.	61
2.11	Dress, taffeta, early 1890s, label in neckline 'Mrs. Grimaly', David Jones, Sydney, Ref.: H7423. Photograph: Penelope Clay, Powerhouse Museum, Sydney.	62
3.1	Maids cleaning a carpet in garden of 'Rosebank', Elizabeth Street, Hobart, Tasmania, c.1888. Photographer: Russell Young. Ref.: 1999.29.10.2. Collection: Tasmanian Museum and Art Gallery.	89
3.2	Living room, possibly in Allahabad, India, c.1890. Photograph by kind permission of Centre of South Asian Studies, University of Cambridge.	89
3.3	Living room, Sialkot, 1895, home of Col. F. W. and Mrs Egerton, Ref.: Y302200, Royal Commonwealth Society Collections. Photograph reproduced by kind permission of the syndics of Cambridge University Library.	90
3.4	Living room, homestead 'Devanah', Queensland, pre 1915, Photo ID 02720. Photograph reproduced by kind permission of James Cook University Library, Helen Dyer Collection, North Queensland Historic Photographic Collection.	93
3.5	Living room, 'Monomeeth', Landsdown Crescent, West Hobart, Tasmania c.1910. Ref.: PH30/1/9593. Photograph courtesy of Tasmanian Archive and Heritage Office.	94
3.6	Ceiling rose decoration, Clarendon House, Tasmania. Photograph: D. Lawrence. Reproduced by kind permission of the National Trust of Australia (Tasmania).	98
3.7	Zinc panel for ceiling and wall decoration, c.1905, Victoria Esplanade, Hobart, Tasmania. Photograph: A. Melrose, Private Collection.	99
3.8	Hand-painted wallpaper, Government House, Hobart, Tasmania. Conserved 1972 during restoration work, Ref.: NS1309–1–1. Photograph: D. Lawrence. Reproduced by kind permission of the Tasmanian Archive and Heritage Office.	101
3.9	Wallpaper frieze, Runnymede House, Hobart, Tasmania.	

LIST OF ILLUSTRATIONS

	Photograph: D. Lawrence. Reproduced by kind permission of the National Trust of Australia (Tasmania).	102
3.10	Sofa of colonial cedar, double-ended with a Palladian-shaped carved back, on turned legs, secondary timber of huon pine, with gold-regency striped upholstery, c.1835, Clarendon House, Tasmania. Photograph: D. Lawrence. Reproduced by kind permission of the National Trust of Australia (Tasmania).	111
3.11	Detail of 3.10, showing decoration on the arm rest. Photograph: D. Lawrence. Reproduced by kind permission of the National Trust of Australia (Tasmania).	111
3.12	Armchair of Tasmanian blackwood with pink upholstery and matching stool c.1850. Made by either 'Brown' of Launceston or 'Pearson' of Hobart for Clarendon House, Tasmania. Photograph: D. Lawrence. Reproduced by kind permission of the National Trust of Australia (Tasmania).	112
3.13	Mantel drapes of red velvet with white velvet appliqué and chenille embroidery. Photograph: D. Lawrence. Reproduced by kind permission of Narryna Heritage Museum, Hobart.	121
3.14	Needle-run lace depicting kangaroo and apple, made by Miss Ada Wilson, c.1910. Ref.: P1938.49, item 49 in exhibition 'Tasmanian Lace-making: Ada Grey Wilson Lace Collection'. Collection: Tasmanian Museum and Art Gallery.	121
3.15	Sawn weather-board house with timber over-frame, man and two women and children on front verandah, Roma, Queensland. Photo ID 28829. Photograph reproduced by kind permission of James Cook University Library, Architecture North and Western Queensland Collection, North Queensland Historic Photographic Collection.	123
3.16	Living room, possibly Allahabad, India c.1890s. Photograph by kind permission of Centre of South Asian Studies, University of Cambridge.	126
4.1	'The Rector's Garden: Queen of the Lilies', 1877 by Grimshaw, John Atkinson (1836–93), ID: HMP86659, Harris Museum and Art Gallery, Preston, Lancashire, UK/ The Bridgeman Art Library.	139
4.2	Garden in Wellington, India, as painted by Miss Pilkington in her Commonplace Book, 1894. Book comprised of watercolours, annotated pen and ink and colour washes, photographs and mounted ephemera.	

LIST OF ILLUSTRATIONS

	Reproduced by kind permission of Centre of South Asian Studies, University of Cambridge.	143
4.3	Plants of North Queensland, watercolour album, 1888–92, provenance unknown, Rare Books Collection, James Cook University. Photograph: D. Lawrence. Reproduced by kind permission of James Cook University Library.	144
4.4	Front gardens, The Strand, Townsville, 1907, Photo ID 00155. Photograph reproduced by kind permission of James Cook University Library, W. J. Laurie Collection, North Queensland Historic Photographic Collection.	149
4.5	Front of house and garden, 'Omana House', Ref.: G-3156-1/1, date unknown. Photograph reproduced by kind permission of the Auckland Star Collection, Alexander Turnbull Library, Wellington, New Zealand.	150
4.6	Packet of flower seed, c.1900, J. H. Taylor, Launceston, Tasmania, Ref.: TCP631.521TAY, Photograph: D. Lawrence. Reproduced by kind permission of Tasmanian Archive and Heritage Office.	153
4.7	Verandah with rich plant life, 1900, Photo ID 08832. Photograph reproduced by kind permission of James Cook University Library, North Queensland Historic Photographic Collection.	176
5.1	'The Table Tasteful', *The House*, London, 1897. Reproduced by the kind permission of the Museum of Domestic Design and Architecture, University of Middlesex.	195
5.2	Wedding cake and table possibly set for the marriage of Thomas Young to Catherine Foley in 1891, Tasmania, Ref.: 1999.29.10.1. Photographer: Russell Young. Collection: Tasmanian Museum and Art Gallery.	197
5.3	Two women seated at a dining-table on a verandah, Queensland, 1907–9. Photo ID 00575. Photograph reproduced by kind permission of James Cook University Library, Frederick Charles Hall Collection, North Queensland Historic Photographic Collection.	199
5.4	Watercolour sketch of Eva Gray fishing, Queensland, Eva Gray Journal, c.1881. Photograph: D. Lawrence. Reproduced by kind permission of John Oxley Library, State Library Queensland.	218
5.5	Watercolour sketch of Eva Gray shooting, Queensland, Eva Gray Journal, c.1881. Photograph: D. Lawrence. Reproduced by kind permission of John Oxley Library, State Library Queensland.	219

LIST OF ILLUSTRATIONS

Table

3.1 Domestic goods exported from London to sites across the British Empire, November 1894, adapted from *Furniture and Decoration with which is incorporated The Furniture Gazette*. No. 12, vol. 5, December 1894. Copy held at the Museum of Domestic Design and Architecture, (Ref; BADDA 651).   87

GENERAL EDITOR'S INTRODUCTION

It is a special pleasure to introduce this book. The doctoral thesis on which it was based was examined in the study of my home in Perthshire. This happened because I had recently undergone surgery and my convalescence had not proceeded far enough to permit me to travel. In any case, there was a curious appropriateness about the surroundings. While Dianne Lawrence's book is about the maintenance of female gentility in the British Empire, we sat in a house redolent of Scottish Victorian gentility. Old Bank House was built in 1850 by a country solicitor and bank agent as a 'gentleman's residence' appropriate to his status and it exudes the style and tone of that period. No doubt the ladies of the family of this solicitor, William Yeaman, set about some aspects of a form of the gentility which Dianne Lawrence charts. The rooms, the gardens, the original coach house and servants' quarters (no longer part of the main residence) would all have invited it. With the successful conclusion of the 'viva', we were able to withdraw to the formal dining room and indulge in a lunch party which reproduced at least some of the genteel 'foodways' and presentational aspects of Chapter 5. It all seemed a good deal more agreeable than the impersonal surroundings of university offices and restaurants.

But it would be giving an entirely false impression of the arguments of this innovative work if it were to be imagined that genteel women in the Empire were merely struggling to disseminate the cultural and social norms that must have been followed in Old Bank House – and its many English equivalents – in the nineteenth and early twentieth centuries. The central focus of the book is upon environments, the physical environment of the colonial territories covered, and the social (and also racial) environments of settlers in parts of Australia, New Zealand and the Cape, as well as administrators and other 'sojourners' (temporary residents) in India or West Africa. These various environments homed in, as it were, on the residences and gardens of such settlers and expatriates. They were expressed in the character of the rooms, the scale and nature of the verandahs, the furniture, the interior décor, the use of textiles, and much else. They were also reflected in the gardens, the flowers, the vegetables, the social lives, the modes of entertainment, the food, and the relationships with the servants of such people. Within such varied environments, women expressed their gentility through clothing, through efforts at cleanliness, through visiting and entertaining, through gardening and flower arranging, through food preparation and presentation.

Lawrence considers that 'gentility' is a more useful category than social class in these contexts, not least because gentility cuts across gradations of class, of occupation, of income, and varieties of place. Moreover, she demonstrates that the practice or 'performance' of gentility constituted much more than the simple attempt to reproduce forms of Britishness overseas. It was a dynamic process which varied according to environmental and chronological contexts. It incorporated elements of taste, of pride, of gender identity, all of which contributed, for its practitioners, to vital characteristics of moral tone and therefore worth. Moreover, it had many aspects of hybridity about it. It constituted a set of cultural norms which responded to climates, places, and the botanical, culinary and racial situations in which it was practised. Thus gentility was able to accommodate, even promote, aspects of cultural and environmental interaction. In addition, the arrangement and delineation of gentility was dependent upon design fashions and economic forces, upon the importation of textiles, aspects of décor (such as linoleum, carpeting, wallpaper etc.), flower and vegetable seeds, adornments for clothing, tinned foodstuffs and much else. It was also connected with the appearance of new trades at the frontiers of empire, the arrival of dressmakers, cabinet makers, various types of shop, even piano tuners.

The book charts these phenomena through the medium of dress and the presentation of the body, through the vital domestic space of the living room (in which such dress would be displayed), through gardens as the outdoor expression of the home, equally central to the establishment of the genteel frontiers against the dangerous and alien environment beyond, as well as through the preparation and almost ritualistic serving of food within the home or upon the verandah. The range of sources used to arrive at this analysis has been remarkable. They include family letters, newspapers, trade directories, museum collections and the striking visual evidence of photographs. The full list can be found in the bibliography, but suffice it to say that the images and dynamics of gentility have been assessed in striking ways that should help to guide other researchers.

Of course the study is by no means comprehensive – what book can be? – but we do get hints of other aspects of gentility such as the presence and the role of males, the upbringing of children, the physical forms used to facilitate reading and writing, the appearance of new technologies and so on. Future studies may well move on to an examination of genteel bedrooms and dressing rooms, bathrooms and the rituals of washing and bathing, the presence of horses or other animals,

GENERAL EDITOR'S INTRODUCTION

the genteel use of carriages, traps, ultimately bicycles and motor cars. And of course other questions arise such as the spread of these aspects of gentility to the working classes and to indigenous peoples (or their outright rejection as a form of resistance to social or racial colonisation), as well as the manner in which such concepts and practices were modified, rejected or protected in the twentieth century. Gentility constitutes a rich seam which requires a great deal more mining. But Dianne Lawrence's book offers signposts for the ways in which this can be developed. Its great value lies in the fact that it addresses issues of gender, of colonial social life (including relationships with servants of a variety of races), of reactions to environments, of architectural and design modes, of gardening, and of the economic dimensions of the imports necessary for the maintenance of genteel manners. A rich seam indeed.

John M. MacKenzie

ACKNOWLEDGEMENTS

This book is a natural development of my doctoral thesis and it is appropriate to thank the Arts and Humanities Research Council for their generous funding of that initial project. I also welcome this opportunity to thank Lancaster University and its History Department for their subsequently appointing me as an Honorary Research Fellow, a status which has eased my access to archival and library sources and has helped me to keep involved as an independent scholar in the wider academic community.

A substantial part of my research has been conducted in Australia, and for their help I thank Michael Lech of the Caroline Simpson Research Collection, Sydney, Glynis John, Powerhouse Museum, Sydney, the staff of the Tasmanian Archive and Heritage Office[1] and Vickery Avery of the Tasmanian Museum and Art Gallery. A most special thanks are in order to Alison Melrose of Hobart, who has been astonishingly giving of her time, and from whom I have learnt much about Tasmanian cultural history. My work in Queensland would not have been so fruitful, nor yet so enjoyable without the assistance of the staff of the Library of James Cook University, particularly Bronwyn McBurnie who has been so very helpful in securing for me permission to use images from the North Queensland Historic Photographic Collection. For their warm hospitality, kindness and support I thank Alison Melrose, Blair Gamble and Les Bishop in Hobart, Toni McDowell in Bothwell and Alan and Jean Dartnall in Townsville.

Within Britain numerous individuals have provided me with professional assistance and I thank in particular Kevin Greenbank and his colleagues at the Centre of South Asian Studies, Cambridge University, Elizabeth Gilbert of the Lindley Library, Royal Horticultural Society, Diane Backhouse at the Unilever Archives and the staff of the Lancaster University Library. I am grateful to Sue Womersley for her careful reading of the final text, and to Emma Brennan of the Manchester University Press who has so admirably supported this work from proposal to press.

Throughout this enterprise I have been blessed to have the encouragement and support of a host of friends. I thank them one and all – for dinners cooked, for fire-sides shared – and for their indulgence in the face of my obsession with old wallpaper!

I am also delighted to have this space to voice a particular thank-you to my colleague and friend Professor Stephen Constantine of Lancaster

ACKNOWLEDGEMENTS

University. Not only have I profited enormously from his expertise, he has been encouragement itself; urging me on when the task seemed impossible. I am deeply grateful for his help.

For their technical support I thank Marco and Tom Lawrence, whilst appreciation of all else they give is expressed in the dedication.

My acknowledgements of the various personal and professional debts I owe would be incomplete if I did not also grasp this chance to thank Professor John M. MacKenzie, for his introduction to this book. In it he tells of the deliciously toothsome luncheon we shared in the elegantly appointed dining room of his home in rural Perthshire. In so doing he gives due recognition to the value of the domestic within the world's grander concerns, and the genteel women whose lives are considered here would certainly join with me in applauding those sentiments.

Note

1   As from January 2012 the Archive Service of Tasmania, including the Tasmania Library and related collections, have merged to form the Tasmanian Archive and Heritage Office.

1

Introduction: gentility and the performance of self

In 1837 Georgina Malloy wrote from her new home in western Australia declaring 'I must have been all this time now nearly three years without a female soul of my own rank'. Mary Hobhouse was living in the South Island, New Zealand in 1860 when she burst forth in a letter saying, 'Oh dear, how I should have liked to be with you at Fortnum and Mason's before Xmas! All the artificialities to which one attaches so little value when one is in the midst of them change at this distance into blissful and almost poetic visions', and Ada Slatter, not long arrived in the Transvaal Colony in 1904, declared herself to be 'the only lady here and it's pretty awkward at times'.[1] Missing familiar faces, practices and places is a commonplace amongst all who relocate, an inevitable response as old as human migration itself, but in the examples given the longing expressed is less for loved ones, but rather for certain forms of social interaction, set amidst most particular material circumstances. In brief, these women were feeling the lack of a refined terrain. This work scrutinises the processes involved in relocation and resettlement as experienced by such women as Mrs Hobhouse, Mrs Malloy and Mrs Slatter – women of genteel persuasion. Although the model for their aspirations and practices may have been a British one, as experienced first hand or through the filter of preceding generations of migrants, local circumstances called forth notable adaptation and modification of existing norms, and hence the evolution of new forms of gentility. It will be shown that for genteel women their response to the shock of the new and the resultant refashioning of their identities were to find expression through their material culture and its associated practices.[2]

The women investigated lived in the temperate zones of Aotearoa/New Zealand,[3] southern Australia and southern Africa and in the sub-tropical and tropical regions of northern Australia, India and West Africa. This extensive geographical base makes possible an examination of gentility faced with varying climates and terrains, and hence allows consideration of the ways in which aspects of the women's physical environment became part of their cultural landscape. The period of the study circa 1840–1910 permits the inclusion of women in long-established British communities in India, expanding and consolidating colonies of southern Australia and New Zealand, and newly emergent settlements in West Africa and northern Australia.[4] As this study is insistent that local circumstances stimulated place-specific responses, it is both appropriate, and indeed necessary, to include data from this wide spatial and temporal range.

All the women discussed in this work were migrants, but some were sojourners whilst some expected their relocation to be permanent. Hence the terms colonist, migrant and settler are all employed here, and whilst they each have distinct meaning they cannot be taken as absolutes and in terms of the psychological adjustments to be made by the individual there is definite overlap. Certainly the anticipated duration of stay would have some bearing on the migrant's behaviour, affecting the relationship both with the new site and with the metropolis, but it is highly questionable whether it was ever the determining factor in their daily lives. It may appear at first glance to be of prime importance, but only if one foregrounds time over all other factors involved in the migrant's life and such weighting would be highly suspect. Much more crucial to those who relocate, for whatever period of time, is the desire, indeed the profound psychological need, to be at ease in one's surroundings, to have control of one's personal space and develop at least some measure of competency in the locale. Moreover the expectation of others – that of both local peer groups and those of the former home – was arguably as significant as the duration of residence. If there were pressures upon you on all sides to commit yourself to the task of colonisation and demonstrate your worth in the cause of civilising and domesticating the British Empire, then such was the case whether it was for a two-year stint in West Africa in 1910, or a likely fifteen years in North Queensland in 1875, or a probable lifetime in Tasmania in 1835. Thus it is that in the development of their domestic culture one cannot make a critical distinction between sojourner and settler.

This combination of a need for a sense of well-being and a response to peer and family pressure would apply equally to second and subsequent generations of migrants, who in a sense had an even tougher job, having to follow on from their parents and grandparents who had carried out the tasks of primary settlement and now passed on the baton of colonisation. Thus the second generation migrant who left her parents in southern Australia to set up home in North Queensland, and the gen-

INTRODUCTION: GENTILITY AND THE PERFORMANCE OF SELF

erations of women who supported their menfolk in India were subject to many of the same influences and pressures in their drive to establish genteel standards in their new homes as the first wave migrants.

Central to this work is an analysis of the concept of female gentility as enacted in colonial settings. Gentility is a term used to describe a system of values, a highly nuanced form of knowledge. It can usefully be understood as having had two constituent parts. Firstly it had a theoretical stance, from which viewpoint genteel individuals deemed themselves to be in a position of superiority, elevated above those around them, who were, by definition, considered to be 'vulgar'. In women, gentility was characterised by notions of restraint. Although its outer manifestations were a preoccupation with control of body and personal space, in addition and crucially those behaviours were held to be indicative of control of inner, and by implication undesirable, passions. This meant there was a strong moral aspect to gentility, which naturally upped the stakes for all participants as its loss meant loss of character and virtue. In turn this made it harder for non-genteel elements of society to challenge its worth and furthermore it made it more desirable to emulate. In view of its cultural weight it is scarcely surprising that it was a term used by women themselves. It was spoken with pride, and appears to have taken precedence over other means of self-definition.

That it was dominant in the woman's identity is the key to understanding the second strand of the phenomenon; its crucial characteristic being that gentility was performative in nature. Gentility was at the core of the subject, and it found expression through modes of behaviour in conjunction with material means. Indeed it should be stated more strongly: it would wither without material means of expression, for as expression of subjectivity it was essential to the genteel woman's vitality, and it is no coincidence then that those unable to sustain their performance have often been described as 'decayed gentility'.

In this work it will be shown that the internalised values of female gentility were enacted and asserted through endlessly changing performance. Russell argues that if the public parade of social values was the sum and substance of gentility it could have been so readily imitated that it would not have retained its power. She holds that 'something had to be withheld, and that something was the conviction that ultimately the performance was irrelevant. What mattered was the true, innate gentility which the performance revealed'.[5] This surely is to misunderstand the nature of performance. To interpret it as little more than mannered artifice and empty consumption is to underestimate the profound nature of meanings underlying these seemingly trivial concerns. The woman's meticulous attention to presenting a

[3]

genteel image not only expressed her inner values; in turn her values were constructed by her performance. As the environment changed so too did the performance and here therefore is the connection between ideology and behaviour made explicit.

Because the performance took material expression it can be seen that gentility had a clear and visible link with consumption, which in turn demands access to funds, and hence it is tempting to say we are speaking of those commonly referred to as middle class. However, as a means of identifying the boundaries of colonial refinement this term of reference simply will not suffice, is as dangerous as it is slippery, and leads to comparisons being made between parties which are in fact utterly dissimilar. Class may be identified by birth, but the social weight of such happenstance is likely to be subject to erosion when shorn of its initial context and shifted to new locations. Alternatively class is conventionally defined by income, and/or by material markers. The former obviously varied to such an extent across the British Empire during the period 1840–1910 as to limit its usefulness as a means of assessing relative social positioning, whilst material markers must also be approached with due caution as in some sites, at some dates, such markers were not to be had for love or money irrespective of the household's income.

An obvious alternative to the term class is to identify the women in question by the occupation of the man of the house. This has some validity, for the women investigated here were all relocating and setting up homes in the company of a man to whom they were related by blood or marriage. Many of the women who are discussed were married, but there were also unmarried sisters, widows living with unmarried sons, and daughters accompanying their widower fathers. It was with and for these men that they were homemaking, and indeed one of their primary functions was to support their menfolk in this endeavour. Thus his successes and failures would have been hers, but so too her contribution could either develop and extend or even undermine their joint enterprise. Hence reading them first and foremost as a single entity, with his occupation as a critical feature of the structure has some value.

Furthermore an awareness of the occupation and related status of the man of the house serves to alert us to the competition, jostling and snobbery amongst the members of any one 'set' but also between the various groups in any given society. Certainly we will see here how much harder Sarah Terry, whose husband was an agent to a merchant in Bombay, had to strive to keep 'up to the mark' compared with Clementina Benthall who lived in the same region and was married to a judge. In relation to Melbourne society, Russell notes that colonial merchants and bankers were anxious to distance themselves from those who worked in retail trade or manufacturing and 'bore the stigmas of "the shop" or industry'.[6] Clearly a hierarchy of material and cultural circumstances was always present, between those at the very top of any society and those positioned in the middle. At any time within any given colonial society there were those who aspired to join or gain promotion within a tribe, and simultaneously there were those who were fearful lest they fail to retain their position. Thus there were gradations of gentility, and such distinctions were based not only upon financial capital but also upon cultural capital.

The high value accorded to cultural capital is why neither class nor the occupation of their menfolk is entirely satisfactory as a means of defining the parameters of female gentility. In view of the fact that the very notion of empire imbued the activities of colonisers with moral authority, how much more influential then were those whose moral stature was highly valued by virtue of their sex. All women were held to be the guardians of moral worth, but those who were elevated by gentility were making a double claim for leading the way in establishing and maintaining morally sound communities. Here it will be shown that whilst gentility was a determinant of female status in Britain, in locations across the British Empire the ideology acquired additional value and purpose. In colonial sites it invariably fell to the woman to establish a cultural aesthetic, to lay down markers in new or uncertain landscapes.

In making the case for the influence and power of gentility the intention is not of course to deny other influences simultaneously at work in colonial societies, nor yet does recognition of broader frames of reference negate the significance of gentility. Rather the discussion serves as a reminder that along with the oft-stated importance of such concerns as political and military matters ran other cultures, without acknowledgment of which studies of migration and identity remain incomplete.

That gentility was a concept which had currency over the English-speaking world throughout the nineteenth and twentieth centuries is testimony to its enduring value. As such it was recognised by others in different sites, though not in the form favoured by Linda Young, who speaks of 'global Anglo middle-class gentility', as if it were a singularity.[7] Young's stated intention is to 'open up new understandings of some commonalities of history' and takes 'the larger focus of a continuous, transnational Anglo culture [which] avoids the perils of exceptionalism'. In consequence of this reductive frame of reference all the complexities and tensions of emergent identities in different times and places are condensed to mere 'characteristic localisms'.[8] It is more helpful to recognise that, as with any system of knowledge, gentility was not fixed and absolute; rather was it highly sensitive to environmental circumstances – indeed therein lay its strength – and is therefore to be understood as a process rather than an entity.

Of course, Young is far from being the only writer to make comments on gentility in the British colonies. Women who would doubtless have identified themselves as genteel are frequently the subject of works with a rather different focus. For example, Procida in writing of the contribution made by married European women in establishing and maintaining British rule in India is almost invariably discussing genteel women but that aspect of their persona lay beyond her brief.[9] Similarly Buettner's work on European elites in late imperial India provides useful commentary on the possible psychological impact of being a member of what she judges to have been an arcane society, but other readings of the routine enactment of daily life are not considered.[10] It is in the Australian context that female gentility has attracted the greatest attention, with the most valuable publications for the purposes of this study being Russell's finely focused examination of gentility in nineteenth-century Melbourne, and Floyd's work on genteel practice in rural settings.[11] There has, however, been little or no comparative work on genteel performance in sites across the British Empire, a gap in historical enquiry which this work seeks to remedy.

If women were to establish themselves and remain secure in their standing within society as upholders of genteel values, all facets of their performance had to be suitably controlled. It is possible to identify aspects of the women's lives which seem to have been of common concern not only in Britain but also across all the colonial genteel societies investigated. These were dress, living rooms, gardens and food management and, as described below, this work is structured around those topics. The material culture of these areas of their lives emerges as a critical mechanism for ideological expression. It follows therefore that the ability of material culture to both make and express cultural meaning can usefully be analysed to cast light on the ways in which these particular migrants mediated their colonial circumstances. It is of course not enough to speak of the interactions of people and objects. It is the practices associated with the objects which hold the key, for they animate and provide contextual meaning. As Miller *et al.* state, 'Material culture is not something that exists just in the materiality of place or objects. Nor is it an internalised fantasy of these places or objects. It is called material culture because it exists in the practices which involve both those things'.[12] So in speaking of material culture having agency, one refers to the networks of meanings and allusions within which the objects are sited. These will include, though this list is not exhaustive, utility, exchange value, powers of evocation,

INTRODUCTION: GENTILITY AND THE PERFORMANCE OF SELF

symbols of other objects and other cultures, and of new affiliations. It can be seen that it is because the objects were both representative of and evocative of such a complexity of meanings that they had so much power, and from the point of view of this enquiry have so much to offer as a means of mapping cultural mores.

Pivotal in these interpretations of the behaviour of migrants has been the stress on memory in the process of relocation. Readings of the human psyche which foreground early-years experiences as the only significant formative influence of life tend to prioritise the place of memory in the behaviours and decision-making of adulthood.[13] In such approaches, memory and the part it plays in fashioning identity is understood as immutable. More illuminating is an understanding of memory as a constructed entity with moral force and power. Memory says this is how we were and how it was. It seeks to justify and explain the past. It makes sense of the tangle of life as lived, tidying up what Zemon Davis refers to as 'the uncertainty of truth', asserting this is how we did it before and it was the right and proper way to do things, so must be replicated.[14] Seen in this light, memory emerges as something to be harnessed as and when, where and how it was needed. So memory has multiple and changing functions. With their roots ripped from their previous soil and not yet established in the new, the migrants had to look to their past for both consolation and guidance. They needed that history and they drew on it extensively. Such were the needs of the individual but also of course of the wider imperial enterprise, for it was vital that they should be of one accord. So rather than notions of collective memory it is more meaningful to speak of agreed collective interpretation.

Such a stance was adhered to only as long as it was deemed to be useful, for from the moment of the colony's inception the new inhabitants had to work to create a viable society. It was essential that they focused on the here and now and formed new attachments to place, for it was equally vital to establish a history for the new colony, a history which could be drawn upon in times of individual or national crisis. Memory and the objects and practices through which it is expressed will only be to the forefront for as long as it has a purpose; thereafter the objects move to the back of the cupboard, and the associated practices and the social mores they represented are seen as the faintly quaint customs of ancestors soon to be superseded by the new. Thus memory played a role for individual and society alike, but it was a changing role. It did not form the new identities but they were informed by memory and interpretation thereof. So the past is reinterpreted in the light of the present situation and so the new site has direct bearing on the form that reinterpretation will take.

Parkin's words on those who suffer enforced migration have merit for explaining the initial lot of all who relocate: 'departing ... is to be exposed to a vulnerability which is as existential as it is material, the two being fused, for it is through the skills and objects one may take that one's future may be given shape, at least from the perspective of the departee'.[15] At the onset the migrant is adrift, and all-importantly for the group under investigation here, temporarily disempowered. However, their role was clear cut, for such women were the custodians of the coloniser's more refined social and domestic traditions, and also therefore the gatekeepers for the entry of change, determining if, when and how it was allowed in. The material aspects of their life were a means of expressing the form change was to take and was taking, and hence they offer a means of reading not only continuity but also change and inevitably conflict.

This work explores these processes of resettlement, questioning whether, and to what extent, their material culture and related values were reproduced or made anew in their various settings. It can be said that the values associated with objects they elected to take with them were subject to change. The very fact that the objects had been selected to form part of the new home conferred on them additional status, and they took on a mediating function in relation to the loss of the migrant's former home.[16] The intimacies and complexities of the women's relationships with their material culture were a means by which they expressed enduring attachments to the past and their changing perceptions of that past state. Equally the meanings attributed to items of material culture acquired *in situ* can be understood as elements in new forms of gentility which developed in direct response to the challenges and demands of the locale, and of formulating and expressing emergent affiliations with the new homeland. It can be said that the women, their belongings and the space they inhabited all had a considerable degree of interpenetration. This is not merely to speak of objectification but rather that the interactions between the component parts of their lives actually determined the form of the whole.

In his seminal work on the concept of 'taste' in mid-twentieth-century France, Bourdieu speaks of 'an acquired disposition to "differentiate" and "appreciate"', and he articulates precisely the connection between the material expression of such choices and the construction of social hierarchies.[17] Thus he explicitly links together the material and cultural worlds. He also makes due allowance for gender as a determinant of social mores, particularly in the construction of insider and outsider groupings. In consequence, Bourdieu supplies much of the theoretical underpinning for this work which in turn largely determines the methodologies employed in seeking to locate, identify and discuss

INTRODUCTION: GENTILITY AND THE PERFORMANCE OF SELF

various forms of genteel female 'differentiation' and 'appreciation'. Bourdieu is not, however, specifically and explicitly concerned with the meanings and worth of items and collections of material culture; rather is his preoccupation with the values which engender such assemblages. It is therefore to the work of Miller that this enquiry turns for theoretical thinking about material culture *per se*.[18] Miller's discussions of the ways in which the meanings of objects change, dependent upon their manner and place of use, have obvious application here. Equally useful is his articulation that as place contributes to meaning so there is an implicit link between the materiality of object and the materiality of the space wherein the object is sited. This study also benefits from other work on space, and the gendering of space itself. Writings which have been helpful in this regard have been Ardener *et al.*'s early insights into the potential of gendered space to empower but equally to constrain behaviour, and Attfield's more recent work on the constructive and destructive force of everyday items within domestic spaces.[19]

The historiographic tendency to understand the genteel women as emblematic of idealised 'Britishness' must inevitably be self-referencing and circular in nature, for seeing people as fixed entities renders them immune to meaningful analysis. In reality the act of migration limits the chances of maintaining the status quo, but equally creates the possibility for the refashioning of self. In taking relocation as a force for change, adaptation then becomes the norm and the likelihood of reinvention and reconstruction is seen as integral to the new life. Rather therefore than judging only on the basis of their finished performances, this study focuses on the processes within genteel performance and indeed refutes the idea that a performance can ever be said to be 'finished'. As vital expression of her subjectivity the ideology was adhered to every bit as fiercely, indeed perhaps more so, by those who were constrained in the performative aspect, because they were financially stretched and/or, critically for this work, because they were sometimes thwarted in their need to access the knowledge or material means of expressing their superiority. The fine-grained analysis carried out here reveals the extraordinary ingenuity displayed by colonial elites, and by those who aspired to join their tribes, in order to create a genteel performance. Far from these women endlessly looking in a rather passive fashion to Britain to supply their vitality, it is clear that there was a far more complex dynamic to their lives, and that they were active and engaged with the challenges and rewards of their circumstances, and that animation can be read through their material culture and its associated practices.

The four areas of the women's lives explored here have been selected because they were seen by contemporaries as being the quintessential elements of true genteel womanhood. Chapter 2 considers dress, which is taken to be the most intimate expression of self. Dress was a highly developed means of expressing difference and status of race and rank, and thereby it had agency in the exercise of British power along social and racial lines. The discussion lays emphasis on the responses of the women on finding themselves a conspicuous and significant sight in alien territory. Chapter 3 examines the creation of the living room, a critical space on the basis of which a woman would be judged as to whether she had succeeded in creating a respectable, refined and genteel household. Chapter 4 focuses on gardens and ways in which the spaces contributed to other aspects of genteel performance and how the very physicality of gardening served to foster attachment to site. Chapter 5 explores food and how the repetitive nature of its sourcing, preparation and presentation generated a multitude of ways for signalling genteel distinction. It is appropriate that the four topics should be handled separately as this enables the investigation to be conducted in depth and thereby to identify the relative positions and values attached to all aspects of the subject. Thus each chapter contributes differentially to a greater understanding of the challenges the women encountered and the subtleties of the strategies they developed in order to present themselves and their households in a manner consistent with their genteel interiority.

In concentrating on the process of adaptation for just one type of migrant this study focuses on activities so often dismissed as prosaic, but which here emerge as profound and indicative of ways in which the inner self changes and is made manifest through outer performance and practice. Female subjectivities are viewed from a perspective which sees identity as fluid and organic and domestic processes as a key expression of the adaptation and modification of self. Scrutinising the practices of female gentility also serves to highlight how the culture's innate sensibility to social conditions made it such a controlling device in colonial society, thereby bringing into sharp focus a particular form of female culture which has hitherto been prone to misrecognition. In turn it is hoped that examining the specificities of colonial experiences for this distinct group serves to cast useful light more generally on the processes of relocation and resettlement which prove to be such a distinctive feature of modern life.

Notes

1   G. Malloy, Port Augusta, February 1837, D/KEN/3/28–9, Kennedy Papers, Cumbrian County Archive Service, Carlisle; A. and L. R. Drummond, *At Home in New*

INTRODUCTION: GENTILITY AND THE PERFORMANCE OF SELF

Zealand: An Illustrated History of Everyday Things Before 1865 (Auckland, B. & J. Paul, 1967), p. 150, Mary Hobhouse February 1860; S. Strickrodt (ed.), *Women Writing Home 1700–1920: Female Correspondence Across the British Empire. Vol. 1 Africa* (London, Pickering & Chatto, 2006), p. 208, Ada Slatter, November 1904.

2. For a discussion of the process of resettlement in a national group of migrants see J. M. MacKenzie, *The Scots in South Africa: Ethnicity, Identity, Gender and Race, 1772–1914* (Manchester, Manchester University Press, 2007); and for an assessment of the working and significance of the phenomenon of migration within the British Empire both 'home and away' see S. Constantine, 'Migrants and Settlers' in J. M. Brown and Wm. R. Louis (eds.), *The Oxford History of the British Empire*, Vol. IV, *The Twentieth Century* (Oxford, Oxford University Press, 1999) and M. Harper and S. Constantine, *Migration and Empire* (Oxford, Oxford University Press, 2010).
3. Henceforth referred to as New Zealand, as befits a study of British colonialism.
4. For the purposes of this work North Queensland is taken as a distinct region, being the land north of the 22nd parallel and that which many 'separatist settlers' aspired to make an independent colony.
5. P. Russell, *A Wish of Distinction: Colonial Gentility and Femininity* (Melbourne, Melbourne University Press, 1994) p. 91.
6. Russell, *A Wish of Distinction*, p. 8.
7. L. Young, '"Extensive, Economical and Elegant": The Habitus of Gentility in Early Nineteenth Century Sydney', *Australian Historical Studies* No. 124, 2004, pp. 201–20.
8. L. Young, *Middle-Class Culture in the Nineteenth Century: America, Australia and Britain* (Basingstoke, Palgrave Macmillan, 2003), pp. 33, 7.
9. M. A. Procida, *Married to the Empire: Gender Politics and Imperialism in India, 1883–1947* (Manchester, Manchester University Press, 2002).
10. E. Buettner, *Empire Families: Britons and Late Imperial India* (Oxford, Oxford University Press, 2004).
11. Russell, *A Wish of Distinction*; E. Floyd, 'Without Artificial Constraint: Gentility and British Gentlewomen in Rural Australia' in R. S. Kranidis (ed.), *Imperial Objects: Essays on Victorian Women's Emigration and the Unauthorized Imperial Experience* (New York, Twayne, 1998).
12. D. Miller, P. Jackson and M. Rowlands, *Shopping, Place and Identity* (London, Routledge, 1998), p. 287.
13. For discussion of attachment theory and its implications see I. Bretherton, 'The Origins of Attachment Theory: John Bowlby and Mary Ainsworth', *Developmental Psychology* No.28, 1992, pp. 759–75.
14. N. Zemon Davis, *Fiction in the Archives: Pardon Tales and their Tellers in 16th Century France* (London, Polity Press, 1988), p. 113.
15. D. Parkin, 'Mementoes as Transitional Objects in Human Displacement', *Journal of Material Culture* Vol.4 (3), 1999, pp. 303–20.
16. J. S. Marcoux, 'The "Casser-Maison" Ritual: Constructing the Self by Emptying the Home', *Journal of Material Culture* Vol. 6 (2), 2001, pp. 213–35; Marcoux, 'The Re-furbishment of Memory' in D. Miller (ed.), *Home Possessions: Material Culture Behind Closed Doors* (Oxford, Berg, 2001).
17. P. Bourdieu, *Distinction: A Social Critique of the Judgment of Taste* (Cambridge, University of Massachusetts, 1984), p. 466.
18. D. Miller, *Material Culture and Mass Consumption* (Oxford, Blackwell, 1987); Miller, *Why Some Things Matter* (London, University College, 1998).
19. S. Ardener (ed.), *Women and Space: Ground Rules and Social Maps* (London, Croom Helm, 1981); J. Attfield, *Wild Things: The Material Culture of Everyday Life* (Oxford, Berg, 2000).

2

'Dress indicates mind':[1] the art and practice of appearance management

Introduction

Dress is the first and arguably key way in which individuals connect with their social surroundings. The presentation of the dressed self is therefore of immense social consequence. Self-evidently the body is the bearer of the messages of dress, with dress imparting to the body a degree of plasticity, enabling the individual to promote a chosen image. The dressed body is therefore an amalgam of person plus dress. It can be understood as both the physical representation of the subject, and a representation of the values to which the subject subscribes. It follows in fact that the dressed body is site of both consumption and production, constituent of its cultural context. As the dressed self is the most intimate expression of subjectivity, it is appropriate that this work should commence with analysis and discussion of the meanings of dress amongst genteel women.

Gentility was essentially performative in nature, and because of its visual immediacy dress lay at the heart of genteel performance. For the genteel woman dress had discreet meanings; how she presented herself was read by peers and wider society alike as being indicative of her character as well as her social standing. Thus the malleability dress lends to the body assumed a particular intensity of meaning in genteel circles, signifying as it did group affiliations and one's relative position within the group. To that end the woman needed to have both breadth and depth of dress expertise to assist her in making countless fine judgements about her presentation. It can be seen therefore that no examination of genteel behaviours, certainly of female gentility, would have credibility without analysis of dress.

For a long time work on dress in a historical context, particularly that of the modern period, suffered neglect as it was deemed to be frivolous and not to warrant rigorous academic enquiry. When enquiries were undertaken, they usually focused on 'costume' collections, with the implications of 'otherness' and theatricality which the term can imply. Drawing on isolated garments held in museum collections created as many problems as it solved. Such holdings were weighted in favour of the exceptional, such as ball-dresses and wedding gowns. Admittedly there is a degree of inevitability in this; they are the garments made from the fabrics of the best quality available, they have the least amount of wear and are the best cared for items, whereas the 'every day' garb has largely perished. Nonetheless privileging 'best dress' not only implies that the value is primarily based on the textiles employed, but also makes it harder to read wider social meanings of dress. Early works on colonial dress tended to be of that type, guilty of what Maynard refers to as 'dress-blindness', privileging male activities, including their dress practice, and suggesting women adhered to modes of dress inappropriate to the climate or their circumstances.[2]

It is the more pleasing therefore that recent work of an empirical nature has been carried out within the museum sector. Most notable, for the purposes of this enquiry, are object-based investigations at the New Zealand museums Te Papa in Wellington and the Auckland Museum, and also at the Powerhouse Museum in Sydney, Australia. At the latter they have a policy of generating 'statements of significance' regarding items within their collections which serve to site dress within a broad social context.[3] Exhibitions, such as the National Gallery of Victoria's 'Australian Made: One Hundred Years of Fashion' and on-going research at the Queensland Museum, Brisbane which explore the provenance of garments within their respective holdings are also making valuable contributions to object-centred work.[4] In a similar way Cumming *et al.*'s forthcoming work on dress in New Zealand, in which the authors use the methodologies of material culture to interrogate and contextualise European dress from the mid-nineteenth to the mid-twentieth century, serves to illuminate the specificity of local circumstances, and hence cite the garments within their biographical context.[5] Projects of this nature make explicit the economic, social and political grid within which the garment is positioned; thereby reinforcing the argument that it is utterly inappropriate to view dress as in any way inconsequential, the more so indeed in new and developing societies.

The reader should be aware of the necessity to approach with caution the concept of fashion in relation to genteel dress. It is not the case that fashionable women were guaranteed to be genteel, nor yet that genteel women were necessarily fashionable. Fashion, by its very nature, delights in novelty; gentility was preoccupied with 'taste', a very different form of knowledge. So although changes in dress style must inevitably loom large it is important not to overstate fashion as a prime mover. Knowledge of fashion and the extent to which it was or was not taken up by the genteel woman has to be examined within its ideological context, rather than being seen as separate to or in any way imposed from above within a 'fashion system'.[6] Structuralist explanations of that type are reductive and effectively side-line the woman as a self-determining entity.

That said, more recent work on fashionable dress has adopted methodologies which are of immense value, exploring the practices of individuals in specific settings. Examining dress *in situ* in this way enables readings which allow for dress being in Miller's phrase 'expressive of highly individualised presencing'.[7] Finkelstein emphasises that in order to gain an understanding of the meanings of dress it is necessary to have an appreciation of the relevant cultural discourse, stating: 'identities are interpreted through processes of social construction, as individuals supply one another with feedback, thus identity is symbolic and reflexive'.[8] Equally Entwistle's focus on 'the body as the environment of self' provides a vital means of mapping the routes of dress practice in colonial settings. By recognising that all activities are bodily situated in time and place, and hence that the body is always dressed for that situation, she too gives readings of dress as dynamic and responsive to external influences.[9] Dress then emerges as having critical agency in how the subject negotiates relations with the surrounding world.

This chapter will pursue just such an integrated approach by examining dress and its associated practices *in situ*, thereby making the case for place and practice being paramount as determinants of the meanings of dress. The first section of the chapter considers the dress practice of the genteel woman in Britain. It provides an overview of the depth and range of her dress expertise and how she acquired her knowledge and sourced her dress. Also discussed are the meanings which her peers and wider society ascribed to her appearance. Valuative conclusions of a moral and social nature were made on the basis of her presentation. Highlighted therefore are ways in which that influenced her behaviours – specifically with regard to her dress and its associated practices. Having established the cultural background, the discussion turns to the position of the appropriately attired woman in colonial societies, and how and why developing and maintaining her genteel appearance took on added significance in the face of various site-specific challenges. The detail of female dress practice is then subjected to close scrutiny, revealing the strategies which were developed in response to such challenges. Factors analysed are: the challenges of changing climates, the responses to shortages of textiles and other supplies, the making and maintenance of the garments, the tricky matter of style, various technological developments, and geographic and demographic features. This detailed analysis of the women's practice reveals not only complexity and variety but also intense subjective involvement in all aspects of their appearance, and hence the chapter concludes with discussion of ways in which dress emerges as vital for the individual in making her way in her new community. It is also demonstrated that far from being of exclusively female interest the presence of the genteelly attired woman had an emblematic significance in colonial locations, and was therefore of interest to all around her.

The analysis is supported throughout by reference to contemporary sources, namely: journals, letters, newspapers, periodicals, mail-order catalogues, photographs and garments. Of these the items of dress are of paramount importance; material survivors of the past, the garments stand as metaphor for their wearers drive to survive, and indeed prosper, with varying forms of their gentility intact.

'A favourable or unfavourable impression is made according to the appearance presented by every lady':[10] genteel dress in Britain

The statement quoted above typifies a number of works published in Britain during the latter half of the nineteenth century. Their authors made explicit that they considered it a woman's duty to dress in a manner which accorded with prevailing notions of femininity, and furthermore that conclusions would be drawn regarding her integrity and moral worth based primarily on her dress. By extension the very presence of the tastefully dressed woman was held to be a force for good. In *How to Dress as a Lady on £15 a Year by a Lady* (presumably for women in somewhat straitened circumstances who yet sought a genteel wardrobe) the author asserts: 'no remark is truer than that a woman is more or less judged by the style of her dress; and further that half her influence for good or bad depends upon it ... that careful consistent and tasteful dressing induces a feeling of self-respect; this gained, the respect of others is sure to follow'.[11] Although her work is aimed at a more affluent readership, Baronne Staffe strikes a similar tone in linking the managed self and character: 'mortals are led by appearances, and the more beautiful good women are the better equipped they will be to guide aright a world whose future depends upon the moral worth of its mothers and daughters'.[12] These two works serve to highlight that although inevitably there were gradations in the material expression of gentility, as determined by the individual's material circumstances, the moral tone was a constant feature. Evidently then there was a body of opinion across both the genteel populace and its aspirants. Admittedly, as these are essentially guidance manuals, caution must be exercised in assuming that the advice was followed. Nevertheless, as the ideas underlying these works were propounded in so many fields, from religious texts to poetry and painting, it can be said that there was both a moral and social imperative to present oneself with care and attention to detail.

Although guidance manuals about dress were so numerous – as indeed they were on all aspects of women's lives, hence they are therefore referenced again in subsequent chapters – yet their advice is curiously imprecise. The very lack of precision was calculated to induce anxiety in their readers, and of course this was most acute in those for whom a refined appearance was the foundation stone of their performance, but who were either financially vulnerable, or *nouveau riche* and hence newcomers to the genteel scene. To varying degrees concerns were also experienced by those seemingly in a more secure position, for the competitiveness inherent within gentility meant one could never quite assume one's status was permanent.

To be successful at appearance management required a considerable, and it must have seemed to those participating, ever-expanding knowledge. All aspects of dress, from head to toe, required painstaking care, for the elements had value separately as well as contributing to the whole performance. Women of genteel background developed their knowledge of dress as part of their education. Sewing (ideally fine work but the skills for plain sewing were usually taught as well), a sensitivity to the uses of textiles, an appreciation of style and an awareness of how to care for one's wardrobe were all part of their formative learning. Armed with such knowledge they could then make and purchase appropriate commodities and present themselves in a manner which accorded with their values. Far from this making them secure in their positions of dress dominance, they felt constantly under threat by those whom they held to be social inferiors dressing in ways too similar to their own. Of course, anxieties of this sort had always beset elites, but there are certain combinations of circumstance which heighten such fears – such as periods of economic expansion and – all-important to this enquiry – the process of relocation.

By mid-century onwards all sectors of the dress industries were experiencing growth, both stimulating and benefiting from a range of innovations and inventions which in turn released on to the market an astonishing variety of dress commodities. It seemed the needs of the customer were inexhaustible, leading a draper of Bond Street, London to recall in his memoirs that it was his trade which had led to the department store, 'and for one building which is devoted to men you will find twenty that are devoted to women's wear. Woman has thereby become a dynamo of demand, and it is what woman wants that set the wheels of industry going throughout all this whirling world'.[13]

It is evident that the genteel woman was a highly visible feature of the cultural landscape. She had an oft-stated duty to provide a model for other women, both of the next generation and those of lower status, and to that end her dress had specific function and meaning. Clearly those functions fostered tendencies to conform and it seems many women did have a well-developed sense of responsibility regarding that feature of their dress. Although this overview has identified tensions and anxieties in her situation, it should also be noted that along with the pressures and responsibilities of her position came power; both the hedonic power which accrued from presenting herself in a manner others found pleasing and that which arose from her moral standing within the community. Equally, having ready access to a rich abundance of commodities encouraged nuanced practices and thereby gave openings to dress creatively and to express personal preferences. That there were constraints and conformity in matters of dress does not negate pride in achievement and high self-esteem. Little wonder that dress was a focus of careful consideration when women of such heritage were relocated in sites across the British Empire.

'In a hot climate a pretty frock is a great asset':[14] dress in the colonies

Genteel women going to the colonies were moving into truly alien territory. Whilst in Britain, most of the situations in which they found themselves were relatively familiar; the social scripts were in place, and even if some aspects of the situation were being encountered for the first time there were enough recognisable features for them to pick up clues as to how to behave and therefore, all importantly, how to dress. The rupture of migration and relocation – and we must remember this would also be the case for those who moved within the Empire, such as from India to South Africa or Tasmania, or from the well-established cities in the south of Australia to the later colony of North Queensland – would impact on every aspect of genteel women's performance and threaten inner stability. There would be a definite need to draw on and assert their core values, and to make full use of that primary means of expression of subjectivity, their wardrobe.

The sense of vulnerability brought about by the alien scene stimulated a need to seek out the reassurance of the familiar – in this instance similarly dressed women. By concentrating on local forms of dress, members of sub-cultures quickly became recognisable to one another, and received confirmation that their appearance was acceptable.

Maynard speaks of individuals achieving 'social authenticity' through their clothes, and in colonial settings it seems that to be seen to dress in an appropriate manner was the first step towards acceptance within a group, and through that to forming an attachment to place.[15] It can be seen that the new arrival had much to gain by adopting such mode of dress. It sent out clear signals and helped to foster alliances with others judged to be similarly genteel. Conforming in this instance meant dressing and behaving in accord with local mores. A wise newcomer was sensitive to such nuances; for whilst she may initially be admired for her smart ways from 'the old country', local loyalties would quickly take precedence over her novelty appeal, and if she were to secure social space in her new location she had to adapt accordingly. When 'Mrs T' appeared at the Governor General's party in thick thread mittens with black velvet bracelets, Emily Eden, who as sister to the unmarried Governor General of India, Lord Auckland, presided as hostess at such functions, remarked: 'she may have genius and many good qualities but, you know, it is impossible to look for them under those mittens' – making one wonder was Mrs T only on the fringe of genteel society, or was she a member of another circle, perhaps in business, or was she indeed simply a new arrival not yet fluent in reading local style.[16]

Though a woman may seek to make herself visible to the elites of the European community, theirs were not the only eyes watching and making judgements. Accustomed as she was to a gaze that was gendered and hierarchical, to encounter a gaze that was also racialised was an additional and troubling challenge. In most locations the presence of the racially different was all around her, sometimes even living in her household if she was their employer, threatening her self-assurance by virtue of their 'otherness'. Dress had agency in helping her to contend with that test of her control. The meaning of one's dress and presentation is constructed not only by the wearer, but also by the observer. The gaze of the racial 'other' could be experienced as an intrusion into her space. All that genteel dress stood for in Britain in terms of social superiority, advanced femininity and elevation of character came to her assistance in her new location in asserting her right to control her space. It must also be stressed that in her colonial setting her dress underlined that she was a member of the racial elite; her dress serving to emphasise not only that she was different, but that her difference was white. Here then can be seen not a change in dress, but a change in meaning ascribed to dress, and therefore presumably some internalised adjustments in attitudes to her appearance. Doubtless for some women at some times dress must have acted as a mask, enabling them to present an air of composure, irrespective of what lay within.

Thus far the discussion has identified meanings dress had for individuals. Of equal weight though, and needing to be understood simultaneously, was the importance and high regard the well-dressed woman held within the European colonial communities. At the centre of the colonising vision lay the desire to convert the wilderness. To have sited within the 'disorder' of the alien scene a woman whose attire and personal space are controlled in every detail was a clear statement of cultural achievement and of further intent; the more effective indeed in settings where there were so few other signifiers. Here Douglas's analysis is apposite: 'when the human body is regarded as emblematic of its social context, then it becomes a repository of a society's ideals of human conduct'.[17] This of course is the elite woman in colonial locations which is most oft-cited – formally garbed in inhospitable territory. So often read as a passive symbol, in truth she was an active constituent in the new locale, both making and changing reality through the direct agency of her dressed self. This awareness of the power of dress is nicely articulated by Mrs Tremlett in her memoir of time spent in Nigeria accompanying her husband on a geological surveying trip:

> In a hot climate a pretty frock is a great asset, and exercises a particularly beneficent influence upon the temper of a properly constituted female, to say nothing of the inspiring effect it has upon the beholder; and I always think that a woman is a poor thing if she can't turn up at dinnertime looking as fresh as paint, whatever she may be obliged to look like all day.[18]

It can be seen that their dress was of the essence if the women were to be successful in the colonies, for both individual and communal reasons. If material culture can be said to be active in facilitating social interactions it can never be more so than in relation to dress. Bourdieu, in recognition of this transformative power of dress, wrote: 'attention devoted to it, awareness of the profits it gives and the investment of time, effort, sacrifice and care which they actually put into it are proportionate to the chances of material or symbolic profit they can reasonably expect from it'.[19] The key concept in Bourdieu's analysis is 'investment', and for the purposes of this work it can be seen that the agency of their dress provided the women of genteel persuasion with a vital means of negotiating their new circumstances. By making these ongoing investments of time, money and energy, positioning within the social hierarchies was secured and sustained and, furthermore, the women maintained and adapted their sense of self. Dress, because of its intimate relation to core subjectivity, is very sensitive to the reflexive element of identity. In their attention to their dress the women were not clinging to out-of-place behaviours, nor yet being merely reactive in the face of the gaze, rather were they taking ownership of their own space in a manner compatible with their values, but values which were subject to changes determined by local circumstances. The following examination of elements of their dress practice explores some of the challenges they faced in their various locations and the strategies they developed in response to such challenges. Dress emerges as dynamic agent for the development of new forms of female gentility.

'The climate is a good disciplinarian – heat 96 degrees at 3 p.m!':[20] genteel dress for all weathers

Photographs of European women in the British colonies which were produced mid-century often give the impression that, irrespective of their location, they were permanently enveloped in heavy and unyielding clothing. Admittedly some of the seeming stiffness of these images can be explained by the technical constraints of early photography. More importantly, however, was that they were produced either to send back to their previous home, or for their *cartes-de-visite*. Hence they were statements of achievement and/or ambition, self-conscious in their intent, so it was perhaps logical that they would elect to pose in their most formal attire. Equally however, when photographic advances made it possible to expose plates more rapidly, records were made of women outdoors wearing much lighter attire. See, for example, Figures 2.1 and 2.2: of three ladies in a North Queensland garden, and that of Mrs Spencer Hopkins on the verandah of her home in Townsville, North Queensland. Evidently then there was a mixture of dress worn, suggesting that to some extent dress was adapted to suit climates so very different to Britain's.

All colonial sites had periods of hotter weather than that which was normally experienced in Britain, and it is perhaps inevitable that in personal writings the heat gets more mention than the cold, simply because of that contrast. This is not of course to say that they were all hot all the time, and some sites, notably the South Island of New Zealand and Tasmania, have harsh winters and are prone to highly unpredictable weather. So some settlers doubtless had to modify their dress to cope with lower temperatures than they had been accustomed to, such as those settlers in Tasmania who had previously lived in India.[21] It is unsurprising therefore that the market for imported heavy textiles continued, as evidenced by advertisements in 1907 editions of the Hobart newspaper the *Mercury*: 'Fitzgerald's Drapers: winter velveteens, tartan plaids – both clan and fancy, for ladies who do not like the conspicuousity of clan Tasmanian tweeds' – see Figure 2.3 of ladies taking tea on a verandah in Hobart clad in relatively warm dress – and 'Furs: Russian sable, American possum'.[22] Jocic notes that the demand

THE ART AND PRACTICE OF APPEARANCE MANAGEMENT

2.1 Women wearing lightweight dresses in garden, Queensland, c.1904–9.

for fur in southern Australia was such that it stimulated an interest in indigenous fauna, citing by way of illustration a woman's cape of Tasmanian platypus, c.1890.[23]

Maynard makes the case for the development in Australia of distinct forms of behaviour in relation to hot weather, arguing that in public at least it had to be endured. She cites Trollope: 'One does not allude to heat in a host's house anymore than to a bad bottle of wine . . . You may call an inn hot, or a court-house, but not a gentleman's paddock or a lady's drawing room'.[24] Katie Hume's letters from Queensland certainly appear to support that view. She spoke of modifying her dress because of the demands of the heat – 'Of course I cannot wear anything but a black barege skirt, and white body indoors – washing bodies are indispensable in the heat'. And yet note how sharp is her criticism of one of her acquaintance: 'I must describe to you Mrs Nevill's toilette, when I called at the Parsonage for the Church key. A light silk faded-looking skirt, with *low* black velvet body and dirty tucker, bare neck and arms, blue and silver ribbon tied round a head of rough shorn hair' – making concessions to the heat seems only to have been acceptable in private.[25]

Nor was the belief that appearances had to be maintained in public only found in Australia. Lady Curzon, Vicereine of India, made explicit

2.2 Mrs Spencer Hopkins wearing lightweight dress with matching parasol, posed on the back verandah of her home 'Devanah', Queensland, c.1908.

2.3 Elegantly attired women taking tea on the verandah, 'Rosebank', Hobart, Tasmania, c.1910.

both her concern for standards and the effort it cost her: 'Oh! The heat, the heat. Dressing in it is simply awful and with broad rivers running down all over you, it is hard to appear dry and smiling at a daily dinner-party'.[26] Curzon's attitude cannot be attributed solely to her very high-profile role, for in a similar manner Constance Larymore, when writing advice for those embarking on a life in turn of the century Nigeria, is emphatic that in relation to corsets to 'leave off wearing them at any time for the sake of coolness is a huge mistake ... *Always* wear corsets, even for a tête-à-tête home dinner on the warmest evening; there is something about their absence almost as demoralizing as hair in curling pins!'[27] Isabella Russell, writing from Bathurst, Gambia at the turn of the century described how with the temperature at 96 degrees her husband David 'is sitting writing in his shirt sleeves – I wish I could strip a bit!'[28] These latter two remarks certainly suggest that, even for an audience of one, standards must still be maintained, but also serve to remind us how closely the manner of self-presentation is linked with the interiority of the subject, with much more at stake than disappointing or shocking one's husband with a *déshabillé* appearance.

GENTEEL WOMEN

2.4 The elegantly attired mistress of the house presiding over tea-time on the verandah of her Queensland home, c.1907–9.

The sources cited in the preceding paragraph also illustrate that notions regarding dress and demeanour when in public seem to have remained strict across both time and place. Equally they remind us that what distinguishes between private and public has cultural specificity. Constance Larymore and Isabella Russell, and their husbands – Resident and Judge respectively – presumably considered the verandah or living rooms where they were seated as semi-public areas, with the likely presence of at least servants if not chance visitors, and therefore they had to dress with decorum.

Those two women writing from West Africa, and the photograph produced at around the same date of the group of men and women taking tea on a verandah in North Queensland (Figure 2.4) highlight that there appears to have been a strongly gendered aspect to what constituted acceptable dress in the heat. In relation to mid-century Australia, Maynard spoke of 'the disjunction between the casual nature of the man's clothing compared to the formality expected of the woman'.[29] This photograph, produced c.1907–9, suggests the convention was still in place, indeed actually heightened in some circumstances, such as when the climate was challenging. To women fell the prime responsibility of establishing social standards, and the

[24]

visual impact of the fully-covered and restrained women cannot be overestimated. Whilst the men could more readily adopt less formal dress, no such latitude could be tolerated in women, for it carried with it the suggestion of lack of control and improper, indeed uncivilised, behaviours.

In her expressed wish to be able to 'strip a bit' Russell was presumably referring to both the multiple layers which formed women's dress and the convention at that date that day dress should cover all but the hands and face. Certainly it was customary to wear a quantity of substantial underclothes, partly to protect the outer garments from soiling. The Godden sisters, in writing of their childhood in early twentieth-century Bengal, provide a vivid recollection of their 'comfortable faded everyday cottons' being replaced when they were dressed for the afternoon in:

> clean vests, liberty bodices with dangling elastics and white kid suspenders, white cotton stockings . . . white drawers buttoned on to the bodices, the buttonholes stiff with starch so that there were crises at certain important moments, while the legs had ruffled lace edges that, starched again, chafed our groins. Our white petticoats had more starched lace that tickled armpits and necks; over all went clean dresses.[30]

As there is no mention of corsets, the Godden girls were presumably prepubescent, despite which they were already being initiated into the ritual of changing into more formal dress, with all that symbolised in terms of the decorous behaviour which would be expected of them as adult women.

Most women do seem to have been in accord with Larymore's directive, and corsets remained customary as their absence was considered vulgar. Steele's work on corset use in Britain states that the idea that corsets should be comfortable was not even considered until mid-century.[31] However, if that was the case it soon changed as 'Gossamer Swan Bill Corsets designed for warm climates' were advertised in the *Brisbane Courier* in 1877, and even Larymore's strictures on corset wearing do advise 'the coolest kind obtainable', suggesting lightweight models were widely marketed by the turn of the century.[32] Steele also asserts that throughout the century debates in relation to corset use revolved around whether only moderate corseting should be used, not about ceasing to wear them at all.[33] It is tempting to suggest that in hot climates there may have been less inclination to lace corsets tightly, but no evidence has come to light to support such a suggestion, possibly unlacing being associated less with sexual abandonment and more with slovenliness, the very antithesis of gentility. Interestingly Jane Bardsley, who lived on a cattle farm in the far north of Queensland, is decidedly frank on the subject of her corset: 'I have to squeeze into number 19 waist, when I really think by the agony I suffer I should wear one yard. I am not at all slim, my weight is 8st 2lb and height 5 foot 1 inch, so know that the fat has to go to some other part of the body when I get my waist to number 19'.[34]

Contemporary readers who find the thought of such restrictive dress a complete anathema should be mindful that until the 1950s the majority of British women wore some form of 'foundation garment', and at the time of writing wearing a brassiere is still customary practice amongst most western European women, irrespective of the temperature. Bourdieu cites choice of clothes as being one of the items most strongly linked to early-life role models, and this ongoing use of corsets may well be a case in point.[35]

Crinolines, the metal frames worn to support exceptionally wide skirts, can be said to constitute underwear in so much as they were hidden from view. Although they appear cumbersome to modern eyes, and were indeed a source of much mockery to mid-century cartoonists and commentators, they did reduce the necessity for wearing numerous heavy petticoats, and were therefore cooler and more comfortable. Georgina Bowen wrote from South Island, New Zealand in 1862 to her sister in England complaining that 'I have had a succession of atrociously bad ones lately – by the way it would be as well to send me one in the next box, a large one please', indicating that at that date the fashion in that far-flung settlement was largely in step with that of the metropolis.[36] It is interesting to note then that they retained a much longer-term popularity in the tropical north of Queensland, a practice noted by resident Charles Eden's observation made in the late 1870s that 'these under-structures were an extremely fast-selling commodity in Queensland station stores although they had ceased to be fashionable a decade previously'.[37]

In addition to some modification to underwear it is evident that outer dress was adapted to suit local weather conditions. There were changes made in terms of both the weight of the fabrics used, as discussed below, and the colours worn. In 1870 Katie Hume in Queensland received from her family in England what she described as a 'pretty "Fish'ook"' commenting 'it will do very nicely to wear out of doors next summer, the present fashion of "having nothing on" being very suitable for this climate'.[38] The photographs included here demonstrate that white and pale shades were in popular use in North Queensland during the 1890s and beyond, at least for dress worn in public. Note particularly in Figure 2.2 the light and lacy dress worn by Mrs Spencer Hopkins who, as wife of the proprietor of Townsville's largest drapery store, would presumably have had the pick of the stock. Emily Eden commented that in India 'No milliner will sell silks or satins during the damp months, because they cannot expose them to the air', and Emma Roberts advised taking to India 'plenty of muslin dresses, for silks, satins and heavier fabrics are endurable only during the short winter months ... the first hot season is very trying, and demands all the alleviation which thin garments can afford'.[39]

It should be noted that the use of 'tropical white' was not, however, universally popular, largely it seems because of the difficulties of keeping it clean. Constance Larymore did not favour its use in Nigeria, saying 'white gowns, cool and dainty as they are, I do not recommend very strongly, as a dusty path or a shower of rain will make them unwearable after half-an-hour'. Similarly Lucy Gray's main reservation about Cape Town was the disagreeable wind that meant 'an inch of one's dress and petticoats, as well as stockings, are dyed with red sand at the end of a walk'.[40] Thus that which made white garments theoretically desirable – they were harder to keep clean and therefore supposedly denoted a leisurely existence – was actually their undoing, the more so when the wearers had to contend with less than ideal laundry facilities, as discussed in further detail below.

The other consequence of living in warmer climes is that exposure to the sun darkens the skin. The women's cultural heritage expected that they present pale pink face and hands to the world; for that not only equated with an existence free from manual labour, but also implied a delicacy and purity of disposition. It seems reasonable to assume therefore that hats with veils were probably more popular amongst elites and those with ambitions to join them.[41] It is surely significant then that the subject of having darkening complexions is rarely mentioned in personal writings, and when it is it is in surprisingly stoical tones; such as when Elizabeth Jacobs and her family became 'burned rich red brown colour' on their journey from Bombay to Zanzibar, and Rachel Henning noting that she and her sister looking 'ancient' under the hot climate 'though it agrees with me so well'.[42] Admittedly Henning was living on relatively remote homesteads, firstly in New South Wales and then in central Queensland, but as there was an insistence on genteel practice in some other aspects of her performance this is to be understood less as a decline of former standards than as a development of new ones.

Indeed this latter phrase of Henning's exemplifies the attitude many women living in hot climates seem to have had towards their appearance. It is important not to overstate a view of the women compelled to be always sweltering and miserable in hot and heavy clothes. Such readings rob them of agency. Dress use needs to be understood contextually. Although the women were entirely serious about setting and maintaining standards it does not follow that they did not take pleasure from living in warmer climes or that they did not modify their dress accordingly.

Thus numerous references are to be found of adaptation to site-specific circumstances. For example, just as Henning seems to have enjoyed a sense of well-being, so too did this anonymous writer in Cape Town in 1861 revel in the more relaxed mode of living: 'no need for careful toilet, no unnecessary anxiety as to boots or gloves! We have no neighbours within a mile of us, and if we had they would not care a bit!'[43] Miss Lowndes, who lived in South Africa at the turn of the century, declared 'The colonial rule for clothing is to wear only thin garments such as are right for the middle of the day, wearing an extra wrap if chilly'.[44] Miss Lowndes worked as a governess and it may be that the demands of her employment compelled her to adopt a pragmatic approach to her wardrobe, whilst still working hard to present herself in a genteel manner. Eustace Kenyon recorded of his wife: 'Ethel is getting very keen on bicycling now and is determined to buy a machine with some money she had kept from her wedding presents'. One gathers from this that Ethel Kenyon did not feel so restricted in her dress that she could not venture out on her bicycle into the streets of Calcutta. Doubtless she changed her attire, possibly at this late date adopting 'rational dress' but that would in no way be at odds with her genteel persona.[45] Isabella Russell in Gambia did write to her sister describing as 'a bit trying' that 'there was never a dry garment on you (forgive my vulgar frankness)', but still went horse-riding regularly.[46] In some sites women who engaged in cycling, horse-riding and archery may also have made use of the feminine but robust woollen fabrics which were available from mid-century onwards. Taylor argues that the incentive for the development of such textiles was the changing social mores which encouraged women to be more physically active, and therefore both the stimulus and the market for these goods was the middle and upper classes.[47] In colonial settings the great advantage of the fabrics was that they did not require the cotton wadding previously needed for interlinings, hence the garments were lighter – an obvious advantage in warmer climes – and their use can be regarded as another form of adaptation.

Of course, offering constructions of themselves as coping with the rigours of the climate was part of their self-presentation as capable colonisers, and equally to complain of the heat was vulgarity itself, but nonetheless it does appear that the women did not feel utterly constrained by arbitrary convention, rather do their accounts indicate that conventions were changing. It is important to remember it was the women who wore the clothes, and not the other way round.

THE ART AND PRACTICE OF APPEARANCE MANAGEMENT

'Ribbon, Buttons, Braid, Frilling, Needles, Elastic, Black Lace, Mending-card':[48] recycling, adapting and modifying dress

Whichever colonial site the women inhabited during the latter half of the nineteenth century the range and depth of dress commodities they could access would not replicate those that were available in Britain. Indeed in remote settings and where communications and supplies were severely constrained, it is no exaggeration to say they experienced textile deprivation. In some settings this prompted the development of a socially acceptable and highly visible second-hand clothes trade. For example, in Van Diemen's Land in 1832, Mrs Allport noted in her journal that she had 'called at Elliston's and he has sold our things (coarse bush clothes, old coats etc) for £23 . . . it is double what we expected', and certainly a sizable sum for the date concerned.[49] The editor of the journals asserts that the family 'never acquired huge wealth'; be that as it may, Morton Allport was a partner of one of the colony's leading law firms, and the family were high-profile members of society and most assiduous in their genteel performance. That such a household sold their unwanted garments and that it warranted a mention in her journal says much of the challenges faced by the new settlers and the strategies developed in response. Similarly some thirty years later the Reid Scott household accounts have an entry from 1868 of 'sale of old clothes: £12', and even as late as 1878, Mrs Butler noted how she 'had spent the morning packing up old clothes', suggesting that in that colony there was still a call for such goods and she was not averse to mentioning her involvement in such dealings.[50] Similarly when Sarah Greenwood was in childbirth at her home in Nelson, New Zealand, in 1845 she commented of her attendant '*she* is delighted to be paid in old clothes and I to save the cash'.[51]

It is no surprise that the ladies cited above were *au fait* with selling on of unwanted dress as in Britain the second-hand clothes trade was extensive, highly structured and long-established. For example, in 1843 one Mr Isaacs opened the 'Old Clothes Exchange', in Cutler Street, London, where some 7,000 square feet were devoted to various aspects of buying, cleaning, altering and selling on of used garments. Although Ginsburg stated that 'the upper classes were surreptitious in their dealings', it could equally be argued that rather than 'recycling' being considered shameful the genteel woman had simply developed a more appropriate way of sourcing and disposing of items.[52] Thus the *Englishwoman's Domestic Magazine* ran advertisements such as 'E.B. has a handsome ermine jacket, large size, cost £3.00, would take a useful morning dress, furs sable or ermine. Open to offers'.[53] This is not to suggest that women in the colonies employed the magazine directly to exchange items with Britain, but rather that they were familiar with such strategies and, as the publication was sent to Tasmania, it seems reasonable to assume that on a modest scale the practice may have been re-established there as a form of genteel practice. In addition, communities in which commodities were scarce were frequently characterised by transactions which involved barter rather than money. So in some locations those behaviours may have coincided. Such may have been the case for Laura Wright whose diary entry of 1865 from rural Tasmania notes 'Exchanged two dozen pattipans for old clothes'.[54]

It is hard to gauge how extensive the used dress trade was in colonies established at a later date, such as that of North Queensland. Certainly it seems likely that in the initial stages of settlement such textiles would be used as packing for fragile items being transported by sea from the cities of southern Australia. However, as the coastal town of Townsville was slow to expand, and up-country settlers were effectively isolated from such a source of supply, it may be that other aspects of practice would dominate the use of second-hand dress. In addition, the genteel end of the market would presumably require a sizable population base as otherwise one would be in danger of simply exchanging dress with one's neighbour, which would surely strain the credibility of the effortless genteel performance, of which dress formed such a critical component.

The demographic factor largely accounts for the lack of references located regarding second-hand dress practice amongst the Europeans in West Africa. With scarcely more than 300 of such incomers in 1870, only rising to about 2,000 by the turn of the century, such modest numbers in such a large land mass must inevitably have constrained mechanisms such as the marketing of all second-hand goods within the British elites, including dress.[55]

One of the other consequences of textile shortages was that dress did not 'percolate down' the social ladder as rapidly as it did in Britain. Genteel women either exchanged dress with their peers (at a suitable remove), or sold to those who aspired to a genteel appearance. The practice in Britain of passing items on to the servants effectively ground to a halt in such situations. Georgina Bowen's maid left her post in South Island, New Zealand in 1866, apparently telling her employer that amongst her grievances 'I don't wear out or give her enough dresses that she has made more in situations at home by selling things that her mistresses have given her!!!'[56]

It must be stressed that using second-hand dress did not equate with any lack of interest in their appearance. Just as the woman advertising in the *Englishwoman's Domestic Magazine* cited above is very precise in her requirements, so the purchasers of second-hand items in colonial locations selected items which accorded with their preferred persona. It is also possible that knowing or even half-knowing the provenance of the garment more than compensated for it having been worn by another. Dress worn by a woman of known genteel standing would surely do much to enhance the self-esteem of the next owner, particularly if she was one who was striving for social promotion. Another reason why there was no stigma attached to second-hand dress was that for most women carrying out alterations and modifications were core needle skills. The majority of women developed the necessary expertise when they were young, such knowledge being valued as an indication of their refinement. Added to which, in Britain the cost of the fabric often far exceeded that of making up the garment, particularly if the material was of good quality, and none but the very highest echelons of society were able to purchase their dress without some regard to cost. It was therefore entirely customary to adapt dress to accommodate changes in body shape – as for maternity wear for example – or to fit entirely different people.[57] These skills often proved of vital importance in colonial settings, both because of textile shortages and because where there is social jostling for position then all markers of distinction take on heightened meaning. Having the ability to make such changes to one's dress could add individuality and distinction and make all the difference when commodities were limited.

Mrs Allport, despite a demanding domestic routine, noted in her journal how she had 'unpicked my blue muslin to wash and modernise it'.[58] As the colony of Van Diemen's Land remained entirely reliant upon imported textile goods for many decades, a 'feast or famine' situation seems to have prevailed in the shops. When the ships came in the 'packages' of goods were duly advertised; meaning that all the women were purchasing from the same limited reservoir of merchandise at the same time. Being in a position to make up something different or a bit smarter might well have been perceived as giving a woman the 'social edge' – particularly if she was something of a newcomer to genteel performance. Ginsburg argues that those who were respectable, but could not afford to aspire very far up the social ladder, could still demonstrate their moral virtue by making and remaking their garments.[59] This would certainly explain the frequency with which descriptions of alterations appear in women's writings, for altering and recycling was then elevated and given a moral meaning, rather than being a 'last resort'. Equally, to complain of having to employ such tactics would identify one as vulgar.

A shortage of textiles would sometimes directly influence style. For example, a narrow fabric intended for bonnets, such as a twenty inch satin, could, if commodities were scarce, be pressed into use as a dress material. In such a case some eight or ten widths might be required and the time taken and labour involved would be considerable, though of course if a style such as organ pleating was in vogue it would be seen as a desirable feature. Similarly the use of detachable yokes, or inserting panels of a different fabric into the bodice or the skirt could be an effective means of making a small quantity of material 'go a long way'.[60]

The prevalence of making and modifying dress also explains why haberdashery stores seem to have flourished so rapidly. It is interesting to note that it is that aspect of commodity supply over which an anonymous lady in Cape Town enthused in 1861: 'our shopping is very complete, Fletchers is our Marshall & Snelgrove and they will supply you in anything in haberdashery from a button to Brussels lace'.[61] Similarly in 1887, little more than twenty years after the commencement of white settlement in North Queensland when the population of the town was recorded as only 350, the *Townsville Daily Bulletin* ran an advertisement for the Beehive Store which included 'choice millinery, trimmed and untrimmed hats, lace flourishing from 12–40 inches, Spanish, Oriental, Chantilly and Deutelle', suggesting the presence of women who were seeking ways to give 'finish' to their dress.[62] Even as late as 1879, by which time the British were long established in India, the *Englishwoman's Domestic Magazine* recommended that those going to the sub-continent should take all the necessary 'braids, buttons, ribbons, belts, linings and trimmings as none of these things will be procurable out there even at double the price, and when you begin to make up your dresses it would be too provoking to have the work brought to a standstill for want of the proper articles to match'.[63]

That existing garments would tolerate remodelling tells us much regarding the durability of their original manufacture. Until 'off the peg' came to dominate supply it was customary for most dress to be made with the use of substantial facings and interfacings, and generous hems and selvages; all of which served to reinforce and strengthen the garment. Such attributes ensured the garments had an in-built longevity and of course meant they had scope for significant adaptation. Thus dress was meant to last, and was expected to last. Indeed Lockren argues that when ready-made items first became available women were reluctant to purchase them, primarily because they were not made in such a substantial manner, and therefore lacked that all-important potential for remodelling.[64] Where an item of dress has survived to the present day it is not only indicative of the value the garment had for the wearer or wearers, but is also testament to its inherent strength and stability.

THE ART AND PRACTICE OF APPEARANCE MANAGEMENT

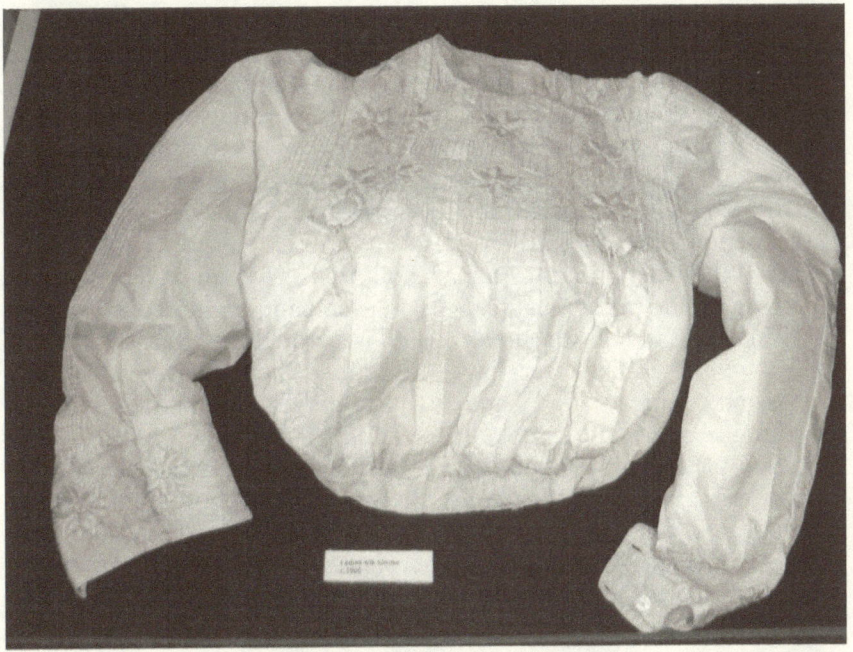

2.5   Lady's silk and lace blouse, Queensland, c.1900.

For example, a striped cotton day dress and embroidered lawn shawl held in the Narryna Costume Collection in Hobart, Tasmania, said to have been worn by Mrs Butler on her arrival in Van Diemen's Land in 1824, was subsequently altered to the style of 1840.[65] Similarly there is a ladies' ivory silk blouse c.1900 held in the Local History Collection in the Townsville Library, North Queensland, see Figure 2.5.[66] It is handmade and the waist band is heavily sweat-stained and worn, but the body of the garment is in very good condition and has evidently been well cared for. Later additions have been made to the bodice in the form of lace work and buttons. It is also possible that the fastenings are of a later date. It is a most delicate and elegant garment and was presumably much valued, having been protected from the ravages of attacks by moulds and termites, to which textiles in the tropics are highly vulnerable. Being able to reference directly such items *in situ* serves to deepen appreciation of both the work involved and also the meaning invested in these material items in their various locations.

In all the sites examined the element of the wardrobe which seems to have been subject to constant appraisal was that of hats and bonnets.[67] This is understandable as hats make such an important contribution to one's performance. A hat can act as a framing device for the face, and by implication the person within. It can be used to accentuate or minimise feature or shape, and can add height and increase the wearer's presence and stature. When going shopping, attending church or making calls one had to present oneself with the utmost care and some form of hat was customary. Modifications to headwear could rejuvenate an all-too-familiar outfit and, if executed with care and skill, gain the admiration and approval of one's peers. Little surprise therefore that it is such a recurrent topic in personal writings.

Jane Williams, living in Poona, India in 1832, had evidently taken exception to the purchases made by her husband on her behalf during his time in Bombay, for surely there is a touch of exasperation, or perhaps of hurt in his letter: 'but how could I know whether a Bonnett was a good colour or a bad – and as to the shape, you did not tell me to get it *uncut*. I thought it looked charming'.[68] Georgina Bowen in New Zealand in 1863 accompanied a friend to choose a hat and declared later 'I am afraid it is not very pretty but there is so little choice here', which may suggest some modification was in order.[69] Miss Rutherfoord, writing from Cape Town c.1853 to her sister in India, gives illuminating detail on the nuances of hat design:

> Ellen and I have fancy straw bonnets lined with blonde, and trimmed with white ribbon with a straw-coloured and black sort of fringe, and straw over the curtains ... I thought the bonnet you sent Mama very pretty and becoming but she said it was all too bright. However now it is lined with blonde and a pretty lilac cap with a trimming outside left and looks very nice.[70]

That Miss Rutherfoord's sibling selected a bonnet as an item to send home to Cape Town, and that it was the subject of such animated discussion certainly does suggest that hats were high-status items with meanings far beyond any utilitarian function. It is no doubt significant that Mr Rutherfoord's work as a shipping agent meant the household had a wide circle of acquaintance and were obliged to keep themselves in the public eye, and therefore that his daughters' mode of presentation had implications for all aspects of their lives, both business and social.

Perhaps the most eloquent cases of dress modification are those where an item belonging to one family member is adapted for another, absent relation. Mrs Allport's journal contains a number of references to making clothes for her son including 'Made Morton a nice morning dress and trousers with part of my mother's scarlet chintz gown'.[71] Here can be seen the coming together of a range of experiences and responses. Mrs Allport's work with a dress worn by her mother to create a dress for her son has a particular intensity. The dress provides a means of continuing the family nurturing process that the absent grandmother had started so long ago. The past is drawn into the present through the agency of the dress and Mrs Allport's seamstress practices; rarely can recycling have more creative and profound meanings.

It has been shown that recycling and modifying dress appears to have been customary practice in most sites across the period examined. By making their mark on it, literally as well as figuratively, dress contributed to women's performance. Far from it being a hardship to work on their appearance, the evidence suggests that the women saw the adaptability of dress as a positive attribute, and the very processes of alteration and modifications were mechanisms which helped them to absorb it into their chosen persona. Thus the new practices denoted changes taking place to their identity – an identity as genteel as its predecessor, but adapted to meet the challenges of the new location.

'My ironing is something superior in its way':[72] *caring for dress*

Possessing a suitable array of dress was not, of itself, sufficient. Keeping their wardrobe in sound order – by which was meant clean, pressed and in good repair – was of equal, if not greater, importance to women. In colonial sites, white British notions of cleanliness took on an added significance, being equated with purity, and positioned in sharp contrast to all those regarded as socially inferior, but most notably to indigenous peoples whose 'otherness' was articulated in terms of lack of cleanliness. Their failure to accord with European standards in this regard was seen as symptomatic of their fundamental disorder, lack of development and ungodliness. Small wonder then that for the white elites presenting a well-ordered appearance lay at the heart of their practice and was held to be symbolic of bodily and indeed moral control. It followed that the very processes and procedures involved in dress maintenance were also imbued with moral meaning. These tasks were labour intensive and many demanded considerable skill. Irrespective of whether the women had servants to perform the work or whether circumstances necessitated they have more than a supervisory role, having some degree of knowledge was part of their expertise.

Until well into the twentieth century the textiles used in dress were cottons, linens, silks and woollens. Being natural fibres, not all responded well to washing. For example, if left to steep woollen fibres become waterlogged, causing the garment to become misshapen. Similarly silk threads are inclined to 'give' when wet, which is why it was customary for items to be taken apart prior to washing and then re-sewn afterwards; see the reference made to Mrs Allport's unpicking of her muslin dress, as cited in the previous section. Prior to the late 1850s when aniline dyes started to become available, most dyes were not colour fast, so fixative had to be added to the wash. These tended to be fabric specific; thus bran was used for brown linen and raw ammonia for blue linen. Some fabrics required the use of stiffening agents: isinglass for light muslins and a solution of glue for the heavier chintz as used for mourning dress. Textiles which would not tolerate washing at all, such as velvets, were dry-cleaned with stale bread and then steamed to lift the pile.[73] It can be seen from this detailed account of just a single aspect of dress maintenance that it was no easy matter to keep their wardrobe 'up to the mark'. Indeed in early periods of settlement soap itself was sometimes in short supply, as when Mrs Allport recorded 'Washed two dozen clothes, having still a great many dirty as have been without soap for several weeks'.[74]

In Britain the women of the house could reasonably expect to draw on the competences of a lady's maid or laundress. In many colonial sites there was either a shortage of servants altogether or, of equal concern, a shortage of labour with the requisite skills. In addition to advertising in the local newspapers, it seems likely that genteel groups searched for servants of proven quality amongst their own circle.[75] For example, Mrs Meredith in Tasmania received a letter from one of her acquaintance, a Mrs Grueber, asking: 'How does your new laundress get on? Have you heard anything of her from Mrs Lyne? I told Mrs Forster that I had hired a woman for you. There is no harm in my telling you that I shall always be glad to look out for domestics or anything else I can do for you'.[76] A possible sub-text here is that Elizabeth Grueber sought to improve her status by being associated with the wife of a high-profile lawyer, and so this communication provides a small glimpse into the working of genteel society, and how even basic elements of dress practice had agency within such groups.

It seems possible that in sites where the servants were more likely to be male – India and parts of Africa particularly – laundering was of particular concern. As explained above, adherance to culturally-specific notions of cleanliness was an important aspect of British colonising ideology. There may have been a certain hesitancy, if not actual distaste, among the women for having their dress, particularly their underclothes, handled by the men of the very people from whom they were at such pains to distance themselves. Was there perhaps a tension in being obliged to have a hint of quasi-intimacy with the males of 'the other'? (This would be akin to the ambivalence sometimes expressed in relation to the servants who handled their food, a theme pursued in Chapter 5). In published works male servants are all too frequently presented as being inherently foolish and incompetent, and that included their supposed inability to do laundry. Thus, in an article purporting to provide guidance for those embarking for life in India, a former resident describes how 'your *dhobi* ties stones into your linen, or at least into such garments as he intends to operate on, and then proceeds to thrash them against the flat stone or board ... , you can readily fancy this is an eminently destructive process to linen in general'.[77] As the washing techniques employed in Britain until well into the twentieth century relied largely on abrasion and soaking, it was an exaggeration to suggest that laundering in colonial settings was so very different. This would therefore support the suggestion that what were being articulated here were deeper concerns.

On the other hand, given the volume and work of dress care, surely many women must have been at the very least pragmatic, possibly deeply appreciative, of having their dress cleaned for them, irrespective of who took on the burdensome task? Certainly that is implied in Robert Gray's remarks bemoaning the consequences for Europeans living in North Queensland of the compulsory repatriation of the potential labour of Pacific Islanders.

> Domestic servants are difficult to procure, coloured labour is prohibited, and domestic duties in a climate where for many months the thermometer for many hours a day ranges from 95 degrees upwards, becomes irksome even to womenfolk who are accustomed to it. I have often thought how much more endurable the life of womenfolk in tropical north Queensland would be if each carrier or settler's wife could have a coloured woman to assist at the wash-tub and other domestic duties.[78]

Of equal importance to having one's dress clean was to have it well ironed or pressed. Presenting a smooth appearance was held to be indicative of a serene and smooth inner self. (A calm and unruffled presentation was also the aim of the genteel living room, as discussed in the following chapter.) As dress was held to be indicative of character, it followed that if one had control of dress so one was said to have control of passions and irrationalities. Conversely, crumpled and creased dress spoke of inner discord, lack of control, and hence – vulgarity. Thus ironing, which may seem to be an essentially cosmetic activity, had a moral dimension and was integral to the process of gentility.

That the process and results were highly valued is indicated by Mrs Allport's journal entry of 1832, noting that she had spent the day ironing, even though, or arguably because, she was at that stage living in decidedly basic accommodation.[79] Similarly Eva Gray in North Queensland recorded one summer's day in 1881 that the temperature stood at '108 in the shade' despite which she had spent the morning ironing.[80] Note that the women were undertaking this important work themselves, for just as aspersions were cast on the ability of 'native servants' to perform the washing with adequate care so too was there doubt that they could be entrusted with ironing. In giving advice to women going to Nigeria at the turn of the century, Constance Larymore stated 'It is decidedly useful to bring out from home one or two flat-irons, and make a point of "getting up" one's most cherished muslin blouses, etc, for oneself'.[81]

Ironing was undeniably a skilled activity, as witness the development of different sorts of irons for specific tasks. Box irons were used for collars, Italian irons – which had different sized tubes mounted on a pedestal and heated by a poker – were used for ruffles, and flat-irons were made with heel plates of varying weights for textiles of different weights. In relation to households in Australia, Webber states that it was common to own several irons to meet the complexity of the task.[82] The very fact that there was such a range of irons available speaks of the high store set by appropriately pressed items. By mid-century, cottons and silks were within the price range of so many that, if she were to make those all-important distinctions, the genteel woman had to take additional care with the presentation of her dress. The photograph of the ladies in a North Queensland garden – Figure 2.1 – gives a vivid illustration of the magnitude of maintaining and presenting a clean and smooth appearance.

In handling dress care and presentation discreetly, it has been argued that dress maintenance had significance well beyond the dictates of hygiene. The frequency with which the topic occurred in both personal writings and published works has served to show that the practices involved as well as the final product lay at the heart of genteel performance. Adjustments to such practices can therefore be understood to have been part of the adaption to the changing circumstances.

'The shot or rather wavy patterns were most expensive, 14Rs for a piece of nine and a half yards':[83] *sourcing the right textiles*

When genteel women set about selecting the textiles required for new dress they brought far more to bear on the subject than merely individual preferences for particular colours and patterns; they also brought a range and depth of knowledge which they had developed concurrently with their needlework skills. They possessed an expertise and sensitivity to the material qualities of textiles which arose directly from handling and working with an extensive range of fabrics.

So, in addition to admiring the fineness of vivid silks or the softness of mellow-hued woollens, their appreciation of textiles was more informed, as they also knew how fabrics hang and drape and therefore their suitability for specific sorts of garment. Just as a previous section of this chapter looked beyond the static image of the studio portrait to highlight that the women were active participants in their own lives, whatever the climate, so here there is a need to recognise that dress was worn on animated bodies. Dress is dynamic in a quite literal sense and the inherent qualities of textiles can, when correctly used, enhance or disguise the moving body. Silks cling and mould the frame whilst a stiff cotton has more integrity and hence hangs quite differently. Equally dress is not silent. For example, at the turn of the century taffetas were popular not only because of the bright colours, but also because the addition of metal salts to the dyeing process contributed to the rustle as the skirt was swished by the movement of the woman's legs. See Figure 2.6 of a dress made of just such a fabric which still retains its glowing amethyst hue.

These material qualities of textiles obviously affect the experience of the wearer, and in turn those who observe the wearer. So in her choice of textile the genteel woman was making yet another decision about how she was going to present herself physically to her world; thus textiles can themselves be understood as part of her performance and therefore sensitive to changes to their wearer's environment. As dress was part of the moral framework of gentility, so too were textiles imbued with moral meaning. Clementina Benthall, who was married to a judge and hence fairly well advanced on the ladder of Anglo-Indian society, commented on fabric for sale in Moulmein market: 'the cotton cloths made for the poorer people were many of them pretty but so coarse that I did not buy any, as they would be quite useless' – this refers to more than just the weave.[84] Benthall's words referenced a whole raft of behaviours within which the textile would be sited. Her perceptions can usefully be set alongside those of Sarah Terry who lived in Bombay in the same period and was obliged to resort to any number of stratagems if she and her husband were to 'live up to the mark' on the modest salary he was paid as a merchant's agent. Terry recorded how she sent her Portuguese maid to the bazaar to purchase cheap clothing fabric on her behalf as she could not risk being seen to shop in 'the native quarters'.[85]

In *How to Dress as a Lady on £15 a Year by a Lady* the author advocated that older women should adopt heavier fabrics; the implication being that just as they were of greater substance as the moral arbiters within the female community, so too did they require more substantial dress.[86] (This is comparable to Mrs Lucy Orrinsmith's advice that curtains for the living room should be made of 'honourable fabric', a

2.6 Taffeta dress, c.1875, Tasmania.

point developed in the following chapter.[87]) As the rituals surrounding the wearing of mourning dress seem to have been observed in most sites across the period examined, this too would presumably reinforce the custom of older women wearing heavier textiles. However, in colonies in their infancy there was initially a demographic imbalance, with fewer older women. This raises some interesting though currently unanswerable questions as to whether that thrust on to younger women the responsibilities of being the 'elders' of their groups, and therefore fostered a premature adoption of more 'matronly' textiles. Conversely did the women in India, many of whose children spent most of their time in Britain, wear more 'girlish' attire as there was limited place for the matronly role?

By the mid-nineteenth century, world trade in textiles was well established, and women who had lived in Britain, or in long-established centres within the British Empire, and who subsequently went to take up residence in other sites would have been accustomed to using textiles from a variety of countries. The editor of Miss Rutherfoord's 1850s letters from Cape Town states that there was 'a large variety of materials in [the] stores; silks from the East as well as cottons and woollens from Europe. Barège was a French silk muslin, only one of a large number of names now quite forgotten; silk-striped orleans, printed corahs and surahs, sarsnet and plummet ribbons, cassimere and balzarine'.[88] At roughly the same date Clementina Benthall assiduously searched for and finally purchased some Burmese silks, a local speciality, though she did complain that they were 'generally such excessively gaudy colours'.[89] In similar fashion in 1900 Rawdon Reilly wrote from India to his wife in Britain that he had seen a piece of 'Assam silk[,] ... makes such charming ladies dresses for the summer. The piece was 50 inches broad by about six yards long – whether that is enough for a dress I don't know – you will know better than I do'.[90] In relation to the Australian context, Broadbent et al. argue that prior to the 1840s India was the main source of textiles, listing amongst others punjums, izarees, nainsooks, Luckypore Hummums, Bengal calamancoes, nankeens, palampores and baftas. They argue that thereafter Britain was a source of cheaper goods, until the colony's expanding population created a demand for fine silks and crêpe shawls from China.[91] It should be noted though that this list includes not only such seemingly Indian sourced fabrics as Luckypore Hummums and Bengal calamancoes, but also baftas, a term applied in West Africa to an assortment of plain and fancy cloths, which implies that textile sourcing was not as clear cut as they would suggest. Similarly by 1905 in the developing colony of North Queensland a store in the booming gold-rush town of Charters Towers – 'Aridas All Nations Warehouse' – was able to advertise that they stocked 'French Woollen Cashmeres, Japanese Silk, Pongee Silk, Indian Muslins and Indian Linens'.[92] Thus Aridas actually celebrated and capitalised on its world-wide sourcing. See also Figure 2.7 of Mrs Alphen's ladies store in Charters Towers which gives visual indication

GENTEEL WOMEN

2.7 Mrs Alphen's dressmaking store, Charters Towers, Queensland.

of the size of the market and the range and complexity of commodities involved.

It is evident from the sources given that selection of textiles amongst genteel women was characterised by eclecticism, and is comparable therefore to changes in behaviour which are identified in the following chapters in relation to living rooms, gardens and food. Dress textiles are an example of objects which in some settings were adopted out of necessity, then become acceptable, and then, by dint of being used by elites, become *de rigueur*. Shrimpton argues that the use of local textiles 'remained a significant feature of dress amongst generations of Europeans in India, reflecting their unique circumstances and distinguishing them from their countrymen at home'.[93] Thus the textiles changed in meanings by and through the context of their use; in this instance being used to make European-style dress. The ease with which this aspect of the supposed 'exotic' had been absorbed into genteel performance serves to caution against claims that those of British heritage who lived in the colonies were intent upon re-enacting an idealised notion of Britishness. For not only was textile practice in Britain itself changing all the time, but in colonial settings that which was deemed to be 'exotic' and possibly viewed with suspicion one day was willingly embraced the next. Indeed Rawdon Reilly's words quoted in the previous paragraph, which is part of a passage in which he is trying to persuade his wife to join him in India, offers a reading that some items

[42]

were valued precisely because they were acquired at a remove from the metropolis.

It is the more interesting therefore that no references have been located of use of African fabric for dress purposes, although such commodities were valued for household textiles, as will be seen in the chapter on living rooms. The reluctance to employ locally made textiles for such an intimate purpose as dress was perhaps in part because of their physical properties; often coarsely woven and designed for drawing around and draping the body, rather than the close-fitting moulding of the form as was customary in European dress. In addition, however, local fabric was deemed too gaudy, too crude – ultimately too 'other'. Rather than resort to such commodities the women seem to have used textiles imported from Britain or from India. Thus Cape Castle merchant F. Swanzy's accounts of 'Goods on Hand, 1st March 1854' include such luxury items as satins and French nicanees (a lightweight striped fabric) which may well have been used by members of the small British community.[94] Later residents in West Africa were able to benefit from improved transport links with the metropolis to purchase the readily available 'off-the-peg' items – an aspect of dress practice discussed below. Those women living in the cities in the south of Africa were well supplied with goods, as already mentioned above in relation to the woman enthusing about Cape Town's shopping possibilities in the 1860s. Indeed Lewis and Foy state that even as early as 1811 there were some forty-two retail shops in Cape Town and that 'snobbery flourished from then on', a reminder of how quickly the competitive element of gentility finds expression.[95]

The only exception to the pattern of shunning local textile unearthed to date is that of Isabella Russell who sent to Britain from Gambia 'a few yards of the butcher blue linen the Mohammedans wear here', in order that her sister could make an overall for Isabella's daughter who was in her care.[96] It is clear from the tone of Isabella's letters that she found the separation from her child very painful and sending the small but intimate gift can be understood as an act of nurturing and an attempt to connect those aspects of her emotional life through the textile.

Locally-made textiles with a rather different cultural aura were the merinos and other wool yarns produced in Australia and New Zealand by the European settlers themselves.[97] Naturally these goods were of immense importance if the colonies were going to expand, and the domestic markets, though not as economically important as the export trade, had value in furthering emerging nationalism. Certainly retailers made much of the association. Anthony Hordern & Sons, a Sydney-based department store, took as their motto 'Trade follows the flag, while I live I'll grow' and continued '[it is a] true saying as History proves. Wherever the flag of an English-speaking race is planted, prosperity and happiness are foregone conclusions, and when an enterprising house of business spies out the land, the pioneers are hailed with delight'.[98] Much was made of local manufacture, or even applying local sounding names to items imported from overseas. Anthony Hordern claimed that colonial-made 'even if they cost a little more are infinitely superior'. Of course how much they were taken up by the genteel sector is harder to quantify. However, as the goods became more sophisticated it seems they would have been adopted and indeed even acquired the cachet that Hordern's extravagant advertising literature claimed. Such fabrics are therefore a good example of patterns of use changing through time as they competed with produce from overseas.

This analysis of textile practice and preference demonstrates that one cannot speak simply of 'fine fabrics worn by fine people'. Local circumstances prompted various strategies. Georgina Malloy stated that 'I never wear anything but dark cottons and a muslin kerchief and a lighter print for Sundays', suggesting that this was a modification to her dress very likely called forth by changes in her lifestyle brought about by moving to the small and isolated settlement of the Swan River, Western Australia, in the 1830s.[99] Conversely when faced with the showy dress of those whose menfolk had quite literally 'got rich quick' in the mines, Mrs Allport in Van Diemen's Land wrote of having to wear prints 'which ladies must be contented to wear now, if they would be distinguished from the "slumocracy". Mr Harnett told me he had just sold eighteen yards of bright yellow satin to a digger's wife for a dress'.[100] In that instance quieter dress served to emphasise her refinement; Mrs Allport and her circle could not afford to be seen to be in any sort of competition with their social 'inferiors'. It seems possible that the dramatic success of the goldmines around Charters Towers, North Queensland some decades later may have prompted similarly understated dressing on the part of local genteel elites. What these women saw as constraints on their choice of textiles and how they responded can be understood as another aspect of their adaptation to their changing circumstances.

By teasing out the behaviours of a number of individuals in different sites this discussion has shown that sourcing of textiles was a complex and sophisticated activity which varied across both time and place. As an element of dress practice it demands attention for all the reasons discussed, not least of which being that it reminds one of the physicality of dress, and the intimate relationship between the textile and the body.

THE ART AND PRACTICE OF APPEARANCE MANAGEMENT

'The Indian tailors are a very intelligent race, work well and make any garment you like if they have a pattern, they have no powers of origination':[101] *devising new dress*

There were three methods by which women could obtain completely new dress: by making it themselves, using the services of a dressmaker, and buying 'ready-to-wear' or 'off-the-peg' items. In Britain and other sites with a manufacturing base the ready-to-wear trade expanded rapidly during the nineteenth century though a relatively small percentage of the output was for women, much less indeed for the 'top end' of the market. This is, however, only one reason why it was that within colonial genteel circles there was not a linear progression from one approach to another. Rather did local circumstances as well as those from further afield combine to prompt a range and mixture of practice, possibly greater than in Britain.

As sewing was considered to be a quintessential feminine activity, as discussed above in relation to alterations and recycling (see also discussion in Chapter 3 on needlework for adornment of the living room), it is scarcely surprising that their personal writings contain numerous references to dressmaking. What must also be noted was the sheer volume of sewing the women carried out. Mrs Allport's journal for 1832 not only lists making curtains, mending her husband's trousers, mending nine pairs of stockings, doing various alteration tasks for all the family and constantly fashioning dress for her young son – it also records making a chemisette, a cambric collar, a muslin dress and a silk scarf. Making those refined items for herself in the face of all her other work was an important achievement and material statement of her gentility. Katie Hume writing from Queensland in the late 1860s sounded rather despairing of her workload: 'I am overwhelmed by needlework as usual! I wish it were possible ever to come to the end of it, just for the sake of the novel sensation, but as soon as one thing is polished off, something else rises up at the end of a long vista of "must be done immediately"'. Having then itemised all the sewing she had to do for her husband and baby daughter she concludes: 'Then there are lots of my own dresses to gore and modernise but those always get pushed into the background'.[102] This suggests that for some women in sites where little help was available making new dress could not be a priority, and other means of genteel expression may have come to the fore.

Some women do appear to have decided that the end result of having a new garment was not worth the trouble. Rachel Henning wrote from her rural home in North Queensland that when a dress did not fit 'I left the making for another winter and did without, ... such misfortunes are likely to make one contented with any wearable garment'. As with Hume, though for different reasons, this suggests that for Henning other aspects of her genteel persona took greater priority in 'the bush'.[103] Whether Henning was unusual in her attitude is hard to assess; certainly her candid words were unusual. However, Maynard notes that Henning had known little of sewing before she migrated to Australia and had only learnt out of necessity, so she cannot be taken as typical of her kind; rather was sewing at all part of her personal adaptation.[104]

Certainly one must be cautious about assuming that those who lived in geographically isolated sites ceased to be concerned about maintaining a genteel wardrobe. Allingham, writing of pioneer families in the Kennedy District, North Queensland suggests that there were more social interactions amongst the women living in the back-blocks than one might expect: 'The two Mrs Hanns and Caroline often made social visits by horse or buggy to Burdekin Downs and Hillgrove, to Mrs James at Nulla Nulla and to Mrs Daintree, visits which were of course returned'.[105] These were sizable journeys and would presumably call for the hostess to extend considerable hospitality, so an adequate wardrobe would be needed to meet the requirements of a range of activities, both when acting as hostess and when as a guest.

One imagines sewing must have been very trying during hot weather. In some situations the women seem to have had little choice; in early settlements dressmaking services of good standard took time to become established and such may have been the case for Mrs Allport in Van Diemen's Land in the early 1830s as mentioned above. Certainly it was so for Mrs Melville in Sierra Leone in the 1840s who spoke of how 'the difficulty of getting a person to assist in even the plainest sort of needlework is great'. So she struggled on, despite her dwindling supplies of 'tape, ribbon, thread, needles and pins' and the frustration that 'the damp of the climate is such that nothing saves needles from rusting – except that they be kept in a phial of oil'.[106] And when in 1832 Georgina Malloy describes how her neighbour on the Swan River, Western Australia, lost her home in a fire, she notes in particular 'all their shoes, needles and thread destroyed, which in this far distant clime is really irreparable'.[107]

Equally in households which were working to consolidate their standing within the community the woman may not have been able to afford the services of a dressmaker, even when they might have wished to do so. One senses this was the case for Katie Hume, who noted in a letter to Britain that she was about to employ a dressmaker: and this was some three and a half years after her arrival in a well-established area of Queensland.[108] Similar strain is noted by Miss Rutherfoord in

Cape Town who bemoaned to her sister that 'Papa will allow us each £20 per annum for our dress[;] ... without our seeking it Papa's position has thrown us more into society so that once or twice a week the afternoon is spent in visiting. All these things mount up milliners bills, gloves etc'.[109] In the light of earlier comments regarding the abundance of good shops in the city, and their father's position as shipping agent in the ever-expanding port, one can readily imagine that the Miss Rutherfoords felt keen anxiety as to whether their wardrobes were of an acceptable standard, and this would explain why a visit by the dressmaker is spoken of with particular pleasure and satisfaction. This instance of concern around dress practice serves to remind us of the marked overlap between the worlds of home and business, and how aspects of the women's lives, which have all too frequently been read as being of exclusively female interest, actually had relevance and value far beyond that designated sphere.

Later writings from Africa are of note specifically for the infrequency with which home dressmaking is mentioned (lack of interest in local textiles for dressmaking having been commented on above), which also supports the suggestion that women there adopted other approaches, such as using mail order, visiting dressmakers and buying 'off the peg' when trips to the metropolis permitted.[110] In view of the women's attitudes to their appearance as cited above in relation to adaptation to climate, the absence of home dressmaking cannot be construed in any way as a lessening of interest in their dress.

Charlotte Wortley Corbett, living in India in the 1860s no doubt had plenty of opportunity to draw on the services of the local *dirzees*, despite which we do find reference in her diary to sewing, including cutting out jackets, a task demanding some degree of technical expertise.[111] As the cost of having dress made for her would not be high, it suggests that Corbett preferred to do at least some such tasks herself, implying that the process of making and the creativity involved were important elements in her practice. Using a mixture of approaches seems to have been customary in many sites across the period examined. In India this idea is further supported by the example of Clementina Benthall in Calcutta in the 1840s who spoke of having to take on another *dirzee*, and later of a purchase of a thimble, presumably for her own use, and the Godden sisters who described how at the turn of the century the *dirzee* and their mother and aunt made all their dresses – 'in fact a perpetual dressmaking went on' – and as there were four daughters as well as the two adult women this is scarcely surprising. The Godden sisters' autobiography hints at a degree of financial strain in the household. Their father was a shipping agent in the bustling, and doubtless highly competitive, Bay of Bengal and it may be that the women's performance was subject to similar pressures to those discussed in relation to Cape Town's resident Emma Rutherfoord.[112]

There appears to have been a degree of prejudice against the Indian tailors, as witness the quotation employed in the title of this discussion. Those sentiments were regularly expressed in published work, with even the seemingly liberal-minded Godden sisters saying of their mother's and aunt's dresses that 'They were probably *dirzee*-made, but to us they were creations, the zenith of fashion', suggesting they too had absorbed some of the contemporary attitudes to local workmanship.[113] If the local workers were considered in some ways inferior, it raises the obvious question of why the women employed them, given what an important task they took on, other than for the sake of convenience, of course. One is left with the suspicion that what is being articulated is actually further expression of fear of intimacy with 'the other', as discussed above in relation to laundering and other dress care.

Such 'drawing away' from the local, which after the events of 1857 became such a marked feature of Anglo-Indian society, may well have favoured the European owned department stores which opened in those towns and cities where there were large Anglo-British populations – for example, Whiteway, Laidlow and Co., who established premises in Calcutta in 1882, and subsequently opened branches in Madras, Lahore and Simla. Similarly Hall and Anderson's Calcutta Emporium catered almost exclusively to the tastes of the European elites and boasted departments specialising in outfitting and dressmaking, millinery, drapery and footwear.

A valuable illustration of the combination of practice some women adopted has been provided by Margery Wood, who in recalling her childhood on the Andaman Islands in the early years of the twentieth century noted how her mother made a lot of her own clothes as 'needlework was her greatest pleasure', but also how she:

> had a cousin who had been apprenticed to the court dressmaker and told her to go to Woolams in Knightsbridge, and she arranged for a catalogue to be sent every year then she would buy one evening and one afternoon gown. There was also a resident *dirzee* to copy your clothes from bazaar bought fabric. When King Edward VII died she was the only woman on the island with a black satin evening dress.[114]

The main Andaman Island was a penal colony and as Mr Wood was a senior officer his wife held an important position within the small European community. Her life was dominated by the club, concerts, bridge and an endless round of entertaining – all of which necessitated having a wardrobe which not only was smart and stylish, but was also regularly updated.

THE ART AND PRACTICE OF APPEARANCE MANAGEMENT

In mid-century Tasmania, James Reid Scott's accounts include entries for his wife's clothing with bills from drapers, dressmakers and merchants, suggesting Lilly acquired dress by a variety of means, including a payment of '£9–1 shilling for Mrs. Worthy, Dressmaker'.[115] Matilda Hale's diary of 1875 is sparse but does include more than one entry for a visit to the dressmaker, as well as entries in her accounts book for paying the dressmaker and clothier. Her husband worked for the Hobart brewery and she appears to have had a very small social circle. Her diary offers us glimpses of a carefully constructed genteel persona, though possibly working within some financial constraints. That she should employ a dressmaker is therefore the more interesting and suggests that dressmakers' charges were low, that there was a cachet attached to using such services, or possibly, though less likely, that Mrs Hale lacked the necessary seamstress skills.[116] Thus her practice provides an example of gentility at work in a household where the head of the house was in trade. It also gives a useful illustration of how the material expression of gentility could be accessed at many socio-economic levels. Mrs Meredith, as wife to a leading lawyer was much higher up the social scale. She is fairly reticent about her dress but her 'accounts to be settled' show purchases made from drapers and dressmakers alike in Hobart but also in Melbourne, suggesting either mail order or, more likely, purchases made on her visits to the mainland.[117] Laura Wright's extensive diary, in which she implies that her Tasmanian farming household was comfortable rather than overly prosperous, is replete with references to making dress for herself and her young adult daughters, but in addition an entry from 1863 records 'Mrs Drysdale (dressmaker) left this evening, in the four days was here made 4 dresses and the best part of a silk jacket for Geraldine, her terms are half-a-crown a day'.[118]

Evidently there was a similar mixture of practice in North Queensland, for by 1877 there were nine drapers and eight milliners and dressmakers in Townsville and by 1900 those services had increased to twelve dressmaker-milliners and eleven drapers and clothiers.[119] It seems to have been quite a common practice for the drapers to run a dressmaking service, as shown in an advertisement W. P. Waller ran in 1877: 'Dressmaking, as usual, is under the management of a good Dressmaker of ability, and therefore, Ladies can rely on good Style and Finish'.[120] As noted in Tasmania, peripatetic dressmakers found a ready market for their services in up-country locations. The Kelso family out on the Hervey Range had a dressmaker who made at least one trip per year out to their station during the 1890s, and the McLaughlin family in the same district record similar visits, possibly by the same dressmaker.[121]

As North Queensland was not subject to significant white settlement until the late 1860s, the speed with which services and supplies were in place provides a vivid illustration of how much the communication and transport industries had expanded since the early days of settlement of Tasmania. Of equal significance for this discussion are the findings of the 1876 census which record only 5,582 white females in the north, and even by 1900 the total population of Townsville was only 13,000.[122] That such a limited number of women could act as a stimulus for such a rapid expansion of growth can of course be accounted for in some large part by the success of the goldmines. But it also raises the question of whether by late in the century the genteel woman in the north felt a keener sense of deprivation than those early arrivals in Tasmania, knowing as she did the rich resources which were to be found in the south. Given that expectations of what was necessary to sustain a genteel appearance had changed so much during the century, were her perceived needs greater, particularly when challenged as she was by the new money of the digger's wife?

Maynard notes that the gold rush in the south of Australia during the years 1848–53 prompted a fourfold increase in the import of 'off the peg' clothing, and suggests that this supply prevailed against local produce and in favour of a more uniform manner of dress.[123] There is clearly useful work to be done on the import and consumption of dress in the north of the continent at later dates, and on whether, as arguably would be the case, the welter of imported items of dress encouraged the development of more nuanced practice amongst the genteel, with perhaps greater reliance on etiquette and decorum. Thus increasingly what you wore might not have been enough; it was how you behaved within the dress which perhaps became more telling. This latter point is forcibly taken up by Floyd, who argues in relation to rural Australia that dress 'was of trivial significance when compared to more internalised signifiers of status – one's demeanour and one's status'.[124] It should be borne in mind of course that even if there was an increasing standardisation of dress it does not follow it was British in style and tone. Dress was increasingly being manufactured locally and the larger stores in the cities, such as the Brisbane store Finney Isles & Company, had agents overseas who purchased the styles, fabrics and colours deemed appropriate to their customers' requirements. Similarly in the south of the country the Melbourne department store Buckley & Nunn sought to capitalise on its locally made garments: 'visit our Establishment and Inspect our Large and Varied Stock of Australian-made Apparel, made on our Premises by Australian Workers for Australian Wearers'.[125]

The dress and textile industries of the latter half of the nineteenth century are characterised by numerous technical developments and innovations, but the two which arguably had the most profound effect on the genteel woman were the domestic sewing machine and the paper pattern, both of which became more readily available. Webber notes the power of the sewing machine was that it provided the means for making ever more complex and potentially genteel items.[126] In any society where appearance was seen as *the* marker of status, being able to make a genteel wardrobe may not have been a guarantee of social success, but equally it was certainly a prerequisite. In Tasmania sewing machines became available during the 1860s and, whilst initially they were rather costly, sales rose steadily. In 1877 the *Tasmanian Mail* advertised 'Hand-Machines £5 5 shillings, Family-Machines £7 10 shillings'.[127] Both Katie Hume in southern Queensland in the 1860s and Eva Gray in the north in the 1880s just mention in passing using their machines, suggesting they had been so absorbed into their practice as to no longer warrant elaboration.[128] Emma Rutherfoord had a machine in the 1860s, and her editor suggests it was one of the first in Cape Town, and, coupled with the advent of the paper pattern, it must have made immense difference to that hard-pressed genteel performance.[129] Presumably the genteel woman must have felt rather ambivalent about the ready availability of the sewing machine, for though it enabled her to expand her wardrobe it also provided the same opportunities to those who challenged her position of social dominance, so the technology fed in to the competitive nature of gentility. The *Englishwoman's Domestic Magazine* unwittingly put their finger on this very dilemma when describing the sewing machine as 'one of the means by which the industrious labourer is as well clad as any millionaire need be, and by which working girls are enabled to gratify their women's instinct of decoration'.[130]

The paper pattern is such a simple concept and yet had an immediate success. In 1852 the *Englishwoman's Domestic Magazine* started to include paper patterns, and as references have been found to the journal having had readers in Tasmania, various sites on the Australian mainland, Cape Town and across India its potential for impacting upon dress practice should not be underestimated. (It would, for example, be interesting to know if Mrs Drysdale, the dressmaker employed by Laura Wright as described above, made use of paper patterns). Other magazines soon followed suit. By the 1880s McCalls and the Butterick Pattern Company had distribution agents over most of the Australian land colonised by Europeans.[131] As these patterns allowed for a more rapid dissemination of information about ideas of style and fashion they may well have had the same effect as an influx of 'ready-to-wear' dress, namely an erosion of difference and a greater preoccupation with notions of centralised fashion. So here too one may imagine that careful and critical judgements had to be made by those of genteel sensibilities to decide which patterns to adopt, and how if necessary they should be modified to accord with the notion of taste which prevailed within their particular genteel 'tribe'.

This discussion has identified that even the manner of dress manufacture played a part in genteel performance. As with all elements of dress practice, how it was made was determined by the context, and therefore contributed to the meaning of the dress.

'Doing good at every stopping place, showering blessings and imparting information':[132] *vital knowledge for assembling the genteel 'look'*

Women who wanted to occupy positions of high status had to make very careful decisions about what sort of styles they should adopt. This was not necessarily because they wanted to dress in the latest fashions as determined by Paris, London and New York; chasing the latest trend would have been a risky business anyway, even allowing for steadily improving communications and transport. Rather did they need to know what was in fashion so they could position themselves accordingly; never overly dressed in such a showy manner as to run the risk of being thought outlandish, never clad in such outmoded garments as to appear to lack either the knowledge or resources to update one's dress.

Equally there are also tensions to be identified with the women wanting to be regarded as being of genteel appearance within their peer group and within wider colonial society. This called for negotiation of local circumstances and embracing of local norms, whilst also retaining at least the notion of having dress which would be suitable for the metropolis. Conflict between the two was inevitable, and added to the pressures involved in making decisions about dress style. The Tasmanian example cited above of Mrs Allport's wearing of print dresses because of her concern to distance herself from the 'slumocracy' is a case in point. Georgina Malloy's husband articulates very clearly the distinction as it applied to male attire. He wrote from their home in Western Australia to his mother in Britain requesting she send 'a good cloth waistcoat or two such as one would not be ashamed of wearing in England'.[133]

It can be seen that for many the quest for knowledge would be unceasing, particularly if uncertain of their position within the hierarchy. One of their sources of information was the new arrival. Sarah Selwyn, who travelled out to Auckland, New Zealand in 1842, and was initially rather horrified by the local dress, wrote to her female cousin, 'you will judge that fashions are slow of travelling hither when I tell you that some years ago all the ladies were dressed in tight skirts! A great start has been made since then'. One can hear her pleasure when, some two years later, she was able to write of a visitor from Sydney: 'Then she is so wonderfully well-dressed, so exceedingly soignée and fashionable and so ready and able to impart information on this important topic'.[134] Selwyn also commented on what a long time it had been since she saw an unmarried woman of that age – most of the migrants tending to marry young. This may imply that marriage was a determining factor in a woman's style of dress and supports a comparable point made in relation to textile choice. In similar vein Charlotte Godley wrote from Wellington in 1850 requesting her family to 'send us a chapter on fashion. Mrs Eyre in her trousseau, got a year ago nearly, is at present our model', suggesting that Godley felt sadly out of touch.[135]

Initially the main formal source of information on Selwyn's 'important topic' was periodicals sent from Britain. As mentioned in the previous section, the *Englishwoman's Domestic Magazine* is known to have had a flourishing overseas market. Other publications aimed at a similar readership included the *Englishwoman's Domestic Journal* – which seems to have been a rather drabber version of the *E.D.M.* – and the *Young Ladies' Journal*. It is reasonable to assume that for every copy actually arriving in foreign parts it had countless more readers.

As well as written descriptions of styles, these periodicals carried fashion plates, a valuable source of knowledge, albeit an idealised one. Prior to the early 1860s, constraints on cheap colour printing meant the hand-coloured illustrations were in muted washes of pink, green and yellow. Rarely was the whole garment coloured, often it was just a trim or a hair ornament and there was no attempt made to indicate either the fabric or the draping, other than by grey shading. Thereafter it was possible to produce brighter colours and actual models of dress were depicted, rather than merely generic shapes. An impressive piece of sales organisation can be seen in the *Englishwoman's Domestic Magazine* of 1863: 'The newest fashions for Spring and Summer months expressly designed for the *E.D.M.* The garments illustrated in the colour plates may be seen and purchased at "Msrs. Farmer & Rogers'" establishment, Regent Street, London'.[136] Thus the advancements in printing, in the 'ready to wear' trade and, presumably, in mail order were co-ordinated to both stimulate and satisfy market interest.

Taylor makes the point that fashion plates are not to be taken too literally as indicators of dresses worn, that they were, as stated above, idealised and need to be understood contextually.[137] Furthermore Taylor is speaking of dress practice in Britain. How much more important then that they be approached with caution in the context of dress practice empire-wide. Here, therefore, they are being taken as an indicator of interest in *ideas* about dress, and how that could be incorporated into broader ideologies regarding a genteel appearance in a variety of locations over a period of time.

When there was a sufficiently large population base, local periodicals appeared. Of course this development meant ideas about and knowledge of dress could be circulated much quicker, doubtless prompting the same mixed responses in the minds of the elites as did the paper patterns and sewing machines, namely they were welcomed but it could so easily mean knowledge about this all-important subject was in the hands of the 'wrong sort of people'. In most colonial settings a limited British population meant the women remained reliant on periodicals and newspapers sent from 'home'. In Australia, however, with its rapidly developing population, twelve such fashion magazines were published between 1880 and 1900, including Madame Weigel's *Journal of Fashions*.[138] In addition many newspapers in Australia had a 'Ladies Page', and it was evidently seen as an important feature, with the *Tasmanian Mail* including it from the first issue in 1877. On that occasion it contained news of Paris fashion and described a dress in sufficient detail for it to be copied. A subsequent issue ran a piece from the *New York Herald* and provided very detailed dress news, including a reference to the French designer 'Worth', and advocating the use of Indian silk. Clearly the paper saw itself as the disseminator of important news. It is interesting therefore that some fifteen years later the emphasis was on the events and dress practices occurring in Hobart. For example, an edition of 1893 reported on the local race meeting and described in great detail the dress of those present. On that occasion at least, the only overseas item was a report about a Hobart woman who had recently been married in Paris.[139] Similar patterns of coverage seem to have been the norm in North Queensland where by 1905 the *Register* gave far more attention to the dress details of those attending local picnics, tennis balls and afternoon teas than to the *haute couture* of Europe.[140] The implication is surely that there had developed a confidence about local genteel mores, and there was less reliance on confirmation from the metropolis.

Similarly distinct behaviours were observed in India by long-term resident Margaret Fowke. Although she was writing half a century before the period of this enquiry, she made a significant observation: 'Many of the ladies of Bengal dress very well, as it is impossible to follow strictly the fashion of England they are in general much more guided by their own taste than by fashion, or at least as far as it is becoming'.[141] So she identifies that taste is a separate and internalised entity quite separate from notions of fashion and also that local behaviours were inevitable. Although she interpreted it as being the result of isolation from the metropolis, and did not give the recognition to local circumstances which is so crucial to the argument made here, she did identify and describe a local form of gentility, and one which was recognised, valued and participated in by residents.

In some sites another important source of information as well as actual dress was the mail order business. The system that was in place in Victoria, New South Wales and Queensland by the closing decades of the century offers a striking example of the moral tone adopted by stores in relation to their potential customers. This is amply demonstrated by Anthony Hordern & Sons' catalogue of 1894:

> Our silent traveller passing from point to point, doing good at every stopping place; showering blessings and imparting information; dropping useful hints; clearing up doubts and settling controversies; is embedded in THIS BOOK, WHICH IS DESIGNED to instruct people dwelling in the country in the theory and practice of SHOPPING BY POST.[142]

Thus the stores sought to position themselves as key agents within the woman's decision-making regarding purchase of dress. Admittedly there is little evidence to suggest that firms on the mainland had a large impact on the consumers in Tasmania; it would simply not be worth their while to send a traveller on such a slow and indeed uncertain journey to serve such a limited population.[143] However, Hobart merchants established their own mail-order service for within Tasmania. Scripps states that Mathers the drapers supplied diagrams to advise customers on how to take correct measurements when requesting dressmaking by post, and Fitzgeralds the retail store ran an advertisement in the *Tasmanian Mail* making the rather grandiose claim that they had 'an extensive mail order business' and their 'tailor made costumes' were said to be 'preferred by ladies all over Australia to anything available in Adelaide, Sydney, Brisbane or Melbourne'.[144]

For women living in isolated sites, all shopping was in effect done by mail order. In many places in rural North Queensland the carter delivered only twice a year until well into the twentieth century, so receiving dress knowledge and dress commodities was correspondingly slow. Maynard notes 'The lack of current fashion information meant that styles changed abruptly, though infrequently, in remote areas'.[145] Dress practices in such locations were akin to those experienced some decades earlier by settlers in Tasmania, the chief difference being that when women did make the journey to the city greater quantities of ready-made dress were on offer.

No discussion of dress style for the genteel would be complete without consideration of the part played by items from family members in Britain, be they sent on request or as gifts. Inevitably requests were made more often by women in new settlements where services and supplies were limited. So Georgina Malloy's appeal for 'if not too expensive, also twenty yards of *good black cotton velvet*, as much as would make me a *very full dress* and some over for children's frocks' was made because she really was deprived of all but the most basic of requirements. In 1835 the Swan River settlement was so undeveloped that Malloy wrote 'indeed we *suffer materially* from this place being so little known as it makes our numbers so small we have no opportunity for progressing'.[146] It is questionable whether Malloy's intention to make a full-skirted dress was based on fashion knowledge, or whether it was because she was obliged to undertake so much physical work that she needed that, above all else, her dress should permit ease of movement. Included in the archive of the Malloy family papers in Britain is a published document entitled 'Equipment for a Lady going to India'. If Georgina Malloy did indeed take this as her model then one can only wonder how useful in the Swan River in the 1830s she found the 'twelve white dressing gowns, silk stockings and frilling for twelve habit shirts'.[147] This provides a most telling illustration both of how site-specific were the requirements of dress, and of how, inevitably, many of those early migrants must surely have been woefully ill-prepared.

Charlotte Godley's requests are revealing: in 1850 she asks for gloves, 'two pair black, four rather dark, and six quite light, and three pair of long white'. Her statement that 'I find I wear more gloves than I expected, being out so much' is presumably a reference to an unexpected degree of formality in Wellington's burgeoning community. Later in the year she wrote asking 'you to send me out a silk gown of some rather dark, cheap kind; a made up skirt with flounces if they are still to be had, would be thought beautiful here and cannot be bought'. This is a good example of Godley drawing on previous dress knowledge to assist her in establishing herself in a new genteel circle.[148] It is also noticeable that more requests were sent when the women first arrived in the colony and that as they became more established so their requests seem to have declined, presumably as they developed some degree of ease in their new surroundings, adjusted to local standards and looked to the immediate environment to meet their dress needs.

Unsurprisingly, gifts from Britain were especially valued. Katie Hume in Queensland commented that an 'elegant present of lace was pronounced lovely. It will "vastly" set off my new dresses!' – suggesting that the gifts made a significant contribution to her presentation, just as Godley's flounced skirt was going to aid her performance in New Zealand.[149] Equally one can hear the bitter disappointment in Emily

Eden's words when her gift was lost en route for India: 'My poor box is at the bottom of the sea . . . I particularly grudge the gown Lady G had worked for me. I was wishing to see it so much. It is an inconvenient loss, for if we arrive on Saturday, as we expect, I shall have no bonnet to wear on Sunday'.[150] However, it is Sarah Greenwood, writing from New Zealand in 1843 whose words highlight the other crucial aspect of dress from the old home. In describing attending a dinner party, she wrote: 'I wore my pretty silk dress and thanked the giver in my heart. I often think to myself "I will tell Mama how useful this or that has proved" but you all loaded me with benefits, that though I think of and thank-you for them every day and hour their very number prevents my singing them out'.[151] The incorporation of past experiences into present circumstances has already been discussed in relation to dress modification. Here it is seen again in a different form when the migrants speak of the arrival of the 'box of delights' from their former home and how and where they wear the contents. It is the very intimacy of dress which makes the gifts so poignant; to dress one's body in a garment chosen by a loved one so far away is an act of emotional intensity. The sheer physicality of dress invites the act of remembering, of experiences shared, an undeniable past as a force in the present. Ash, in speaking of dress belonging to the deceased, used the phrase 'the aesthetics of absence'. It can usefully be applied to migrants' dress sourced from families never entirely left behind.[152]

As this discussion has made abundantly clear, the style of dress worn by genteel women was a complex matter, in which overseas fashion, local circumstances and the tastes of absent family all played a part. The last influence which needs acknowledgement is that of the women's menfolk, particularly their husbands. The women's ambitions to present a genteel appearance were for their family's standing in the community as much as to satisfy their individual needs. It follows therefore that for social as well as personal reasons husbands sometimes participated in the decision-making process. Thus Jane Bardsley noted in her diary, c.1896, 'I have a beautiful green dress and toque from Finney's of Brisbane. It is Tom's choice. He says I must dress differently now I am a married woman and buy materials one cannot see through. The choice is a bottle green, almost as thick as a billiard tablecloth, trimmed with black velvet, and a very severe toque'.[153] Bardsley's words offer a reading that suggests her pleasure in her new dress – presumably sent by carter all the way up to their property in Normanton in the far north of Queensland – was somewhat muted by the matronly nature of the garment. Katie Hume recounted that when her sister-in-law, in southern Queensland, gave a 'grand party . . . Marion had a handsome bright green silk for the occasion, trimmed with fringe. She may not wear a low dress', one of several references to her brother-in-law's guiding hand.[154] Few men can have been as involved as Charles Bowen in New Zealand, whose wife wrote at length about his interest, which seems not always to have been entirely welcomed. She wrote to her sister in Britain that 'he makes my life a burden about my dress' and 'You really must send me relays of bonnets, one *cannot* get them here and Charles makes more fuss about head gear than anything else – except perhaps crinolines'.[155] *The New Zealand Dictionary of Biography* lists Bowen as an 'administrator, politician, poet, magistrate and educationalist'. Equally revealing perhaps is his biographer's comment that Bowen 'relished nothing so much as recognition as a gentleman', and with such a public and self-aware profile it is no surprise that he placed a high store by the contribution Georgina's dress made to their joint performance.[156]

It is evident that information about style of dress was obtained from a wide variety of sources. One's peers, shops, mail-order catalogues, newspapers and new arrivals supplied knowledge locally, whilst from the metropolis came letters, parcels and periodicals. The sheer range of the sources of information highlights the enduring interest women had in style. When taken in conjunction with the other elements of dress practice analysed in this chapter it is clear that style made an important contribution to the genteel appearance. Equally it is evident that it was not slavishly followed, but rather were aspects of fashion adopted and or modified as befitted local and personal circumstances.

Examples of dress actually worn in specific locations can be seen in Figures 2.8–2.10. These show *cartes-de-visite* as used by women in Tasmania and North Queensland when making social calls. Such items are material indicators of the high value accorded to dress, and also hint at the way in which the practice of leaving such cards functioned as a means of disseminating ideas about desirable dress.

It is appropriate, if poignant, to conclude this discussion of dress with reference to a garment that was never worn, as shown in Figure 2.11. At some point during the early 1890s a Mrs Grimaly commissioned the dressmaker at the Sydney-based department store David Jones to make this elegant burnt-orange silk and silk-brocade frock.[157] The dress and its additional set of sleeves were never collected. Was the customer unable to settle her account, or dissatisfied with the goods? Did she simply move away and forget to send for it? Or did she become pregnant, or – for it is a dress made for a mature woman rather than a young figure – perhaps she died? At the time of writing no supporting documentation has been located and the garment, suitably stored, sits in the archive, testament to the importance of genteel dress as a sign of cultural currency.

2.8 Woman wearing checked dress with white collar and cuffs, the latter items possibly detachable, Tasmania, c.1850s.

2.9 Woman wearing dress with bustle and lace trim, the latter possibly a later addition, Queensland, c.1870s.

2.10 Woman wearing dress with frilling, long buttoned cuffs and decorative hemline, Queensland, early 1890s.

GENTEEL WOMEN

2.11 Mrs Grimaly's unworn taffeta dress, Sydney, New South Wales, early 1890s.

'The people here think of little besides dress, . . . we shall have enough to do to "look like others", as Mama says':[158] *in conclusion*

This chapter has examined female genteel dress in a variety of locations across the British Empire. It has made the case for dress being a critical mechanism in negotiating self-identity in new surroundings. This has proved to be infinitely more helpful than adhering to old orthodoxies of assuming the women were intent merely on replicating a notion of Britishness, with its strong implication that they behaved with unquestioning conformity. Such interpretations lay the emphasis on the constraints and prohibitions in the women's lives. This analysis has cut a swathe through such narrow readings. By taking an integrated approach and considering structural, developmental and personal factors at play it has been possible to isolate and explore both individualised responses to specific circumstances and the broader grids in which dress was situated. The wide-ranging enquiry has challenged readings which have taken the final ensemble as being dress's only meaning, and scrutinised instead the practices associated with that finished 'look'. Thick contextual detail has been amassed and the routine enactment of behaviours has been examined, thereby illuminating the determining rationale which lay behind those behaviours.

Dress stands revealed as dynamic; critical in the women's expression of identity and, because of its complexity and intimate relationship with the body, particularly sensitive to changes in their circumstances. The extreme contrivance of genteel dress which has hitherto so often been dismissed as trivial emerges as a meticulously stepped performance, a highly developed way of expressing social difference. Delineating their genteel distinctiveness lay at the heart of the identity of genteel women and their dress was their primary marker. Challenges to their gentility were a constant feature of such women's lives – indeed responses to recurring challenges are a characteristic of genteel societies and hence a theme addressed throughout this work.

First discussed in this chapter in relation to the expansion of commodity markets in Britain, anxieties regarding fear of erosion of difference clearly ran throughout the women's experiences, largely irrespective of time or place. Maynard makes the case for such insecurities being a particularly contentious issue in Australia, arguing that waves of prosperity arising from the plundering of the country's rich natural resources had generated buying power amongst those from whom the genteel drew away with distaste. It seems though that although the triggers for anxieties had temporal and spatial specificity, concerns of not being able to dress differently, by which they meant 'more tastefully', were a perennial feature amongst most female migrants as we have seen it expressed in sites as contrasting as New Zealand and India across the period under investigation. It suggests that the over-arching explanation was the absence of other signifiers, either because the colony was in its early stages of settlement or because other markers were effectively denied to the women – such as in India where for the women whose menfolk worked in officialdom regular household moves had to be made and they were therefore constrained in other means of expressing gentility, such as furnishing their living rooms and creating gardens.

In the light of the above it is the more interesting that those women in West Africa towards the turn of the century made fewer comments regarding their dress practice. It is difficult to gauge to what extent this might be attributed to the relatively short duration of most residencies (though surely no genteel woman worth her salt would consider going even a year without some modification or alteration to her wardrobe) or to the increasing ease with which many items, including ready-made dress, could be purchased by mail order.

Equally it could be argued that their disinclination to write about their dress practice even in semi-public documents is indicative of changing attitudes to what constituted being 'a lady out in the colonies'. Developments in the fields of education, communication and transport ensured that the women, be they District Officer's wife or trader's daughter, had a greater awareness of the world and the significance of the imperial project within it than had their predecessors. Whilst their role remained broadly the same – that of selfless devotion to the cause of maintaining standards and acting as prime movers in the transmission of cultural values – notions of how they were to achieve those ends had shifted. The women may have felt a desire and a pressure to present themselves as playing an active part in the wider imperial project, active by arguably more male-determined terms of reference. Mrs Tremlett wrote of how in the 1890s most men, be it in official or business circles, were reluctant to have white women in Nigeria at all, saying they were only tolerated there 'under sufferance', an attitude Laura Boyle said was still common amongst British men living on the Gold Coast more than a decade later.[159] With pressures upon them to contribute in a much more androcentric manner this may well explain the paucity of dress detail, and why instead the following chapters will reveal much more discussion of their creations of homes and gardens, with a particular emphasis on training servants.

It has become clear that dress as the most intimate expression of subjectivity took on added and different meaning in colonial locations. By pursuing and modifying their dress practice the women acquired the means of anchoring themselves, of developing a sense of 'self' in a new place. Working, sometimes indeed struggling, to maintain their appearance can be understood as the women grappling with their change of circumstances. Deciding which dress to don had profound psychological meaning, far in excess of the seeming simplicity of the act itself. So dress had agency for the individual in the stepped process of identity formation.

THE ART AND PRACTICE OF APPEARANCE MANAGEMENT

It has also been shown that dress was a means of aligning oneself with a particular local identity group. By dressing in a manner which accorded with the local genteel set that was appropriate to the woman and her household's position (or that to which they aspired), other behaviours would come to accord with the values of that set. Furthermore, so would your attitudes to other groups, namely 'outsiders'. By dressing to comply with the local look your view of the world was determined, as was the world's view of you. The woman's peers read her dress and took it to be a definition of the themes of her life. Equally the 'other', be it indigenous or social inferior, was excluded and hence the beginnings of a place-specific identity started to develop. Dress can therefore be understood as integral to social ordering. The positive reactions of others with specific regard to dress consolidated social relations and favoured the evolution of nuances in local dress. Thus dress had a mediating function between the individual and her peers, but also wider society. The intense formality of the women's dress, which seems to have been retained in public across all sites during the period concerned, spoke volumes as to the body and self in a state of control. This discussion has identified that this was both recognised and encouraged by contemporaries because a woman's dressed self and the image it presented were a highly visible and valued contribution to the marking off of space in the name of empire. Thus the genteelly dressed woman was at the very centre of the social arenas of her site and an active constituent in the generation of cultural values.

Closely related to this point is the fact that the women's dress and related practices served to reinforce gender roles. The highly stylised forms of femininity as performed in public with their emphasis on supposed effortlessness and ease stood in marked contrast to the masculine roles with their expectations of action and displays of physical activity. So the women's dress did much to preserve the status quo in this regard, reinforcing the thrust of the previous paragraph which argues that their presence and spheres of activity were of paramount importance within the imperial project.

This chapter has shown that dress had agency as a means of expressing self-worth, of participating in chosen social groups and contributing to wider colonial society. However, it has also become evident that dress was a material means of expressing some of the conflict of being an in-comer. The all-important sensitivity to local mores could sometimes be at odds with the current or imagined notions of dress in Britain – hence Rachel Henning's expression that her new dress was 'too good for the bush'.[160] Clashes between affiliations to being a colonial and being British overlapped with tensions of a more personal nature between a sense of belonging 'home' or 'away'. This work argues

GENTEEL WOMEN

that the latter dichotomy, though not of course of the women's making, was more often directly articulated by women through their personal and domestic practices. It took on a special intensity in relation to dress with the flow of knowledge and supplies tending to be largely, though certainly not exclusively, one way from Britain out to the colonies. (It has also been shown that the informational exchange was largely, though again not solely, the province of women.) Material culture of this type has proved to have been highly evocative of 'elsewhere', but also had social force in the colonies when amalgamated into the recipient's performance.

This discussion has been positioned from the perspective of the women themselves, rather than that of the observers. The 'gaze' has been seen as one factor at work, but by no means the only one, in determining women's dress behaviours. The notion that the women were merely reactive in matters of dress has been forcefully rejected. In identifying discreet meanings of her dress, this chapter has shown that the genteel woman developed a performance eminently suitable to her setting. She took ownership of and structured her own space and by so doing exerted a strong influence on the behaviour of others and on other spaces over which she had profound influence.

The next chapter enters the living room, the area of the home which ideally was both the creation and province of the mistress of the house. Used for a range of family and public/private activities it was the ultimate setting for the woman of genteel appearance. The meanings dress had for the women and the values it conveyed to their observers were in turn reinforced and further structured by the genteel living room.

Notes

1. H. Southgate, *Things a Lady Would Like to Know* (London, William P. Nimmo, 1874), p. 480.
2. C. Flower, *Clothes in Australia: A Pictorial History 1788–1980s* (Kenthurst, NSW, Kangaroo Press, 1984); M. Fletcher, *Costume in Australia 1788–1901* (Melbourne, Oxford University Press, 1984); M. Maynard, *Fashioned from Penury: Dress as Cultural Practice in Colonial Australia* (Cambridge, Cambridge University Press, 1984).
3. www.tepapa.govt.nz   www.aucklandmuseum.com   www.powerhousemuseum.com
4. www.ngv.vic.gov.au   www.qm.qld.gov.au
5. D. Cumming, B. Labrum, J. Malthus and K. Merrick, *Framing Dress in Aotearoa New Zealand, 1850–1950*, forthcoming publication.
6. R. Barthes, *The Fashion System* (London, Jonathan Cape, 1985).
7. D. Miller, *Why Some Things Matter* (London, University College, 1998), p. 8.
8. J. Finkelstein, *The Fashioned Self* (Cambridge, Polity Press, 1991), p. 23.
9. J. Entwistle, 'The Dressed Body' in J. Entwistle & E. Wilson (eds.), *Body Dressing* (Oxford, Berg, 2001).
10. Southgate, *Things a Lady Would Like to Know*, p. 480.

THE ART AND PRACTICE OF APPEARANCE MANAGEMENT

11 Anon., *How to Dress as a Lady on £15 a Year by a Lady* (London, Warne & Co., 1873), pp. 4, 8.
12 Baronne Staffe (trans. Lady Colin Campbell), *My Lady's Dressing Room* (London, Cassell, 1892), Introduction.
13 C. Cavers, *Hades! The Ladies! Being Extracts from the Diary of a Draper* (London, Gurney & Jackson, 1933), pp. 18–19.
14 Mrs H. Tremlett, *With the Tin Gods* (London, Bodley Head, 1915), p. 5.
15 M. Maynard, *Dress and Globalisation* (Manchester, Manchester University Press, 2004), p. 16.
16 P. Barr, *The Memsahibs: The Women of Victorian India* (London, Secker & Warburg, 1976), p. 28.
17 M. Douglas, *Natural Symbols* (Penguin, Middlesex, 1993) cited in Finkelstein, *Fashioned Self*, p. 51.
18 Tremlett, *With the Tin Gods*, p. 5.
19 P. Bourdieu, *Distinction: A Social Critique of the Judgement of Taste* (Cambridge, University of Massachusetts, 1984), p. 202.
20 Isabella Russell, Letters from the Gambia, Bathurst, 10 April 1899, British Empire and Commonwealth Museum, henceforth BECM.
21 That said of course the weather is very variable in some parts of India. Emily Eden commented on its changeability when, after crossing the Ganges at Gurmukteser Ghaut, she noted 'On Wednesday morning the thermometer was at 41 degrees and on Thursday at 78, so we had to rush from fur coats and shawls and stoves, to muslin gowns and fans; and as far as I am concerned I do not think it is very wholesome'. E. Eden, *Up the Country: Letters Written to her Sister from the Upper Provinces of India by Emily Eden* (Oxford, Oxford University Press, 1930), p. 87.
22 *Mercury*, 14 March 1907, 11 April 1907.
23 L. Jocic, *Australia Made: One Hundred Years of Fashion* (Melbourne, National Gallery of Victoria, 2010), pp. 13–14.
24 A. Trollope, *Australia*, P. Edwards and R. Joyce (eds.) (St Lucia, University of Queensland, 1967), p. 67. Cited by M. Maynard, '"A Great Deal Too Good for the Bush": Women and the Experience of Dress in Queensland', in G. Reekie (ed.), *On the Edge: Women's Experiences of Queensland* (St Lucia, University of Queensland Press, 1994), p. 59.
25 N. Bonnin (ed.), *Katie Hume on the Darling Downs: A Colonial Marriage* (Toowoomba, Darling Downs Institute Press, 1985), p. 98, 17th January 1868. 'Barège' – a silky gauze muslin as made in Barège, France; 'body' – a sleeveless garment for the upper torso; 'tucker' – a detachable yoke, worn over the breast, as with a low cut dress.
26 Lady Curzon, Bombay, cited D. Kincaid, *British Social Life in India 1608–1937* (London, Routledge, 1938), p. 260.
27 C. Larymore, *A Resident's Wife in Nigeria* (London, Routledge, 1911), pp. 299–300.
28 Isabella Russell, 1899, BECM.
29 Maynard, *Fashioned from Penury*, p. 107.
30 J. and R. Godden, *Two Under the Indian Sun* (London, Macmillan, 1966), p. 67.
31 V. Steele, *The Corset: A Cultural History* (New Haven, Yale University Press, 2001), pp. 87–111.
32 *Brisbane Courier*, 19 September 1877, cited in Maynard, 'A Great Deal Too Good for the Bush'; Larymore, *Resident's Wife*, pp. 299–300.
33 This debate is exemplified by Mrs Fanny Douglas, *The Gentlewoman's Book of Dress* (London, Henry & Co., 1894–95) in which she asserted a 'tight lacer ... person who respects herself and is careful in all departments', p. 107.
34 J. Young (ed.), *Jane Bardsley's Outback Letter Book: Across the years 1896–1936, Pioneer Life in Australia's Tropic North* (North Ryde, NSW, Angus & Robertson, 1987), p. 25.
35 Bourdieu, *Distinction*, p. 78. For further discussion of the use and meanings of corsets see S. J. Vincent, *The Anatomy of Fashion: Dressing the Body from the*

Renaissance to Today (Oxford, Berg, 2009), pp. 38–48; for a rich array of corsetry and its manufacture see 'The Symington Collection', www.leics.gov.uk/museums

36 C. Macdonald (ed.), *Women Writing Home 1700–1920: Female Correspondence Across the British Empire. Vol. 5 New Zealand* (London, Pickering & Chatto, 2006), p. 339, Georgina Bowen.
37 Maynard, 'A Great Deal Too Good for the Bush', p. 56, citing C. H. Eden, *My Wife and I in Queensland: An Eight Year Experience in the Above Colony, With Some Account of Polynesian Labour* (London, Longmans, Green & Co., 1872).
38 Bonnin, *Colonial Marriage*, p. 183. Fish-hook is a type of crochet hook, suggesting Hume's gift was a lacy item, possibly a wrap or stole.
39 E. Roberts, *The East India Voyager* (London, J. Madden & Co., 1839), p. 15; E. Eden, *Letters from India*, Vol. 1 (London, Richard Bentley, 1872), p. 132 cited by J. Shrimpton, 'Dressing for a Tropical Climate: The Role of Native Fabrics in Fashionable Dress in Early Colonial India', *Textile History* Vol. 23, 1992, pp. 55–70.
40 Larymore, *Resident's Wife*, pp. 299–300; A. F. Hattersley (ed.), *A Victorian Lady at the Cape, 1849–51* (Cape Town, Maskew Miller, [194?]), p. 21.
41 The cultural value of hats is discussed in the following section.
42 Y. Bird (ed.), *A Quaker Family in India and Zanzibar, 1863–186: Letters from Elizabeth and Henry Jacobs* (York, William Sessions, 2000), p. 148; D. Adams (ed.), *The Letters of Rachel Henning* (Harmondsworth, Penguin, 1969), p. 166.
43 Hattersley, *Victorian Lady*, p. 17.
44 E. E. K. Lowndes, *Everyday Life in South Africa* (London, S.W. Partridge & Co., 1900), p. 43.
45 Eustace Kenyon, Letters from Calcutta, 10 May 1896, Centre of South Asian Studies, University of Cambridge, henceforth CSAS.
46 Isabella Russell, 1899, BECM.
47 L. Taylor, 'Wool, Cloth and Gender: The Use of Woollen Cloth in Women's Dress in Britain 1865–1885' in A. de la Haye and E. Wilson (eds.), *Defining Dress: Dress as Object, Meaning and Identity* (Manchester, Manchester University Press, 1999), pp. 36–41.
48 James Morris Draper; bill sent to Mrs Meredith 1 July 1885, NS23/4/6, Tasmanian State Archives, henceforth TSA.
49 J. Richardson, 'An Annotated Edition of the Journals of Mary Morton Allport', Ph.D. Thesis, University of Tasmania, 2006. 7 November, 1832.
50 James Reid Scott, Household Accounts, Ledger Page 118, 1868, NS52/1/1, TSA; , Mrs Butler, Diary, 1 January 1878, NS2089, TSA.
51 Macdonald, *Women Writing Home. Vol. 5*, p. 123, Sarah Greenwood.
52 M. Ginsburg, 'Rags to Riches: The Second-hand Clothes Trade 1700–1978', *Costume: The Journal of the Costume Society* No.14, 1980, pp. 121–35.
53 *Englishwoman's Domestic Magazine*, Vol.8, 1871, p. 60, copy held in Private Collection, Hobart, Tasmania.
54 L. P. Wright (ed.), *Laura's Brookville Diaries: 1819–1894* (Launceston, Greenhill, 2003).
55 R. R. Kaczynski, *Demographic Survey of the British Colonial Empire*, Vol. 1: *West Africa* (London, Oxford University Press, 1948), pp. 2–17, as cited by Harper and Constantine, *Migration and Empire*, p. 111.
56 Macdonald, *Women Writing Home. Vol. 5*, pp. 371–2, Georgina Bowen, August 1866.
57 N. E. A. Tarrant 'A Maternity Dress of about 1845–1850', *Costume: The Journal of the Costume Society* No. 14, 1980, pp. 117–20. In addition, the Bernberg Costume Collection, Museum Africa, Johannesburg lists in its holdings an 'Edwardian turquoise maternity gown', a rare survivor given both the hard wear such items were often subjected to and the ambivalence at that date towards bodies swollen with child.
58 Richardson, 'Allport Journals', 4 September 1832.
59 Ginsburg, 'Rags to Riches', p. 122.
60 My thanks to Alison Melrose for alerting me to this practice.

61 Anon., *Life at the Cape One Hundred Years Ago, by a Lady* (Cape Town, C. Struik, 1963), p. 11. Marshall & Snelgrove – a smart department store in London, established 1848, which supplied each and every dress commodity a well-turned out lady could require.
62 *Townsville Daily Bulletin*, 3 October 1887.
63 *Englishwoman's Domestic Magazine*, 1879, copy to be found in Central Public Library, Leeds, UK.
64 P. Lockren, 'Why Were Women of the 1900s Slow to Take Up the New, More Economical Ready-made Clothing?' Unpublished paper, Pasold/Chord Conference, University of Wolverhampton, 2010.
65 'Bicentennial Exhibition Album Notes', Narryna Costume Collection, Hobart, Tasmania.
66 Thanks to Dr Judith Jensen, Townsville Library Service for bringing this item of dress to my attention. Regrettably at the time of writing no more is known of the provenance of this item.
67 The significant exception to this is amongst the European women living in West Africa, where, from mid-century onwards, the pith helmet or sola topee became *de rigueur*.
68 P. L. Brown (ed.), *Clyde Papers*, Vol.1 (Oxford, Oxford University Press, 1941), Prologue, p. 155, with thanks to Roslyn Hill for bringing this work to my attention.
69 Macdonald, *Women Writing Home. Vol. 5*, p. 332, Georgina Bowen 5 November 1863.
70 J. Murray (ed.), *In Mid-Victorian Cape Town: Letters from Miss Rutherfoord* (Cape Town, A. A. Balkema, 1953), p. 33, 'blonde' probably refers to bleached lace.
71 Richardson, 'Allport Journals', 20 November 1832.
72 A. Drummond (ed.), *Married and Gone to New Zealand* (Hamilton, Paul's Book Arcade, 1960), p. 75, Sarah Greenwood, Nelson, August 1843.
73 C. Walkley and V. Foster, *Crinolines and Crimping Irons: Victorian Clothes, How They Were Cleaned and Cared For* (London, Peter Owen, 1978).
74 Richardson, 'Allport Journals,' 15 September 1832.
75 *Mercury*, 8 January 1867, 'laundress wanted'.
76 Elizabeth Grueber, Battery Point, Hobart to Mrs M. Meredith, 19 January 18? , NS123/192, TSA.
77 *Englishwoman's Domestic Magazine*, January 1879, p. 90. Copy held in the Central Public Library, Leeds, UK.
78 R. Gray, *Reminiscences of India and North Queensland* (London, Constable & Co., 1912), p. 254. By 'womenfolk' Gray refers to European women.
79 Richardson, 'Allport Journals', 18 September 1832.
80 A. Allingham, 'Victorian Frontierswomen: the Australian Diaries and Journals of Lucy and Eva Gray, 1868–1872 and 1881–1892', MA Thesis, James Cook University, 1987. 28 December 1881.
81 Larymore, *Resident's Wife*, p. 206. Although this work does not examine British Central Africa, readers may also be interested to know of a photograph produced in H M Consulate, Nyasaland in 1886 which records a European man demonstrating ironing to two African women, whilst another African woman works a mangle. See Royal Commonwealth Society Collection, University of Cambridge.
82 K. Webber, 'Romancing the Machine: The Enchantment of Domestic Technology in the Australian Home 1850–1915', Ph.D. Thesis, University of Sydney, 1996, p. 201.
83 Burma silk prices in bazaar in Moulmein 1849, Mrs Clementina Benthall, Diary, CSAS.
84 Clementina Benthall, Diary, 1849, CSAS.
85 Barr, *The Memsahibs*, p. 82. The financial strain upon Sarah and Sidney Terry is further indicated by Barr's note that of the £600 p.a. paid to Terry by Higson & Caldwell of Calcutta the couple felt obliged to spend £200 p.a. on life insurance.

86 Anon., *How to Dress as a Lady*, p. 10.
87 Mrs L. Orrinsmith, *The Drawing-room: Its Decoration and Furniture* (London, Macmillan & Co., 1878).
88 Murray, *Mid-Victorian Cape Town*, p. 29: orleans – heavy woollen; corah – plain un-dyed silk; surah – twill-weave silk for dress or blouse; sarsnet – soft silk; cassimere – wool of suit weight; balzarine – soft dress textile with cotton warp and worsted weft.
89 Clementina Benthall, Diary, 1849, CSAS.
90 Col. Rawdon E. D. Reilly, Letters from India, BECM.
91 J. Broadbent, S. Rickard and M. Steven, *India, China and Australia: Trade and Society, 1788–1850* (Glebe, NSW, Historic Houses Trust of New South Wales, 2003).
92 *North Queensland Register*, 1905.
93 Shrimpton, 'Dressing for a Tropical Climate'.
94 F. Swanzy Collection, UAC/2/33/AG/2/1/1, Unilever Archives and Record Management, Port Sunlight.
95 R. Lewis and Y. Foy, *The British in Africa* (London, Weidenfeld & Nicolson, 1971), p. 90.
96 Isabella Russell, 1901, BECM.
97 The fleece of the merino has a short staple with a finer yarn than that of the harsh long staples of English breeds, and hence could be used to make higher quality wools and worsteds.
98 *Anthony Hordern & Sons Stores*, Haymarket, Sydney, Catalogue 1894, p. 1. Copy held in the Caroline Simpson Library and Research Collection, Sydney.
99 D. Coleman (ed.), *Women Writing Home 1700–1920: Female Correspondence Across the British Empire. Vol. 2 Australia* (London, Pickering & Chatto, 2006), p. 167, Georgina Malloy, January 1835.
100 Richardson, 'Allport Journals', 11 January 1853.
101 'On Indian Outfits', *Englishwoman's Domestic Magazine*, January 1879, p. 132.
102 Gore – to cut to shape. Bonnin, *Colonial Marriage*, p. 160, 20 December 1869.
103 Adams, *Rachel Henning*, p. 143.
104 Maynard, 'A Great Deal Too Good for the Bush'.
105 A. Allingham, 'Pioneer Squatting in the Kennedy District', *Lectures on North Queensland History*, Department of History, James Cook University, 1975, pp. 77–96.
106 Mrs E. H. Melville, *A Residence at Sierra Leone by a Lady* (London, John Murray, 1849), p. 132.
107 Coleman, *Women Writing Home. Vol. 2*, p. 157, Georgina Malloy, 1 October 1832.
108 Bonnin, *Colonial Marriage*, p. 183, 13 May 1870.
109 Murray, *Mid-Victorian Cape Town*, p. 29.
110 Decima Moore does, however, speak of spending some of her time mending clothes. D. Moore, *We Two in West Africa* (London, Heinemann, 1909), p. 249.
111 Charlotte Mary Wortley Corbett, Diary, Ormsby Papers, CSAS.
112 Clementina Benthall, CSAS; Goddens, *Two Under the Indian Sun*, p. 67.
113 Goddens, *Two Under the Indian Sun*, p. 79.
114 Margery Wood, Audio tape 599, BECM.
115 James Reid Scott, Accounts, NS52/1/1, TSA.
116 Matilda Hale, Diary, 1875, Tasmaniana Collection, State Library of Tasmania.
117 Mrs John Meredith, Accounts, TSA, NS123/81.
118 Wright, *Brookville Diaries*, 8 December 1863.
119 *Willmett's North Queensland Almanac: Miners, Settlers and Sugar Planters Companion* (Townsville, T. Willmett, 1877); *Pugh's Queensland Almanac and Directory* (Brisbane, Pugh, 1900). Copies held at Local History Library, Public Library, Townsville.
120 *Willmett's Almanac*, 1877, capitalisation in original.
121 Oral History Collection, Local History Collection, Townsville Library Service.

My thanks to librarian Dr Judith Jensen for bringing this information to my attention.
122 G. Bolton, *A Thousand Miles Away: A History of North Queensland to 1920* (Canberra, Australian National University, 1972). Note that the indigenous peoples were not recorded.
123 Maynard, *Fashioned from Penury*, pp. 97–8 and 131.
124 E. Floyd, 'Without Artificial Constraint: Gentility and British Gentlewomen in rural Australia' in R. S. Kranidis (ed.), *Imperial Objects: Essays on Victorian Women's Emigration and the Unauthorized Imperial Experience* (New York, Twayne, 1998), p. 87.
125 'Table Talk', 17 January 1907 cited by Jocic, *Australia Made*, p. 14.
126 Webber, 'Romancing the Machine', p. 224.
127 *Tasmanian Mail*, 1877.
128 Bonnin, *Colonial Marriage*, 20 December 1869; Allingham, 'Victorian Frontierswomen', Eva Gray, July 1881.
129 Murray, *Mid-Victorian Cape Town*, p. 29.
130 *Englishwoman's Domestic Magazine*, 1867. Copy in private collection, Hobart, Tasmania.
131 From 1873 to 1937 the American company Butterick also published a fashion and society journal, *The Delineator*, copies of which are held at the Australian National Library.
132 *Anthony Hordern & Sons Stores*, Sydney, Catalogue, 1894, p. 2. Copy held at Caroline Simpson Library and Research Collection, Sydney.
133 Captain Malloy, 5 April 1837, D/KEN/3/28-9, Kennedy Papers, Cumbrian County Archive Service, Carlisle.
134 Macdonald, *Women Writing Home*. Vol 5, pp. 23 and 67, Sarah Selwyn, c.1844. Soignée – well groomed.
135 J. R. Godley (ed.), *Letters from Early New Zealand by Charlotte Godley, 1850–1853* (Christchurch, Whitcombe & Tombs, 1951), p. 91.
136 Sanderson Collection of Fashion Plates, Vol. 2, 1841–62, Vol. 3 1863–1909. Copies held at the Central Public Library, Leeds.
137 L. Taylor, *The Study of Dress History* (Manchester, Manchester University Press, 2002), p. 136.
138 Webber, 'Romancing the Machine', p. 280.
139 *Tasmanian Mail*, 1877 and 1893.
140 *North Queensland Register*, 1905.
141 D. E. Blum, 'Englishwomen's Dress in Eighteenth Century India: The Margaret Fowke Correspondence, 1776–1786', *Costume: The Journal of the Costume Society*, No. 17, 1983, pp. 47–8.
142 *Anthony Hordern & Sons Stores*, Haymarket, Sydney, Catalogue 1894, p. 2.
143 The population of the state of Tasmania in 1867 was 101,592, as against 546,000 for Melbourne alone.
144 *Tasmanian Mail*, 22 December 1906. Cited by L. Scripps, *The Industrial Heritage of Hobart, Vol. 1 Historical Study* (Hobart, Hobart City Council, 1997), p. 81.
145 Maynard, 'A Great Deal Too Good for the Bush', p. 55.
146 Coleman, *Women Writing Home*. Vol. 2, pp. 158 and 167, Georgina Malloy 21 February 1834 and January 1835.
147 'Equipment for a Lady going to India', D/KEN/3/27, Kennedy Papers, Cumbrian County Archive Service, Carlisle.
148 Godley, *Letters from Early New Zealand*, pp. 99, 122.
149 Bonnin, *Colonial Marriage*, p. 183, 13 May 1870.
150 Eden, *Up the Country*, p. 394.
151 Macdonald, *Women Writing Home*, Vol. 5, p. 118, Sarah Greenwood, 4 October 1843.
152 J. Ash, 'Memory and Objects' in P. Kirkham (ed.), *The Gendered Object* (Manchester, Manchester University Press, 1996), p. 223.
153 Young, *Across the Years*, p. 85.

154 Bonnin, *Colonial Marriage*, p. 148, 8 July 1869.
155 Macdonald, *Women Writing Home. Vol. 5*, pp. 345 and 339, Georgina Bowen, 5 November 1863.
156 *New Zealand Dictionary of Biography*, www.dnzb.govt.nz
157 Powerhouse Museum, Sydney, H7423. My thanks to Curator Glynis Jones for bringing this item to my attention and to Alison Melrose for further assistance in dating the dress.
158 Coleman, *Women Writing Home. Vol. 2*, p. 123, Fanny Leonora Macleay, Sydney, 1826.
159 Tremlett, *With the Tin Gods*, p. 280; L. Boyle, *Diary of a Colonial Officer's Wife* (Oxford, P. Alden, 1968).
160 Adams, *Letters of Rachel Henning*, p. 128.

3

'The arrangement requires much taste and judgement':[1] creating critical space, the living room

Introduction

During the latter half of the nineteenth century there developed a notion that in any household which made claim to refinement the living room was a quintessentially female space. This idea, expressed in steadily more forthright terms, gathered in momentum over the decades, prompting the mistress of the house to lavish increasingly anxious care and attention on this most critical of domestic areas. It can therefore be understood that for the genteel woman it was an area which provided a crucial means of both formulating and expressing her identity. By and through these rooms women made clear statements to their households and beyond regarding the standards they set and the position they intended to occupy, or at least aspire to, on the ladder of gentility. To contemporary society each element of the room had moral significance, so that which was held to be a perfectly appointed arrangement carried with it moral authority. These were private spaces into which selected individuals were invited. Thus the rooms were laid out for display and subject to scrutiny. The choice of material items was therefore never arbitrary; rather was it a question of 'taste', notions of which lay at the heart of gentility and which were expressed through endlessly changing performance.

This chapter will examine that performance as it was enacted in these vital spaces, and consider ways in which the value systems to which the women subscribed found expression in material terms. It will thereby argue that the material culture of the rooms is to be understood as eloquent expressions of contemporary site-specific female genteel subjectivities. The objects and related practices will be analysed as a means of understanding ways in which genteel norms and ideologies were modified and/or reproduced in a variety of colonial sites across a period of time.

It will be argued that the room was a pivotal space in the woman's life; the process of its creation and its subsequent uses another means by which the woman established herself in her new location, both psychologically and socially. It is because gentility is essentially performative in nature that social relations are an all-important part of the phenomenon, but equally it must be understood as central to the identity of the individuals within the social group. So the case is made for giving greater weight to ways in which individuals sought to develop points of anchorage for themselves and their household in a new genteel society. Furthermore, examination of the living room provides a means of politicising the domestic, for though the room was in the private sphere it had relevance far beyond the home and can also be understood as expression of broader discourses regarding the imperial enterprise and women's contribution within it.

It is evident from the above that the contents and practices of genteel colonial homes merit consideration, and yet relatively little work has focused on this subject, much less directly on the living room. Many works on European women in Asia have drawn extensively, and largely uncritically, on the personal writings of those whose self-conscious narratives were an uneasy mixture of advice manual and memoir.[2] In such accounts social distinctions are subsumed within a generalised mythical memsahib, snobbish and inflexible, whose life, it is implied, largely conformed to the image as presented in the guidance manuals. In the Australasian context there has been a plethora of works which saw women's preoccupation with the detail of refined domesticity as being incompatible with notions of egalitarianism, and elect instead to generate stories of heroine helpmeets whose lives were considered to be only subsidiary to the 'real work' of colonisation undertaken by their menfolk.[3] None of these works engaged directly with the phenomenon of gentility, though, by dint of the sources used, many of their subjects would have almost certainly defined themselves as such.

Rich and informative work on the Australian domestic interior has been carried out by Lane and Searle, though as they aimed to cover the entire country local patterns of practice are inevitably overlooked, and the status of the room's creators is not a central element of the survey. Russell's seminal publication on female gentility in Melbourne is invaluable, and lays the ground for examining such behaviours in a broader context, but her focus is on attitudes and behaviours rather than on material aspects of the home. Young's work on the material expression of gentility does acknowledge the need to explore the 'expressive and symbolic meanings' of objects, but in seeking to make the case for a global gentility effectively loses sight of localised adaptations.[4]

CREATING CRITICAL SPACE, THE LIVING ROOM

The museum sector continues a long-established tradition of producing fruitful work on domestic artefacts. Jaffer's work on furniture from British homes in India as held in the Collections of the V&A, London, and numerous projects carried out by the Historic Houses Trust of New South Wales, Sydney, Australia and by The Otago Settlers Museum, Dunedin, New Zealand are all outstanding contributions to the field of colonial home histories.[5] To explore the living room thematically this work draws on the methodologies of such studies, whilst also making due reference to the work of Ardener and of Massey, both of whom examine the gendering of space, and of Chattopadhyay and of Miller, who place the design and construction of the house and the spaces within at the centre of their explorations of gendered domestic behaviours.[6]

Jones, in his study of interiors of the Indian sub-continent, alerts us to the many male-only households within the British community, certainly an important element in the history of domestic consumption in that location, as indeed such arrangements were in many African colonies, but of significance for the incoming genteel women only in so much that they sought, with some urgency, to establish homes of a quite different order. This chapter considers the relationships that developed between the rooms, their material contents and the women and the spaces that they sought to occupy. In so doing it casts light both on the genteel interiority of the mistress and on the ways in which her genteel practices acted as mechanism for structuring and furthering social hierarchies.

The opening section of this chapter considers the living room in Britain, and how that model contributed to cultural expectations in colonial settings. This in turn paves the way for examining the genteel living room in those locations, its functions in emergent genteel societies and the challenges faced by the in-coming homemakers. The elements of the room are then analysed in detail, with due consideration given to the ways in which each part both had value and meaning in itself and also contributed to the whole ensemble. Central to the discussion are the strategies developed by the homemakers to overcome the challenges of their new environments. Their ingenious and imaginative approaches often resulted in interiors of astonishing complexity and eclecticism, interiors which can be read as material representation of the process of change occurring within their creator's identity. It will be seen that the material culture of the room had agency for the woman to negotiate the endless variables and complexities of the ever-changing circumstances she encountered in her new location. Aspects discussed are floorings and ceilings, walls and furniture – with the piano calling for discrete handling, needlework and craftwork, and the use of flowers and plants. The chapter concludes with discussion of ways in which this exploration of the living room has furthered understanding of how and why material culture proved to be a critical mechanism for ideological expression. Emerging as a site for the adaptations and modifications to which female gentility was subject, the room also proves to be an arena for enactment of their vital contributions to the process of successful colonisation, and hence a base and source of social power.

'A room that holds our dearest treasures, and sees little of the seamy side of life':[7] the living room in Britain

This description of the ideal living room is typical of a widely stated view that the home was the seat of all that was civilised and virtuous within society, and within the house no area was more highly regarded than the living room. It was held to be the setting for the modelling of perfect behaviour, for the benefit of the household and society alike. Hence the room was seen not only to contain reassuring symbols of lifestyle and status, but indeed as an embodiment of moral standards. Opinions regarding the influence of the room were regularly articulated in contemporary publications, such as 'There can be little doubt that the surroundings of our daily life are largely instrumental, not only in affording pleasant sensations, but actually moulding our natures and characters in many important respects'.[8] It followed that moral value would also be accorded to the process of arranging and maintaining the room and that responsibility for creation of this elevated space would lie with the woman of the house, as she was held to be the embodiment of all that was pure and good.

The line employed as the title for this chapter continues 'the arrangement requires much taste and judgement, so that, in their disposal, the whole may be in perfect harmony'.[9] The harmony it refers to is much more than an aesthetically pleasing disposing of the objects within the room; it carries with it notions of moral, as well as material balance, all parts in congruity, controlled and at ease. Gentility's self-appointed position at the top of the social hierarchy was a precarious one indeed. Much more hung on the colour of one's curtains than 'mere' fashion. Qualification for tribal dominance necessitated full cognisance of complex and ever-changing standards, for the successfully appointed room was a source of power, denoting affiliations and exclusions.

Scarcely surprising then that there was a plethora of detailed material published about all aspects of the room's décor, works which were invariably didactic and prescriptive in tone. Of course, one must exercise caution in assuming that advice as given was life as lived, much less would all readers take the same meaning from the works. However,

Kinchin, in making the point that the women were not as 'witless, passive and angst-ridden as some of the authors would have us believe', nonetheless finds the publications useful for being 'indicative of the complex webs of cultural meanings woven by women in interiors that were multi-layered, not only in terms of fabrics but in terms of affectivity, sensibilities and associations'.[10] Equally, that there was an ongoing market for such advice speaks of the inherent insecurities of gentility, and also that there was a perceived need for guidance by those who felt themselves to be on the fringe of genteel society, ambitious but uncertain of how to proceed. Note how this author 'helps along' the novice, assuming no prior knowledge of the niceties of genteel life:

> Fine manners are a necessity, and a certain amount of fine manners is maintained by the use of a room that holds our dearest treasures, and sees little of the seamy side of life. It is on little things that our life depends for comfort, and small habits, such as a changed dress for evening wear with a long skirt, to give the proper drawing-room air, the enforcement of the rule that slippers and cigars must never enter there, and a certain politeness maintained to each other in the best room, almost insensibly enforced by the very atmosphere of the chamber.[11]

From this extract can be deduced not only that the room was to be a sphere of feminine authority, but also that the space, the objects within and the behaviours of the occupants were deemed to have a mutually reinforcing influence. The notion of the room as hallowed ground was an idealised construction, and therefore there was inevitable conflict as the reality was largely unattainable; such complex environments were labour intensive and difficult to control. If one is also mindful that by mid-century homemakers in Britain were theoretically able to be active participants in a material world of ever-increasing complexity, little wonder living rooms became such significant points of conspicuous but anxious consumption. As every element of the space was understood by themselves and peers as essential to such a high-status lifestyle, so the material culture was endlessly and increasingly nuanced, every detail codified and replete with meanings.

During the period under examination the visual appearance of the rooms changed dramatically. Technological developments in the paper and textile and chemical industries enlarged the range of wallpapers and soft-furnishings. Improvements in communications and manufacturing, both in Britain and in many sites overseas, ensured an ever-increasing variety of goods was on offer to the homemaker. Expanding knowledge of the world was eagerly seized upon by designers and manufacturers, and contemporary publications were characterised by enthusiasms for a diversity of styles. Thus new forms of knowledge did in turn inform the behaviours of the homemakers, and seemingly incongruous items entered the genteel home as the 'exotic' was invited in and rendered acceptable. Irrespective of the decorating style adopted, the centrality of the room in the woman's life remained a constant feature in the genteel portion of society.

Further appreciation of the value of the room lies in understanding it was the setting for a number of socially vital activities. Not only was it used for private practices, intended to reinforce the family as the basic unit of civilised society, it also functioned as the site for 'calling'. This institution, which was largely, though by no means exclusively, pursued by women, was pivotal in establishing and maintaining social connections and hierarchies. It was another topic on which advice manuals rushed to provide guidance. Mrs Beeton was specific on how the mistress should dress for receiving calls: 'It is as well to be neatly attired, for a costume very different from what you usually wear, or anything approaching an evening dress will be very much out of place'; and also on activities during the calls: 'If a lady be engaged with light needlework, and none other is appropriate in the drawing-room, it may not be, under some circumstances, inconsistent with good breeding to quietly continue with it during conversation'.[12] This latter point of Beeton's highlights that the room was to be an appropriate arena for the display of the hostess's accomplishments and also that being witnessed engaged in the creation of such work would also contribute to the feminine refinement of the space. Equally there were activities which were held to be unsuitable, such as smoking, and loud, unruly and unseemly behaviour. Guidance was also given on the nature of the conversation which was and was not deemed to be appropriate, the duration of the calls, and the etiquette to be observed regarding the return of calls. It can be seen that 'calling' operated to structure genteel society and therefore there was a social value to the interactions, which belies the seemingly rather empty nature of the dialogues. 'Calling' was part of their habitus; 'subjective but not individual system of internalised structures, schemes of perception, conception and action common to all members of the same group or class'.[13] Thus it can be seen that there was a reciprocal relationship between the room and the activities which took place within the room, with the space determining behaviours. Hence the room is to be understood as a controlling and controlled environment, necessity for which lay at the heart of genteel performance.

Such then was the aesthetic and behavioural heritage against which the woman with genteel ambition set out her stall when she commenced homemaking in the colonies. As noted in relation to dress practice, whether the woman was first generation migrant in 1840s

Tasmania, second generation moving in the 1870s from a family base in the south of the country to establish a home in the new colony of North Queensland, or perhaps a turn of the century settler in southern Africa – she would reference many of the same aesthetic traditions and 'material attitudes', albeit filtered through successive generations and/or varying experiences. This touchstone of taste, whether experienced first hand or vicariously, accounts not only for some similarities in the rooms empire-wide, but also explains some of the seeming anomalies, as the women responded to such factors as restrictions on communication with the metropolis, availability of commodities – or lack thereof – and varying complexities and efficiencies of infrastructure. Conflict was also inherent within their lot as gentility fought for survival. It had to adapt or to perish; initially at least both could be troubling possibilities for the woman of genteel persuasion.

No woman who held herself to be genteel, or had ambitions in that direction, would dream of making a life in the colonies without a living room. It is perhaps not overstating the case to say that without a genteel interior she may experience breakdown of her genteel interiority; certainly her subjectivity would be placed under severe strain. To prosper she had to develop strategies for occupying her space psychologically as well as physically. This required her to dig deep into her cultural capital, and it is on the basis of that understanding that her colonial living room is examined.

'Our house was English streaked with Indian, or Indian streaked with English, it might have been an uneasy hybrid but we were completely and happily at home':[14] *living rooms for changing lives*

Ideally the colonial living room was to function in the same way as its idealised form in Britain; namely it was to be the woman's throne-room, centre of hearth and home and hence a moral as well as physical space. Evidence suggests that it was recognised as a priority for the woman of the house and that her menfolk were willing to defer to her opinions and preferences regarding its appointment. Andrew Morrison, writing to his fiancée in Britain prior to her journey out to India, described the house and the basic living room furniture, but assured her that he would wait on her arrival before making more purchases as her taste and judgement were required. Similarly Rawdon Reilly sent his wife a diagram of the home that she would have on her arrival, and newly married Eustace Kenyon told his mother that he thought his wife 'was very much looking forward to having her own house and doing her own housekeeping'.[15]

The room was also to be used for social gatherings comparable to those which took place in Britain. So again it can be understood as a private/public room, site of display of the woman's homemaking expertise, which both consolidated and extended her genteel practice, instrumental in positioning the household on the ladder of gentility. In colonial societies, however, where so many of life's social certainties were called into question, such activities as the culture of calling took on added and absolutely vital significance. Certainly its ritualised behaviours were frequently parodied, and even its participants seemed sometimes to find it a bind. Evelyn Beeton who took a year long trip to northern India in 1912 spoke of 'paying calls on everyone in the Cantonment, which is the duty of the newcomer (a deadly business – paying 40 calls of 3 minutes each on 40 strange ladies)'.[16] Nevertheless as Beeton's words make admirably clear, as a disseminator of knowledge and social attitudes it was a remarkably effective tool. Calling worked to establish and reinforce rules of conduct, created affiliations with those who met with approval, and equally utterly denied access to others. A new arrival in Cape Town commented that 'The ladies here have a very excellent plan of calling upon all desirable strangers within a week after new arrivals have been seen in church. This enables the ladies of the garrison especially to make a rapid acquaintance, if they are so minded, with the proverbial hospitality of Cape residents'.[17] The woman could thereby be acknowledged in the community and gain social gravitas. It could make or break her credibility and claim to membership of the elite. Lewis and Foy cite the experiences of an anonymous resident at the turn of the century in an unspecified colony in tropical Africa:

> Africa was probably never as rigid as India nevertheless the newcomer had to learn the code and abide by it. On arrival the mysteries of calling were first performed, especially in the smaller stations. You called on your seniors, while your equals and juniors called on you. This involved the whole paraphernalia of hats, gloves and stockings, not to mention visiting cards.[18]

Such was the value of this social mechanism it seems to have been adhered to even in remote locations. Allingham, drawing on family diaries of homemakers in the Kennedy District in Queensland, reports an unexpected amount of contact as 'despite their isolated situation the early settlers made concerted efforts to maintain social contacts and preserve the niceties of the society from which they came'.[19]

That the living room was valued by herself and her peers is indisputable, and yet in striving to create and maintain her space, the genteel woman met with innumerable challenges. As noted in the previous chapter and although a generalisation, it is accurate to say that the colonies of the British Empire had warmer climates than Britain. This prompted the development of styles of housing fundamentally different to those which were the norm in Britain, and the resulting quantitative and qualitative changes to the interior spaces had a profound effect on how the women experienced and occupied their homes. Lucy Gray's description of her home in North Queensland in the 1860s is restrained, but certainly hints at how the house challenged her expectations of a home:

> It consists of three rooms in a row all opening into the verandah, before and behind, which answers for halls and passages[;] between the top of the walls and the roof there [are] about two feet open, which has the advantage of letting in plenty of air and the disadvantage of making it impossible to shut out cats etc. The partitions between the rooms being the same height as the walls leaves the whole length of roof open from end to end that a person at one end has the benefit of conversation going on at the other.[20]

Similarly Violet Jacob, on seeing the house she and her army officer husband were to occupy in Mhow, central India in the 1890s noted of the drawing room 'there are seven windows and seventeen ventilators so there ought to be plenty of air', suggesting it was actually anything but airy, and also thought it worthy of comment that the house seemed 'very open'.[21] Whilst Gray notes the advantage of having a well-ventilated home, rooms which could not be closed to the elements let in many other problems as well as the cats she mentions. Charlotte Stamper spoke of their house in Mussoorie, northern India as having been 'prettily situated and a fair size but the walls streamed with damp all the time', and Mrs Melville in Sierra Leone complained of how the wind was blowing and 'everything in the house is covered with an impalpable red dust ... every article of furniture is shrinking and cracking – paper and the boards of books curling up – [and] veneer peeling off'.[22]

Whereas homes in Britain required small easy-to-heat interior spaces, in warmer climes that which was regarded as spatial intimacy had to give way to large rooms which maximised the possibilities of ventilation and created at least the illusion of cool and airy spaces. Chattopadhyay notes that such rooms, fourteen to twenty feet high, 'refused to grant their residents a private interiority – the space of the "intimate sphere"'.[23] For the woman of the house such unruly space constituted a particular set of challenges; not only in terms of the appointment and maintenance of the apartment, but also to carrying out those very practices for which the room was designated.

As the room was designated for the enactment of such highly valued social practices and interactions, its spatial configuration launched a daily counter-attack on her attempts to impose a restrained tone. Descriptions such as those given here from India and Queensland highlight that space itself must be taken to be a material force, with power to structure the interactions of those within it. If the genteel woman was to assert her persona in the alien environment she had to devise strategies to control the site, or at least create the illusion of so doing.

Living rooms were always labour intensive but expecting to present a controlled and effortless salon under such circumstances was a very tall order indeed. It is interesting therefore that the additional work arising from such conditions is rarely mentioned, presumably for the very reason that gentility demanded that the performance should appear effortless. In some colonies, especially in more remote parts of Australasia, servants were in short supply from the onset of colonisation, thereby threatening that which Young describes as the woman's 'status honour'.[24] More remarkable for being unusual therefore are remarks such as Sarah Greenwood's, who at the prospect of life in her home in New Zealand without a servant said 'as to cleaning of all kinds I confess that I like it most vulgarly'.[25]

In houses designed for cool climes it was very simple to designate areas for different purposes. Buildings of several storeys with halls and passageways leading on to multiple small rooms lent themselves for specialised use. Not only could some areas become gendered, but so too could social hierarchy be made spatially explicit. Servants knew their place, literally as well as figuratively. In colonial homes in warmer climates, servants, still regarded as that most essential of commodities, could so easily be in the wrong place. The mistress of the house could find herself obliged to live on terms of quasi-intimacy with her servants, who frequently were the only representatives of the indigenous peoples with whom she had contact. In many colonies, notably in Africa and India, house servants were male, so the woman's discomfiture had gendered as well as racialised aspects. Ardener comments that in 'cultures where there is little expectation of trust beyond the family circle, the domestic environment represents a sanctuary from the perils outside'. Clearly in many sites such 'sanctuaries' remained elusive throughout the period of colonisation. Ardener extends her point with the suggestion that 'where the hostile line is drawn close to the front door, the importance of the home and the status of the woman inside, as its symbol and guardian, become correspondingly greater'.[26] Thus there was increased pressure on the mistress to create a haven, but so too were there more obstacles to her success.

One of the most troublesome features of many colonial homes

was the verandah, commonly employed as an outdoor living room. If life in tropical or sub-tropical climes was to be made tolerable an area protected from the harsh sunlight but open to any chance breeze was a godsend. Of course this meant 'the house imposed an outward looking orientation and a dynamic relationship with the environs', the very antithesis of the inward looking and contained living room of the northern hemisphere.[27] In addition, as a living area it was difficult to control or to impose the requisite softening aesthetic said to denote genteel femininity. It also fostered a range of informal and relaxed behaviours, which challenged the idealised notions of standards of femininity. In practice many households had an interior living room in addition to the verandah space. The very fact of having two areas with the same supposed function compelled the woman to adapt her genteel standards: either remain in her formal but stifling space within or modify her performance on the verandah. Figure 2.4 in Chapter 2, 3.16 in this chapter and Figure 5.3 in Chapter 5 are representations of such modifications of behaviour. So for the mistress the verandah was a problematic and slippery space and her attempts to occupy it and the objects and practices she introduced can be understood as reflecting that inner dilemma.

The very dimensions of verandahs and interior living rooms taxed the homemaker's ingenuity. King notes that the chairs designed for relaxation (with men expressly in mind as they accommodated sprawling inelegant legs), 'took up areas of fifteen square feet; with space added to allow bearers to circulate'.[28] Decima Moore gives us an insight into the huge floor space she had to tame in her home in Accra, West Africa, and how some attempts seem to have been made to subsume the verandah within the overall relaxed seating area:

> The verandah we fitted up with a few basket chairs we had brought from Las Palmas, a hammock and some native rugs and mats ... We stained and polished the floor of the billiard room, placed our round gate-legged oak table on a Turkey carpet in the centre, an oak writing-desk in one corner, a piano in another and two solitary looking basket-chairs in the remaining spaces of the wilderness.[29]

Moore's choice of language, most specifically 'wilderness', serves to emphasise the scale of her civilising task. We see how the very dimensions of the external and interior rooms scorned the homemaker's attempts to conquer and domesticate the space. In Moore's account there is an unmistakable touch of the heroic in the careful positioning of a few choice items amidst the vast and undeniably 'alien' expanse.

Also of interest and significance here is that Moore gives centrality – both in the room and in her description – to 'our round gate-legged oak table'.[30] In electing to take with them pieces of furniture and other items the homemakers were according great authority to the objects. Items from previous homes are to be understood as a distinctive form of material culture which materialised memory. Such is the power ascribed to objects that they have almost endless mobility of meaning. Possessions transported in this manner acted as mechanism for the past to reside in the present, for past practice to be accommodated in a new location. Marcoux's work on elderly people dismantling their homes prior to moving into residential care speaks of the disposal of objects as a form of pre-death inheritance.[31] This idea can usefully be applied to belongings transported by migrants; the presence of the 'inherited' object, and the people it was connected to, live on in the process of making a new home. Similarly Hallam and Hockey, in their analysis on meanings and values of family mementoes, state that 'The perceived duration of an object, its capacity to endure time and to operate across time by encoding aspects of the past or future in the present moment is crucial to its memory function'.[32] Implicit here is that responses to objects are individualised *and* will change through time. The items from the old home would be valued for sustaining traditions as well as for memories of specific people and places. Initially the migrant must, of necessity, inhabit those objects as much as the site to which they have moved. However, as strategies are developed for psychological occupation of the space, so the objects took on different meanings.

Items sent as gifts would always be particularly poignant. From Lady Nora Scott's journal comes an eloquent account of her response on the arrival in India of a bookcase made by her son in England:

> We unpacked it this morning. It is beautiful – so nicely made, and so brilliantly polished. The mahogany is a rich colour and shows the grain ... It will stand by John's side, by his chair, as he works, and whenever we leave India wherever we live, Leslie's bookcase will be with us, and after belong to our grandchildren (if we have any) and be precious to them as dear Leslie's work when he was a boy of fourteen, the outcome of love and perseverance.[33]

Scott articulates so clearly the layering of meaning carried within the object, and its power to contribute to the continuance of family feeling.

The living room was also the home for a variety of objects which were acquired in the new locale. They offer readings of an appreciation of the exotic, of signs of the woman's capacity to adapt and hence be a good coloniser, and are therefore arguably expressive of the process of making new site-specific components of identity. Sylvia Leith-Ross, after visiting the home of Isabelle Vischer, actually articulated this hybridisation of cultures remarking that she had 'gathered together the finest Kano cloth and mats and leather-work so that there was not a jarring note in the shadowy rooms, cool and still like pools of water after the violence of the daylight'; suggesting it was an 'intelligent creation based on the country's riches, belonging to it, issuing out of it, and at the same time harmonising with our own ideas of simple comfort, order and cleanliness'.[34]

Leith-Ross saw the room as having precisely that harmony of component parts which so identified the tasteful interior, unknowingly echoing the very language of the British guidance manual. Equally such spaces can be read as sites of conflict, with all these objects wrestling for space, their incongruities reflective of the homemakers internal and possibly irresolvable dilemmas. Jones, in his analysis of Anglo-Indian homes, acknowledges this tussle: 'Instead of stimulating remembering (of the domestic interior of the homeland), the material culture of the colonial bungalow continually cut across the construction of [that] meaning and interrupted the process of evocation which the notion, as well as the reality, of home promised'.[35]

Of course most sense of conflict is expunged from the women's representations of their rooms, be they written or pictorial. Theirs are stories of achievement and pride, with little or no acknowledgement of other truths to be told. In consequence the rooms under investigation may seem elusive and incomprehensible, and photographic representations appear oddly static. Some of this is attributable to the technological constraints of contemporary photography, some to the genteel emphasis on control and restraint which also seems to deny change and action. The aim here is to reanimate those spaces by means of considering the process of their creation, as performed by its prime users, the genteel colonial woman. The discussion turns next to various elements of the room, which offer readings of their discrete meanings and which also had cumulative value in making a feminine genteel space.

'A pretty drawing room with crimson damask furniture and a rich carpet in the centre':[36] *elements of gentility – floors and ceilings*

In homes of European heritage there has long been a tradition that in all but the very rudest of accommodation there will be some use of floor covering, albeit of a rudimentary nature. Flooring adornment is a basic marker of domestic intent, with such items sometimes even taking precedence over the floor being level, safe and cleanable.

For homes with any pretension to gentility, however, floor coverings in the living room were an essential element in the domestic ensemble. The very act of stepping on to a covered or treated surface serves to distinguish the space from its surrounding environment. It was the first surface with which one had contact when entering the room and hence a reminder of that difference, as preparation for touching other select surfaces, and also that one's behaviour should be modified accordingly.

Flooring in such colonial homes seems to have ranged from painted stones and polished *chunam* with artfully strewn mats, to sumptuous silk and woollen carpets, but, whatever the handling, it was accepted that flooring required careful consideration – signifying attention to detail and the all-important control of space.[37] Equally the softening effect of a floor covering was equated with femininity, and so the practice of using floor coverings lay at the heart of the female genteel aesthetic, and was therefore underpinned by ideology quite as much as any practical considerations, sometimes indeed even in defiance of practicalities.

For these reasons flooring practices cannot simply be categorised in terms of the dictates of cold and warm climates, nor yet solely on the basis of ready availability versus scarcity value, rather do a range of factors need to be taken into account, both material and symbolic. The use of oilcloth, a forerunner of linoleum, is a case in point. Manufactured in Britain, it proved immensely popular empire-wide, though particularly in colonies where no other form of floor covering was readily available. See Table 3.1, where the 'Furniture Trade Barometer' records that in a single month in 1894 some 20,000 yards were sent from Britain to Adelaide, and all but 70,000 yards to Sydney and Melbourne respectively, whilst even the more modestly sized Wellington took delivery of some 13,000 yards. Oilcloth and linoleums (for a while both were marketed until oilcloth was superseded by the technically superior linoleum) were ideal for covering coarse and newly made floors, and certainly satisfied all of Mrs Orrinsmith's concerns regarding gaps in floorboards which she feared 'become traps for dust, inlets for draughts, homes for insects and hindrances to wholesome scouring'.[38]

Furthermore in addition to its many practical qualities such material also had the virtue of being able to simulate other, more highly regarded, surfaces. In 1906 Williamson & Cole, Clapham, London, were advertising 'newly glazed floor cloth, specially adapted for surrounds, giving the appearance when laid of oak floor parquetry'.[39] Such an item could quickly and easily give an air of permanence and appropriate 'finish', when other, more elegant commodities, specifically carpets, were not yet available, or for some households could not yet be afforded. McGufficke also notes the use of floor cloth in North Queensland, stating that it was customary to mimick carpet designs by painting or stencilling designs on to the plain surface.[40] Thus distinc-

Table 3.1 Domestic goods exported from London to sites across the British Empire, November 1894.

Destinations	Furniture £	Oil Cloth Yards	Paper Cwt	Carpets Yards
Adelaide	2,319	20,000		5,000
Auckland	56	3,800		6,500
Bombay	933	4,800	3	1,700
Brisbane		25,700	52	2,600
Bundaberg		100		
Calcutta	702	770		5,870
Cape Town	2,717	2,192	732	1,310
Christchurch	21	360		1,133
Cooktown		92		
Corunna		1,360		263
East London	1,331	4,076	33	2,024
Fremantle	873		53	
Geraldton				80
Greymouth	133			
Hobart	486	50	11	77
Invercargill		656	41	
Kurrachee	201			210
Launceston		2,760		
Lyttleton	165	610		500
Madras	18	1,098		
Maryborough	165	3,660		
Melbourne	1,077	70,010	867	20,200
Napier	19	1,900		
Nelson	19			
Oamaru				150
Otago	1	1,150	826	587
Perth	31	950		
Port Natal	1,528	2,675	49	2,288
Rangoon	19	60		
Rockhampton		1,000		
Sydney	1,165	69,946	206	11,335
Townsville		1,600		
Wanganui		200	20	
Wellington	292	12,900		3,400
Zanzibar	33			

tions of taste could be displayed even within a relatively commonplace commodity.

By the latter half of the century when and where carpet was employed, it does seem to have been customary to have a border between it and the wall; Mrs Orrinsmith is quite categorical on the subject: 'no carpet should *entirely* cover a floor'.[41] As with so many domestic practices we see here the dictates of practicalities elevated to become virtues, for prior to the invention of mechanical sweepers carpets had either to be cleaned *in situ* or to be regularly lifted and removed for beating, so it was not workable to have them covered with heavy items of furniture, a piano for example, unless one had the requisite labour supply. Well-presented floor borders spoke of a well-regulated household, and imply labour was available to undertake that 'wholesome scouring'. (See Figure 3.1 of two women outside a home in Tasmania in the process of carpet cleaning – a rare visual record of household maintenance.)

That this style of a central carpet was much admired is shown by its frequent use even in warm climes, where the insulating properties were of no appreciable consequence. Clementina Benthall noted after attending one of Miss Emily Eden's 'At Homes' at Government House, Calcutta during 1842 that 'the apartment was a pretty drawing room with crimson damask furniture and a rich carpet in the centre'.[42] That Mrs Benthall, as wife of a judge, should express admiration of the décor of Government House is scarcely surprising, but her singling out the carpet for special mention is rather more noteworthy. See also Figures 3.2 and 3.3 for the extensive use made of carpet in rooms in Allahabad and Sialkot. Both photographs were taken c.1890, suggesting the use of carpeting remained desirable.

The Indian situation is particularly interesting as, despite having a well-developed local carpet industry, there was a considerable demand for British manufactured carpet, with 5,870 yards reportedly imported into Calcutta during November 1894 (see Table 3.1). Of course by that date not all of the carpet was used in homes of Europeans; doubtless much of it was used by wealthy Indians. Lady Nora Scott noted in her journal of 1885 a visit to a 'native woman's house . . . She took us into the drawing-room, a large cheerful room, the windows overlooking the scarlet roofs of the good town beyond. The furniture of the room was mostly European and the carpets gaudy but there is always something about these rooms in Indian houses that tell you you are not in Europe'.[43] The implication was that the home of the Indian family lacked the inherent good taste of a European home, as 'gaudy' carpet can be understood as tantamount to vulgarity. (The reader will recall in the previous chapter Clementina Benthall's use of the self-same adjective to denigrate dress fabric sold at the local bazaar). The adoption by indigenous elites in India of practices which the Europeans considered to be markers of their own superiority is a material indicator of one of the conflicts inherent in the genteel homemaking project, and was perhaps a tension peculiar to that site.

3.1 Maids cleaning a carpet in the garden of 'Rosebank', Hobart, Tasmania, c.1888.

3.2 The mistress of the house in her living room, possibly Allahabad, c.1890.

3.3 The living room of Colonel and Mrs F.W. Egerton, Sialkot, 1895.

Not all European homemakers in India at this time adhered to the use of carpets. In Calcutta in 1896 Ethel and Eustace Kenyon elected not to cover their living room floor because it was made of marble, a highly regarded surface which, as well as being a cool surface, spoke of luxury, and it was entirely appropriate to expose it to view. Doubtless to the recipients of their news back in Britain their decision must have sounded most impressive, if alien, for there marble was only to be found in the very grandest of houses. For the newly wed middle-income Kenyons making their home in India it can be seen as another example of local adaptation, for though it was still a high-status material, with the same cultural resonance, it was attainable, and a clear marker of refinement to display to their peers.[44]

For some early settlers in Australasia, scarcity of supply meant they put great store by obtaining any carpet at all. Charlotte Godley, homemaking in the North Island, New Zealand in 1851 described a satisfying find: 'it was a grand affair for us, being real Brussels, and quite a pretty carpet, if it had not a pattern that is twice too big for our room. We were glad to pounce on the only bit in Wellington, though it was a piece in short remnants, and had been bought at Sydney for cutting up into rugs'.[45]

In relation to flooring we do get occasional glimpses of the labour behind the processes involved in the living room, for it was Godley's Maori servant who altered the carpet to fit her room. Similar reference to her servant's value is made by Georgina Bowen, setting up home in the South Island in 1862, who commented that her companion-maid Soper 'is now hard at work on the drawing-room carpet. She really has been very useful, we have had all the carpets made at home'.[46] Even when carpet was more readily available it seems it was still sold in fixed lengths and widths, and it fell to the woman of the house, or her family or servants, to modify it to fit the rooms. Here then is further evidence that all aspects of flooring arrangements fell within the mistress's remit. Entries in Laura Wright's Tasmanian diary of 1864 note that her daughters 'Laura and Gussie went to get carpet for me'; and the following day she reports 'busy making carpet before six. Finished carpet' and then the next day 'commenced cleaning rooms by half past five and had both carpets down by 12 but all very busy'.[47] Although Mrs Wright had servants she and her daughters do seem to have undertaken a lot of domestic tasks. This may be construed as the household struggling to attain and maintain genteel standards, though equally Mrs Wright may have been engaged in passing on her expertise to her daughters, as their work usually seems to have been of a fairly creative nature. It is surely evident from the descriptions of Godley, Bowen and Wright that it was accepted that there would be both compromise and work involved in sourcing and preparing carpet – efforts well worth while with carpets having attributes far beyond the purely practical.

Carpeting remained a popular commodity in many areas of Australasia, as can be gauged by the 20,200 yards off-loaded in Melbourne and the 6,500 yards in Auckland during November 1894 (see Table 3.1). In the face of its increasingly ready availability, shades of gentility were achieved in carpeting, as with so many commodities, by an increase in range. Thus Brownalls, merchants of Hobart, were able to offer their customers in 1877 a choice of 'tapestry, real Brussels, Kidderminster, Felt, Indian Matting'.[48] However, during the late 1880s and 1890s economic recession bit hard across Australia, though it was felt sooner and the more keenly in Tasmania. In 1887 Brownalls' advertisements focused on sale items and linoleums, suggesting a decline in sales of more expensive items. Such economic details serve as a reminder that gentility was a precarious affair, prone to suffer in periods of economic downturn, as the conspicuous consumption which generally underpinned high-status living could not be sustained.

In contrast to behaviour in commodity-laden sites is that found in the homes of early homemakers in rural North Queensland. There, in the face of absence of manufactured materials, a remarkable example of adaptation of flooring practice was to be found in their adoption of ant-bed floors. This feature of the house, which seems to have been in common use until late in the century, was often mentioned rather admiringly by visitors, presumably because its creation and maintenance was labour intensive and taken to be indicative of domestic ambition. Charles and Lucy Eden had just such a floor, and he gives a precise description of the manufacturing process:

> Get a couple of dray-loads of the conical nest of the white ants, of which there is sure to be plenty – indeed too many – within a short distance; pound this up finely and mix it with water until it becomes the consistency of mortar; then having smoothed all inequalities in the ground, spread it over to the depth of three or four inches, smoothing it with a piece of heavy plank let into a handle, and leave until thoroughly hard.[49]

That Eden elects to include the description in his memoir of their homemaking processes suggests pride in their ability to extemporise and in their achievement. Eden does not record who did the actual physical task of laying the floor, but as his knowledge is so detailed it suggests he may have carried out the work himself, or at least been involved in supervising its execution.

When access to sawn timber became available, polished planking came to be highly valued, as seen in the photograph of 'Devanah', c.1912 (Figure 3.4). As with the use of non-fitted carpets discussed above, this prizing of exposed flooring can be understood as necessity becoming virtue, as any floor covering – even something as robust as linoleum – was susceptible to attack by the voracious white ants, and prone to mildew during the wet season.[50]

These treated floors, be they ant-bed or polished boards, could then be further enhanced by mats and rugs of various sorts. Isaacs notes, in relation to Australia, the popularity of rag-rugs, or waggas, and suggests that although they are generally associated with poorer homes it seems likely that in sites of textile shortage their use may have been more widespread.[51] Animal skins – kangaroo, possum and wallaby – all seem to have been in frequent use, though whether any one of them was seen as being particularly sought after seems unlikely. They were all abundant species, hunted for bush food, and as trophies carried relatively little cachet. Of course, in some colonies animal skins were associated with experiencing the exotic and with hunting prowess, particularly if they were species perceived to be ferocious. Such skins could be viewed in a very positive light, as indicated by the Goddens's memory that

3.4 Living room of the house 'Devanah', Queensland, pre 1915.

their East Bengal home had a 'bearskin with a stuffed snarling head', whilst a photograph of a turn of the century house in Tasmania has a proudly positioned cheetah skin, possibly indicative of time spent in Africa (Figure 3.5).

In North Queensland, flooring imported from China seems to have been highly regarded. The photograph of the elegant 'Devanah' shows careful positioning of three rugs, which look commercially made and may well have been Chinese in origin. With flooring material, as with many domestic and personal commodities, their being of Chinese provenance was a positive attribute. Ships from Asia called at the northern settlements before proceeding south to the larger cities, thus North Queensland could boast of having today what Sydney and Melbourne would not have for quite some time.

This discussion of genteel flooring practice concludes with some consideration of the widespread use of various forms of grass matting.[52] Such materials seem to have retained their appeal, in a range of circumstances and sites, over an extended period. It is arguable therefore that their use can be understood as an example of a really quite modest piece of domestic material culture acquiring status through its absorption into the performance of particular groups. Thus when

3.5 Living room of the house 'Monomeeth', West Hobart, Tasmania, c.1910.

in the 1890s Bardsley visited a neighbouring homestead in the far north of Queensland, one rather larger and grander than her own, she commented it had fourteen rooms with 'an ant-bed floor covered in Chinese matting'.[53] The term 'china matting' came to be used to refer to woven fibre flooring as made in Australia, so Bardsley may have been admiring an item imported from the south of the country. Equally, given that by 1900 *Pugh's Almanac* listed twenty-four merchants in Townsville, of which at least six appear to have had Chinese proprietors, it seems likely that they would have imported various forms of flooring materials direct from China. Certainly McGufficke records an advertisement in an 1875 edition of the *Townsville Times* for Chinese matting, which further supports the point made above in relation to North Queenslanders' satisfaction in the acquisition of Asian-made, perhaps lower priced but faintly exotic items.[54]

In similar vein Leith-Ross and Larymore, homemaking in Nigeria at the turn of the century, both speak very positively about the locally made grass matting. Larymore is expansive on the matter: 'nothing is nicer or cheaper than an Indian dhurri or cotton carpet, but, as the bungalows are all fitted with linoleum, no more is really needed than a few of the artistically coloured grass mats, made chiefly at Bida, and found almost everywhere; they cost about three shillings each, rising to six shillings, according to the distance from Bida, and are quite delightful'.[55] Larymore had lived in India for some four years prior to her husband's posting to Nigeria. Thus, in addition to her willingness to embrace grass matting, we see here how Indian artefacts had become so much part of her domestic ensemble that it is surely not overstating the case to suggest she rather regretted the supply of linoleum.[56] Larymore's practice is a particularly rich illustration of the layering of identity construction, and the way it finds expression in the reconfiguration of home.

Eliza Errington, in her water-colour of her living room in Port Arthur, Van Diemen's Land in 1844, depicts her matting with exquisite care, suggesting it was a valued aspect of the room.[57] It seems likely that the matting was Indian in origin. Broadbent *et al.* record that by the 1830s matting was imported to Australia in a variety of weaves and colours, lengths and widths and in considerable quantities.[58] Lane and Searle note that migrants would sometimes purchase such matting en route for the colony, either in India itself, or at the Cape, where in the 1840s it sold for two shillings a yard.[59]

In Christchurch, New Zealand Georgina Bowen purchased matting to use as bordering for her living room carpet: 'It is hempen with a little red stripe in it. I think it will look well enough but it was tremendously expensive as anything imported is here'.[60] It seems likely that Bowen's matting was also made in India, possibly in Madras as the matting made in that region was particularly highly regarded. She was writing in 1862, but the item she describes is not dissimilar to that depicted by Errington, and no doubt by the 1860s comparable goods would be either sent direct or re-exported from Australia on to New Zealand. That Bowen elected to use the matting, despite its cost, speaks of its desirability, which cannot adequately be accounted for in solely practical ways.

This survey of flooring has revealed a complexity and range of both practice and sourcing. It has shown that flooring had symbolic meanings for the genteel mistress, as she prepared the ground, both literally and figuratively, for this important feature of her domestic space. The flooring practices of such consumers give further reminder of the need to consider both developmental and structural factors when analysing the consumption of material objects.

'Our drawing-room boasts of a real lath and plaster ceiling in the form of a dome.'

This remark was made by a British resident of Sierra Leone in the 1840s; she was the more pleased with its appearance as 'few apartments here are furnished above, otherwise than by planks and beams painted white'.[61] This brief comment tells us much, not only with regard to the construction of the houses and the labour and materials available, in that site at that date, but also of what the writer deemed to be of value. Her home, her words convey, was both unusual and superior. This remark seems to have typified women's attitude to the ceilings of their homes across both time and place: it was another feature of the room which required 'finishing'.

Houses in tropical locations were often built, as noted above, with large interior spaces to facilitate movement of air and give at least the impression of airy comfort. The high ceilings – anything from ten to twenty feet high – were not always viewed positively, however, seeming as they did to negate the intimacy of the domestic space. Constance Larymore, who, as noted above, had lived for some four years in the Indian sub-continent, was accustomed to the notions of interiority commonly found in hot climes, and yet she still described the Residence at Kano, Nigeria as 'a great vault-like apartment'.[62] Having initially been unable to locate any references which suggested women in West Africa made significant attempts to alter their ceilings, this author had assumed that the white painted beams of Sierra Leone were the accepted norm. The more interesting therefore, not least for its scarcity, is a set of instructions for decorating his and his wife's home sent by F. Swanzy to his agent in Cape Castle, Gold Coast, whilst on a visit to London in which he requests that 'the boards of the roof of the Gallery [be] painted blue'.[63] As Swanzy was a merchant and presumably had easy access to materials and labour he was in a strong position to implement such refining touches. For most homemakers dwelling in houses with rooms so high and commodities so limited it is hard to imagine what sort of refinements they could have employed, though the practices of North Queensland and India are illuminating.

Homemakers in North Queensland during the closing decades of the century made imaginative use of textiles to give appropriate 'finish' to their coarse newly made ceilings. Charles Eden described 'the inside of the drawing-room being most tastefully lined with light-blue linen, forming a canopy and keeping the rough sides of the room out of sight', with his use of 'canopy' suggesting the ceiling was covered as well as the walls.[64] Similar description of fabric use comes from Bardsley who, as always, constructs her biographical account with studied care: 'I have made the two main rooms so artistic by lining them and ceiling them with art muslin that has a greyish background with pink roses and green foliage'.[65] Both Eden and Bardsley run together their treatment of the ceiling and walls, suggesting they considered those elements of the room to be of equal importance.

Attempts to 'improve' some ceilings of houses in India were hampered by the presence of punkahs, the vast fans which were suspended from ceilings or high up on the walls, and which were powered by the efforts of a servant seated outside the room. The punkah was thus a dominant element in the space and constant reminder of the necessary but irksome presence of the servant, so it was both a limiting factor on the aesthetic arrangement and a symbolic reminder of the 'other'. The electric fan, which came to replace the punkah, did not of course carry the same meaning, but in spatial terms was still something of a constraining feature in the aesthetic lay-out of the room. Despite this constraint, grander houses tended to adopt the decorative styles of comparably grand houses in Europe, with moulded friezes and central roses. In relation to slightly more modest households, Mrs Clemons described the early use of textiles in houses in Madras, where the homemakers would 'procure strong and coarse white cloth, which is sewn together, and form a sheet, that extends the whole length of the room; this is placed from wall to wall, and stretched and nailed across; frequently a deep frill is put round it, which forms a kind of cornice'.[66] Such an approach presumably influenced the North Queensland practice described above.

It is in the homes in cooler climes that genteel distinctions in ceilings are perhaps most nuanced. Very grand households in the southern states of Australia and in New Zealand could afford to import plaster ceiling roses and other decorative features. As well as being heavy and prone to breakage the installation of such items also required the services of a skilled plasterer. When papier mâché fixtures were developed, with all the virtues of being cheaper, lighter, less prone to breakage, and easier to fix in place, they quickly superseded plasterwork. Initially they were imported from Britain, and Capon reports a very early advertisement for imported papier mâché ornaments appearing in the *Sydney Morning Herald* in 1837.[67] A Tasmanian example of imported papier mâché is to be found at Clarendon House, Figure 3.6. When Australian manufacturing of such items developed, they came within the reach of a much wider section of society, and hence became a contested marker of gentility, prompting a proliferation of styles with a range of motifs employed.

The other technical development in ceiling décor which fostered genteel practice was that of pressed or stamped metal ceilings. The technology was developed in Germany in the 1880s but soon spread, with manufacturers in America, Britain and Australia. In the latter, the largest and best-known company was 'Wunderlich', whose products were made of zinc from the mines in Broken Hill, New South Wales. They were a highly successful company, selling their goods through

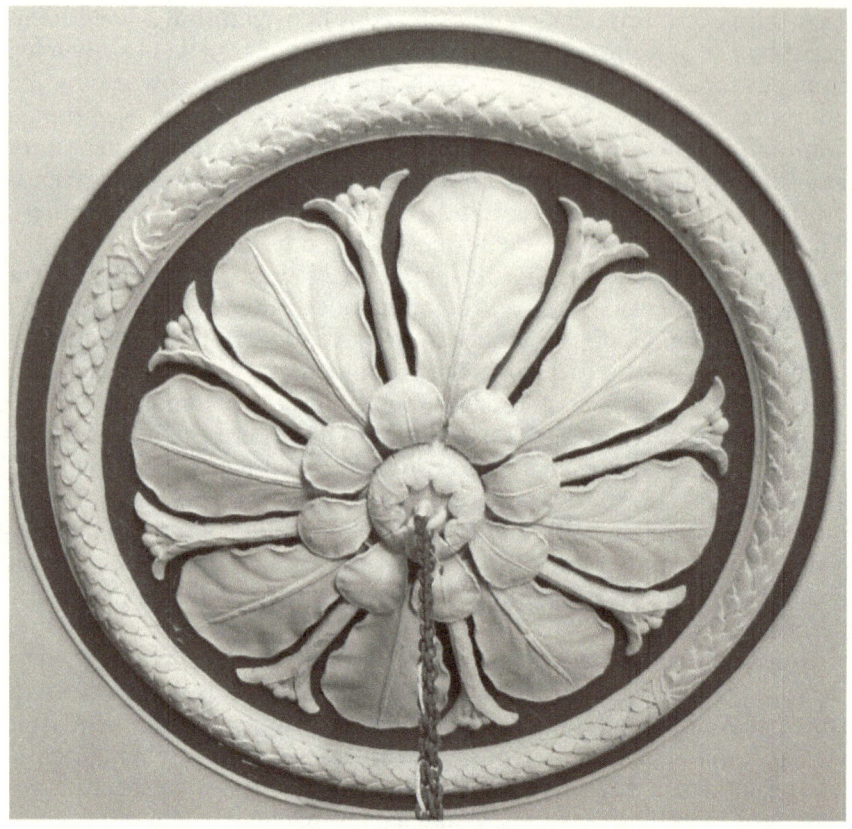

3.6 Ceiling rose, Clarendon House, Tasmania.

agents to sophisticated homes in a variety of locations across the country.[68] As zinc is so malleable it was the perfect material for making a range of decorative features – friezes, roses, cornices and full sheets – and could be fitted by any reasonably competent decorator, see Figure 3.7.[69] It could be painted in the customary light tones, or to resemble more expensive metals. As always gentility both stimulated and fed off the ensuing complexity of choice.

This overview of the decoration of ceilings within the genteel living room has demonstrated that where possible it was another element which received improving treatment, to which end the homemakers drew on technological developments and on improvements in communications. Even in this one feature of the room one can see how gentility was ever sensitive to local conditions and possibilities.

3.7 Zinc panel for ceiling and wall decoration, as used in a house on Victoria Esplanade, Hobart, Tasmania, c.1905.

'Oh, Lincrusta you will turn us grey!':[70] *elements of gentility – wall coverings*

Mrs Orrinsmith is as didactic on the subject of walls as on all other aspects of living room décor, laying stress on the value of wallpaper as a unifying factor within the decorating scheme. In taking wallpaper manufacturers to task for producing *'purely* ornamental designs, the patterns hideous and meaningless, suggestive of nothing but confusion and unpleasantness', Orrinsmith, whilst commenting on fashion, is imparting a moral weight to her subject.[71] Although British advice manuals can never be taken as direct evidence of actual behaviours at 'home', much less in the colonies, in the use of wallpapers there does seem to have been a general acceptance amongst homemakers of European heritage that it was an essential element in the living room, and that its absence was felt as a lack, for it carried meaning and value far beyond its decorative function.

Until mid-century much of the social value of wallpaper was attributable to its price. Until the early 1840s papers or 'pieces' were printed by hand, and such a labour-intensive process meant supplies were limited and prices remained high. Entwisle comments in relation to the order books (1824–38) of the London-based company Cowtan and

Sons: 'They read like an extract from Debretts. It is apparent that nearly everyone in London and the provinces with any pretension to distinction or social eminence, used wallpaper in their homes', a remark effective for highlighting that wallpapers were a highly codified commodity.[72] Only with the development of the rotary printing machine was it possible to produce wallpapers in relatively large quantities. In addition, from 1712 until 1861 British-made wallpapers were subject to taxation. During the Napoleonic Wars the tax was raised to one shilling per square yard, a levy that remained in place until 1847, when it was reduced to two pence, and ultimately discarded, whereupon there was a dramatic expansion in the social range of those who could afford wallpaper.

The expansion of the market in Britain and in her colonies, and the increasingly nuanced use which accompanied such growth, triggered anxiety in users employing wallpaper in this key area of their home. Equally, although the advice manuals appear highly prescriptive, in reality there was a deal of latitude in what was deemed acceptable. Kerr urged that the aim of the living room should be 'especial cheerfulness, refinement of elegance, and what is called lightness as opposed to massiveness ... comparatively delicate ... entirely ladylike'.[73] The vagueness of such directives, and Kerr's chosen examples are typical of many such publications, played upon the inherent insecurities of gentility. Was the living room cheerful, refined, delicate and ladylike enough? Wallpaper, being such a visually dominant element in the room, had disproportionate power within the space. Little wonder then that so many homemakers, in so many spatial and temporal locations, set high store by its presence and, initially at least, commented with regret where its absence was unavoidable.

Colonial supplies of wallpaper were sent from Britain and America, but in their absence, in Australia at least, stencilling was a frequently employed technique, either directly on to the wall or on to plain paper, and examples of such early practice have been located in Tasmania.[74] Although the provenance of these decorations is unknown it seems most likely that the early stencils were cut and the work undertaken by the women themselves, especially if the household was in a remote location. At the opposite end of the social scale in some very high-status rooms hand-painted wallpaper was made, and Government House, Hobart had some magnificent pieces with *trompe l'oeil*, creating architectural features, swags and sprays of flowers – the whole aglow with delicate blues, lemons and pinks and rich gold highlighting. See Figure 3.8.[75]

Most households made use of commercially manufactured papers as and when available and, again drawing on Tasmanian practice,

3.8 Hand-painted wallpaper, Government House, Hobart, Tasmania.

advertisements in the Hobart press indicate that by the 1850s a supply of wallpapers had been established. In 1856 Huybers Wine & Spirit Merchant and General Importer advertised 'paper hangings', but by 1877 Brownalls offered '4,000 pieces room Papers from 7½ d. to 2s. per piece'.[76] At no stage however did the advertisements carry any detail

3.9 Wallpaper frieze with hand-painted in-fill, Runnymede House, Hobart, Tasmania.

about the designs of paper they had in stock. This may suggest that for the early homemakers having a papered wall at all was such a marker of refinement that the pattern was not to be quibbled over.

Allport does make a reference in her 1852 journal that 'the papering men forgot to come yesterday, but are very busy today', but many more references were located in which the women did the decorating themselves, with or without the aid of help from their daughters or their servants, as for example in Laura Wright's comment 'Geraldine and self up early, very busy papering little room etc'.[77] Mrs Bayley at Runnymede House showed one of the most impressive examples of ingenuity displayed by a genteel homemaker. She and her husband had ordered a deep and highly decorative frieze of complex design for their living room. When it arrived it was found to be short by approximately one foot – so the determined homemaker set about painting in the missing section. The paper is still there, in astonishingly good condition and the only reason the 'join' is apparent is because the hand-painted colour has darkened whereas the coloured paper has faded, see Figure 3.9.

By the 1880s there was a huge choice of wallpapers available in most of the colonised areas of Australia. By this date a large percentage of households of all classes had adopted the tripartite style of wall décor; of dado – filling – frieze. This gave infinite flexibility to the decorating scheme. More affluent households could indulge in complex combinations of papers, a complete scheme, to give richness to the room, whilst less prosperous homes could select cheaper papers for the dado and filling and be more extravagant in the border. So again the commodity gave ample opportunity for the expression of genteel preference. The patterned metal sheeting used for ceilings was also adopted for wall use, being both elegant in design and having the added advantage of disguising less than perfect walls, particularly useful in new settlements where impression management had to be a rushed affair.

By the end of the century there was a notably lighter tone to decorating schemes, in advice publications and homes alike. There was a resurgence of interest in stencilling, with commercially available hand-blocked papers, produced by firms such as Rottman and Co. and Shand Kydd. As such products were imported from Britain they catered very much for the top end of the market, and it seems most likely that in more modest homes local decorators carried out the work.[78] However, as there had been such a rich practice of home-stencilling in earlier days of settlement one should not rule out the possibility that some later generations of women had learnt the art, and that in less affluent households, the practice was reinstated, the more so as it was entirely in keeping with other branches of the Arts and Crafts Movement.

This discussion has presented a quantity of evidence which demonstrates that in temperate climes wallpaper remained highly valued, and that it played an important part in the homemaker's genteel performance.[79] Their peers in colonies in tropical locations had to contend with serious challenges to this aspect of their aesthetic. In North Queensland no source material has been found to suggest that wallpaper was in use amongst the homes of early settlers. The oft-cited illustration of the Henning family wallpapering their living room in Exmoor, central Queensland in 1863 is the sole example which has come to light, and it may well be that they simply lacked the local knowledge to be aware that the paper, 'an extremely pretty one [with] a very light green ground with a white pattern of wild roses and ivy-leaves on it' was unlikely to survive the following wet season.[80] More telling therefore is that no advertisements for wallpaper have been found in the local press and no photographic evidence has come to light of wallpapered interiors in the north of the state. This is in marked contrast to the Tasmanian findings, and as access to supply was equally restricted in both sites – indeed would have been potentially rather better in North Queensland as international transport and communications had improved so radically by the closing decades of the century – one must look to other factors to explain the absence of the use of wallpapers.[81]

The most likely explanation is surely that of climate; year round high humidity would cause the paper to mildew, mould and rot. In consequence it seems there was a 'wallpaper line', above which its use was impracticable in all areas with a prolonged wet season. In addition to the climate, pests such as silverfish and white ants – the latter the scourge of the homemakers in the tropics – would eat not only the paper but also, it is assumed, the glue; early adhesives were organically based, being either the home-mix of flour and water, or based on animal products such as bone and skin. Finally paper is notoriously heavy of course, and for those living in the back-blocks the loading costs would have added dramatically and preposterously to the unit costs.

As indicated earlier, those homemaking in North Queensland in the closing decades of the century came from a variety of backgrounds. Many migrated directly from Britain, whilst others arrived following a period of service in India, or were indeed of Australian birth and had moved north from the southern states. In all cases their cultural heritage would have had the aesthetic expectation that for domestic spaces to have 'finish' the walls needed to be softened with wallpaper. So that particular marker of distinction being denied them, imaginative use seems to have been made of textiles.

The earliest such reference found in North Queensland was Charles Eden's description of their living room cited above in relation to ceiling décor. Similar practice was adopted by Lucy Gray, who made a brief entry in her diary that she had spent her day 'putting calico on the sitting-room'. As she does not mention any design on the textile one could assume it was plain unbleached cloth and was put in place to keep out the fine dust which would penetrate between the wooden slabs of the walls when the winds blew during the dry season. The same technique was employed by her sister-in-law Eva over ten years later, 'the rooms lined with striped hessian machined together and nailed up over the walls'.[82] These examples of practice in North Queensland demonstrate how inventive homemakers were in striving to 'civilise' and take ownership of their domestic space, and how they made use of practices from other sites, in this instance the use of fabric in homes in India, cited above.

To those of European heritage the dimensions of rooms in many colonial homes in tropical sites could seem cheerless and lacking in intimacy. Wall coverings, particularly coloured and patterned styles, 'shrink' a room and draw in the space, fostering a sense of enclosure. Their value in generating a sense of controlled genteel space cannot therefore be overstated. Walls devoid of treatment effectively scorned so much of their work to establish a soft feminised space. Emily Eden told how she overcame the bleakness of her house in Simla: 'I got a native painter into the house, and cut out patterns in paper, which he then paints in borders all round the doors and windows and it makes up for the want of cornices and breaks the eternal white walls of these houses'.[83] Mrs Melville in Sierra Leone spoke of the shock to the newly arrived person whose eyes were 'accustomed to rest on ... papered and pictured walls and capacious window drapery' and how necessary was the use of 'a handsome mirror, in gilded frame [which] takes off the bareness of a *dead* wall'.[84] Her very choice of vocabulary suggests a perception that papers were needed to enliven the space. Similarly Constance Larymore writing of her home in Kano, Nigeria considered the room much improved by distempering the walls in a bright colour, 'pinky-red walls decorated with sketches and prints, a few gorgeously hued Japanese paper wall hangings scattered about'.[85]

Larymore is not only speaking of the visual effect of her decorating scheme, she is anxious to inform her readers that she created a controlled environment, in which all elements received due care and attention. It was a long time before the bare polished planks of North Queensland's 'Devanah' or the plain colour-washed walls of African homes acquired the same standing as the papered wall in temperate locations. Until such time its absence could so easily give the impression of a half-hearted domestic intent and lack of control.

In seeking to tease out the precise values to the woman of her papered wall the practical merits cannot be underestimated. Wall pieces were an effective means of introducing colour and pattern and contributed hugely to the aesthetic of the room, also serving to cover rough walls and aid insulation. As has been shown here, identifying those practical aspects does not negate their crucial value as an element within the genteel performance. Wall coverings are to be understood as a means of enveloping the space within, and marking it off in gentility's name – exemplified in Mrs Selwyn's words when she visited her friends in Taurarua, New Zealand: 'ladies and gentlemen coming to call, a papered room and a return to old familiar habits impressed me strongly'.[86]

'The carpenter made me a bush sofa':[87] *elements of gentility – furniture*

As this work makes explicit the act of leaving familiar surroundings and re-establishing oneself in a new society took on a particular material dimension for those seeking to create or recreate an elegant household. Items of furniture taken from the old home would therefore have a specific value. Not only would they resonate with memory of people and places left behind, they would also serve a 'seeding' function in setting about creating a new genteel space. Unsurprisingly such objects loom large in letters 'back home', acting as coded reassurance to their loved ones that, though far away, in some sense they were never entirely 'left behind'. Evidently there was pleasure to be had in the inclusion of the old home within the new – the decision-making as to their placement within the ensemble, polishing of familiar surfaces and their daily use could be very effective in making the woman feel at home.

Clearly, to describe such items solely as 'family heirlooms' is reductive and misses much of the psychological meanings the items have in the subject's negotiation of circumstance. It is the biographies of such items, and the part they played in the practices of other cherished homes which, when sited in new spatial and temporal locations, makes them so eloquent. Note how Sarah Selwyn describes this very process: 'The way in which our old Eton furniture fits with our present room is curious. In said room, above about and underneath, is nothing but Kauri wood, so that as Mr Whytehead says it is very like being inside a box'.[88] Here we see the objects in another chapter of their lives, one in which they occupy spaces which initially seem alien – note the absence of wallpaper, the unaccustomed timber – but within which they settle down. Personifying objects in this way is not merely a stylistic device – rather is it a reminder of the strong narrative position they occupied in the lives of those to whom they belonged.

In addition to the furniture which accompanied the homemakers, further items would be needed on arrival. Selecting and arranging furniture for such an important room was always given a high priority. Furniture was not only visually and spatially dominant within the room, it had to satisfy practical and aesthetic needs. In situations where judgements were going to be made about their choice it is little wonder the women gave such priority to the selection and arrangement of this all-important room. All sites posed challenges to the genteel aesthetic and prompted a variety of coping strategies.

Lack of access to furniture always called forth a deal of ingenuity. In the homes of early settlers in Tasmania, where access to manufactured items was limited, even upholstery work often had to be carried out by the mistress of the house, or her household servants. Mrs Meredith's Housekeeping and Account Book notes in 1820 the purchase of 'canvas for sofa 9s, tin tax [sic] 1s thread 1.5d'.[89] Similarly Anna Nixon notes in a letter to her father in 1845 how a gift of 'two pieces of a very pretty red and white chintz' was made into curtains as well as providing covers for two sofas, an ottoman and eight chairs.[90] No doubt the textile having come from Lady Franklin, the wife of the governor, contributed to the desirability of the gift. Naturally as local manufacturing developed there became less need for the women and their immediate staff to do such exacting work as upholstery.

For homemakers living in isolated spots access to commodities was often constrained by poor communications and freight costs. For example, in 1889 a carrier in North Queensland charged £17 per ton to transport goods up-state, which seems an exorbitant figure and must have been particularly prohibitive in relation to heavy items of furniture.[91] Mrs Anning, establishing a home in Reedy Springs, North Queensland, spoke of how:

> A loading arrived of purchases we had made in Sydney and Townsville, and some of my personal treasures too, so I had plenty to occupy my mind and hands ... we had bought the most necessary and useful things for our house being built before we left the towns, but it was one thing to buy, quite another to get the things landed on the station ... [It was] three months before our loading came, and another year before we had our own home.[92]

An alternative strategy was to recruit station labour to manufacture items. Anning describes how 'the carpenter made me a bush sofa for which I made a grass mattress, and we made extra beds and everything that was necessary for a comfortable bush home'.[93] Her wording suggests that having moved to the bush she had changed her expectations as to what constituted an acceptable home. Similarly Jane Bardsley, homemaking on a cattle station in the Gulf Country to the far north of the state, describes how 'Sim the Chinaman is a cabinet maker as well as a cook'. She explains how he 'helped to build my home which is very nice, making verandah squatter chairs, little rustic tables, bookshelves and a linen press', and how in addition to the little chairs and tables he had made 'large ones to serve afternoon tea'.[94] Eden also describes how he and Lucy had in their living room a 'sofa stuffed with bush hay and covered with blue blankets' and Lucy Gray how 'the carpenter is at work making tables, shelves etc'.[95] As these homemakers all included these details in their diaries and memoirs it can be deduced that an ability to extemporise was a source of pride.

Similarly positive approaches are described by women in West Africa. Thus Decima Moore gives a detailed account of a 'find' for their home in Accra, Gold Coast at the turn of the century:

> An enormous chest, 12 feet long by 4 feet high and 4 feet broad, with six large drawers. This had been originally used for holding uniforms, and the drawers were still marked in large painted letters, faint from age, with the words 'Fezes', 'Jackets', 'Breeches' etc ... In a few days it was the making

of the whole room as it stood there – scraped, stained and polished, its top reflecting the shiny silver bowls, lamps and flower vases. It was a joy – the finest sideboard ever seen.[96]

This item was evidently a source of satisfaction and certainly Moore seems not to have felt her gentility to have been unduly compromised; rather is she making the point that it rose to the occasion. This is evidenced by the way she gives the piece a narrative position, foregrounding it in her memoir, even including a photograph of herself and her husband seated in the room, and commenting on the presence in the image of the self-same chest of drawers. Constance Larymore described how in the face of the 'utter gloom and desolation' of her living room in Kano 'an extraordinary improvisation was effected in a couple of hours by an improvised sideboard, boxes piled up to serve as tables, and covered with gaily-coloured cloths', and also how she made use of 'a coarse kind of muslin [which] can be purchased locally, and, when faintly dyed with indigo, becomes quite a pretty pale blue, very cool looking, and can be constantly renewed when faded'.[97] Larymore and Moore's pride in their achievements is the more understandable if we remind ourselves that at this date there were very few Europeans in West Africa, of whom just a handful were women.

In most if not all locations it seems to have been common practice to obtain furnishings from a range of sources. Thus cane work, though certainly fashionable in European homes empire-wide, had a special appeal in tropical sites. Unlike upholstered work it was less prone to suffer damage in the wet season and less likely to harbour insect life. For those living in up-state North Queensland who had to pay for freight from the towns it must have been an advantage that it was light in weight. It is noticeable that it was not merely relegated to informal use; see for example the elegant living room of 'Devanah' (Figure 3.4), where cane work was blended with more formal upholstered pieces, with a cane chair positioned next to the grand piano. Initially, it seems, much cane and bamboo furniture was imported from China, and in 1900 there were eight merchants of Chinese heritage in business in Townsville, which may suggest that supply continued.[98] In addition there was a shop in Charters Towers, a hundred miles west of Townsville, which specialised in bamboo and cane work.

In Tasmania many of the early settlers were former members of the military in India, who went seeking a congenial climate and environment, and naturally took with them household items, which in turn fostered an interest in such amongst other homemakers.[99] Broadbent has argued that many items long-assumed to be British imports were actually of Indian manufacture. The household inventory produced on Maria Meredith's death in 1831 includes a 'handsome cedar sofa, carved with blue Moreen with two pillows' and a 'small cedar work table with turned pillar and claws'. This change in furnishing practice is unclear, however, for Broadbent states that Australian cedar is taxonomically indistinguishable from Indian cedar, and if such is the case then it is impossible to know whether those pieces were imports from India, from the Australian mainland or made locally from timber imported from New South Wales. Similarly the 'mahogany tea-caddy' and the 'handsome mahogany sofa table on castors' might, given the early date, have been brought over from Britain, but equally could be of quite different origin; the more so as the term 'mahogany' was applied to almost any timber with comparable graining, as it was deemed to be a marker of quality and carried a certain cachet.[100] Anna Maria Nixon, for example, boasted that 'The very nice round mahogany table was of colonial make – £8, really as cheap as in England'.[101]

Shortage of a commodity often creates take-off for a second-hand trade, as seen in the previous chapter in relation to dress. Nowhere exhibited such a structured second-hand furniture market as India where the fluid demographic of many European residents, notably those employed in the military and officialdom, prevailed against settled long-term homemaking. Many housekeeping guides recommended that all substantial items be purchased *in situ*, usually from the previous homemaker. Chattopadhyay has argued that 'in such a context choice and arrangement of furniture became less a mark of individuality than a sign of Englishness', which arguably fails to make enough allowance for the drive on the part of the mistress of the house to express her interiority.[102] Rather did she employ a range of tactics to personalise her home, of which purchasing from her predecessor was only one aspect. Jones describes how many women saw furnishing their homes as 'an adventurous activity', and such would certainly seem to have been the case for Clementina Benthall and Charlotte Wortley Corbett. They each wrote of making trips to furniture bazaars and warehouses, displaying both initiative and involvement in the appointment of their homes and suggesting a concern to create a genteel setting, irrespective of whether some of the items were 'previously enjoyed'.[103] There are some parallels to be drawn here between the use of second-hand dress and such recycling of furniture. For example, there would doubtless have been occasions when knowing the provenance of a piece would add to the pleasure and satisfaction of the next owner, particularly if it had hailed from a somewhat higher-status household. By and large, however, as with garments, it was not how and where one acquired the items so much as how you adapted and arranged your possessions. Therefore Jones's claim that 'second-hand Anglo-Indian furniture acquired the role simply of domestic apparatus within the colonial bungalow' must be approached with a considerable degree of caution.[104]

Of particular interest in identifying changes in genteel practice is the adoption of locally made furniture. In Tasmania a number of carpenters and joiners were found amongst the convict population, and knowledge of local timbers soon developed. Indeed Scripps notes that 'by 1820 there was sufficient knowledge for the overseer at the King's Yard in Hobart to identify eighteen species of timber and the uses to which each could be put'.[105] Whilst cedar was initially imported from New South Wales it was soon supplemented and even replaced with blackwood and huon pine – species found only in Tasmania.[106] Huon pine grows very slowly and produces a fine-grained timber which can be made into very attractive furniture. Although the furniture was made in the familiar styles, not all the woodworkers had been high-quality craftsmen in Britain, and therefore there emerged a slightly 'homely' local vernacular, see Figures 3.10 and 3.11, and in contrast the more elegant piece made just a few years later, Figure 3.12. The ongoing success of the local furniture trade can be gauged partly by the modest quantities imported from Britain – by the 1860s just a few hundred pounds worth per annum.

Nor was this practice of buying those locally made pieces merely rationalisation prompted by costs of imported items as the Tasmanian furniture trade continued to flourish. Although it is not readily possible to identify who was buying what, that a range of goods was available and that so many were of local manufacture suggests the development of new purchasing patterns across society, and hence more nuanced use at the 'top end'. William Bros, established 1887, were able to declare 'we manufacture the bulk of our stock', and their chief competitor Coogans claimed in 1913 to be 'the largest furniture warehousemen and manufacturers in the Commonwealth'. By 1909 Williams Bros were offering rooms of furniture on an instalment plan; perfect for those on a limited income who yet aspired to create a genteel look to their home.[107]

In North Queensland the furniture trade developed in Townsville in response to the needs of the new settlement. In 1880 J. L. Morgan established his business as a furniture warehouseman and upholsterer and in an entry in *Aldine's History of Queensland* stated: 'Mr Morgan turns out a large quantity of furniture, all of which is carefully designed to suit the climate. The wood used in this industry is mostly local, though a considerable importation is done with England and America for the purpose of obtaining rarer woods. Mr Morgan imports large quantities of furniture'.[108] By 1900 *Pugh's Queensland Almanac* entry for Townsville listed five furniture dealers and four manufacturers, seven

3.10 Sofa of colonial cedar, double-ended with Palladian-shaped carved back, on turned legs, secondary timber of Tasmanian huon pine, Clarendon House, Tasmania, c.1835.

3.11 Detail of 3.10, showing decoration on the arm rest.

3.12 Armchair of Tasmanian blackwood with pink upholstery and matching stool, Clarendon house, Tasmania, c.1850.

cabinet makers and furniture warehousemen (though there was some overlap with some names having entries under different headings) and eight Chinese merchants, some of whom may well have stocked furniture, curios and household items. Thus it is clear that a supply of goods was established with extraordinary rapidity, and again this is indicative of potential for the expression of a local form of gentility.

Comparable hybridisation of practice can be identified in Georgina Bowen's enthusiastic description of 'one of the most beautiful wedding presents we have had – it is a small round table made of every kind of New Zealand wood most beautifully inlaid'. At this point in the letter Bowen gives a sketch of the seven pointed star-shaped design, though alas it is omitted from the published work.[109] So again indigenous materials were used, almost certainly by European craftsmen making furniture of European design.

Particularly complex practice developed in India, where items were made by local craftsmen for the local British market, in a manner which was actually an amalgam of European and Indian styles. Thus the shapes and sizes were made with European domestic spaces in mind, but the flamboyant decoration was 'exotic', if not necessarily authentic.[110] Thus Eustace Kenyon wrote to his mother of 'a handsome addition to our own furniture in the shape of a very fine brass table ... the legs are wood, just like your teatable at R [?], the uprights and crosspieces are all polished black and only the ornamental part remains white, and the brass tray is a very handsome one of the Jeypore work'.[111]

Furnishing practice in a different type of home in India is explored in Jones's analysis of inventories of planters' belongings from households in rural sites in Bengal. His findings would suggest that those who were able to establish long-term homes, but were not very high up the social ladder, were more likely to purchase furniture made from local timbers. Thus Mary Shillingford's home contained pieces made of 'sissoo', 'camphor', 'mangoe' and 'teakwood' – all native trees.[112] These timbers have distinctive and pleasing colours and graining, so rather than seeing them as necessarily a substitute for better-known timbers their use can be understood as a distinct form of adaptation to local circumstances.

All the signs are that across both the temporal and spatial range examined the genteel living room was able to accommodate furniture with a range of provenance. Items came from their former homes, were sourced through private sales, from hawkers, from auctions, new, second hand, by mail order, imported and made from a variety of materials in a variety of styles. Far from being a poor relation, eclecticism was sometimes seen as a positive attribute. The ability to be able to make use of what was on offer is indicative of the women's self-positioning as adaptable and able colonisers. Their representations of their rooms carry no note of apology, rather are they celebratory. Anchored in time and place amidst the rich material variety of their room, they are exemplars of the fluidity of identity construction.

GENTEEL WOMEN

'I am very tired, as I have just had a "bout" of pianotuning':[113] *elements of gentility – the piano, needlework and floral arrangements*

To modern eyes the piano can appear to be merely another item within the furnishings, whereas such was the discrete meaning of the instrument that it is more appropriate to consider it separately. There was a long-established convention that music tuition, generally in the shape of piano lessons, should form part of a young lady's education, and some degree of competency was expected in any woman who professed a degree of refinement. It follows that for the woman the very fact of having a piano sited in the room was an expression of her genteel subjectivity, and its presence even when silent spoke of that interiority.

As well as its psychological meaning for the individual, the piano also had agency for social interactions, an element within the networking that was part of the woman's 'work' at which she had to succeed if the household were to prosper in their new setting. So the instrument and its associated practices must also be understood as a force for cohesion in emergent genteel societies.

The value many women accorded to their pianos is directly expressed in their personal writings, in which they catalogue at some length how they sought to overcome the environmental challenges to which their poor instruments were subjected. Thus in New Zealand in the 1840s Charlotte Godley chronicled how:

> We were lucky enough to get our pianoforte tuned by a passenger from the *Mariner* . . . He has really done it very well though it is not perfect; but it was so bad before that it was a great thing to have got him at all . . .We called at Mrs Fox's where he was tuning her pianoforte which is a very good one; which kind office he did for Mrs Gold, who had brought out a new semi-grand one from Broadwood by the *Lady Nugent*. I believe that if anyone wanted to bring out a pianoforte, a square one is the best, because the machinery is much more simple than in one like ours (a low cabinet P.F.), where, if anything got broken, a mere tuner cannot repair it as he can the square ones. And I think too, that if anyone was coming out here for good, it would answer to bring out a more expensive kind than ours (£28 in its packing case from Wornham), for they seem to bear the voyage far better.[114]

Godley has been quoted at length because this passage describes so vividly the challenges faced by the would-be music-maker, the limited availability of services – only the chance arrival of a skilled stranger rescued them all from ongoing discord – and the dominance of the instrument within her genteel circle.

In Swan River, Western Australia in 1832 Georgina Malloy was so anxious to get a piano that she had sent for one from Cape Town. Whether her order went astray she does not explain, but when the following year her neighbour's house burnt down and her piano came to reside with Malloy during rebuilding she wrote 'you may well conceive my gladness at this acquisition, as I have not heard the sound of music for four years'. However, by 1840 Malloy reported 'I have a little organ as it is called, or a sort of instrument like an organ and piano combined. It is like a work table in appearance, and being a wind instrument has the advantage of not getting out of tune'. Her response to the environmental challenges was to adapt her music practice to a change of instrument – a harmonium presumably – and to embrace the possibilities of the new. She continues: 'This the children often dance to, and at dear Augusta, I used to take it out on the grass plot, and play till late by moonlight, the beautiful broad water of the Blackwood gliding by, the roar of *the Bar*, and ever and anon the wild screams of a flight of swans going over the Fresh Water Lakes'.[115] This most self-aware construction of her and her family's behaviour reveals the development of dramatic strategies to overcome the alien world in a refined manner.

The market price of the piano also gives indication of its cultural value. In Van Diemen's Land in 1852 Mary Morton Allport reported that 'someone left town and sold up, all her furniture sold very high, the piano fetched 85 guineas', surely an extraordinary sum for such an early date.[116] Little wonder Mrs Meredith took such great care with her piano when she moved house within Van Diemen's Land: 'My piano, carefully replaced in its English case, and laid upon a dray well padded with bags of straw, and drawn by six oxen, moved away with a grave and solemn demeanour, as if conscious how important a part it played in the procession'.[117] Even allowing for Meredith's florid literary style it is clear that the piano had a very special meaning – signifying to those around her its owner's high status. Given the demand for pianos it is no surprise to find that by 1840 there was a piano manufacturer in Hobart. From 1840 to 1860 William Williams assembled imported models, but he also made his own 'which are said to stand the climate better'.[118] This must have been a marketing strength as they had to compete with British manufacturers, who also sought to extend their market, as seen by an advertisement in the *Home News for Australia* for 1854: 'Pianofortes for the Colonies and India, John Cheek, London'.[119]

If the climate of Tasmania was found to be a challenge how much more so was that of Northern Queensland. Katie Hume's detailed account of tuning her own piano reveals what a problematic affair it could be to maintain one's instrument:

I am very tired, as I have just had a 'bout' of pianotuning. This is the first time I have tried to tune it *throughout*, altering the pitch and I find it dreadfully perplexing and tiring, but I think I shall manage it, with the help of my tuning forks, which give a whole octave. I have often drawn up certain notes, but never before altered the pitch, so this is quite an experiment. I am sorry to say it *stands* very badly now. I pay 2 guineas to have it tuned, and in ten days it is as bad as ever, but I suppose no instruments will stand the sudden changes we have here and the older they get, the more it affects them. I hope I shall make it *passable* for Xmas, but those buzzing base notes are very puzzling!![120]

Despite this seeming obstacle the piano business seems to have developed in tandem with European colonisation. McGufficke gives a very early example of interest in music-making from the *Port Denison Times* of 1866: 'Piano-fortes of excellent tone and workmanship made expressly to withstand the climate at 30 guineas'.[121] Presumably quite a number of the householders must have had pianos as by 1877 an advertisement in the *Townsville Herald* stated 'pianos tuned and repaired'. *Willmett's North Queensland Almanac* of 1888 lists three pianoforte dealers, and in 1889 'Rooneys' of Townsville advertised having 'taken a load of Ronisch pianos'.[122] *Pugh's Queensland Almanac* of 1900 lists two piano dealers and tuners in Townsville and by 1906 'Miss Kerry, importer of music and musical instruments' was advertising her services in the *Townsville Illustrated*.[123] That the availability of pianos was established so rapidly in North Queensland speaks clearly of the instrument's power as a signifier of social achievement, and serves as a reminder that colonial societies in their infancy were, first and foremost, aspirational societies.

The benign climate of Cape Town was evidently kind to pianos, as witness Malloy's order and Miss Rutherfoord's reference to 'mak[ing] the old piano rattle to the astonishment of occasional visitors'.[124] However, the harsh weather in West Africa seems to have proved a considerable challenge to the would-be pianists, with Mrs Melville in Sierra Leone in the 1840s describing how the Harmattan wind caused the strings of the pianoforte to break.[125] Possibly some individuals took pianos with them or ordered them from afar, just as Godley, Meredith and Malloy had done in Australasia, as during the period investigated European women were so very low in number that there was not the critical mass to foster and support a supply business. Equally of those who went, very few expected to stay for any length of time, and it is perhaps understandable that the piano was not high on their list of priorities. Of course, households of the early part of the twentieth century may well have been able to draw on pre-recorded musical entertainment, as the wind-up gramophone became more readily available.[126]

CREATING CRITICAL SPACE, THE LIVING ROOM

In India the piano faced the climatic challenges discussed in relation to other warm weather sites. Charlotte Corbett's diary of 1862 is typical in noting, when dining at a friend's, 'nice house, music, piano wonderfully out of tune'. Equally the temporary nature of many households amongst the military and civil service must surely have constrained the contribution pianos could make to the genteel performance of early nineteenth-century homes. Unsurprisingly the harmonium found a ready market in India. As noted above, wind instruments had the advantage of not going out of tune, plus they were lighter and generally more robust and therefore easy to transport. It is also, reputedly, rather easier to master than the piano. From mid-century onwards therefore, in many homes the harmonium occupied the same niche, both literally and figuratively, as the piano did elsewhere. Corbett noted in her diary that whilst in Calcutta she and her father 'Chose our Harmonium at Harrodon's – a very sweet toned "drawing-room Alexander" with knee well'. And when they reached her father's next post she wrote in large letters at the top of the page: 'Harmonium arrived', suggesting it was a source of great pleasure and a significant contributor to her genteel persona as she and her household were ever on the move. Although Corbett had a very spare writing style she is unusual in including occasions when the genteel performance was marred by the challenge of the locale, details normally expunged from most personal writings. Thus she notes not only that her acquaintances' piano was out of tune, but also that 'Mrs Carmichael's song interrupted by the fall of a lizard in her neck'.[127]

The material presented has surely demonstrated that the piano retained its significance for the woman who aspired to or wanted to retain her social standing, and the lengths she would go to in order to overcome sourcing and environmental challenges. The piano and all that it represented is therefore exemplar *par excellence* of the woman digging deep into her cultural resources to anchor herself within a new genteel circle. The instrument spoke of high European culture and hence her and her household's position in relation to their European heritage. The music-making the instrument facilitated provided a link with their previous home and family, links that were reinforced by the repetition of tuning, practising and playing. Equally her musical proficiency ensured the woman had another area of strength in staking her and her household's claim amongst the local elite.

The significance of music-making in the genteel performance is also indicated by the way the instrument is dominant within the space of the living room and yet subsumed into the overall arrangement by being decorated with other objects. Examples of the woman's craftworks, framed images, flower and plant arrangements were among the most popular selections, and it is to such items in the room that this discussion turns next.

'I would sit happily for hours over this work':[128] *accomplishments with needle and craft*

The ability to work well with sewing needles and other related tools, and thereby to make functional and decorative objects was central to female identity, both in the metropole and in colonial settings. Which work-forms were pursued would depend on personal preferences and skills, on access to materials, what was considered to be desirable by publications of the day and by one's peer group, plus presumably wider mainstream artistic trends, such as the Arts and Crafts movement. Isaacs notes that in Australia no one work-form was practised by a particular class, that they were all prone to changes in fashion, and that the quality of material they could afford to use could either upgrade or downgrade a piece.[129] This would make even these supposedly serene pastimes a potential hotbed of anxiety and competition for those seeking to display their genteel expertise and creativity. Louisa Meredith was particularly sharp about fashionable behaviours in Hobart, declaring:

> I found that the prevalent fashionable epidemic, instead of betraying symptoms of the ancient Berlin-wool influenza or the knitting disorder, had taken on an entirely new turn, and that a landscape sketching and water-colour fever was raging with extraordinary vehemence. All the young ladies, and many elder ones, immediately discovered (or coveted, which is nearly the same) a great taste for drawing.[130]

It is true to say that all but the poorest of living rooms in homes with female occupants would be expected to contain items of needlework and craftwork made by the woman of the house. That said, it was inevitable that those women of genteel persuasion, or with ambitions in that direction, would seek to produce a greater number of more complex items. These works would be made specifically for the living room, as this was the critical space where the woman was expected to display her expertise.

In areas where homemakers settled for some time there can be found development of local forms. Isaacs identifies a number of crafts which evolved in Australia during the nineteenth century: shell-work, grottos, decorated emu eggs, miniature animal models, and picture framing and furniture adorned with botanical items. In addition she notes the ongoing practices of work-forms of British tradition including embroidery, sewing, quilting, appliqué, lace and beadwork, crochet, knitting and rug-making.[131]

In Tasmania site-specific work-forms developed and interests in local natural history were reflected in the women's work. Laura Wright's diary records 'invented book-markers of periwinkle shells', and the value she accorded to her creativity and ingenuity can be gauged by an entry later that same month: 'very busy all morning preparing our little parcel to send to England by the Marths. It consists of moss shells, dried specimens of flowers and seaweed stalactites, shell markers etc etc'. The moss work to which this entry refers seems to have been a particular enthusiasm of Wright's and she makes several such entries including 'gathered a little bouquet for my moss basket as a memento' and 'gathered the first spring nosegay before breakfast for my moss basket'.[132]

Incorporation of natural forms into their designs was a distinctive feature of their work. Isaacs comments of a piece produced by Elsie Maria Benjamin of Perth, Tasmania in 1865 that 'it is typical of the embroidery being done in Tasmania at that time by a circle of women who followed the style and teaching of Louisa Ann Meredith. The flowers are worked in heavy silk and chenille thread, on silk. They include the blue-berried Dianella sp., Tasmanian banksias bottle-brush and Eucalyptus Globulus, the Tasmanian Blue-gum'.[133] Whilst Isaacs does not offer any direct evidence of Benjamin's connection to Mrs Meredith it is the case that by that date Meredith, who was most self-aware in her constructions of gentility, had established herself within Tasmanian society and beyond, as both writer and artist. Her paintings of local botanical specimens were accurate and skilful.

Local botanical forms were also a source of inspiration for painted items such as tea-trays and work tables. A magnificent-sounding piece was entered in the 'Tasmanian Juvenile and Industrial Exhibition' held in Hobart in February 1883. Helen Bell (c.1862–?) painted a table top which depicted (clockwise):

> Tasmanian waratah, a wreath which includes cheese berry (cyathodes glauca), kangaroo grass (themeda australis), grasstree (richea dracophylla), native cherry (exocarpus sp.), silver wattle (acacia dealbata), clematis (clematis aristata), blue lovecreeper (comesperma volubile), purple bottle-brush (melaleuca squamea), blue gum (eucalyptus globulus) and mountain laurel. Waratah, cheeseberry, grasstree and mountain laurel are all endemic to Tasmania.[134]

Although not all work was of the same level of accuracy as that described above, there was perceived to be a clear connection between the women's art, needle and craft works and contemporary interest in botany, the language of flowers and their horticultural interests. Scourse notes the fashion throughout the Victorian period for botanical identification books published with ladies in mind, in which 'the remotest improprieties were scrupulously avoided, [and] heavy facts were diluted'.[135] Interests in botany and horticulture were seen as being a natural extension of the woman's nurturing roles. Just as the garden and the woman were considered to be mutually enhanced by association, so too did artistic pursuits in the living room which drew on 'the flower kingdom' elevate the creative process, the space and the artist. Belief in the language of flowers, in which specific meanings were attributed to individual species, became in turn a source of inspiration for their art-work. Of note is how in *Embroidery*, a five-part journal published in London in 1908–9, the stated aim is to 'encourage a good type of work' and the magazine emphasises the 'purity and virtue' of the activity. The first issue included a pattern for 'a vest and cuffs decorated with trailing campanula' and went so far as to imply that the delicacy of the work was comparable to the detail in Botticelli's *Primavera*.[136]

An interest in other aspects of natural history was also considered a suitable activity for women. Knowledge of the natural world was held to equate with a greater understanding of the Divine Order and Purpose and hence 'gained a pious aura'.[137] This interest and knowledge was extended and reflected in various representations of an artistic nature in living room furnishings, as for example a fire-screen worked in Berlin-wool with a design of parrots found in Tasmania made by local resident Emily Swan in 1845, and a spectacular mantel drape of red velvet with white velvet appliqué work and chenille embroidery, which included within the design a lyre bird. Although the lyre bird was not native to Tasmania, it was an image which was regularly published, hence it was an exotic and yet familiar animal, see Figure 3.13.[138]

Another craft activity which was very popular amongst some women in Tasmania at the turn of the century was that of woodcarving. Although woodcarving is physically demanding work – the more so when working the notoriously hard local timber blackwood – there was relatively little work produced by men. In Tasmania carving was deemed to be a feminine pursuit, and hence is an example of changing attitudes to the use of the body which were still compatible with gentility. (This topic is explored in greater depth in the following chapter in relation to gardening.) The practitioners who are best remembered are Sarah Squire Todd and Nora Ellen Payne, both members of well-known local families. They made screens, sometimes incorporating dyed and embossed leather panels, fireplaces and seats. Once again local flora and fauna were recurrent motifs, with the blue-gum being a particular favourite.[139]

Perhaps the most self-conscious construction of a Tasmanian form of genteel work is that of lace-making, see Figure 3.14. In 1910 an

3.13 Mantel drapes of red velvet with white velvet appliqué and chenille embroidery, Tasmania.

3.14 Needle-run lace depicting kangaroo and apple, made by Miss Ada Wilson, Tasmania, c.1910.

exhibition of Tasmanian lace-making was held at the Masonic Hall, Hobart. Under the patronage of Lady Barron with the support of the local Arts Society and Arts and Crafts Society, Miss Ada Grey Wilson mounted a display of lace made by her and a group of companions. She later said of their work that 'we were desirous of making our own designs from Tasmanian flowers etc and could then call them Tasmanian points. The designs were intended not only for lace but also for embroidery'. That they met with approval is indicated by the report in the *Mercury*: 'one of the most pleasing features of the display was the number of competitors who departed from the stereotyped designs, and took as their subjects native flora and fauna, and portrayed them excellently'.[140]

Given their cultural heritage there is every reason to think that the women who settled in North Queensland would be as motivated and as able in needle skills as their cousins in Tasmania, yet they have left relatively few traces of their industry. McGufficke notes needlework, pokerwork and painting were popular pastimes for women 'who were able to display their accomplishments and simultaneously produce functional and decorative items for the house'.[141] *Willmett's Almanac* of Townsville listed in 1888 two suppliers of Berlin-wool, suggesting that that was still a popular form of work. A photograph of the interior of 'Moss Vale' station, North Queensland, taken in 1918 shows a tapestry-worked cushion and an example of what is probably a montmellick worked table-cloth.[142] Another image of a rural home in North Queensland depicts a group on the verandah, with one of the women sewing, and the sewing-box given pride of place in the composition, see Figure 3.15. Evidence such as this is, however, thin on the ground. Nor does the mere fact of being in an isolated setting with limited access to materials seem a full and causal account. Suppliers in Britain made much in their advertisements of the willingness to cater for overseas trade, as with George Hogg Art Needlework, suppliers of silks, patterns and materials who advertised 'special attention to Foreign Orders'.[143] Adela Stewart, homemaking at a comparable date in a relatively isolated site in the Bay of Plenty, New Zealand noted in her memoirs how in 1893:

> I got, by post, from Providence Spinning Mills, Bradford, Yorkshire, a great bundle of giant and other wools; the former to make a *'tricot couvrepieds'* for my sofa, imagining that such a big piece of work would keep me busy for weeks. But the wool and the needle being so thick, I began the rug on one Saturday and finished it the next, and possess it still, as good as ever.[144]

One might conclude that the paucity of remaining items in tropical locations is directly attributable to the rigours of climate and insect

3.15 Family group on verandah of sawn weather-board house with timber over-frame and bark kitchen extension, Roma, Queensland.

damage, and naturally those do have to be factored in, but yet the absence of references to such work in the women's personal writing is also intriguing. Certainly early homemakers and those in remote sites would be obliged to spend a lot of time making clothing for themselves, their children and even their menfolk. Under such circumstances the time available for fancy work would obviously be limited. Another factor might be that such very ladylike behaviours did not and have not accorded with constructions of the woman as 'frontierswoman', and therefore few references were made to such work at the time and the items created have not been subsequently valued and conserved. Thus the absence of such traces in North Queensland could be as telling as their presence was in the Tasmanian context.

Equally, however, there is also a notable lack of mention of craft and needle work in personal writings from India and Africa. Of course many of the women in the African colonies were homemaking by a date when many household textiles were available commercially, which may well have had the effect of devaluing the handmade items, or at least discouraged the women from allocating their energies in that direction. Arguably the items being factory-made, and hence reproducible, would not, however, devalue them in the woman's eyes, as it is the act of 'belongingness' within the genteel interior which gives the item meaning. Perhaps it is rather that the Edwardian fashion for more lightly furnished rooms meant there was less appreciation for the plethora of handmade items which so characterises the high Victorian living room in Britain and some colonial homes.

Such is obviously not the case for the woman in India during the earlier decades under investigation. Can one therefore conclude that shortage of stay in any one house for those in civil or military circles prevailed against making adornments for the living room? If that is the case then one might expect to come upon more references to needle and craft work in longer-term homes, as, for example, in those whose owners were involved in business. Jones's work on the possessions of planters in rural locations, as discussed above in relation to furniture, would seem to support this idea. He reports that the widow of an indigo planter and factory manager in Chapra in north-east India had a range of textiles in her drawing-room, and whilst some of them sound as if they would be of local manufacture, as in 'table cloth ... maroon colour, silk border', equally the antimacassars and the mantel drape may well have been worked by hand by the mistress of the house.[145] It seems plausible that the temporary nature of some homemaking compelled the women to give greater attention to other aspects of their genteel performance, as perhaps with Charlotte Corbett's eagerness to obtain her harmonium. It is also possible that the exotic and unfamiliar nature of their surroundings fostered greater interest in other art-forms such as drawing and painting. Perhaps the greatest bar to needle and craft works in homes in Africa, India and North Queensland is that the majority of those homes had verandah-based living rooms, and as such the lack of enclosure limited the possibilities for formality and for display. The consequences of such 'open-plan' living, which may seem so attractive to modern eyes, can be understood as a source of conflict for the genteel mistress, striving to control her environment and establish and retain her feminised space.

'He arranges flowers very well for an Indian':[146] *plant material in the living room*

This discussion of the living room would not be complete without due reference to the place of cut flowers and plants within the decorative scheme, and their significance for the mistress of the house. Artistic flower arrangements were regarded as another female accomplishment, and as noted by Blackes 'the multiple tables so beloved of genteel homes provided ideal sites for floral display'.[147] Although Blackes is speaking of the British home, it was a feature of the living room ensemble which was retained in many colonial settings, though arguably its meaning became more complex. The presence of flowers in the woman's throne-room served to showcase another aspect of her femininity, to provide a reminder of the 'wilderness' beyond, and hence how she contributed to civilising and taming that world, and how therefore her sphere of influence extended well beyond the enclosure of the living room.[148]

Her expertise would be noted and commented upon by her peers, and in turn bouquets of flowers were frequently taken as gifts when making calls. Alice Massey's letter from India, describing her day, places arranging the flowers at the top of her list of housekeeping tasks, ahead of instructing the servants.[149] The Goddens recalled how at their home in India their mother, in the company of her most highly regarded servant, would walk around their garden selecting the blooms for the house.[150] Mrs Jacob's begrudging remark, as quoted in the title of this section, would suggest that it was a task to which she would have been more naturally suited.

These references also remind us of the value of the living room even in sites where so much of daily life was 'verandah-based'. In this, as in all other aspects of homemaking, published works were available to guide the novice, such as Miss Maling's *Flowers for Ornament and Decoration* which not only suggested which species to use on which occasion (drawing on the language of flowers once again) but even gave direction as to the sort of receptacle which should be used.[151] Such was the status of floral arrangements that a range of vases were manufactured, designed for everything from the single bloom to vast sculptural displays, and from tiny delicate blossoms to showy flamboyant specimens. Although that work was written for the British market, the methods it extolled seem to have had wider application. Photographic records indicate that in tropical sites, where cut flowers were harder to come by, more use was made of 'house-plants'. Alternatively the flowers were grouped in small tight bunches and distributed around the room in a manner considered to be 'dainty', see Figure 3.16. An unknown lady from the Cape mentions the inclusion of wild flowers in the bouquets of her callers.[152] This incorporation of the indigenous species can be read as gentility finding another means of establishing itself in the locale. In sites where garden flowers could grow in abundance it was common practice to grow material specifically to be cut for the house, as was the custom in grand homes in Britain. This enabled the woman to respond to changes in fashion, as during the Edwardian period when it was fashionable to display massed single species. Scourse describes the living room in Britain as 'a cocoon of nature'.[153] The genteel woman in her colonial home was somewhat more ambivalent about the surrounding natural world, but in her living room we see

3.16 Living room, possibly Allahabad, c.1890s.

how she drew on the local environment in addition to the European heritage to inform her artistic accomplishments, and this was a major element in her negotiation of circumstances.

As has been amply demonstrated, any examination of the material culture of these genteel women must accord due weight to those activities which have often suffered in analysis, with the term 'womanly arts' used pejoratively and handled dismissively. Even the specialist works by Scourse and by Isaacs cited here focus on the individual and domestic setting for the women's works, without considering their wider meanings and values. In consequence it has been all too easy to see their accomplishments as lightweight, of no great consequence, part of the equally undervalued domestic world.

This discussion has shown that for the women and their peers the processes and products of needle, craft and floral work were highly valued. The work was frequently of a high calibre, and a key aspect of homemaking only relinquished when circumstances were radically changed. Although the form of their work did indeed change according to local circumstances, the principle of their applying womanly finishing touches to the room continued to loom large in their allocation of their time and energies. As such these arts lie at the heart of their feminine genteel identity and performance. Russell comments that in relation to these female accomplishments women had their only opportunity to display gentility and taste in a positive way, rather than by the avoidance of display.[154] Whilst this is surely somewhat of an overstatement as their lives are to be understood as replete with genteel signalling, certainly the self-effacement expected of them in so many situations could rarely be set aside, and it is therefore true to say that the arts discussed here are of special importance in offering a reading of a significant area of power for articulating both social distinction and feminine interiority.

'Simla grows rhododendrons and pines and violets, but nothing else – no damask, no curtain rings, no glazed cottons for lining – nothing':[155] *in conclusion*

This chapter has subjected to scrutiny the living rooms of genteel households in colonial settings. In so doing it has attested to the influence and power of the contents and spaces of such rooms and their associated practices. The elements of the room have been shown to have both discrete and cumulative meanings, and to have expressed and structured adaptations made by the women to their new locations. That said it has also become evident that such is the power ascribed to objects that although they had agency for the woman in her negotiation of circumstances they were not impartial in that mediation.

Many of the tensions in the woman's situation found expression in and through her material culture and some of those tensions were peculiar to the living room. The living room as sanctuary was contested space in Britain, but in colonial settings it encountered yet further challenges. Attempts to create and maintain controlled genteel spaces were often rendered problematic by aspects of the local environment. This chapter has considered such factors as architectural design, climate, lack of services and supplies, and geographical and social isolation. It has become evident that the idea of the living room as an idealised space was retained but that the realities of life demanded on-going adaptation and modification of both design and use.

It has also become clear that of equal significance in her creation of the room were memories of former homes, memories which found expression through her material practices. Thus it is apparent that her performance was in part informed by memory. Far from being a constant source of comfort, however, the presence of the past within the present can be a source of tension, as the migrant strives to negotiate the reminders of the 'then and there' with the daily demands of the 'here and now' – ground which has to be endlessly reworked in order to be at ease if one is not to remain forever an outsider in exile. Hence the meanings of the woman's material culture had, of necessity, to change over time. It cannot therefore be said that memory was the only, or indeed the prime mover in the women's performance. It follows that readings of colonial living rooms which argue they were little more than poor attempts to replicate British interiors fail to take into account the interiority of the rooms' creators.

A central theme of this work is that analysis of material culture provides a means of reading the actual process of refashioning identity. It was inevitable that given her ever-changing circumstances the woman's genteel subjectivity would itself be in a state of flux. In this chapter it has been argued that the rooms stand revealed as both expressive of, and representative of, identity formation in action. Instrumental in this reading have been the representations she generated of her living room: her personal writings and visual depictions. The detailed care with which some described the making of their living rooms evidenced their desire to give their material culture a narrative position, and that in turn speaks of its centrality in their lives. Such fragments of their lives have been taken as having directly contributed to the formulation of identity – indeed they cannot meaningfully be understood as being other than integral to the construction process.

The living room gives opportunities to observe the synchronicity of elements of genteel practice – the space and the contents therein, the appropriately attired bodies engaged in appropriate activities. So the rooms are both display and performance, evidence of the woman's expertise and an arena for the confirmation and consolidation of genteel practice. Readings of the individual room can be extended to understanding the creation of a number of such in other homes as a collective investment in community needs, the rooms being active in contriving an appearance of unity and thereby furthering social cohesion of the elites. This foregrounding of the living room has thus politicised the space and the women's stage-management of the activities within the space.

These rooms were the arena for both household affairs and those of a semi-public nature, and as such were the site of much of the women's influences in the colony and hence their contribution to the wider imperial cause. It was by bringing into contact those two spheres of activity that the women were able to extend their authority beyond the home, and steer not only their household but wider society along genteel pathways. It is appropriate that the next chapter should examine the area which lay beyond the immediate confines of the house, but still within the domain of the home, namely the garden. It will be shown that the practices of the garden made vital contributions to the women's role as animators and consolidators of colonial society.

Notes

1. H. W. and A. Arrowsmith, *The Home Decorator and Painters' Guide* (London, 1840) cited by J. Banham, S. Macdonald and J. Porter in *Victorian Design* (London, Cassell, 1991), p. 38. The term living room is employed throughout this discussion. It is taken to refer to the space variously described as the parlour, sitting room or drawing room. These descriptors are slippery terms and their use was to some degree subjective, as often based on family preferences as on specific architectural features or social status. My thanks to Michael Lech for reading and commenting upon an earlier draft of this chapter.
2. D. Kincaid, *British Social Life in India 1608–1937* (London, Routledge, 1938); M. Shennan, *Out in the Mid-day Sun: The British in Malaya 1880–1960* (London, John Murray, 2000).
3. H. M. Simpson, *The Women of New Zealand* (Wellington, Department of Internal Affairs, 1940); E. S. Coney, *Stroppy Sheilas and Gutsy Girls: New Zealand Women of Dash and Daring* (Birkenhead, Tandem Press, 1998); E. Pownall, *Mary of Maranoa: Tales of Australian Pioneer Women* (Sydney, F. H. Johnston, 1959).
4. T. Lane and J. Searle, *Australians at Home: A Documentary History of Australian Domestic Interiors from 1788–1914* (Melbourne, Oxford University Press, 1990); P. Russell, *A Wish of Distinction: Colonial Gentility and Femininity* (Melbourne, Melbourne University Press, 1994); L. Young, *Middle-Class Culture in the Nineteenth Century: America, Australia and Britain* (Basingstoke, Palgrave Macmillan, 2003).
5. A. Jaffer, *Furniture from British India and Ceylon: A Catalogue of the Collection of the V & A Museum and the Peabody Essex Museum* (London, V & A Publications, 2001); www.hht.net.au/ www.dunedin.govt.nz
6. S. Ardener (ed.), *Women and Space: Ground Rules and Social Maps* (London, Croom Helm, 1981); D. Massey, *Space, Place and Gender* (Cambridge, Polity Press, 1994); S. Chattopadhyay, 'Goods, Chattels and Sundry Items: Constructing Nineteenth Century Anglo-Indian Domestic Life', *Journal of Material Culture* Vol. 7 (3), 2002, pp. 243–71; D. Miller (ed.), *Home Possessions: Material Culture Behind Closed Doors* (Oxford, Berg, 2001).
7. Mrs J. E. Panton, *From Kitchen to Garret: Hints for Young Householders* (London, Ward & Downey, 1889), p. 86.
8. 'Artistic Homes or How to Furnish With Taste', 1881 cited by J. Calder in *The Victorian Home* (London, Batsford, 1977), p. 193.
9. Arrowsmith, *Home Decorator*, cited Banham *et al.*, *Victorian Design*, p. 38.
10. J. Kinchin, 'Interiors: Nineteenth Century Essays on the "Masculine" and the "Feminine" Room' in P. Kirkham (ed.), *The Gendered Object* (Manchester, Manchester University Press, 1996), p. 24.
11. Panton, *From Kitchen to Garret*, p. 86.
12. Mrs I. Beeton, *Beeton's Household Management* (London, Ward, Lock & Tyler, 1869), p. 10.
13. P. Bourdieu, *Distinction: A Social Critique of the Judgement of Taste* (Cambridge, University of Massachusetts, 1984), p. 86.
14. J. and R. Godden, *Two Under the Indian Sun* (London, Macmillan, 1966), p. 46.
15. Andrew Morrison, Letters from India, 1895,; Col. Rawdon E. D. Reilly, Late 28th Pioneers and India Staff Corps, Letters from India, British Empire and Commonwealth Museum, henceforth BECM; Eustace Kenyon, Letters from Calcutta, 1896, Centre of South Asian Studies, University of Cambridge, henceforth CSAS.
16. Evelyn Beeton, Journal, 1912, CSAS.
17. Anon., *Life at the Cape One Hundred Years Ago, by a Lady* (Cape Town, C. Struik, 1963), p. 6.
18. R. Lewis and Y. Foy, *The British in Africa* (London, Weidenfeld & Nicolson, 1971), p. 152.
19. A. Allingham, 'Pioneer Squatting in the Kennedy District', *Lectures on North*

Queensland History, Department of History, James Cook University, 1975, pp. 77–96.
20 A. Allingham, 'Victorian Frontierswomen: The Australian Diaries and Journals of Lucy and Eva Gray, 1868–1872 and 1881–1892', MA Thesis, James Cook University, 1987, Lucy Gray XXXI Journal, 1868.
21 C. Anderson (ed.), *Violet Jacob: Diaries and Letters from India 1895–1900* (Edinburgh, Canongate, 1990), p. 21.
22 Charlotte Stamper, Memoirs, 1864, S. Laughton Papers, CSAS; Mrs E. H. Melville, *A Residence at Sierra Leone by a Lady* (London, John Murray, 1849), pp. 14–15.
23 Chattopadhyay, 'Goods, Chattels and Sundry Items', p. 249.
24 Young, *Middle-Class Culture in the Nineteenth Century*, pp. 54–5.
25 C. Macdonald (ed.), *Women Writing Home 1700–1920: Female Correspondence Across the British Empire. Vol. 5 New Zealand* (London, Pickering & Chatto, 2006), p. 113, Sarah Greenwood, 1843.
26 Ardener, *Women and Space*, p. 19.
27 J. Craik, 'Verandahs and Frangipani: Women in the Queensland House' in G. Reekie (ed.), *On the Edge: Women's Experiences of Queensland* (St Lucia, University of Queensland, 1994), p. 146.
28 A. D. King, *Colonial Urban Development* (London, Routledge Kegan Paul, 1976), p. 151.
29 D. Moore, *We Two in West Africa* (London, Heinemann, 1909), pp. 55–6.
30 Moore may also have chosen to itemise the 'gate-legged oak table' and the 'Turkey carpet', to indicate that she was *au fait* with the aesthetic of the Arts and Crafts movement, very much in vogue in the metropolis at that date.
31 J. S. Marcoux, 'The "Caisser-Maison" Ritual: Constructing the Self by Emptying the Home', *Journal of Material Culture* Vol. 6 (2), 2001, pp. 213–35.
32 E. Hallam and J. Hockey, *Death, Memory and Material Culture* (Oxford, Berg, 2001), p. 48.
33 Lady Nora Scott, Journal, Bombay 1882, CSAS.
34 S. Leith-Ross cited by H. Callaway, *Gender, Culture and Empire* (London, Macmillan, 1987), p. 176. Isabelle Vischer, author, whose works included the cookery book *Now to the Banquet* (London, Victor Gollancz, 1953).
35 R. D. Jones, *Interiors of Empire: Objects, Space and Identity within the Indian Subcontinent, c.1800–1947* (Manchester, Manchester University Press, 2007), pp. 60–1.
36 Mrs Clementina Benthall, Diary, 1842, CSAS.
37 *Chunam*: burnt lime, sometimes used in conjunction with aggregate to create a chequer-board design.
38 Mrs L. Orrinsmith, *The Drawing-room: Its Decoration and Furniture* (London, Macmillan & Co., 1878), p. 59.
39 P747.5WIL, Museum of Domestic Design and Architecture.
40 C. M. McGufficke, 'Parlours in North Queensland Houses: 1861–1920', MA Thesis, James Cook University, 1992, p. 19.
41 Orrinsmith, *Drawing-room*, p. 51.
42 Clementina Benthall, Diary, 1842, CSAS.
43 Lady Nora Scott, Journal, April 1885, CSAS.
44 Eustace Kenyon worked for the Telegraph Office and though he subsequently rose up the ranks he started off in quite a modest way. At this stage Ethel and Eustace employed three servants plus a cook.
45 J. R. Godley (ed.), *Letters from Early New Zealand by Charlotte Godley, 1850–1853* (Christchurch, Whitcombe & Tombs, 1951), p. 153. 'Brussels carpet' is a worsted carpet with a heavy pile formed by uncut loops of wool on a linen warp.
46 Macdonald, *Women Writing Home. Vol. 5*, p. 307, Georgina Bowen.
47 L. P. Wright (ed.), *Laura's Brookville Diaries, 1819–1894* (Launceston, Greenhill, 2003).
48 *Mercury*, 13 February 1877.
49 C. H. Eden, *My Wife and I in Queensland: An Eight Year Experience in the Above*

CREATING CRITICAL SPACE, THE LIVING ROOM

     Colony, With Some Account of Polynesian Labour (London, Longmans, Green & Co., 1872), p. 65.
50 Tamara Lavrenic, Collections Manager, Historic Houses Trust of New South Wales reports difficulties trying to stabilise oilcloth in which termites 'have devoured the support in places, leaving only the medium and design layers'. www.palimlest.standard.edu.au
51 J. Isaacs, *The Gentle Arts: Two Hundred Years of Australian Women's Domestic and Decorative Arts* (Sydney, Lansdowne Press, 1987).
52 Grass matting was a generic term used to describe a range of fibres, grass-like in appearance, such as flax, hemp, jute or sisal, all of which were admirably suited to weaving and dyeing. Usually designed and made by the indigenous peoples of the locality, they tended to be cheap and more readily available than other, supposedly more sophisticated, items.
53 J. Young (ed.), *Jane Bardsley's Outback Letter Book: Across the years 1896–1936, Pioneer Life in Australia's Tropic North* (North Ryde, NSW, Angus & Robertson, 1987), p. 70.
54 McGufficke, 'Parlours', p. 21.
55 C. Larymore, *A Resident's Wife in Nigeria* (London, Routledge, 1911), p. 197. Bida, Nigeria, long-established site of manufacture of brass, glass and other craftwork.
56 Jones goes so far as to state that 'The use of grass matting in the Anglo-Indian interior was a near-universal phenomenon.' Jones, *Interiors of Empire*, p. 55.
57 Eliza Errington, Port Arthur, Tasmania, 1844 cited in Lane and Searle, *Australians at Home*, p. 68.
58 J. Broadbent, S. Rickard and M. Steven, *India, China and Australia: Trade and Society, 1788–1850* (Glebe, NSW, Historic Houses Trust of New South Wales, 2003), p. 157.
59 Lane and Searle, *Australians at Home*, p. 68
60 Macdonald, *Women Writing Home. Vol. 5*, p. 312, Georgina Bowen, 1862.
61 Melville, *A Residence at Sierra Leone*, pp. 24–5.
62 Larymore, *Resident's Wife*, p. 197.
63 Letter from F. Swanzy to G. Inglis, 2 June, 1852, UAC/2/33/AG/1/2/1, Swanzy Collection, Unilever Archives and Record Management, Port Sunlight; my thanks to Diane Backhouse, Archivist, for bringing this item to my attention.
64 Eden, *My Wife and I in Queensland*, pp. 134–5. See also the following section on wall coverings for further discussion of Eden's practice.
65 Young, *Across the Years*, p. 130.
66 Mrs Clemons, *The Manners and Customs of Society in India* (London, 1841), p. 11, cited Jones, *Interiors of Empire*, p. 52.
67 J. Capon, 'The Development of Decorative Wall and Ceiling Ornament in the Colonial Period' in M. Stapleton (ed.), *Historic Interiors: A Collection of Papers* (Sydney, Sydney College of Arts, 1983), p. 24.
68 *Wunderlich Ltd, Abridged General Catalogue of Metal Ceilings, Wall linings and Stamped Metal for Exterior and Interior Decoration*, Crowther Library, State Library of Tasmania, henceforth SLT. By 1913 Cathcart & Ritchie, Townsville, North Queensland was agents for Wunderlich.
69 See also following section on wall coverings.
70 Lady Curzon on seeing the interior of her Vice-Regal's Lodge, Simla. She continued 'It looks at you with pomegranate and pineapple eyes from every wall', cited by Kincaid in *British Social Life in India*, p. 257. This rather suggests that the heavy and ponderous style of décor considered desirable for the public/private spaces in the homes of the elite at the turn of the century was not to everyone's liking.
71 Orrinsmith, *Drawing-room*, p. 10.
72 E. A. Entwisle, *Wallpapers of the Victorian Era* (F. Lewis, Leigh-on-Sea, 1964), p. 8.
73 R. Kerr, *The Gentleman's Home* (London, 1864), p. 107 cited by Kinchin in 'Interiors', p. 14.
74 Examples of stencilling directly on to the wall are located in an old homestead, 'Grantham', and in the Castle Hotel, both in Bothwell, Tasmania.

75 Good-sized fragments of the paper are to be found in the State Archives. See also J. Searle, 'Government House, Tasmania: An Essay in British Establishment Aspirations' in G. Winter (ed.), *Tasmanian Insight* (Hobart, State Library of Tasmania, 1992), pp. 192–211.
76 *Mercury*, 14 January 1856, 13 February 1877.
77 J. Richardson, 'An Annotated Edition of the Journals of Mary Morton Allport', Ph.D. Thesis, University of Tasmania, 2006. 9 November 1852; Wright, *Brookville Diaries*, 10 January 1876.
78 A. Montana, *The Art Movement in Australia: Design, Taste and Society, 1875–1900* (Carlton, Victoria, Miegunyah Press, 2000), p. 19.
79 For a further discussion of wallpaper use in the temperate regions of Australia see M. Lech, *Wallpaper* (Sydney, Historic Houses Trust, 2010).
80 D. Adams (ed.), *The Letters of Rachel Henning* (Harmondsworth, Penguin, 1969), pp. 136–7, 143.
81 Katie Hume does speak with delight of her bedroom in Drayton, prepared for her prior to her arrival. 'I wish you could see my Bedroom, with its pretty white paper with pink rose-buds': N. Bonnin (ed.), *Katie Hume on the Darling Downs: A Colonial Marriage* (Toowoomba, Darling Downs Institute Press, 1985), p. 30. The more moderate climate of southern Queensland would make papering the walls a more practicable option.
82 Allingham, 'Victorian Frontierswomen', Lucy Gray, Diary June 1870; Eva Gray, Journal 28 July 1881.
83 Eden, 1847, cited by Kincaid, *British Social Life in India*, p. 245.
84 Melville, *A Residence at Sierra Leone*, p. 25.
85 Larymore, *Resident's Wife*, p. 197.
86 A. Drummond (ed.), *Married and Gone to New Zealand* (Hamilton and Auckland, Paul's Book Arcade, 1960), p. 110.
87 Anning Family Papers, AFRS/MEM/1, Special Collections, Library, James Cook University, Queensland.
88 Macdonald, *Women Writing Home. Vol. 5*, p. 11, Sarah Selwyn, 19 January, 1843.
89 Mrs Meredith Housekeeping and Account Book, 18 July 1820, NS123/192, Tasmanian State Archives, henceforth TSA.
90 Cited in Lane and Searle, *Australians at Home*, p. 69.
91 R. L. Atkinson, 'The Long Trail', fol. 16r, unpub. MS, Special Collections, Library, James Cook University, Queensland.
92 Anning Family Papers.
93 Anning Family Papers.
94 Young, *Across the Years*, p. 35.
95 Eden, *My Wife and I in Queensland*, p. 29; Allingham, 'Victorian Frontierswomen', Lucy Gray, XXVIII, 1868.
96 Moore, *We Two in West Africa*, p. 57.
97 Larymore, *A Resident's Wife*, pp. 196–7.
98 *Pugh's Queensland Almanac and Directory* (Brisbane, Pugh, 1900).
99 Broadbent et al., *India, China and Australia*, p. 102.
100 'Household Inventory of Maria Hammond (Meredith) deceased, 1831', NS123/192, TSA.
101 Anna Maria Nixon 1845, writing to her father. Cited by Lane and Searle in *Australians at Home*, p. 69.
102 Chattopadhyay, 'Goods, Chattels and Sundry Items', p. 251.
103 Clementina Benthall and Charlotte Wortley Corbett Diaries, CSAS.
104 Jones, *Interiors of Empire*, p. 86.
105 Scripps, *The Industrial Heritage of Hobart, Vol. 1 Historical Study* (Hobart, Hobart City Council, 1997), p. 65.
106 An outstanding collection of nineteenth-century huon pine furniture is to be found in the Tasmanian Museum, e.g. a work-table of huon pine, blackwood, musk casuarina and textile. Cat Ref.: P2006.70.
107 William Bros, *Complete House Furnishers and Retailers*, 1909 Catalogue, *William*

Coogan, *Furniture Manufacturers and Retailers*, 1913 Catalogue, Crowther Library, SLT.
108 *Aldine's History of Queensland* (Sydney, Aldine Publishers, 1888).
109 Macdonald, *Women Writing Home. Vol. 5*, p. 314, Georgina Bowen, New Zealand, 1862.
110 A. S. McGowan, '"All that is Rare, Characteristic or Beautiful": Design and Defence of Tradition in Colonial India, 1851–1903', *Journal of Material Culture* Vol. 10 (3), 2005, pp. 263–87.
111 Eustace Kenyon, 1896, CSAS.
112 Jones, *Interiors of Empire*, p. 109, citing L/AG/34/27/163 Estate of Mary Shillingford, Bengal Wills, 1867, British Library.
113 Bonnin, *Colonial Marriage*, 20 December 1869, p. 169.
114 Godley, *Letters from Early New Zealand*, p. 101.
115 D. Coleman (ed.), *Women Writing Home 1700–1920: Female Correspondence Across the British Empire. Vol. 2 Australia* (London, Pickering & Chatto, 2006), pp. 157, 199, Georgina Malloy.
116 Richardson, Allport Journals, 8 February 1852.
117 L. A. Meredith, *My Home in Tasmania: During a Residence of Nine Years* (Adelaide, Griffin Press, 1932), p. 89, first published 1853.
118 Scripps,*The Industrial Heritage of Hobart*, p. 68.
119 Copies of periodical 1853–98 in Reference Library, State Library of Tasmania.
120 Bonnin, *Colonial Marriage*, 20 December 1869, p. 169.
121 McGufficke, 'Parlours', p. 3; *Port Denison Times*, 3 November 1866.
122 *Townsville Herald*, 22 December 1877; *Willmett's North Queensland Almanac: Miners, Settlers and Sugar Planters Companion* (Townsville, T. Willmett, 1888); *Townsville Daily Bulletin*, 6 April 1889.
123 *Townsville Illustrated* 1906. Copy held at the Special Collections Library, James Cook University, Queensland.
124 J. Murray (ed.), *In Mid-Victorian Cape Town: Letters from Miss Rutherfoord* (Cape Town, A. A. Balkema, 1953), November 1852.
125 Melville, *A Residence at Sierra Leone*, p. 14.
126 The gramophone was invented by E. Berliner in 1887 and became commercially available from approximately 1900 onwards.
127 Charlotte Mary Wortley Corbett, Diary, 1862, Ormsby Papers, CSAS.
128 Eliza Chomley, making reference to her cross-stitch needlework in her 'Memoirs', cited by Russell, *A Wish of Distinction*, p. 98.
129 Isaacs, *The Gentle Arts*, p. 13.
130 Meredith, *My Home in Tasmania*, p. 194.
131 Isaacs, *Gentle Arts*, p. 13.
132 Wright, *Brookville Diaries*, 6 September 1864 and 6 September 1865.
133 Isaacs, *Gentle Arts*, p. 139. Chenille is a silk or worsted yarn that gives a very soft and lush surface.
134 J. Kerr (ed.), *Heritage: The National Women's Art Book* (Sydney, G & B Arts International, 1995), p. 6; *Official Catalogue of the Exhibits of the Tasmanian Juvenile and Industrial Exhibition, 16th April 1883*, Ref.: TCP607.34, Tasmaniana Collection, SLT.
135 N. Scourse, *The Victorians and their Flowers* (London, Croom Helm, 1983), p. 69.
136 *Embroidery* (London, 1908–9). Copies held at MoDA.
137 Scourse, *Victorians and their Flowers*, p. 50.
138 Berlin-wool was a form of work which seems to have had ongoing popularity to judge by a bill for 3 skeins of Berlin-wool from James Morris Draper and Grocer sent to Mrs Meredith 1 July 1885. TSA.
139 Conversation with Peter Hughes, Curator of Decorative Arts, Tasmanian Museum and Art Gallery, Hobart, who suggested that the way in which the Arts and Crafts movement was articulated on the mainland was more 'professional', whereas in Tasmania the work took on a more vernacular quality. March 2007.
140 *Mercury*, 16 September 1910. A. Melrose, *Catalogue: Tasmanian Lace-making:*

Miss Ada Grey Wilson's Lace Collection (Hobart, Tasmanian Museum & Art Gallery, 1990).

141 McGufficke, 'Parlours', p. 5.
142 Moss Vale Station, Ref.: 07633, North Queensland Historic Photographic Collection, James Cook University. Montmellick: a highly textured form of embroidery in which white thread is worked on white fabric, said to be Irish in origin, a popular work-form during the Edwardian period and beyond.
143 *Embroidery*, George Hogg advertised in the first issue.
144 A. B. Stewart, *My Simple Life in New Zealand* (London, Robert Banks & Co., 1908), p. 126.
145 Jones, *Interiors of Empire*, pp. 107–8, citing estate of William Smith, L/AG/34/27/187, Bengal Wills, 1880, British Library.
146 Anderson, *Violet Jacob*, p. 23.
147 M. R. Blackes, *Flora Domestica: A History of Flower Arranging 1500–1930* (London, National Trust, 2000), p. 126.
148 This theme is pursued in depth in the following chapter on the form and meanings of the women's gardening practices.
149 K. Stierstorfer (ed.), *Women Writing Home 1700–1920: Female Correspondence Across the British Empire. Vol. 4 India* (London, Pickering & Chatto, 2006), p. 45, Alice Massey, 1875.
150 Goddens, *Two Under the Indian Sun*, p. 54.
151 Miss E. A. Maling, *Flowers for Ornament and Decoration and How to Arrange Them* (London, Smith, Elder & Co, 1862).
152 Anon., *Life at the Cape*, p. 6.
153 Scourse, *Victorians and their Flowers*, p. 15.
154 Russell, *A Wish of Distinction*, p. 87.
155 Emily Eden 1839 cited by P. Barr and R. Desmond, *Simla: A Hill Station in British India* (London, Scolar Press, 1975), p. 8.

4

'No-one can over-estimate the pleasure of tending flowers':[1] tasteful gardening and growing attachment

Introduction

The previous chapter examined the creation and use of living rooms, and how those rooms, the objects therein and related practices contributed to women's performance of gentility in colonial sites. Their living rooms emerged as recognisably genteel spaces, although the precise form of this aspect of the women's performance was modified by local circumstance. This chapter is an exploration of genteel female subjectivities as developed and expressed in their gardens. Thus it is not a historical overview of women gardeners empire-wide, nor yet is it a survey of colonial gardens. Rather does it examine the refined woman's occupation of, and influence over, the spaces of the garden, and considers ways in which the processes and products of gardening proved to be valuable elements of her performance. It will be shown that there was interaction and interpenetration between the practices of the garden and those of the house, and hence it is appropriate that it should follow the discussion of living rooms and precede that of food. As with the other topics examined in this work their gardens are taken to be an element within the homemakers' habitus, critical spaces through which they reproduced some of the desired values of earlier homes, but also mediated and adapted to new circumstances. Their garden practices therefore had a key role in the formulation of site-specific forms of genteel identity.

Locating traces of such practices over a range of sites has proved far from straightforward, which may in part explain why so little work has been done on the topic, even though bookshops, library catalogues and internet searches would suggest the history of gardens and gardening is an expanding and increasingly popular area of study. One might expect that this would favour a broader range of enquiry, but much of the work takes the form of micro studies on the conservation of large-scale gardens and man-made landscapes, projects with an emphasis on lands prior to the impact of European colonisation, or the undertakings of the common man.² Perhaps then it is also for socio-political reasons that the European woman with elitist ambitions gardening in her bungalow in India or on her sheep farm in New Zealand has largely failed to catch the interested eye of the researcher, and in consequence the form of her garden and extent to which it contributed to her performance are neglected areas of study.

Of the work which has been done on gardens in colonial settings much has been on public gardens, particularly on the botanic gardens which were established across the British Empire along with other institutions such as zoological gardens, libraries and museums. Botanic gardens performed vital tasks in collecting and collating new discoveries, formalising the new knowledge in the name of the imperial cause. For contemporary private gardeners the botanic gardens were sometimes a source of supply of new and exciting plant material, whilst the professional body benefited from the horticultural experiments of the domestic gardeners. It is perhaps inevitable, however, that those private gardens and their creators have received little coverage in works on these public institutions. Thus the Carltons' book on the significance of gardening in India is primarily concerned with various sorts of public gardens, whilst McCracken's richly informative work on the form and function of botanical institutions across the British Empire has too broad a frame of reference to consider the group of gardeners investigated here.[3]

Where smaller gardens have been the focus of attention the vast majority of works present the garden as a finished product, ignore the processes of making and maintaining which lie behind the garden, and are largely descriptive in tone. The more pleasing therefore, in part because it is relatively unusual, is Leach's anthropological approach to the history of gardens. The author analyses elements of gardens and places the domestic garden in a wider social context, and in so doing she reconnects the objects in the garden – both hard design features and plant material – with the processes of gardening and the gardeners.[4] Leach also makes insightful comments as to the ways gardens have been interpreted and some of the myths which have developed in consequence, myths which have in turn predominated in subsequent writing on colonial gardens and their makers. This work will attempt to challenge some of those myths in relation to just one discrete type of gardener. It will question the oft-cited opinion that genteel female homemakers of British heritage were motivated to garden simply in order to replicate a form of idealised British garden, and also that such a woman in the garden was merely another decorative feature.

TASTEFUL GARDENING AND GROWING ATTACHMENT

This chapter commences with an overview of British attitudes to refined forms of gardening, with specific reference to women's place in the garden, and the extent to which that was – or may have been – taken as a model for garden practice in colonial locations. Also discussed are other aspects of genteel women's expertise which aided them in the creation of gardens, such as the cultural reinforcement of an appreciation of beauty and nature, as expressed through knowledge of the language of flowers, and activities such as painting. There follows an examination of the various sections of the colonial garden and the practices therein, which identifies the complexity of values the garden had for the mistress of the house.

It is fitting that we enter at the front garden, as would any caller, as by so doing we can consider the face the genteel household presented to the world. From there we take a guided tour round the flower garden, including consideration of other decorative features such as croquet lawns or ferneries, which were thought to give added value to the garden, and hence to the household. The kitchen garden is handled separately because of its self-evident connection to food and table practices. The verandah is discussed discretely because it is a border territory between the interior of the house and the garden. The outward orientation of the verandah prepares the ground for speculation on the impact that gardens and gardening might have had on the woman's relationship with the world beyond the garden fence. This subject is discussed in the final section, which considers ways in which the gardening practices of these colonial homemakers served to chronicle their changing relationships with the environment, and thereby their attachment to place. It will also be argued that these domestic gardens and the women within them played important roles in the colonising project, acting as metaphor for European notions of civilising alien territory.

By their very nature the women's gardens are long gone. If we are to catch a glimpse of those vivid flower-beds, well-groomed lawns and neat lines of carefully nurtured vegetables we need cast our source net high and wide. The assemblage presented here includes, amongst other items, seed and plant catalogues from Britain, Australia and India, gardening manuals from India and South Africa, memoirs of gardening in New Zealand and in Nigeria, paintings of plants and gardens made in India and Australia, and photographs of gardens from Australia, India and New Zealand. This rich array serves to underpin the argument that the space and practices of the garden had agency for the expression of female gentility, and structured and contributed to the woman's performance.

GENTEEL WOMEN

'People entirely devoid of imagination never can be good gardeners. To be content with the present, and not striving for the future, is fatal':[5] *the female genteel gardener in Britain*

The enduring image most commonly associated with women of the Victorian and Edwardian periods in relation to gardens is that of the fragile maiden in the midst of flowery bower, see Figure 4.1. For contemporaries women's association with gardens was deemed to be 'natural', a logical extension of the nurturing role ordained by their very sex. The garden supposedly reinforced her image as a pure and lovely being, and in turn the garden was enhanced by the innate beauty of her soul. Thus the garden was no mere decorative device, but had a moral force and a strong claim for being to the forefront of the genteel value system, and hence that the woman's presence in it was indisputable. In the garden she was a further conduit of moral worth; it was a site in which she could do good and have a positive influence within society. The woman in the garden can therefore be understood as a material expression of a moral standpoint.

The practical arena in which many of the women worked was the villa garden. 'Villa' was the name given to a style of house built in Britain from the latter half of the century onwards, designed to appeal to the new strata of society: those who had benefited from the expansion of trade and industry and were for the first time in a position to rent or buy a house with a garden. In such households the man worked away from the home whilst the woman managed the domestic affairs. This arrangement did not just provide an opportunity for the woman to garden; the system actually relied on her participation. The garden was to be a marker of attainment, and her presence within in it was of immense value for the status of the whole household.

Inevitably the houses and their gardens varied in size, and if the household purse would stretch far enough a gardener was employed on a full or part-time basis. Horn notes that from 1881 to 1911 domestic gardeners increased in number from 74,603 to 118,739, and one can assume a large percentage of that increase was taken up by villa gardening.[6] Irrespective of whether there was outside help to perform the heavier chores, the women were expected to undertake at least some tasks. Jane Loudon, who went on to became a most outspoken advocate of women as gardeners but was somewhat tentative in her first writings, recommended sowing, watering, transplanting, dead-heading and seed collection as being suitable 'feminine occupations', whilst John Loudon devoted an entire work to advising this new class of gardeners as to how to design, plant and manage their new plot.[7] General works

4.1 'The Rector's Garden: Queen of the Lilies' by John Atkinson Grimshaw, 1877.

on gardens and gardening would frequently allocate a section to villa gardeners and there was a periodical, *Villa Gardener*, entirely devoted to their needs. Of particular note is that this periodical does not appear to have taken a male focus as its default setting. Thus whilst there are gender-specific items – for example a piece entitled 'Plants for the Dining Table' gives particular mention to euphorbias on the somewhat curious grounds that they were also considered a 'suitable adornment for ladies hair', most articles are written in a gender neutral fashion and at least some of the articles were attributed to women authors.[8]

Villa gardens were seen as spaces in which the women could model good behaviour for family and beyond, just as she did in her living room. One writer urged that English boys and girls should be encouraged to garden to deter them from 'the reckless craving for pleasures, often more or less vicious, which is steadily sapping the moral strength of the British race'.[9] The flower garden was used for family recreation purposes and as a space to conduct social gatherings. So it was an area that was very much on display. As an area of female expertise it could be a source of pride, though as with all facets of genteel performance, it had the potential to be a source of anxiety, lest the design, plantings and maintenance prove not to meet the exacting standards of the local genteel circle. The ever-ambitious Mrs Earle, whose assertion forms the title above, also declared 'On first going into a garden one knows by instinct, as a hound scents a fox, if it is going to be interesting or not', words which must surely have caused a twinge of concern in even the most serene hostess.[10] Such was the background against which refined women, and/or socially ambitious women, embarked on gardening in their new colonial homes. Some were experienced gardeners, others complete novices, some met with disaster and success alike, but as will be seen all met with horticultural adventures and seem to have found in their gardens a rich potential for the expression of their genteel interiority.

'If the cottage homes were more generally beautiful with flowers and shrubs greater domestic happiness would often result':[11] garden practice in the colonies

In Britain the right of the genteel women for a place in the garden was accompanied by responsibilities, but in homes across the Empire those pressures to create a refined garden took on a particular intensity. In the so-called 'white colonies' the land itself had an almost mythical significance, for it was to be the tool whereby settlers and even sojourners were to establish a 'better Britain'. However, the land in its natural state was held to be inherently barbaric and it had to be civilised if it were to move beyond being simply territory and make a contribution to the imperial cause. As Byrne notes in relation to New Zealand, there was an impetus to 'claim, tame and re-define the meaning of landscape in specifically English terms'.[12] This point is also nicely articulated by the Resident's wife in Nigeria, Constance Larymore, who declared that 'the planting of useful and ornamental trees is no less than a positive duty incumbent on every householder in West Africa'.[13]

Gardening gave a role and purpose for the women within the colonising project which arose naturally and expanded upon the role and function of the genteel women villa gardening in Britain. Not only were the makers of these genteel spaces to extend the primary colonising work of their menfolk – for that can be said to have been the case for all female gardeners, they were to create havens of loveliness as befitted superior female endeavour. Their gardens were to be microcosms of the aims and intentions the colonisers had for the broader environment. Their endeavours were therefore entirely in keeping with the ideological values of gentility and colonialism alike.

The view of the form and purpose of the genteel garden was an idealised one; just as the living room was supposedly to be the epitome of a civilised interior space so too was the garden to be a perfectly designed, perfectly appointed, exterior space. Ultimate control and a contrivance of effortlessness were the hallmarks of gentility; achieving such heights of perfection in a garden was always a challenge, but in new territories the problems were amplified. Indeed it may be said that female genteel values encountered even greater challenges in their gardens than in relation to the other topics discussed in this work.

The climatic and ecological factors they met with in all colonial sites proved taxing, but arguably the challenges were even greater in tropical regions. In consequence it could be said that establishing an elegant garden in West Africa or North Queensland was yet more difficult than in Tasmania or New Zealand. In some tropical locations the development of local expertise may well have proved more critical, and been accorded higher value, than any amount of supplies and technological developments. To be able to demonstrate you had come to grips with the extremes of the climate, with unfamiliar patterns of growth, and attacks by any number of strange pests and diseases was proof positive that you and your household managed a successful garden. One's peers and surrounding society, all of whom were wrestling with the self-same conditions, would be in a position to have an appreciation and understanding of the scale of your achievement and the work involved to that end. Thus the actual processes were valued, not only the product, and even where there was paid labour involved in the enterprise overseeing the work often fell to the mistress of the house, and her efforts were valued accordingly.

The would-be gardeners who lived in temperate zones had, by and large, better access to supplies than had their peers in the tropics, and were more readily able to take advantage of technological developments and improvements in communication. They were also well positioned to benefit from the work of the acclimatisation societies and the discoveries of plant hunters and botanical institutions. Moreover they were the gardeners who were most likely to be successful in cultivating plants with which they had been familiar in British gardens, or, if they were second generation homemakers, plants they had seen growing in their family's gardens. This last point is critical, for on such garden practices has been based the received wisdom that the prime and sole motivation in their gardening was to reproduce a form of English cottage garden. The complex gardens such homemakers were able to create have a groomed air which is rarely seen in the more exuberant tropical garden. Thus, whilst it may appear that the women gardening in moderate climes were better placed to create the most sophisticated expressions of horticultural gentility, one must exercise caution in reading garden practice, and be ever mindful of the circumstances which determined the gardens' form and function.[14]

Even those women who had no direct experience of gardening

brought a deal of other cultural expertise to support their position of 'the lady in the garden'. It was thought necessary that as part of her education any woman of genteel persuasion should have some knowledge of flowers. Typical of the form this knowledge took was an interest in the notion of the language of flowers, as noted in the previous chapter, which seems to have been highly valued as a marker of taste and to have had some international currency in the English-speaking world.[15] Examples are to be found in Australia where several books were published on the theme, with copies being exchanged amongst friends and family. Laura Wright's Tasmanian diary has an 1864 entry which notes receipt of a copy of *The Language of Common Flowers*, and in 1840 Georgina Malloy wrote from the Swan River settlement in Western Australia to thank a friend in Britain for a gift of *The Language of Flowers*.[16] A volume of *The Language and Poetry of Flowers* is to be found in the Tasmaniana Collection, Hobart, and as it includes plants unlikely to have been found in England prior to 1850 it seems possible that the lists were sometimes updated, and therefore the subject was of ongoing interest.[17] In addition the library holds copies of two more works on the subject, both about local flora and locally published, which suggests that indigenous flora was also being embraced and elevated in this genteel fashion by being associated with behavioural traits.[18] For example, Mrs Meredith's slim volume comprises actual specimens of local flora; all dried, mounted and labelled with loving care. Similar works have been located in other sites, such as South Africa where the University of Cape Town has a copy of Kate Greenaway's *The Language of Flowers*, one of the most popular and widely distributed works of the genre, whilst the National Library of New Zealand has in its collection a locally published volume on the language of flowers, presented in conjunction with a miscellany of poems, thereby linking two areas of refined feminine knowledge.[19]

Knowledge of flowers frequently found expression in other practices, with floral motifs a recurrent source of design in needle and craft work (as discussed in the previous chapter in relation to the material culture of living rooms) and in the production of drawings and paintings. Just as a genteel woman should know how to dress and conduct herself, so too should she know how to create delicate 'likenesses' of flowers. Miss Pilkington, who made a long visit to friends in Ootacamund, India in 1894 made a Commonplace Book, which includes floral illustrations – see Figure 4.2. The watercolours have been applied loosely and the style is impressionistic, yet clearly identifiable are the potted geraniums in the foreground. It may be that Miss Pilkington had a special fondness for the plant with its bright flowers and pungent leaves, or perhaps she lingered over it simply because she recognised it from her

4.2 Garden in Wellington, India, as painted by Miss Pilkington in her Commonplace Book, 1894.

4.3 Plants of North Queensland, as depicted in a watercolour and sketch album, artist unknown, 1888–92.

English home. Equally perhaps she had noted, or been told, that similar pots marched up and down the steps of bungalows across the length and breadth of 'British India', sometimes actually accompanying the memsahibs on their journeys from the plains to the hill stations to escape the hot weather. Whatever the form and extent of the artist's local knowledge not only did she display her genteel skills in making this charming representation of a colonial home, but her compositions featured the very plant which had such iconic meaning in those Anglo-Indian gardens. The other image included here, Figure 4.3, is that of native flowers painted in Bowen, North Queensland and is taken from an anonymous watercolour album produced during a 'Grand Tour' in 1888–92. The artist has depicted the plants with a degree of accuracy and annotated her work in an informative manner; her choice and handling of her subject suggesting her work was a valued form of cultural expertise.[20]

The other area in which women's involvement in their flower gardens found expression was in their personal writings. Georgina Bowen's description of her Christchurch garden suggests keen pleasure in her own knowledge:

It is a large kind of shrubbery of willows, small poplars, acacias, laburnums and native shrubs with a great ti palm left here and there and occasionally a bit of native flax. The flax is more like an aloe than anything else, it has a beautiful scarlet flower but it is over now. The sides of the path are quite gay with flowers, annuals of all kinds geraniums, fuchsia, gladiolus etc.[21]

Sarah Courage's remark that 'whatever the employments of the day, I always contrived to find a little spare time for the flowers' typifies the high value they accorded to their garden.[22] All of the examples cited here serve to emphasise that the sensory aspects of life were held to be within the female sphere and in relation to their flowers in particular were deemed to be an expression of refinement.

In the light of the form and style of many of the fragments which remain of the women's work, most particularly their written work, subsequent interpretations have tended to dwell on the notion of the woman as consumer rather than producer of the flowers, and have foregrounded nostalgia in reading their practices. This discussion will present evidence of an intense involvement in the actual husbandry of their flower gardens, and argue that it was often matched by their enthusiasm for species not at the time associated with gardens in Britain.

Also at odds with the accepted reading of these women and their gardens is the enthusiasm they displayed for their kitchen gardens. It will be shown that although the difficulties they experienced in their floriculture were often exceeded in cultivating fruit and vegetables, the rewards of being able to bring home-grown produce to their tables were immense. Food grown under challenging circumstances carried with it additional kudos, and was a means by which the women could significantly increase the standing of their households.

In their gardening practices can be seen adaptation and the embracing of colonial opportunity in most dramatic form, as exemplified by Adela Stewart, a complete novice on her arrival in New Zealand, who subsequently reported: 'At the end of our 4th year I had become an enthusiastic gardener and so continued, finding far more pleasure in growing flowers, vegetables and trees than in any other occupation'.[23]

'Elegant looking villas with their prettily laid out gardens':[24] the front garden

If the woman was to establish herself and remain secure in her status within society as upholder of genteel values the presentation of her household had to be beyond reproach. The front garden was the face the household showed to the outside world, and it had to be immaculate. Passers-by would receive an overall indication of what might lie beyond, whilst those who came to leave their calling-cards would have the opportunity to make any number of slightly more considered judgements on the precise social standing which the woman occupied or to which she aspired. Indeed Leach argues that the practice of calling was a major influence on the rapid development of European gardens in New Zealand.[25] In many sites, establishing a scrupulously tended front garden seems to have been prioritised, sometimes even when the garden at the back of the house was still of a rudimentary nature. Lucy Gray's diary entry suggests that such was the case in Cape Town: 'Even the most barren wilderness of a garden was neatly hedged off with pomegranate, its rich scarlet flowers sharply edged against dark glossy green leaves'.[26] Only in the most arid settings, where the intensity of the climate precluded the creation of a front garden was the feature abandoned, and then the front verandah took on the same symbolic function (see discussion below).

The most notable characteristic of the front garden, other than its neatness, was the uniformity of style. Colonial houses examined in India, New Zealand, Nigeria and the southern states of Australia all placed the same emphasis on geometrical design; usually a circular drive with a central bed which featured a specimen plant, statuary or an urn. Sylvia Leith-Ross described the bungalow in Zungeru, Nigeria – where in 1907 she and her husband made a home – as having 'a crescent-shaped drive in front'.[27] Within that consistent design, technological developments fostered change and hence permitted expression of genteel difference. Early driveways were sometimes gravelled, which had the advantage of going some way to limiting the amount of dirt trodden into the house. It was also commonly believed that the wide gravel path was an effective means of deterring snakes from entering the house.[28] Mrs Temple-Wright declared that 'gravel in India is not procurable' and recommended instead that the drive be sprinkled with red *soorkee* or *surkhi*, ground brick rubble.[29] Maintaining a gravel or hardcore drive is inevitably quite labour intensive, and therefore suggests servant availability and hence prosperity. Adela Stewart was probably an exception in working on the drive herself. When preparing for a visit by Governor Ranfurly, she spoke of 'hoeing and raking the shell drive with all my might and main'.[30]

In most sites the central bed was cultivated and planted, often with a rapid-growing shrub or tree. Prior to the ready availability of lawnmowers, sowing the bed with grass was not an attractive option as it either had to be cut by hand or grazed by animals. The former approach required the services of an efficient servant to ensure the bed did not become unkempt, and in the latter having wandering beasts so close to the front of the house was anything but desirable. In the case of Australia both Watts and Crittenden stress that lawns were rare until lawn-mowers dropped in price in the early decades of the twentieth century.[31] It is reasonable to assume there would have been an interim stage in which mowers were expensive and only high-achievers could afford them, and therefore that early lawns were themselves a marker of refined living. Similarly lack of access to piped water and limited labour to hand-water would constrain the planting and maintenance of lawns.

Practices from temperate regions differ sharply from those in the tropics. The fine-leaved grasses used for lawns in temperate climes would not thrive in torrid zones, and the broader-leaved species which did prosper may have seemed coarse in comparison, so in some colonies this too may have discouraged some of those who hankered after a genteel green sward. It is possible to discern a note of poignancy in Constance Larymore's words on this subject, written from her home in Nigeria: 'in a tropical country well-kept turf is much to be desired, there is nothing so cool and refreshing to tired eyes dazzled with the glare of sunshine and baked earth, and perhaps nothing that gives such a home-like and cared-for look to a West African compound'.[32] Her sentiments are similar to those expressed by Violet Jacob in India: 'no-one can know how glorious emerald green turf . . . can seem out here in the burnt-looking world'.[33] Little wonder then that Mrs Temple-Wright declared a lawn to be 'an absolute necessity' and well worth the 'one extra rupee a month to your house *bhistie* for watering your grass plot every evening and eight annas per month extra to your grass cutter for cutting your grass plot once a week with the shears you will provide him'.[34] In an attempt to satisfy this European longing for smooth greens, in South Africa Howies nursery of Johannesburg included in their Spring Catalogue of 1912–13 'Howies "Hard-Wearing" Lawn Grass Seed. A *local* grass, tolerates use on lawn-tennis court and croquet lawn – but having a period of dormancy'.[35]

The central bed needed a controlling edging, and there are frequent references by women in New Zealand trying in vain to strike cuttings of the indigenous plant manuka, with the hope of using them for edging plants – an illustration of a structural element of the front garden being transferred from a previous home, but a different plant being employed.[36] In relation to Australian practices, Crittenden notes similar frustrations with attempts to grow box, and Yates Annual Catalogue of 1914 recommended its use be restricted to cooler districts and favoured instead other imported species such as thrift, oxalis and gazanias, whilst for South African gardens Howies suggested using pyrethrum for edging purposes.[37] Equally fashionable, and sometimes employed as an alternative, or in addition to edging plants, was the use of terracotta tiles. These were purpose-made, often glazed, and highly decorative. Examples of locally made items are to be found in the collections of the Historic Houses Trust, New South Wales. Similar goods were made by the Newtown Brick and Pottery Company, Hobart, Tasmania, whose 1880 catalogue lists amongst their wares 'ornamental garden edgings'.[38] Whilst such items were common enough in Britain, that such a specialised object was so widely manufactured in Australia is indicative of their perceived value as contributors to a genteel performance. Those who could not afford items of that type, or could not afford the freight charges if they were living in a more remote site, extemporised with painted rocks, angled bricks or inverted bottles. All such materials ensured a neatness to the approach to the front of the house.

Information regarding the sorts of plants grown in the central bed suggests a variety of localised practice. Leach, in the New Zealand context, speaks of 'the solitary pivotal aloe', Watts of the high status accorded in gardens in the Australian state of Victoria to plants from Britain, whilst Crittenden describes the Edwardian development of a fashion for building raised beds which sloped towards the road.[39] This latter feature created a splendid site of display, and sometimes the actual name of the house was picked out in plants or, around Federation – a time of high national consciousness – the bed might be shaped with the outline of Australia or an emblematic kangaroo.

It would appear that the colonists did transfer the idealised notion of the front garden, for it was to perform the same functions as it had in their former homes. Although inevitably the size and shape of the space varied, and some local features were sometimes introduced, adherence to the traditional design of the British model was largely the norm. The implication is that pressures to conform were greater in the area that was visible to all passers-by than in the screened areas in the private/public domain. That such spaces were successfully established and maintained in the face of such challenges as lack of labour, shortage of water and unforgiving climates is testimony to the high value placed upon them. Figure 4.4 shows front gardens in Townsville in early stage of development and not only indicates the scale of the task to be carried out, but also gives some appreciation of what a difference the neatly cultivated frontages would make to a somewhat harsh terrain.

Despite this obvious importance of the front garden, few direct references to the area have been located in the women's writings. The more interesting therefore, as it seems to have been unusual, is Georgina

4.4 Front gardens, The Strand, Townsville, Queensland, 1907.

Bowen's 1864 account of her front garden near Christchurch, New Zealand. 'The drive to the house is bordered by laurels (the largest in the Province but that's not saying much for them), blue pines and red cedars etc, and bushes of white and yellow broom and Corgoing [?] an Australian shrub, and there are roses and flowers of different kinds in the borders close to the road'.[40] Even here, in her listing of species grown, Bowan stresses, albeit in a slightly self-deprecating fashion, that their laurels are the best in the area, and thereby lays claim to the standing of the household.

This survey concludes with a truly outstanding example of a front garden, see Figure 4.5. So striking is the display at Omana House, Epsom, Auckland, New Zealand that one can scarce imagine that there were further delights behind the house. Again we find the hard design features of the tile-edged path and, as with Adela Stewart's garden in the Bay of Plenty, the paths are made of light-coloured gravel or shell, which acted as a dramatic foil to set off the abundant plant growth. The householder has added further structure to the plot with the use of substantial shrubs, and the herbaceous planting along the side of the path looks varied and was presumably designed to give the visitor plenty to admire as they walked up to the house. As Omana House amply demonstrates, the front garden is to be understood as both presentation of the household and preparation for what lay beyond – the private/public space of the main garden, entered only by invitation.

4.5 'Omana House', Epsom, New Zealand, date unknown.

'There are some beautiful shrubs and flowers here quite new *at home'*:⁴¹ *the flower garden*

The flower garden was the high-profile area of the garden, being the most used, both by the members of the immediate household, and by others who entered by invitation to engage in social activities. It was the setting for afternoon teas, 'at homes' and a range of gatherings of varying degrees of formality. The garden as a whole, but particularly the flower garden, was therefore a key area for genteel performance and had to be maintained to a suitably high standard. There was a 'symbolic profit' to be gained, for individual and community alike, from the bolstering effect of presenting a refined garden. It will be argued, however, that for the mistress of the house the flower garden had a whole range of complex and subtle meanings, being not merely an outside recreation area, but rather an extension of the centre-piece of her genteel performance, the living room, and all the values associated with that space.

There is strong evidence for saying that gardens were seen as a desirable and logical extension of the living room. John Loudon's influential texts spoke of the desire for 'a reciprocal neatness in the garden as in the living room', and Mrs Temple-Wright prefaced her advice manual for gardeners in India thus:

> If you were to receive a letter, the envelope of which was dirty, torn and disreputable, would not you feel disgusted? And would your disgust disappear entirely if, inside that dirty envelope, you found a letter written on dainty scented paper? At least, you could not get over the incongruity between the covering and its contents. In the same way, only to a much greater degree, does one feel the difference in attention bestowed upon the outside and the inside of many of the bungalows in which we live in India. Then let us try to make the exterior of our houses a little more in keeping with the interior, let the beauty of the garden harmonise with the dainty taste of the drawing-room.[42]

Furthermore Leach argues that there was parallel development of the house and garden in New Zealand, noting such customs as the use of foliage to delineate private from public areas, just as in the home all the emphasis was on the private/public space of the living room. These examples from India and New Zealand serve to support the view that the relationship between the garden and the living room was maintained in a variety of sites and periods, and therefore evidently of ongoing cultural value. Chevalier's work on modern homes in England alerts us to the symmetrical relationship of the garden to the living room, and comments on how that symmetry finds expression in material terms.[43] She suggests that the carpet can be compared to the lawn, in terms of its value and function, and speaks of 'colonising' the living room by elements of the garden. This argument has obvious application for genteel homes in colonial sites, and adds further credence to the idea that gardens had discrete meaning within genteel domestic performance.

Just as in Britain by mid-century flower gardening had become an acceptable activity for women of a refined disposition, so too was it pursued in the colonies, and such physical activity was no longer seen to result in a loss of caste. A copy of an 1871 edition of the *Englishwoman's Domestic Magazine*, located in Hobart, includes a list of 'implements necessary for a lady's own use'. Eight items were listed, including a spade, a rake and a hoe. The writer notes that 'these are only required if the lady enjoys practical work, and should be suited to the size of her hands'.[44] Jane Loudon's highly regarded and widely read work on gardening for ladies was essentially practical in nature and decreed that women should not quibble over any of the tasks called for in the garden.[45] Georgina Malloy wrote from Western Australia of her delight at receiving a copy of Loudon's book, declaring it to be 'beauteous and elegant beyond description'.[46] The theme of encouraging women into the garden was taken up in 1859 by the *Sydney Magazine of Science and Art* in an article entitled 'Floriculture for Ladies'. The language is still refined, however, for in addition to explaining the tools required the author suggests that 'ladies might benefit from doing an hour's recreation – I would not call it work – in the garden every morning'.[47] These examples of published materials have all been located from within Australia. In addition Smith Brothers, seed and plant merchants of Uitenhage, South Africa sold 'Popular Boxes of Floral Gems for the Gardens of Ladies and Amateurs' and Howies of Johannesburg advertised 'The Denise Basket or Ladies Gardening Companion, price 17 shillings and sixpence, a most handsome and useful present for a Lady', contents of which included 'Ladies Secateurs and Extra long handled Flower-gathering scissors', whilst Howden & Moncrieff, Dunedin, New Zealand who sold 'Rare and Beautiful Plants' also stocked ladies flower border spades, ladies garden syringes and ladies garden gloves.[48] Mrs Temple-Wright's advice manual for would-be flower gardeners in India was still being advertised some twenty years after its initial publication, which implies yet another generation of Anglo-Indian women considered gardening to be a fitting and rewarding pursuit.

Whatever the romantic representations of the lovely lady in the garden, the reality is that no garden can be created or maintained without considerable physical effort. The amount of physical work undertaken by women in their flower garden must have varied, depending not only upon their personal preferences and strength, but also on their other household demands, the relative isolation of the home, whether any help available had the necessary expertise, and whether the mistress could communicate her needs. It was the case therefore that in some sites, at some dates, servants were responsible for all tasks in the flower garden which called for physical strength.

For many women their gardens provided an opportunity to grow, or at least attempt to grow, cultivars of species familiar to them from gardens in Britain. Indeed the value of gardens as a means of expressing nostalgic longings is well documented. Georgina Bowen's words in a letter from South Island, New Zealand to her family in England are eloquent: 'We have a few blue violets out. If I smell them with my eyes shut I can fancy myself at Horksley or Torquay or anywhere in England, nothing brings back to places one's remembrance so much as some sweet smell'.[49] For Bowen the scent of those tiny flowers transported her back to England, but most especially to places she and her absent loved ones had shared. Cultivating violets in her garden, and describing their sweet fragrance gave her a means of maintaining intimacy with those so far away. Sarah Courage, also in the South Island, expressed a similar idea: 'Average humanity has a liking for something famil-

TASTEFUL GARDENING AND GROWING ATTACHMENT

4.6 Packet of flower seed as sold by J. H. Taylor, Launceston, Tasmania, c.1900.

iar, and the sense of smell is the sense of memory'.[50] And Constance Larymore, giving advice to potential gardeners in Nigeria, acknowledged that 'One's natural instinct is to try to surround oneself with old favourites, sweet peas, mignonette, poppies and pinks', though she continues 'the effort, I fear, is a sheer waste of time and trouble'.[51] See also Figure 4.6 which shows a seed packet of the popular aster as sold by a merchant in Launceston, Tasmania. Sometimes these familiar plants flourished better than they had in Britain, their overseas site being closer to their natural environment, as with Larymore's success with a strain of balsams which she declared 'gave splendid results, thick clusters of delicate rosey pink blossoms. Resembling pink carnations or rosettes of chiffon'.[52] See also the vigorous pom-pom dahlias in the garden of Omana House which have evidently benefited from the warm New Zealand sunshine (Figure 4.5). Katie Hume plainly revelled in the profusion she had inherited in her Queensland flower garden: 'resplendent with gladiolus lilies, four or five feet high. The garden is full of them, for they grow so rampageously'.[53] So it can be seen that memories of other much beloved places found material expression in plants which denoted 'home' by association, irrespective of their actual botanical origin.

Moreover, and this is obviously the only aspect of the women's material culture to which this applies, growing such plants was to have something linked to their former home which was alive. In times and places where communications were slow such a token, progress of which could be duly noted and reported on, was unique in its potential to help the migrants overcome the pain of long-term, often permanent, separation from loved ones. Furthermore, rather than reading the women's desire to grow the plants of a far-away home as borne of hopeless longing, such practice is to be understood as an expression of an aspect of her interiority, a replanting of her identity in new soil, and hence a means of connecting the culture of the former site with that of the new.

In settlements in their infancy, where communications with the metropolis were limited, sourcing plants of such provenance could be a challenge. Friends and family in Britain sometimes came to their aid, as when New Zealand migrant Charlotte Godley wrote to say: 'It is very good of Aunt Charlotte to think of us and our seeds; those she has sent us will be most valuable ... Mr Simeon has sent us the seeds of some quick growing creepers from his old house Colbourne, which will be invaluable in making the house at Port Cooper ... look a little green and verdant'.[54] It is interesting to note that even late in the century some women sent for goods direct from nurseries in England. For example, the balsams which Constance Larymore spoke of with such pleasure and pride had been grown from 'a special packet from Suttons', and in 1883 and 1895 Cannells, plant and seed merchants of Kent, included in their catalogues testimonials supplied by satisfied customers. Thus Mrs Clayton in South Africa wrote that the 'chrysanthemums you sent a little while ago are all growing, having arrived in excellent condition' and Mrs Phillips in Matakana, New Zealand 'begs to acknowledge the seeds, bulbs etc and is obliged for the promptness in sending them. *The Floral Guide* has given great pleasure to both myself and friends'.[55] It does suggest that perhaps there was a certain cachet in ordering goods from the metropolis, Mrs Clayton's chrysanthemums the gardening equivalent of the Marshall and Snelgrove dress or Fortnum and Mason's hamper.

When the population base was sufficiently large, colonial nurseries opened which aimed to satisfy the gardeners' yearning to grow that which was familiar. For example, in Van Diemen's Land, Daniel Bunce set up a nursery in 1836, and was presumably able to supply the European settlers' requirements, initially by importing seeds and then subsequently by growing them on site. In New Zealand, Godley was soon able to report that 'Almost all ordinary garden seeds are to be bought in Wellington, and the roses, etc. are beautiful there', suggesting she sent her orders over from her home in the South Island.[56] Adela Stewart, who was based in the North Island, evidently had a rich local source of supply as she recorded: 'all this wet weather was splendid for planting, and having got £20 of trees from Booth's Hairini Nursery, Tauranga, we had a busy time'.[57] Robert Seth, seed and plant merchant in Calcutta, who by early in the twentieth century was offering an extensive range of familiar species, also included a 'Hot and Rainy Season Collection. Suitable for sowing in the Hot Weather and during the Rain'. The alphabetical list of seeds Seth had for sale has a rich and poetic tone, surely calculated to make any gardener's pulse race: 'Achimenes, Ageratum, Amaranthus, Antirrhinum, Balsam, Canna, Carnation, Celosia, Coleus, Convolvulus, Coreopsis, Cosmos and Dahlia'.[58] As the plants which had been so keenly sought became more readily available there developed in gardening, as with all material practices, the desire for the new. A striking example is to be found in Frank Walker's Catalogue of 1915. In addition to the now commonplace range of flowers, this Tasmanian nurseryman also offered 'novelty carnations, introduced 1914' at the seemingly exorbitant price of two shillings per plant.[59] This argues strongly not merely for personal preference, but indeed for rank within plant selection.

Given a little patience it seems that obtaining the species genteel women were accustomed to cultivating, or had knowledge of, was not overly problematic. Often under-acknowledged is that in addition to those plants there was a deal of enthusiasm for what can justly be described as a global sourcing of plant material. Virtually from his commencement of trading, Daniel Bunce was offering 'seeds and plants, indigenous and exotic' which raises some interesting questions as to what was meant by those terms of reference in Van Diemen's Land at that date, as clearly notions of the 'exotic' have cultural specificity. Did it refer to African species familiar from Britain, or did it, as seems equally likely, mean unusual species from a variety of locations? If the latter then it is interesting to note that forty years later a Californian seed merchant found it worthwhile to send a catalogue over to Hobart.[60] A scrapbook held in the State Archives of Tasmania contains a number of articles from various 1890s editions of *The Garden Journal*, a British periodical which carried descriptions of garden design and practice from around the Empire. That these articles were held to be of sufficient interest to be retained in this fashion suggests sophisticated interests, and although the owner of the scrapbook is not known, the emphasis on flowers and on their use in the house suggests the compiler may have been a woman of refined tastes.[61]

An equal range and variety of flowers grown has been identified in other locations. Georgina Malloy remarks with satisfaction that in her home on the Swan River, Western Australia, 'all Chinese and Cape plants thrive luxuriantly here; many annuals of England are biennial, and *Sweet Peas* and *Hibiscus Africanus* survive the winter'.[62] She also noted an expenditure of the astonishing sum of £7 7s 6d on seeds of oleander, cape gooseberry, pink gladiolus and pink watsonia amongst others, made during their stopover in Cape Town on the journey out from Cumbria, England.[63] This custom of purchasing seed and plants at the Cape en route for Australasia was also noted by Godley in New Zealand, who commented that 'they all do uncommonly well, and bear the wind pretty well, which the roses do not'.[64] The circularity of plant sourcing is graphically illustrated by Jane Williams, who in 1831 sent material from her home in Poona, India to her parents in Van Diemen's Land. She despatched a small parcel 'consisting only of a few seeds which I collected in our compound; but as it is not the proper season, I have not been able to get the seeds of many of the things that I think would grow at the Clyde: all the directions I can give about those I send is to give them as much sun and water and as little frost as possible'.[65] Similarly the editor of Emma Rutherfoord's 1850s Cape Town diaries explains that Emma's brother-in-law succeeded in winning his mother-in-law's approval by dint of sending her plants, including roses, from Calcutta.[66]

Hybridity of practice does indeed seem to have been highly valued, for in addition to casting their net far and wide there is abundant evidence that many women found huge satisfaction and pleasure in cultivating indigenous flora. Louisa Ann Meredith, a high-profile member of Tasmanian society and most self-conscious in her genteel self-presentation, noted of her garden: 'The cultivated flowers are chiefly those familiar to us in English gardens, with some brilliant natives of the Cape, and many pretty indigenous flowering shrubs interposed'.[67] Bunce listed some fifty native species which he considered suitable for garden use when 'intermingled with a few lilacs, honeysuckles and other British Shrubs', which again suggests that in the colony of Van Diemen's Land there was an early development of hybrid practice.[68] Similar 'blessing' was disposed on the New Zealand bush by Jane Deans, who embraced an area of native trees within her garden and surrounded it with a band of conifers, poplars, willows and elms of British origin, and filled the clearings with oaks and other European species.[69] In similar vein, Raine notes that 'Adela Stewart appears to have grown very few traditional European plants outside her vegetable plot'.[70] That Deans and Stewart were not alone in their enthusiasm for growing native species is demonstrated by Duncan & Davies, Nurserymen of New Plymouth, North Island, who by 1917 had several acres of their grounds devoted to raising native trees, some of which, such as *cordyline terminalis* (Ti-pore) or dwarf cabbage tree, were priced rather high at two shillings per plant, whilst Nimmo & Blair of Dunedin,

South Island stocked seeds of native plants, shrubs and trees.[71] Such behaviours suggest not only an ease with eclectic planting but an actual valuing of it as a measure of competency and potential refinement within the setting. Larymore was equally positive about the native flora which she grew in Nigeria, declaring that 'To my mind the wild flowers of the country are by no means to be despised in the garden, many are extremely beautiful' and 'I only wish I had enough botanical knowledge to name half the native flowers and trees I have raised from seed collected casually on the march'.[72]

Ascertaining the extent to which indigenous flora was adopted is complicated by the matter of naming. Simmons notes that in Australia migrants employed 'a device of psychological value [in] the use of old names for the new. Thus the banksia is given the nostalgic euphemism of honeysuckle'.[73] It could of course be argued that rather than being motivated by wistful longings what is seen here is the natural linking of prior knowledge with that newly acquired. Banksias have long stamens, are sweetly scented and many are yellow and red – hence not utterly dissimilar to the most commonly grown honeysuckles.

Sometimes attempts to combine and incorporate local flora met with management problems, as when Georgina Malloy noted that in her Swan River settlement garden in Western Australia, 'I have frequently endeavoured to introduce the native plants among the exotics. They do not succeed, from want of native shelter. The purple creeper alone has consented to be domesticated, and has associated its purple flowers with a very elegant Pink climbing plant from the Mauritius'.[74] Her enthusiasm for native species led to dense planting – that which in temperate climates at that date would have been seen as overplanting – in order to try and create the sort of environment in which the natives would prosper. Malloy's success in this area is a striking example of adaptation to the location and the emergence of local expertise. Comparable overplanting of this type was also the policy in Adela Stewart's garden, 'we planted everything that would look pretty one foot apart', including Australian eucalypts and roses familiar from Britain.[75] This husbandry approach was at odds with the taste for the gardenesque which became increasingly fashionable in Britain from mid-century onwards, and which extolled the virtue of the specimen plant, and therefore required well-spaced planting. Such an approach effectively commodifies the individual plant, and it is understandable that it would gain favour with genteel women in Britain. So the dense planting favoured in some locations – which also, incidentally, went a long way to reducing the need for watering, all-important in sites with hot weather – can be seen as a form of localised gardening practice arising directly out of local circumstances.

McBriar records a long tradition of Australian writing in praise of the use of native plants for ornamental purposes, and identifies brown boronia, flannel flowers and Sturt's pea as having become particular favourites. McBriar asserts that interest in natives became more common after 1890, and was linked to the development of a 'national spirit'.[76] Though doubtless there was at the close of the century a developing consciousness regarding all things Australian, the assumption that the two were linked has to be approached with some caution. Of equal importance surely was that by the turn of the century Australia's urban population dwelt in well-established sophisticated centres with good service and supply networks. Improved communications and easier backyard maintenance arising from technological developments meant more people across society were becoming interested in all sorts of gardening. However, when more people – many of whom of course would be deemed not to be genteel, hence 'outsiders' – engaged in an activity or practice gentility was threatened, and responded by redefining what constituted genteel practice.[77]

All the women cited in this discussion, from Tasmania to Nigeria, Western Australia to New Zealand, embraced the potential of growing plants of types which were new to them, both indigenous and – using the contemporary term of reference – exotic, presumably many of which were new to European horticulture altogether. As with the other areas of practice examined in this work it is the case that gentility retained its dynamism and social power by absorbing, with suitable discretion, the possibilities of the new. This willingness to adapt their gardening practice and adopt the new must surely have carried with it a certain prestige. Not only did it mark them out as innovative gardeners, it also indicated that they were successful newcomers able to set a standard of gardening to which others could aspire. There is therefore an argument to be made for saying that interest in growing indigenous species, and indeed their eclectic approach to planting, were sometimes deemed to be signs of taste.

It seems that all economic upturns prompted development of recreational gardening, particularly of course amongst those who previously had been gardening primarily for subsistence. By 1836 Daniel Bunce of Van Diemen's Land was stating in his catalogue that: 'The garden so agreeably situated in the immediate vicinity of Hobart town, with a very extensive collection of flowers, will be at all times open as a promenade for ladies and gentlemen on the same principle as the popular nurseries around London'.[78] The increase in the popularity of recreational gardening was accompanied by a proliferation of material items which in turn permitted expressions of distinction amongst the gardeners, as witness an 1877 advertisement in the Hobart newspaper the *Mercury*: 'Just imported direct from England ornamental flower pots and expanding pot covers of English, German and Chinese manufacture'.[79] This was an echo of the proliferation of gardening paraphernalia which characterised British garden practice during the latter half of the nineteenth century.[80]

Similar development of the nursery business is suggested by a listing of three nurserymen plus florists and seedsmen in the Townsville section of *Pugh's Queensland Almanac* for 1900, little more than three decades after the commencement of European colonisation. All the examples from Australia suggest that the expansion of interest in gardens and gardening was a characteristic of the maturing colonial site. It does not seem unreasonable to assume that a comparable set of factors triggering take-off of gardening would have occurred in other colonies at comparable stages of development. As gardening became increasingly popular it could theoretically have meant that it had more of a social levelling affect, but because gentility is inherently competitive it responded by making the adjustments in practice discussed above, and therefore this challenges the notion that the increase in the popularity of gardening automatically leads towards egalitarianism.

In addition to the sourcing and husbandry challenges already discussed, the climate was also a frequent trial for the woman trying to create the smooth and perfect flower garden. If the flowers were to contribute to the genteel performance they had to be good specimens, since a poor show was surely worse than no garden at all. When Constance Larymore discovered that growing her 'old favourites' from British seed was a somewhat hit and miss affair she experimented with stock which had been acclimatised in India and reported that: 'the first success was a splendid bed of portulaccas, blazing with crimson, white, mauve and gold, rejoicing in the sun which had shrivelled everything else'.[81] The nurseries were responsive to such needs. Robert Seth's Catalogue from Calcutta claimed: 'The Four Seasons of the Year bring orders for Seth's Seeds and Plants not only from all parts of India, Burmah and South Asia but also largely from every country in Europe and America. The curious Chinese and the progressive Japs. even are our customers, while parcels to Australia and South Africa go to prove that Seth's seeds and Plants are needed all over the world'. In 1905 Smith Bros in Uitenhage were selling 'colonial saved zinnias' and in 1914 Yates offered their customers Australian-saved carnation seeds at five shillings for a packet of thirty.[82]

It is tempting of course to assume that only those gardening in the tropics, particularly the dry tropics, would have experienced difficulties, but Godley's comments about the poor performance of roses in New Zealand, which suggests they suffered from wind-rock, and the general unpredictability of the weather in Tasmania – flood-damage in Mrs Meredith's garden is discussed below in relation to her kitchen garden – serve to reinforce the point that temperate zones are not without serious challenges.

Despite the tests to their patience and skill, one of the reasons why gardening could prove such a source of intense pleasure and satisfaction is that it is essentially cyclical. Whatever the climate, making a garden is a relatively lengthy process. Even in tropical conditions it takes time to establish shrubs and trees and for all the components of the site to meld together. The gardener must wait and watch to see 'how it does next season'. By its very nature therefore the garden requires some degree of commitment, and this is why it makes for such a powerful tool in establishing oneself in a new locale. If they are to prosper both the garden and the gardener must, in a sense, put down roots. Conversely where the home was only of a very temporary nature the mediating agency of the garden was effectively denied to the household.

Clementina Benthall evidently experienced mixed emotions when she and her family moved house, feelings she articulates with particular reference to her garden: 'I sent all my children's flowers to a garden made for Meina and some of my own plants to the other garden. I do not like leaving our beautiful Banion Tree, nor the parting with my children's little gardens, and the rooms they have lived in, but I have had many trials in the house and hope we may be healthier in another'. Benthall's words might suggest the death of a child – 'Meina' possibly, in which case the reference to her children's plants has a particular poignancy.[83]

Benthall's house move was within India, an experience shared by many whose menfolk worked in the military or in officialdom, and it may be that had a significant impact on garden practice. If such was the case then not dissimilar as a constraint upon gardening were the early settlement patterns in North Queensland. European settlement of the north was seen by many individuals, and by government agencies, as a precarious enterprise. Colonisation of the north was therefore very much a stop-start affair and attitudes as to its desirability and practicality remained ambivalent, to put it mildly, until well into the twentieth century. Robert Gray (married to Lucy Gray, whose journal is cited later in this chapter) wrote that:

> Whatever may be said to the contrary, the fact remains that, with the exception of a few localities where the altitude approaches 2000 feet, the climate is a hard one for white women, and those who have resided many years in the country know it to be so, though it is not the fashion to proclaim it, and so long as these conditions continue, it is likely to militate against closer settlement of a permanent nature.[84]

Many of those who lived in North Queensland, perhaps for ten years or more, left for less demanding conditions as soon as they could afford to, or sooner if their health started to decline. It may seem tempting to conclude therefore that such a culture would not be conducive to whole-hearted gardening, but such a reading underestimates the effectiveness of garden practices in the mediating of new circumstances.

If instead one considers Larymore's exhortation that all new arrivals in West Africa had a duty to plant trees and Decima Moore's lamentation on the lack of a garden in her new home in Accra, Gold Coast, then one gains the impression that permanency of settlement was not necessarily the determining factor in choosing to garden. And if one also takes into consideration a comment made in a South African gardening journal, about workers' cottage gardens created in double-quick time along a new railway line, that 'the contrast between the beds of flowers and the barren-looking veld is striking ... little picture spots on the surrounding monotonous veldt', then one can go further and argue that gardening was sometimes prioritised precisely because it can create an air of stability to even the most tentative of settlements.[85]

Where circumstances permitted them to cultivate a flower garden both the process and the end results clearly gave the women immense pleasure. Stewart declared that 'no-one can over-estimate the pleasures of tending flowers. They are the one thing in the world that does not disappoint. They are true friends'. This suggests she found them a source of solace in hard times, affording some measure of compensation when other sources of comfort were in short supply.[86] Katie Hume relished the work so much that even when pregnant she 'spent one whole morning gardening last week (planting out balsams and *weeding*) and was none the worse for it'.[87] And Miss Rutherfoord wrote to her sister recounting how their mother had relinquished all the housekeeping to her daughter and was to be found working 'with more than her usual zeal[;] she is so fond of it she has been rising to garden before breakfast'.[88] Observations of this nature highlight how utterly absorbing many of these women found their gardening. It plainly satisfied a creative urge in ways not fulfilled in any of their other activities. It suggests that their flower garden in particular occupied a psychological space in addition to the literal. The gardens also provided a direct material means of relating to their immediate surroundings, and thereby forming all-important points of anchorage within their new location.

In seeking to identify women's practices in the flower garden this discussion does not wish to disregard those households where the garden was a shared enterprise. For example, Constance Maude, who lived with her parents near Bangalore, where for fifty years her father worked for the Mysore government, recalled that their bungalow 'was most spacious and comfortable. Father built it in 1875 and planned the beautiful gardens himself. Mother was the first to grow many English flowers, specialising in carnations'.[89] Similarly, shared gardening was carried out by Ethel and Eustace Kenyon in Calcutta in the 1890s; they were clearly complete novices and it was Eustace who wrote to his mother, seemingly somewhat despairingly, 'The mignonette that we put in the ground is not coming up, but that in pots has come up fairly well ... some of the other seeds in pots are also coming up but rather slowly and I don't know whether they ought to have more sun, in fact I want a great deal more advice'.[90] In territories where there was a large supply of household servants, as was the case in India, it may have been that families with an interest in gardening had a greater chance of pursuing it together than would have been possible in colonies where the supplies of servants were limited and where the menfolk were engaged in the primary land clearance activities of colonisation. This seems to have been the case in New Zealand, and is elaborated below in association with the kitchen garden.

The successes of the flower garden were often employed to enhance the living room and to decorate the dining table. John Perkins actually compared the look of the table to a flower garden saying that because dining *à la russe* had become so fashionable 'to have a dinner in these days without the accompaniment of Cut Flowers, Plants, Ornamental Leaves etc, would be like dessert without wine'.[91] (See also the preceding chapter on 'Living rooms' and the following chapter on 'Food' for further discussion on the use of flowers and plants for decorative purposes.) Advice manuals on beautifying the home invariably included instruction on the use of floral display, and garden writers echoed their words, as when John Loudon stated that 'a few choice specimens of tall plants in fruit or flower should be distributed in the drawing-room'.[92] This practice of displaying flowers in the house further raised the status of the flower garden, and by implication, its chief manager – the mistress of the house. Such displays would be seen by those exchanging calls, as when this resident at the Cape noted that 'nearly all the people who have called upon me are to be envied the fresh-smelling bouquets of wild or English hot-house flowers that so becomingly bedeck their tables and windows'.[93] Thus the flower garden, in being a site of display, made a significant contribution to the women's genteel performance, which in turn was an element in the establishment and furtherance of the genteel community.

As has been demonstrated, the front and flower gardens provided countless means of signalling difference and ranking within the social hierarchy. The inclusion of additional hard design features to the space of the garden could add yet further value. These could take the form of the showy and ostentatious tennis courts and croquet lawns, or the potentially more modest ferneries, rockeries, sunken gardens, pergolas and arches. In relation to the temperate regions in southern Australia, Hubbard identifies the conservatory as an important site of display, for plants, ornamental furniture and statuary of course, but also for the elegant lady of the house herself, who was duly complemented by being in the midst of her choice blooms. So highly valued was such plant material that the household inventory of Mrs Mary Moriarty of Inverleigh listed and identified all fifty-six of her conservatory plants; they included begonias, cyclamen, fuchsias, geranium, gloxinia and hydrangea, plus ten maidenhair ferns – thereby supplying us with a precise picture of what the great and the good were growing in Victoria in 1912.[94] Leach notes that in urban settings in New Zealand at the turn of the century houses were built with smaller gardens, and yet all these features were still included, though in miniaturised form.[95] The British periodical *Villa Gardener* provided guidance for those who had ambitions for large showy elements and the space to accommodate them, but also for those who had small plots but still preferred 'elegant-habited plants'. This range of practice seems to have continued in colonial sites, for it is a reasonable conjecture that the policy of 'fitting everything in', but on a smaller scale, may well have been a strategy adapted in other sites as well, by those who aspired to gentility but lacked the space or were unsure of their ground. Inevitably the inclusion of additional features in a garden involved more work. For example, caring for croquet lawns and tennis courts requires the sward to be maintained to a high standard involving, ideally, periodic re-seeding, rolling and regular watering. As a generalisation therefore, features designed to give added value were most likely to be found in sites where there was not only a good supply of water but also the labour to carry out such maintenance work.

In the dry tropics the verandah was often the only means of marking distinction and this element of the garden is discussed below. In the wet tropics other strategies were developed, such as using a bush house, which became very popular in North Queensland. The understandable longing for shade experienced by European settlers in such climes prompted the development of structures of lightweight wooden fretwork, which broke up the light and created dappled shady interiors. Such spaces were ideal for growing the ferns, glossy-leaved plants and showy specimen orchids so fashionable in the closing decades of the nineteenth and into the early twentieth centuries. Brouwer's advice on reconstruction of such features in modern North Queensland lists maranta, begonia, allocasia, diffenbachia, fruit salad plant and the native violet as being suitable for such sites.[96] This list can usefully be compared with that of the plants Mrs Moriarty sheltered in her conservatory; in the north tropical specimens needed cool shade, in the south sunshine and warmth. These plants would often be grown in pots or decorative containers, so when they reached their peak they could be taken into the house or verandah, and thereby contribute to the interior performance. Brouwer comments that these structures were so popular that they were even to be found in quite modest suburban gardens, a telling remark, which echoes Leach's comment on the New Zealand model of behaviour.

The additional markers of genteel differentiation discussed here can be understood as examples of that which Bourdieu defines as elements of social capital: 'Different factions of the dominant class distinguish themselves precisely through that which makes them members of the class as a whole, namely the type of capital which is the source of their privilege and the different means of asserting their distinction which are linked to it'.[97] The presence of the pergola and the rockery constituted a jostling for pole position on the slippery scale of gentility.

This discussion has presented abundant evidence that the flower garden made a vital contribution to the genteel women's performance. Buettner, in her work on late imperial India, notes how in their personal writings the women's memories of their time there tended to linger over their gardens, which she attributes to an association with the female sphere of domesticity.[98] Rather than this somewhat prosaic explanation, the case has been made here for the flower garden being for genteel women a site of creativity, a means of relating to their physical and social environment and a source of intense personal pleasure; all of which contributed to developing that all-important sense of being 'at home' in a genteel fashion in a new setting.

'3rd March, 1865 – Dish of peas for dinner':[99] the kitchen garden

Edith Cuthell, on spending her first Christmas in Lucknow, India, was moved to write to her mother in Britain that when she and the 'Captain Sahib' sat down to Christmas dinner they dined on 'soup of tomatoes from our own garden from English seed, also French beans and new peas *not* the tinned article'.[100] It is noteworthy that the vegetables she served had been grown from seed sourced from Britain – possibly even taken over with her – but are here given different meaning and added value because they had been grown under challenging conditions. Cuthell's words clearly imply pride in her various achievements. And what impressive achievements they were: to be able to serve home-grown produce as elements of an elegant dinner on Christmas Day, generally held to be the most important feast of the year, and so soon after her arrival – little wonder she wanted to share the detail with her mother. What greater proof could she supply than that she had indeed established genteel standards 'out in the empire'.

Clearly then the kitchen garden had considerable potential value to the mistress and her household, and its shape and positioning are material indicators of its importance. It had to be near enough to the house to permit ease of access, as the produce could be called on for daily use. The cultivation of fruit and vegetables is labour intensive, so that too necessitated it being placed close by, under the eye of the mistress if she were to supervise gardeners, or so she could have ready access if undertaking the work herself. Equally, however, the kitchen garden was not to be visible from the front or flower gardens, lest it be witnessed in a state of disarray. All stages in the process of food production, be they in the garden, the kitchen or the dining room, contributed to the genteel performance, and as such had to be seen to be effortless. To catch a random glimpse of the kitchen garden whilst taking tea in the flower garden would have marred the performance, as unacceptable as the sight of the mistress actually preparing the vegetables. It was customary therefore for the kitchen garden to be screened from the gaze by hedges, or in the short term, with the aid of trellises or screens. It was also perceived as necessary to have a boundary fence to keep out predators of all types. Be they animal or human, the alien was to be excluded from an area used for growing household food. Clementina Benthall, who set up home in 1842 some four miles from Calcutta, described in her journal how her husband Edward 'has had most of our compound fenced with rails, hired of the Magistrate a great many prisoners, who put our kitchen garden in good order'.[101]

In the light of its value to the household it follows that the area was as rigorously controlled and structured as was the rest of the woman's domain. The space was subdivided into beds and, where the setting permitted, an orchard area. Paths around the garden, generally spoken of as 'walks', were usually some six feet wide. This was not, as might be imagined, to allow ease of access for wheelbarrows, but rather that two people might walk comfortably side by side. Thus we have a spatial sign that on occasion, in a suitably controlled manner, the kitchen garden, as with the flower garden, could be a site of display. For example, Mrs Morton Allport of Van Diemen's Land notes in her journal, 'I took the Butterworths down the garden, where like everyone else, they exalted our fruit above all on the island, especially a new seedling peach'.[102]

Setting up and maintaining a kitchen garden always necessitates a deal of physical effort, the more so in the majority of colonial settings. Unlike the flower garden, where a mature site gives some opportunity for a reduction of physical work, the growing of fruit and vegetables involves a constant cycle of ground preparation, sowing and planting, husbandry and harvest. As with the flower garden it is evident that the amount of work undertaken by the women varied enormously both across the range of and within individual sites, but is not easy to quantify. Rarely do women seem to have written about their gardeners in any detail; certainly they never seem to have been as preoccupied with their personal foibles as when speaking of their other servants. As they did not have to share their domestic space with their gardeners, there may have been fewer tensions in the relationships. For example, Violet Jacob, who seems to have inherited a fine garden at her home in Mhow, Central India, speaks of having three gardeners in addition to a *bheestie* or water servant. She describes their appearance, which would suggest she sees them as important elements within the space of the garden, but makes little or no comment about their personalities, in direct contrast to her attitude to her butler.[103]

It must also be borne in mind that in many locations the woman's responsibilities extended far beyond the actual garden and this too must be taken into account when assessing her work in any one area. Clementina Benthall spoke of her compound as a 'farm', explaining that in addition to poultry it had 'many Rabbits, two Goats and a kid, four Plough Bullocks, four cows and a calf or two', though she did not specify how much 'hands-on' work she did and how much her role was supervisory. Indeed given that her husband was a judge and the household a relatively prosperous one can scarcely imagine that any physical work she did in the kitchen garden was of a systematic nature, rather was it her role as mistress of the house to oversee the management of the compound.[104] Mrs Temple-Wright, whose work on flower gardens has been cited earlier, also published *Baker and Cook*, a guide to keeping house in India, which included advice on supervising the husbandry of cows and other livestock.[105] Adela Stewart, who in consequence of her husband's lack of success on their farm in the Bay of Plenty, extended her spheres of responsibility to a remarkable degree and recorded making 207 lbs of butter during the month of December 1904 alone.[106] It was activities of that magnitude which enabled the Stewarts to pursue the lifestyle they considered appropriate for members of the Irish aristocracy.

For some the kitchen garden was an endeavour shared with their family, as discussed earlier with regard to flower gardens. Thus Alice Massey wrote from Rawalpindi, India of how her husband Lt.-Col. Massey 'has got a nice little vinery in the garden ... Last year the sale of the grapes of it amounted to Rs100. We might get some cuttings and plant them'.[107] Given the status of their household, mentioning the money may be intended to indicate how good the produce was, rather than because the cash was actually needed. A letter Katie Hume wrote from her home in Drayton, southern Queensland shows that on at least one occasion her household adopted a co-operative approach to vegetable gardening: 'I find it difficult to garden here as it is either too *hot* or too *wet*; one morning Walter, Dubs and I gardened from 6.30–8.00 when it was bearable. They cleared the bed of the gigantic weeds ... last night I sowed some carrots and cabbages in the ground Walter had prepared'.[108]

Adela Stewart's account of how she and her female companion undertook the ground-breaking of their garden in the Bay of Plenty, New Zealand is particularly illuminating: 'We pulled up fern-roots, and dug with all our might, feeling exhausted as do all "new chums" at the end of an hour. But that feeling of fatigue has to wear off; as time goes on it becomes evident that gardening must be the women's department, the men being too busy for anything so purely ornamental as flowers, or unnecessary as vegetables'.[109] It could be claimed that Stewart was seeking to justify undertaking such hard manual labour, fearing accusations of unladylike behaviour. McClure, on the other hand, argues convincingly that in the colony of New Zealand there was a re-articulation of what constituted acceptable work, noting that 'A healthy body and a capacity for strenuous physical work were central to the official description of immigrants required by the New Zealand government in the expansive decade of the 1870s'.[110] If one adds to this argument the ever-present shortage of servants in the colony and the expansion of female gardening expertise, it can be seen that there is nothing apologetic in Stewart's words. Far from fearing loss of caste Stewart is surely proud of her achievements in the garden, both on a personal level and within the broader colonial enterprise. Her behaviour was entirely compatible with gentility, indeed it was a new form of gentility which evolved as a direct consequence of local factors, and is discussed again in the following chapter in relation to her work in the kitchen.

Stewart is not an isolated case and in the personal writings of other elite women in New Zealand, and in those of comparable women in North Queensland, the physical work of gardening is frequently mentioned. A case in point is an entry in Lucy Gray's journal in which she describes her satisfaction at being taught how to make bread, in order not to do so herself but rather that 'I can teach others how to do it, which is my chief object in learning such things as I do not pretend to be fond of doing them, if I can get other people to do them'.[111] The picture she presents at this stage is that inside the house she adhered to a strict notion regarding what sort of chores were compatible with her genteel status, though interestingly her attitudes were subsequently modified, as discussed in the chapter on food. At no point, however, does she hesitate to describe in some detail her work in the kitchen garden, tasks which certainly included sowing and harvesting if not the heaviest of work.

The other likely explanation for the frequency with which elite women in northern Australia refer to their physical work is, as shown to be the case in New Zealand, the difficulty of locating and retaining the necessary labour. When the Grays were setting up their home there was a ready availability of servants to work within the house, either people from the South Pacific, referred to collectively as 'kanakas', or the less-highly regarded local indigenous people. There was, however, a shortage of gardeners. Migrants from China, who made the journey to Australia in the hope of meeting with success in the goldfields, sometimes encountered racist abuse and many resorted to their former occupation of gardening, either for private households or as market gardeners. In consequence they were in high demand, as indicated by Eva Gray's 1881 journal entry 'A Chinaman gardener made a good vegetable garden by the creek, but will not stay so we have to try and water it and keep it going'.[112] The social standing of those workers was to suffer greatly when anti-Chinese sentiments led to the passing of the Immigration Exclusion Act in 1901. Treloar wrote in 1915 in *Cottage Gardening in Queensland* urging the growers of fruit and vegetables to erase 'the blot on our escutcheon [it's] a yellow spot', a racist rant aimed at the Chinese-run market garden trade which by that date was well established throughout the north of the country.[113] What impact such opinions actually had on the gardening practices of the women under investigation here cannot be quantified, but might possibly have reduced their enthusiasm for employing men of Chinese heritage. If that were the case more women may have done more of the gardening themselves, which would further the acceptance of the woman working in, not merely beautifying, the garden.

The situation in the north can usefully be compared with the experiences of those living in Tasmania earlier in the century, when there was an initial reliance on convict labour. As the majority of the prisoners had been city-dwellers, they were notorious for their lack of horticultural skills. Over time a pool of local expertise developed, furthered no doubt by the development of the site-specific knowledge of their female employers and the emergence of local nurserymen, as discussed in the previous section of this chapter. The archives of Tasmanian resident Louisa Ann Meredith include a hand-written list, written one gathers by her gardener, of work undertaken from August 1895 to the end of March 1896. Work seems to have been done on a daily basis and included weeding carrots, picking gooseberries, hoeing mangels, cutting firewood, grubbing thistles, picking apples and pears, grubbing and burning gorse in the walnut paddock, digging potatoes and taking bandages off trees. This document suggests Meredith had a complex and extensive garden and orchard, and an adaptable, competent and strong worker.[114] The list is far from comprehensive, leaving a deal of other work to be carried out, irrespective of the season. This might suggest that Mrs Meredith undertook a lot of tasks herself, certainly those requiring more specialist knowledge or a delicate touch, such as taking cuttings and pricking out seedlings.

The reader will have noted that there are many more references cited here to vegetable growing in Australasia than in India and Africa. As there were so few European women living in West Africa during the period under investigation it is difficult to draw other than the most tentative of conclusions regarding the value the women accorded to the act of cultivating foodstuffs and the store they set by the produce – always assuming indeed that those two can be separated. Were they, and their peers in India, less inclined to talk about the vegetable garden if they were not doing any of the work themselves? Did having a ready supply of servants, for both house and garden duties, mean that the connection between the kitchen garden and the dining table was less frequently articulated? Or perhaps it was inevitable that only the product would be valued and not the process.

Larymore's writings are the more valuable therefore because there are so few British female experiences to recover. She was full of enthusiasm for her vegetable garden – 'To my mind the most satisfactory part of garden work in West Africa'. She gives a long list of successes, including French beans, scarlet beans, spinach, cucumber, parsley and spring-onions, all crops that would have been familiar at the British table, though some others, such as melon and egg-plant, would have been associated with affluent households being only half-hardy in temperate climes. She attributes her success to the seed being 'fresh out from England', though as noted above that was not an advantage in her flower garden.[115] Given the unforgiving nature of the climate in West Africa, when successful vegetables were grown there must have been an immense sense of achievement, as with Isabella Russell in Bathurst, Gambia, writing proudly of the inclusion of home-grown lettuce in a dinner to entertain the Bishop of Senegambia, a meal discussed in greater detail in the following chapter.[116]

Whatever the site the women's endeavours to create productive gardens was undertaken in the face of a whole range of environmental challenges. Again it is the women in the more 'hands-on' locations who are most forthcoming on the subject. Thus we hear how some of those challenges were 'friends' turned 'enemies', as with the British gorse introduced into Tasmania, which Mrs Meredith's gardener struggled to eradicate from the walnut paddock, and which was also a grievance to Adela Stewart, as were other plants imported to New Zealand such as sweet briar, kangaroo acacia and hakea.[117] Even in those supposedly benign temperate regions weather conditions frequently impeded gardening, as when Mrs Meredith, having anticipated a successful season recorded that 'my speculations on the future glory of our garden were suddenly checked by a tremendous winter flood, or rather the two successive floods in early July, which caused the rivers to overflow in new places, and drove a raging roaring torrent directly through our neat, precise and just-completed garden'.[118]

In North Queensland the Grays' garden met with comparable disaster. Lucy described how following a tropical storm: 'The next day the garden, or the ground where it had been, was high and dry. How I groaned over the havoc one night made in our flourishing garden, scarcely a trace remained'. Undaunted the Grays elected to replant in the same site, when 'down came another flood, nearly as high as the first, sweeping away the fence and covering the ground with a deep layer of fine sand'. Not until that point did they retreat to higher ground.[119] Only when the Grays were willing to adapt did their garden prosper; persistence had to be tempered with a willingness to learn from experience. Added to the unpredictability of the weather the kitchen garden was prone to attacks by opportunistic local wildlife, as when Lucy Gray's vegetable seeds were gobbled up by crows and rats. First settlers in Townsville, North Queensland found their early attempts at gardening were doomed to failure as without strong fencing wild goats would invade and devour all their produce.[120] All of the examples given highlight that the only workable response to climatic and environmental challenges was to adapt, if need be radically. To be able to bring to the table produce grown under such circumstances was achievement indeed, and how gratifying it must have been for Laura Wright in Tasmania to carry in 'the first peas of the season' and for Katie Hume to watch her 'nice pears now ripening'.[121]

In India the ready availability of labour to water crops and repair storm damage, and the availability of alternative sources of food supply may have meant that losses in the kitchen garden were less critical, certainly they are rarely commented upon. However, Flora Holman does provide a vivid description of unwelcome visitors to their garden in northern India:

> One fine afternoon while we were strolling about in the garden, we saw a large black bear roll up the hillside and climb a large figtree at the end of our lawn. We carried the news to Father inside, who loaded his gun,

but before he reached the door, another bear joined the first intruder and then another. It was no use attempting to talk to three bears, all on one tree, so we were all recalled and the doors shut, as there might have been another contingent coming for the fig feast.[122]

In the light of the general uncertainty of success one is forcibly reminded of the wider value of their gardens and hence the commitment of these indefatigable gardeners. Reducing costs and improving supply of fresh produce were certainly part of their motivation. Katie Hume, for example, was anxious that her carrots and cabbages would grow 'as they are rather expensive to buy'.[123] Eva Gray spoke of how it was 'a great treat to have some fresh vegetables without sending 25 miles to Hughendon and paying a heavy price and then getting them all squashed up off the pack horse'.[124] Flora Holman, in her account of her childhood in India in the 1840s, described living in a most isolated district of Garhwal, Oudh with very few Europeans in the vicinity and no kind of shop for forty miles 'so we started a garden of three large terraces on the hillside and planted it with maize, pumpkins and potatoes', a choice of basic crops which implies the gardening was borne more of necessity than pleasure, and that her father's army salary was not overly generous.[125]

Growing one's own fruit and vegetables also gave women the opportunity to bring added value to their tables. Being able to introduce variety to potentially dull and monotonous diets naturally increased the woman's standing as housekeeper and hostess, a theme developed in the following chapter. In India, Firminger's work on vegetable gardening, whilst initially written for the soldiers of the British army, ran to some six editions, suggesting a rather wider readership.[126] Steele and Gardiner's advice manual for the mistress of the house in India urged the cultivation of a kitchen garden to ensure a regular supply of specifically British vegetables.[127] As with Edith Cuthell's Christmas Day menu cited above, cultivating familiar produce is to be understood not as a slavish apeing of old customs, but rather as part of the process of reconfiguration of genteel practice.

In some sites and at some dates sourcing plant material was another challenge to be overcome. A desire for a supply of plants and seeds for the kitchen garden is certainly a feature of the women's letters to Britain. Georgina Malloy wrote in 1833 requesting culinary seeds for her Swan River garden and Katie Hume makes many references to sowing seeds in Queensland which she had brought from the garden at 'Tott and Barnes', her family home in England.[128] Particularly clear on the subject is Mary Thomas, who in 1838 wrote from South Australia, 'I have read that slips of apple and pear trees have been sent to India from

England in moss with success, and I should like to try the experiment here [...] Likewise a root of rhubarb. I have such a desire for something English that nothing else gives me any pleasure'.[129]

Nonetheless one must be cautious about generalising from such requests. All of those women were writing from Australian settlements in their relative infancy and supplies were presumably limited. Equally the women themselves were only just establishing their gardens and therefore had possibly not yet acquired experience of how to source at a local level, from their peers for example, nor yet how successfully such imported material would grow. It should also be noted that at the time Malloy and Thomas were writing there was a commonly held view that Britain had to be the source of supply for fruit and vegetable material, as witness James Blackhouses published assertion that 'there is not a single plant indigenous to Australia worth cultivating for its fruit, or as a culinary vegetable, unless it is the common mushroom. Most of the European fruit and vegetables however thrive very well'.[130] The women's requests for items from Britain cannot therefore be taken to be fuelled by nostalgia alone, if at all.

An interesting contrast is to be found in Eustace Kenyon's correspondence to his mother and sister on the subject of how, when he and his wife attempted to grow imported seed in their Calcutta garden, they found it lacked vigour 'so one has to get acclimatised seeds from the local native gardeners'.[131] Similarly one of the most enthusiastic and successful gardeners who seems to have embraced both local vegetables and those familiar in Britain was Alice Massey, in whose garden in Rawalpindi she grew both local and 'cold weather' species.[132] No doubt it was common custom to save seed to grow on the following season, just as it was in Britain until well into the twentieth century. In addition, supplies for the kitchen garden would naturally benefit from the expansion of the nursery business that accompanied the growth of European settlements in most sites, as discussed in relation to flower gardens. Of particular interest is the Robert Seth Catalogue of 1919–20, for not only did it offer for sale the brassica, root and salad seeds with which all the British would be familiar, it also had an entire section devoted to 'Indian Vegetable Seed' which listed Jhinga, Kankri, Karela, Sanakaloo and Pulwul-Parbal, plus twenty-six other types. That no English translation is offered for these vegetables may indicate that Seth were catering for an Indian client-base, but equally it does offer a reading that by this late date a lot of the British residents were so familiar with local vegetables that they too were including them in their kitchen gardens. This suggestion is given added credence by a parenthesis in the catalogue: following the listing of Roselle it adds 'Indian Sorrel, most delicious puddings and tarts are made from the thick succulent sepals of this fruit, remarkably fine for jelly'.[133]

Of course such local or exotic fruit and vegetables only merited mention in personal writings when a way had been developed to make good use of them in the kitchen. When the local species could become part of a strategy to provide added value, only then did it become worthy of comment, for only then was the item raised from mere subsistence level to the status of an element within genteel performance. Thus, for example, the anonymous lady at the Cape spoke of the 'pretty little tomato making the most delicious sauce', and Katie Hume wrote that 'our white peaches are just getting ripe. I am about to put them in a pie'.[134] An abundant supply of white peaches would in England be worthy of comment, but that Hume not only grew them successfully but also knew how to prepare them for the table doubled her achievement. Equally Larymore spoke well of 'garden eggs', a generic term for various forms of egg-plant or aubergine, which she found satisfactory when stuffed with various sorts of meat.

It is appropriate that this exploration of kitchen gardens should conclude with consideration of how the individual's practice merged with those of her peers, and hence made a key contribution to making visible, and thereby stabilising, social hierarchies. In some sites gardens and their produce were a form of social currency. In Van Diemen's Land Mrs Morton Allport's journal not only shows much of her making and receiving calls revolved around her garden, but also hints that her evident expertise was shared and valued by her peers, as when she sent a gift of 'Femme de Neige apples and Macon's Incomparable pears'.[135] Similar appreciation of gifts of garden produce is revealed by Laura Wright's Tasmanian diary entries of 1863, which include several references to a kindly neighbour who gave them blackcurrants and gooseberries. In 1876, when her husband was grievously ill, she records gifts of artichokes and a basket of mulberries.[136] In Calcutta, Clementina Benthall noted in her diary that 'our vegetable garden supplies us well and we give one of our neighbours a basketful of edibles daily'. In a later entry Benthall records that friends 'have procured us some wild ducks and teal alive, and we have built a neat Tealery on the back in my garden'.[137] Sometimes produce was exchanged for other items or for all-important expertise. Adela Stewart reports a particularly fruitful trade: 'I made an exchange with a girlfriend in Tauranga of fourteen of my prize chrysanthemums for a fine Brahma cock. Then, for another dozen plants I got from the winner of the First Prize for pastry at the Kati Kati Show, the recipe of how to make it'.[138] Of course, such exchanges rely on living in relative proximity with one's neighbours, and that presumably explains why no such examples have been located from West Africa or upcountry North Queensland, where the women tended to live in remote sites and hence such interactions could not be part of their regular practice.

The examples given serve to illustrate not only the range of competencies of the individual women and the satisfaction they gained from growing food for themselves and their household, but also the investment in the well-being of the community as expressed through their kitchen gardens. This discussion has shown that the kitchen garden's contribution to their foodway practices was only part of its value, and that it had other, equally crucial, values for individual and society alike.

'Affords the opportunity of amusing ourselves when we feel inclined to garden':[139] the verandah

In any colony of the British Empire which had periods of agreeably warm weather, the Europeans and those of European heritage built their houses with verandahs. These structures varied in size and in design. In temperate climates, such as New Zealand and Tasmania, they were generally of fairly modest dimensions, as they were not in use all the year round. Many matched the width of the house frontage, and were little more than three metres deep. In tropical climes, such as in the bungalows of India and the homesteads of North Queensland and stations of West Africa the verandahs were integral to the overall design, sometimes running the perimeter of the entire building, and were anything up to six metres deep. Doors from the interior opened directly on to the verandah, to make best use in hot and sweltering conditions of whatever air movement was available. Houses were often built on 'stumps' or blocks, to discourage invasion by wildlife, protect from floods and encourage up-draughts. In consequence the verandah viewed the world from an elevated position, and in turn visitors stepped up to the verandah.

As has already been examined in some detail in the preceding chapter on living rooms, and will be visited again in the following chapter on food, the verandah was a key space in the lives of the women. Here they conducted much of their social lives, such as receiving callers, taking afternoon tea and holding 'sewing bees'.[140] See Figure 2.3 which shows two ladies taking tea on a partially enclosed verandah in Tasmania. Much of family life was lived out on the verandah and from here the mistress could largely supervise much of the running of her household. Hence they spent time on the verandah in the company of a variety of people, all of whom were involved to some degree and in some capacity in their genteel performance, and therefore it was a site of display. As such it was essential that in hot climes the verandah be a cool and spacious and well-appointed space. Equally in temperate settings a well-protected sun-trap, arranged with an eye to homely comfort, would be highly valued. Hence furnishings in this space were not the material element of greatest value; its value lay in the very space itself. Ardener speaks of space as a means of communication, not just reflecting social rules but as an active constituent in them, as part of a value system.[141] For the woman the verandah was a space she shared with others, but it had a distinct meaning for herself, being an arena in which she performed much of her genteel persona. So even though the verandah may appear cluttered and casual it had significance beyond its apparent informality.

As a contributory element within this space the plants had immense value. The mistress of the house would maintain them to a high standard, as they were a crucial part of her woman's knowledge, and regarded accordingly. So highly did Larymore value plants on the verandah in Nigeria she advocated saving one's bath water to ensure they could receive a daily watering.[142] Of verandahs in India MacMillan's work provides a vivid description of a typical plant display: 'Bamboo trellises – smothered in bignonia, passion-flowers, ivies. Inside the "room" had grass-matting and maidenhair ferns on stands, hanging-baskets, pink creeping geraniums, achimenes with red, white and purple flowers, flower boxes with geraniums, or begonias or violets'.[143] Another description is provided by the Godden sisters who, in recalling their childhood in East Bengal, spoke of 'double steps banked with pots of budding chrysanthemums [which] led up from the drive', which reminds us how in some settings the verandah either formed part of the front garden, or even acted as an alternative introduction to the house frontage.[144]

In North Queensland low-set houses, i.e. those built close to the ground on just small stumps, had shrubs planted around the perimeter of the verandah to cast shade and give privacy. High-set homes might benefit from shade trees, such as rain tree or cabbage tree palm. Verandah plants might include ferns, or temperate species which would be more likely to survive when provided with close and careful management. Figure 4.7 provides indication of the appealing environment which was created on verandahs with the skilful use of plants. Mrs Boldrewood's work on garden advice to ladies in Australia, particularly in the south, was that they grow tree-ferns in pots specifically to decorate the verandah.[145]

In temperate climes a verandah gave the required cover and protection to tender plants, and was therefore employed rather as a glass-house was used in Britain. Some plants would be permanently

4.7 Array of container-grown plants on verandah of low-set house. Em Cavey mounted on her horse Paddy, Burdekin Downs, Queensland, 1900.

situated on the verandah, grown in decorative containers, sometimes displayed to greater advantage on purpose-built racks or stands. These 'living walls' could also be the site for plants imported when at their peak, possibly from the bush house or similar sheltered spot. Emma Rutherfoord described the arrangement in their Cape Town garden: 'on the verandah on each side of the front door we have two flower stands, covered with pretty choice plants from the Botanical Gardens'.[146] That she speaks of 'choice' items and reports the provenance of their plants reminds us that every aspect of garden practice had the potential for an expression of rank and status. (This South African practice can be compared to the marketing in Tasmania of freshly imported, and highly priced, carnation stock, as described in the discussion on flower gardening.)

In addition to the many social interactions the women had on the verandah it was also a space of solitary occupation and invited contemplation. From within this space women looked out across their garden to the land beyond – Meredith spoke of her 'verandah-diorama' – and it was often whilst seated here that they carried out their profuse personal writing.[147] This may in part explain why plants familiar to their readers loom so large in their descriptions of this area. Thus from Cape Town

TASTEFUL GARDENING AND GROWING ATTACHMENT

Emma Rutherfoord wrote to her sister in India about their 'summer garden arrangements ... the pots on the *back stoep*. We went to the Hares the other day and stocked ourselves with violets, polyanthus etc. As we water them they are growing very nicely and we have a beautiful geranium out'.[148] Another writer from the Cape spoke of 'verandahs fragrant with honeysuckle and monthly roses', words evocative of other times and other places, and understood as such no doubt, by writer and reader alike.[149]

In many ways then the verandah seems to have been a delightful area of the woman's domain – surrounded by her chosen plant-life, safe from the alien world beyond, a space in which she could feel secure and relaxed. And yet, notwithstanding its obvious charms, the verandah was also an ambiguous space, for just as it invited the woman to gaze out, so too did it permit the 'other' to gaze in. The alien scene was undeniably close by. This lay behind the veto her husband placed on Alice Massey's desire to grow passionflower on their verandah; 'it will encourage and harbour all sorts of reptiles, snakes, scorpions etc; otherwise I could make it so pretty and shady by growing it round the posts that [support] the roof of the verandah. But he is quite right so I have resigned myself to an ugly verandah in order to be free of reptiles'.[150] In not dissimilar vein Violet Jacob, despite relishing time spent in the Indian countryside, often making trips by herself to collect botanical specimens for drawing and painting, noted that 'even around this civilised house we live in the jackals yell at night and have often been up into the verandah'.[151]

In addition to acting as a literal, and clearly rather leaky boundary marker against the indigenous wildlife, the verandah formed part of the perimeter, a 'front door' to European domestic territory. Therefore it had an important symbolic purpose, serving as a statement of intent, proclaiming that therein was to be found not only safety, but also harmony and order, in short – civilisation. Such a construction defined the world beyond as chaotic and barbarous. In some locales this doubtless really was the case – as for example in areas of North Queensland where angry and desperate indigenous people made attacks on isolated homesteads, in India during the build-up to the horrors of 1857 and beyond, and in virtually all areas of South and West Africa where British peoples were so emphatically outnumbered by African peoples. In such situations even the domestic garden could be a site of conflict, and metaphor for the bigger struggles over land between the colonisers and the indigenous peoples. The verandah was evidently a space with the potential to unsettle one's sense of well-being, and prompt troubling introspection, for from the verandah the alien other was ever in view, both challenging and inviting.

'Wild flowers including single dahlias':[152] in conclusion

This discussion of female genteel garden practices in colonies of the British Empire has taken their gardens to be part of their habitus, each element having discrete meaning, but also contributing to the overall identity. It has been argued that their gardens and associated practices did much to contribute towards the women's physical and psychological occupation of their new space. Their desire to shape at least the immediate environment within the terms of their own aesthetic found expression through the relative positioning of the elements of the gardens, the details of the design and their selection and identification of the material planted. The inclusion of plants familiar from their homes of origin provided a living means of amalgamating their past life into their new circumstances; the past thereby finding a secure space in their future. Equally, placing such *aides de mémoire* alongside indigenous species did much to reduce the sense of the 'alien other' of the locale. Physical work, with or without the assistance of servants, meant a literal investment of energy which also prompted an attachment to the site. This in turn was furthered by the use of garden produce within the home, be it at the dining table or for decorative purposes in the living room. In the light of the findings of this enquiry, women's relationships with their gardens emerge as complex. All sites examined reveal examples of the development of strategies to overcome local challenges, be they climatic, ecological or environmental or the presence or absence of hired-in labour. The garden was evidently a space in which the radical could take place, where change could be negotiated and sometimes embraced.

It has also become apparent that on some occasions in some locations the garden was a contested area. It was invariably enclosed space, its boundaries marked by fencing, hedging or walls. As has already been noted these barriers, intended to keep out intruders in the form of wildlife, were not always successful. They were also designed to exclude unwelcome human visitors, most particularly the indigenous people. The garden as a site of potential danger from anonymous males, usually expressed in terms of veiled sexuality, was a recurrent theme in colonial fiction.[153] That this latter subject is singularly absent from the women's personal writings may be more because it would have introduced a jarring note into their representations of successful colonial endeavour than because the perception of danger did not exist. Clearly then the barriers were not figuratively or literally impregnable, and for the women of genteel persuasion who actively sought exclusivity invasion of their space was doubly unnerving.

It is important, however, not to assume that was the case for all. In

1864 Charlotte Stamper gave the following description of the terrain around their house in Mussoorie:

> The hills first clothed with white roses which caught from tree to tree a mass of scented blossom, then all kinds of wild flowers including single dahlias of every colour, convolvulus, and Japan anemones. The red rhododendrons which there grow into forest trees ... Ferns of course everywhere even all up the tree trunks. Especially sweet was the little maidenhair which followed the track of every dropping rill or streamlet.[154]

Far from presenting the environment as 'other', Stamper's words suggest a reading not of mere detached admiration, but rather of avid involvement, particularly noticeable in her use of self-consciously poetic language. There is scope for suggesting that for many women their relationship with the land was deepened and developed as a consequence of their local garden practices. Just as the garden occupied psychological space beyond its material reality, so too could that world of the imaginary accommodate at least some aspects of the wider environment. Indeed this raises the question as to whether for some women their connections with the land might have been more profound than those of their male colonial counterparts. The mores of the tightly gendered communities of the colonial empire compelled many women to spend much of their time alone, or with those they regarded as their social inferiors. Might not such settings have fostered a more meditative approach to their surroundings? If so, it may have encouraged an appreciation of their natural riches in ways denied to their menfolk obliged to pursue activities of a more overtly exploitative nature. Tyrell asserts that 'assimilation of Australian (native sp.) to the landscape appears alongside the complementary issue of women's specific appreciation of that landscape'.[155] Evidence has been presented which suggests that gardens had the same connecting agency in settings other than Australia, as for example in Constance Larymore's enthusiasm for incorporating Nigerian species into her garden. The sense of urgency some women expressed about their gardening – consider Lucy Gray determinedly replanting in the face of repeated flooding and Katie Hume sowing seeds during the cool hours of the night – can then be understood as arising out of a desire to attach themselves to site as much as for any practical consideration.

The case has been made for gardens and garden practices having mediating agency in giving those women a means of engaging with their surroundings, both within their garden and beyond, and thereby suggesting that through their gardens it is possible to read their most intimate attachment to place. In turn this has furthered the argument concerning the importance and significance of well-being in the life of both the individual and wider society alike. The interplay between individual practice and emergent collective identity is a key aspect of migrant experience. A sense of well-being and emotional investment are hallmarks of a successful migrant. In private gardens we find both expression and representation of female subjectivities, and, thereby, expression of community identity.

The very act of making and maintaining gardens was a means by which genteel women contributed to the imperial cause by creating order out of the chaos of the natural world, and another way in which they worked for successive generations. That their endeavours were conducted in the domestic sphere did not dilute their value. As with their living rooms and food practices that which was carried out in the garden stood as a model for wider imperial endeavour, clear indicator of progress of both household and wider colonial society alike. Colonial societies were first and foremost aspirant societies – to succeed in the garden was to be a successful colonist. Equally to fail in the garden was a double blow, so there was a pressure behind the drive to produce pretty flowerbeds and neat rows of vegetables which went beyond the immediate household, pressure that was of course even more of an issue for those amongst society who wished to proclaim their superiority. Thus beyond the neatly clipped hedges ran tensions as well as celebrations of achievement. Their gardens brought the women some measure of autonomy, but still there remained the pressures of creating a garden of the required standard. Nonetheless it must be borne in mind that those very tensions are indicative of the effectiveness of the women's gardens and their associated practices as a social force. The spaces of the garden may have been physically set apart but their significance was central to genteel women's performance within wider colonial society.

In focusing on the objects and practices of the garden some light has been shed on the obvious interconnections between the garden and the practices around food. It is appropriate therefore that the next chapter should be an exploration of food and its place in female genteel performance. It is also fitting that food should be the final aspect of their performance explored in this work, as dining, particularly when entertaining, gave opportunity for the display of so many aspects of their gentility: the tastefully dressed woman in her well-appointed room, graciously presenting – seemingly without effort – delicate and toothsome fare. To achieve such a synchronicity, often under very difficult conditions, was indeed the very pinnacle of success.

Notes

1. S. A. Courage, *Light and Shadows of Colonial Life: Twenty Six Years in Canterbury, New Zealand*, 2nd edn (Christchurch, Whitcoulls, 1976), p. 90, first published c.1896.
2. See for example the Garden History Society www.gardenhistorysociety.org and the Australian and New Zealand Environmental History Network http://environmentalhistory-au-nz.org
3. C. and C. Carlton, *The Significance of Gardening in British India* (Lewiston, N.Y., Edwin Mellon Press, 2004); D. McCracken, *Gardens of Empire: Botanical Institutions of the Victorian British Empire* (London, Leicester University Press, 2007).
4. H. M. Leach, *Cultivating Myths: Fiction, Fact and Fashion in Garden History* (Auckland, Godwit, 2000).
5. Mrs C. W. Earle, 1897, cited by D. Kellaway (ed.), *The Virago Book of Women Gardeners* (London, Virago Press, 1995), p. 223.
6. P. Horn, *The Rise and Fall of the Victorian Servant* (Stroud, Sutton Publishing, 1990), p. 84.
7. J. Loudon, *Ornamental Annuals* cited by J. Davies, *The Victorian Flower Garden* (London, BBC Books, 1991), p. 215; J. Loudon, *The Suburban Garden and Villa Gardeners* (London, 1838).
8. *Villa Gardener*, January 1873, copies of issues 1872–75 are held at the Royal Horticultural Society, Lindley Library, London, henceforth LL.
9. E. T. Cook, *Gardens of England* (London, A. & C. Black, 1908), p. 13.
10. Mrs C. W. Earle, 1897, Kellaway, *Women Gardeners*, p. 163.
11. Mrs R. Boldrewood, *The Flower Garden in Australia: A Book for Ladies and Amateurs* (Melbourne, Melville, Mullen & Slade, 1893), Introduction.
12. G. Byrne, 'Surveying Space: Constructing the Colonial Landscape' in B. Dalley and B. Labrum (eds.), *Fragments: New Zealand Social and Cultural History* (Auckland, Auckland University Press, 2000), p. 76.
13. C. Larymore, *A Resident's Wife in Nigeria* (London, Routledge, 1911), p. 245.
14. For a discussion of methodological approaches to garden histories see J. Dixon Hunt (ed.), *Garden History: Issues, Approaches and Methods* (Washington, D.C., Dunbarton Oaks Research Library, 1992).
15. It should be stressed that the interest lay in the *idea* of there being another layer of meaning, of poetic or romantic meaning, attached to the floral world, rather than necessarily a literal belief that a nasturtium equated with a fickle mind or a carnation with constancy.
16. L. P. Wright, *Laura's Brookville Diaries 1819–1894* (Launceston, Greenhill, 2003), December 1864; D. Coleman (ed.), *Women Writing Home 1700–1920: Female Correspondence Across the British Empire. Vol. 2 Australia* (London, Pickering & Chatto, 2006), p. 189, Georgina Malloy, January 1840. The endnote to the latter reference notes this was the 'popular floral alphabet of Charlotte de la Tour, pseudonym of Louise Cortambert, first published in Paris in 1818'.
17. *The Language and Poetry of Flowers* (London, Ward, Lock & Tyler, 1877).
18. *Language of the Flowers of Australia, Tasmania and New Zealand*, 4th edn (Hobart, J. Walch, 1877); Mrs L. Meredith, *Language of the Native Flowers of Tasmania* (Launceston, Harris & Just, [18?]), Tasmaniana Collection, State Library of Tasmania, henceforth SLT.
19. K. Greenaway, *The Language of Flowers* (London, G. Routledge & Sons, 1884); L. Von Einem, *Language of Flowers Within the Maze, and Miscellaneous Poems* (Auckland, Brett Print Publishers Co., 1912).
20. Further examples come from New Zealand where Adela Stewart and Sarah Greenwood, despite their household demands, made paintings of their gardens. A. B. Stewart, *My Simple Life in New Zealand* (London, Robert Banks & Co., 1908); Sarah Greenwood, 'The Grange, the residence of Dr Greenwood 1879', watercolour

depicting house and garden with mature trees, E-305-q-055, Alexander Turnbull Library, New Zealand.
21. C. Macdonald (ed.), *Women Writing Home 1700–1920: Female Correspondence Across the British Empire. Vol. 5 New Zealand* (London, Pickering & Chatto, 2006), p. 302, Georgina Bowen, November 1864.
22. Courage, *Light and Shadows*, p. 90.
23. Stewart, *My Simple Life in New Zealand*, p. 74.
24. Courage, *Light and Shadows*, p. 33.
25. H. M. Leach, 'The European House and Garden in New Zealand: A Case for Parallel Development' in B. Brookes (ed.), *At Home in New Zealand: Houses, History, People* (Wellington, Bridget Williams Books, 2000), p. 79.
26. A. F. Hattersley (ed.), *A Victorian Lady at the Cape, 1849–51* (Cape Town, Maskew Miller, [194?]), p. 21.
27. S. Leith-Ross, *Stepping Stones: Memoirs of Colonial Africa, 1907–1962* (London, Peter Owen, 1983), p. 46.
28. Mrs Sheila Warwick, born Uttar Pradesh, India, 1914, Audio tape 405, British Empire and Commonwealth Museum, henceforth BECM.
29. Mrs R. Temple-Wright, *Flowers and Gardens in India: A Manual for Beginners* (Calcutta, Thacker, Spink & Co., 1902), p. 12.
30. Stewart, *My Simple Life in New Zealand*, p. 146.
31. P. Watts, *Historic Gardens of Victoria: A Reconnaissance* (Melbourne, Oxford University Press, 1983); V. Crittenden, *The Front Garden: The Story of the Cottage Garden in Australia* (Canberra, Mulini Press, 1979).
32. Larymore, *Resident's Wife*, p. 244.
33. C. Anderson (ed.), *Violet Jacob: Letters and Diaries from India 1895–1900* (Edinburgh, Canongate, 1990), p. 30.
34. Temple-Wright, *Flowers and Gardens*, p. 14.
35. *Howies Spring Catalogue*, 1912–13, copy held LL.
36. Macdonald, *Women Writing Home. Vol. 5*, pp. 113, 215, Sarah Greenwood, Motueka, June 1843 and June 1846.
37. *Yates Annual Catalogue*, 1914, *Howies Spring Catalogue*, 1912, copies held LL.
38. L. Scripps, *The Industrial Heritage of Hobart, Vol. 1 Historical Study* (Hobart, Hobart City Council, 1997), p. 65.
39. Leach, 'European House and Garden in New Zealand', p. 74; Watts, *Gardens of Victoria*; Crittenden, *The Front Garden*.
40. Macdonald, *Women Writing Home. Vol. 5*, pp. 353–4, Georgina Bowen, November 1864.
41. B. Hamilton-Arnold (ed.), *Letters of G. P. Harris 1803–1812* (Sorrento, Australia, Arden Press, 1994), Letter to his mother in Exeter, England from Van Diemen's Land, 12 October 1805.
42. John Loudon, *A Manual of Cottage Gardening, Husbandry and Architecture* (London, 1830), p. 73; *An Encyclopaedia for Gardening*, 5th edn (London, 1850); Temple-Wright, *Flowers and Gardens*, p. 4.
43. Leach, 'European House and Garden in New Zealand'; S. Chevalier, 'From Woollen Carpet to Grass Carpet: Bridging House and Garden in an English Suburb' in D. Miller (ed.), *Why Some Things Matter* (London, University College, 1998).
44. *Englishwoman's Domestic Magazine*, 1871. Copies located in private collection, Hobart.
45. Jane Loudon, *Gardening for Ladies* (London, Murray, 1841).
46. Coleman, *Women Writing Home. Vol. 2*, p. 203, Georgina Malloy, 14 August 1840.
47. *Sydney Magazine of Science and Art*, April 1859, pp. 197–9.
48. *Smith Bros Catalogue*, 1896–97; *Howies Spring Catalogue*, 1912–13; *Howden & Moncrieff*, 1911, copies held LL.
49. Macdonald, *Women Writing Home. Vol. 5*, p. 314, Georgina Bowen 1862.

50 Courage, *Light and Shadows*, p. 231.
51 Larymore, *Resident's Wife*, p. 240. It will be noted that with the exception of the poppies all the flowers Larymore mentions are scented.
52 Larymore, *Resident's Wife*, p. 241.
53 N. Bonnin (ed.), *Katie Hume on the Darling Downs: A Colonial Marriage* (Toowoomba, Darling Downs Institute Press, 1985), p. 34.
54 J. R. Godley (ed.), *Letters from Early New Zealand by Charlotte Godley, 1850–1853* (Christchurch, Whitcombe & Tombs, 1951), p. 85.
55 Larymore, *Resident's Wife*, p. 241; Cannells Catalogues, Mrs Phillips, Matakana, New Zealand, 1883, and Mrs Clayton, Heilbronn, South Africa, 1895. Copies held LL.
56 Godley, *Letters from Early New Zealand*, p. 141.
57 Stewart, *My Simple Life in New Zealand*, p. 30.
58 *Robert Seth & Co.*, Calcutta, 1919–20, a copy at LL.
59 *Walker Catalogue* 1915, copy held in LL.
60 D. Bunce: *Seeds & Plants Catalogue*, 1836; *Sonntag & Co. Seed Merchants*, San Francisco, California, 1874–75, W. L. Crowther Library, SLT.
61 Scrapbook AB831, Tasmanian State Archives.
62 Coleman, *Women Writing Home. Vol. 2*, p. 177, Georgina Malloy, 1837.
63 H. K. Forsyth, *Remembered Gardens: Eight Women and Their Visions of an Australian Landscape* (Carlton, Victoria, Miegunyah Press, 2006), p. 45.
64 Godley, *Letters from Early New Zealand*, pp. 140–1.
65 P. L. Brown (ed.), *Clyde Company Papers, Part I* (London, Oxford University Press, 1941), p. 144. Jane Williams to Mrs Reid, Ratho, Upper Clyde, Van Diemen's Land, 26 September 1831.
66 J. Murray (ed.), *In Mid-Victorian Cape Town: Letters from Miss Rutherfoord* (Cape Town, A. A. Balkema, 1953), p. 12.
67 L. A. Meredith, *My Home in Tasmania: during a Residence of Nine Years* (Adelaide, Griffin Press, 1932), p. 39, first published 1853.
68 D. Bunce, *Manual of Practical Gardening Adapted to the Climate of Van Diemen's Land* (Hobart, William Gore Elliston, 1838).
69 J. Deans, *Letters to my Grandchildren* (Christchurch, Cadsonbury Publications, 1995), p. 37.
70 K. Raine, 'Domesticating the Land: Colonial Women's Gardening' in Dalley and Labrum, *Fragments*, chapter 3.
71 Examples of these catalogues held by LL.
72 Larymore, *Resident's Wife*, pp. 243, 245.
73 P. Fraser Simmons, *Historic Tasmanian Gardens* (Canberra, Mulini Press, 1987), p. 18.
74 Coleman, *Women Writing Home. Vol. 2*, p. 177, Georgina Malloy, 21 March 1837.
75 Stewart, *My Simple Life in New Zealand*, p. 37.
76 M. McBriar, 'The Use of Australian Plants in Gardens of Federation and other Edwardian Houses in Melbourne 1890–1914', Thesis for Graduate Diploma in Landscape Design, Royal Melbourne Institute of Technology, 1980.
77 P. Bourdieu, *Distinction: A Social Critique of the Judgement of Taste* (Cambridge, University of Massachusetts, 1984).
78 The firm of Cartmels, Kent, England had their nursery laid out in the manner alluded to by Bunce. A copy of *Seeds & Plants Catalogue*, Daniel Bunce, Hobart, 1836 is in the Crowther Library, SLT.
79 *Mercury*, 1877.
80 D. Ledward, *The Victorian Garden Catalogue* (London, Studio Editions, 1995).
81 Larymore, *Resident's Wife*, pp. 240–1.
82 Robert Seth's Catalogue, 1919–20; *Smith Bros Catalogue*, 1905; Yates Annual Catalogue, 1914, copies at LL. Note also the contrast in price between the Australian saved carnation seed offered by Yates and the freshly imported stock on sale at Walker's in Launceston, Tasmania at around the same date.

83 Mrs Clementina Benthall, Diary, Centre of South Asian Studies, University of Cambridge, henceforth CSAS. It is assumed that 'Banion' is a variant of banyan.
84 R. Gray, *Reminiscences of India and North Queensland* (London, Constable & Co., 1912), p. 294.
85 Larymore, *Resident's Wife*, p. 245; D. Moore, *We Two in West Africa* (London, Heinemann, 1909); *Howies Spring Catalogue*, 1912–13, copy at LL.
86 Stewart, *My Simple Life in New Zealand*, pp. 136–7.
87 Bonnin, *Colonial Marriage*, p. 100, 24 February 1868.
88 Murray, *In Mid-Victorian Cape Town*, p. 14, March 1852.
89 Constance Maude, Memoirs, CSAS.
90 Eustace Kenyon, Letters from Calcutta, 17 March 1898, CSAS.
91 J. Perkins, *Floral Decorations for the Table* (London, 1877), cited by M. R. Blackes, *Flora Domestica: A History of Flower Arranging 1500–1930* (London, National Trust, 2000), p. 183.
92 Loudon, *Manual of Cottage Gardening*, p. 43.
93 Anon., *Life at the Cape One Hundred Years Ago, by a Lady* (Cape Town, C. Struik, 1963), p. 6.
94 T. Hubbard, 'Cultivating the Maidenhair and the Maiden Fair: The Social Role of the Late Nineteenth Century Conservatory', *Australian Garden History Society* Vol. 21 (3), January–March 2010, pp. 10–15.
95 Leach, 'European House and Garden in New Zealand', p. 77.
96 C. Brouwer, *Townsville Gardens, Townsville Heritage Kit* (Townsville, Townsville City Council, 2000). With thanks to Dr A. J. Dartnall for bringing this publication to my attention.
97 Bourdieu, *Distinction*, p. 258.
98 E. Buettner, *Empire Families: Britons and Late Imperial India* (Oxford, Oxford University Press, 2004), p. 65.
99 Wright, *Brookville Diaries*.
100 E. Cuthell, *My Garden City in the City of Gardens* (London, Bodley Head, 1905), p. 120 cited by C. and C. Charlton, *The Significance of Gardening in British India* (Lewiston, N.Y., Edwin Mellen Press, 2004), p. 18.
101 Clementina Benthall, Diary, CSAS.
102 J. Richardson, 'An Annotated Edition of the Journals of Mary Morton Allport', Ph.D. Thesis, University of Tasmania, 2006. 5 March 1853.
103 Anderson, *Violet Jacob*, p. 23.
104 Clementina Benthall, Diary, CSAS.
105 Mrs R. Temple-Wright, *Baker and Cook* (Calcutta, Thacker, Spink & Co., 1894).
106 Stewart, *My Simple Life in New Zealand*, p. 89.
107 K. Stierstorfer (ed.), *Women Writing Home 1700–1920: Female Correspondence Across the British Empire. Vol. 4 India* (London, Pickering & Chatto, 2006), p. 50, Alice Massey, 13 June 1875.
108 Bonnin, *Colonial Marriage*, p. 34. Walter Hume was her husband, Dubs possibly another family member.
109 Stewart, *My Simple Life in New Zealand*, p. 27.
110 M. McClure, 'Body and Soul: Work in 19th Century New Zealand' in Dalley and Labrum, *Fragments*.
111 A. Allingham, 'Victorian Frontierswomen: The Australian Diaries and Journals of Lucy and Eva Gray, 1868–72 and 1881–1892', MA Thesis, James Cook University, 1987, p.XXX1.
112 Allingham 'Victorian Frontierswomen', 27 June 1881.
113 H. Treloar, *Cottage Gardening in Queensland*, 4th edn (Townsville, T. Willmett & Sons, 1915), p. 11. The Immigration Exclusion Act was passed 23 December 1901.
114 Mrs John Meredith, Accounts. NS123/81, Tasmanian State Archives.
115 Larymore, *Resident's Wife*, p. 250.
116 Isabella Russell, Letters from the Gambia, BECM.
117 Stewart, *My Simple Life in New Zealand*, p. 34.
118 Meredith, *My Home in Tasmania*, p. 136.

119 Allingham, 'Victorian Frontierswomen', Lucy Gray Journal, Chapter XVII.
120 Brouwer, *Townsville Heritage*.
121 Wright, *Brookville Diaries*, 3 March 1865; Bonnin, *Colonial Marriage*, p. 46.
122 Flora Holman, c.1840s, CSAS.
123 Bonnin, *Colonial Marriage*, p. 34.
124 Allingham, 'Victorian Frontierswomen', Eva Gray Journal, 27 June 1881.
125 Flora Holman, CSAS.
126 H. St John Jackson, *Firminger's Manual of Gardening for Bengal and Upper India* (Calcutta, Thacker, Spink & Co., 1890).
127 F. A. Steele and G. Gardiner, *The Complete Indian Housekeeper and Cook*, 7th edn (London, William Heinemann, 1909).
128 Coleman, *Women Writing Home. Vol. 2*, p. 157 Georgina Malloy; Bonnin, *Colonial Marriage*, p. 34.
129 Coleman, *Women Writing Home. Vol. 2*, p. 312, Mary Thomas.
130 J. Blackhouse, *A Narrative of a Visit to the Australian Colonies* (London and New York, 1843), reviewed *The Gardener's Magazine and Register of Rural and Domestic Improvement*, John Chambers Loudon (ed.), Vol. 19 (London, Longman, Rees, 1843), p. 182.
131 Eustace Kenyon, CSAS.
132 Stierstorfer, *Women Writing Home. Vol. 4*, pp. 65–6, Alice Massey.
133 Robert Seth Catalogue, 1919–20, copy held at LL.
134 Anon., *Life at the Cape*, p. 24; Bonnin, *Colonial Marriage*, p. 46.
135 Richardson, Allport Journals, 21 April 1853.
136 Wright, *Brookville Diaries*.
137 Clementina Benthall, Diary, CSAS.
138 Stewart, *My Simple Life in New Zealand*, pp. 147–8.
139 Clarke and Spender, *Lifelines*, p. 176, Sarah Burnell, Braidwood, New South Wales, 1839.
140 For a vivid account of the role of the verandah in India see P. Barr and R. Desmond, *Simla: A Hill Station in British India* (London, Scolar Press, 1978).
141 S. Ardener (ed.), *Women and Space: Ground Rules and Social Maps* (London, Croom Helm, 1981).
142 Larymore, *Resident's Wife*, p. 248.
143 M. MacMillan, *Women of the Raj* (New York, Thames & Hudson, 1988), p. 78.
144 J. and R. Godden, *Two Under the Indian Sun* (London, Macmillan, 1961), p. 25.
145 Boldrewood, *The Flower Garden in Australia*, p. 19.
146 Murray, *Mid-Victorian Cape Town*, March 1856, p. 19.
147 Meredith, *My Home in Tasmania*, p. 38.
148 Murray, *Mid-Victorian Cape Town*, November 1852. 'Hares' – family friends, pp. 18–19.
149 Anon., *Life at the Cape*, p. 16, September 1861.
150 Stierstorfer, *Women Writing Home. Vol. 4*, p. 50, Alice Massey, 13 June 1875.
151 Anderson, *Violet Jacob*, p. 28.
152 Charlotte Stamper, Memoirs, 1864, S. Laughton Papers, CSAS.
153 See for example R. Godden, *The Peacock Spring* (London, Macmillan, 1975).
154 Charlotte Stamper, Memoirs, 1864, CSAS.
155 I. Tyrell, 'Environment, Landscape and History: Gardening in Australia', *Australian Historical Studies* No. 130, October 2007, pp. 389–97.

5

'The guests being seated at the dinner table, the lady serves the soup':[1] food and household management

Introduction

This investigation of female genteel values and ways in which they were transferred and adapted in various colonial settings understands material culture to be a key expression of identity. It argues throughout that the women's possessions and associated practices can be understood as both a presentation and representation of their subjectivity. It shows that objects and practices, hitherto dismissed as seemingly trivial aspects of their lives, had profound economic, psychological and social meanings. Thus such aspects of their material world offer readings of exactly how the women drew on their cultural capital to position themselves in relation to the initially alien environment and its peoples, and in relation to their peers.

In the preceding chapters on dress, living rooms and gardens this work has been at pains to demonstrate that genteel performance at a remove from the metropolis, far from being a reflection of fixed and predetermined social structures and practices, was an endlessly adaptable and flexible set of behaviours, which not only responded to but actually structured the ever-changing realities. Indeed, if the genteel woman was to establish and retain her position of cultural authority, her practice had to be reflexive; seeking to transfer her former values wholesale was surely likely to be doomed to practical, psychological and social disaster.

Food has particular qualities which give it a heightened sensitivity to its surroundings. Its very physicality ensures a complexity of practice; whether it is eaten raw or cooked, how it is to be prepared and presented and consumed, every stage of this process adds and determines further meaning. Equally, because of its transience, food processes are irrevocably linked to repetition, and constitute a crucial factor in the business of homemaking. Furthermore all these factors – its complexity, physicality and transience, plus its centrality in the household – make food practice a particularly useful means of examining the fluidity of notions of home, and hence change through time in relation to homemaking. Therefore food offers readings of another vital means of constructing female subjectivity in distinct temporal and spatial locations. It will be argued that food practice can be deconstructed in ways which undermine glib readings that suggest that form and style of consumption were primarily exercises in re-enactment of memory fuelled by nostalgia, or merely an unimaginative reworking of all things British. Such readings rob the woman of her agency and rationality. Here the case is made for saying that food practices lie at the heart of discourses about women as colonising agents in their own right.

As the domestic management of the household was invariably the woman's responsibility, and as a high store was set by the efficient provision of food as a key element in the control of the environment, the latter emphasised throughout this work as a cornerstone of genteel performance, it follows that the mistress of the house would have a distinctive relationship with food, quite different to that of other members of the household, who were essentially consumers and beneficiaries of her work. The constant and countless decisions the mistress of the house made with regard to food and its consumption can be seen as a key aspect of her capacity for agency and self-fashioning in her new terrain.

Despite these many arguments for the investigation of food, in this context and beyond, as a field of academic enquiry it has tended to suffer long-term neglect. Prior to the 1980s little serious work had been undertaken other than Barthes's seminal essay.[2] Food had been considered banal, essentially domestic in nature, and its importance was trivialised. Where it was deemed to merit attention it was usually in relation to cookery books and manuals of domestic management. Indeed this was a contributory factor to its neglect because some feminist historians saw food practices as part of a system of female oppression, unworthy of consideration in any other frame of analysis. There was also perhaps a hesitancy to examine food too closely because of its 'troubling' nature, its entering of the body and therefore its intimacy with the other bodily processes of expulsion and decay. Equally the transient nature of foodstuff means it eludes attempts to be elevated and ranked as a form of art, a higher order social activity. Where it had been considered it was usually in relation to banquets and feastings, thus privileging ceremonial performances over the details of everyday preparation, presentation and consumption. And finally, where work has been done on food in a colonial context there has tended to be possibly even more emphasis on notions of replicating Britishness than has been noted in the other topics examined in this work.³

Over the past thirty years, however, there has been the emergence and development of food history and analysis, with a marked emphasis on the cultural mechanisms surrounding consumption. This work has been undertaken primarily by anthropologists and sociologists and has tended to conform to one of two main schools of thought. The structuralists, most notably Barthes, Bourdieu, Douglas and Murcott, understand the meanings of food to be a social force. For example the relationship between the courses of a meal, which is such a predominant feature of meals in western society, or the values placed upon eating in groups as an indicator of social cohesion.⁴ The materialists or developmentalists, as exemplified by Mennell and Goody, focus on historical developments around food, such as the advent or limitations of technology plus biological and marketing factors.⁵ They criticise the structuralists for failing to allow for change over time, holding that they present food as fixed and immutable. The developmentalists in turn are sometimes held to make too little allowance for sociological aspects and the small-scale patterns of human behaviour.

As has been the case throughout this work this chapter pursues an unashamedly pluralistic approach. It takes food to be polysemic, and therefore holds that it cannot be explained with reference to just one over-arching theory but will instead make use of a number of works from a broad socio-anthropological base. Mennell's and Goody's multi-factorial historical approach is useful for developing a contextual understanding of the women's lives, and an awareness that the context would change through time. The discussion will also draw on the work of Barthes and of Douglas who see food as a means of communication, as a key part of the way societies are regulated and controlled, a stance especially helpful for examining the woman as food facilitator and manager. There will also be consideration of the usefulness of the 'food as language' metaphor employed by structural theorists as, despite developmentalists' accusations of universalism, language can surely be understood to have as fluid and responsive an agency as food. Indeed it can be said to share the hypersensitivity of food, and its shared orality is no coincidence. Douglas has been justly criticised for drawing too large a set of conclusions about food on the basis of small-scale studies – her oft-cited work 'Deciphering the Meal' was based on the main meal habits of her own immediate family – but her close focus on the domestic environment and the interactions of the household about and around food serves as a useful schema for examining in other temporal locations that which she terms the 'meal system'.⁶ Although Barthes's work on food was undeveloped, being limited to just one essay, his placing of food on the broader canvas of surrounding society and his recognition of the part played by ritual, association and taboo provides a valuable tool for analysing the complex meanings of food in colonial societies. However, as for the other chapters, Bourdieu's work continues to be of paramount value for this enquiry, for it explicitly links the material world with the cultural. His extensive work on the concept of 'taste' is particularly useful for considering the meanings of ritual in genteel foodways and the ways in which that most hierarchical of worlds was expressed, consolidated and furthered through the hierarchies of practice.

This chapter gives an overview of domestic management in Britain, providing the background against which to set practices empire-wide. The discussion then turns to a close study of aspects of food, not only the ingredients and their preparation, but also a broad range of activities involving labour input (mistress-servant interactions), costings (household accounts and marketing) and presentation (the tableware, menus and the settings). As food is sited within such a broad field it is logical to consider these elements separately, whilst also being ever mindful that, as with all material practices, the meaning of the parts is cumulative. Food practices prove to have been a particularly rich means by which the woman demonstrated her abilities to adapt and survive, and to establish her genteel household and thereby her position of social strength.

'She looked well to the ways of her household, and eateth not the bread of idleness':[7] food and household management in Britain

To manage her household successfully the genteel woman in Britain needed to draw upon a vast body of expertise, ranging from how to manage her servants, the supervision of food preparation (how actively she was involved in preparing food depending almost entirely upon the household income), to the provisioning of the kitchen, the keeping of her household accounts, menu planning and meal presentation. It was assumed that the skills and knowledge for this undertaking would be acquired from her mother and other female members of the family, and/or from the plethora of guidance manuals, all of which had much to say on the subject of the woman's role as household manager.[8] Note the high tone adopted by Mrs Beeton in commencing her instruction with a quotation from Proverbs: 'Strength and honour are her clothing, and she shall rejoice in time to come. She opened her mouth with wisdom, and in her tongue is the law of kindness. She looked well to the ways of her household, and eateth not the bread of idleness'. This lofty exhortation is then supported with this organisational and managerial point: 'As with the Commander of the Army, or the leader of the enterprise, so it is with the mistress of the house'.[9] A similar tone was adopted by Mary Jewry in *Warne's Everyday Cookery* published some thirty years later: 'the mistress of a family commands a small realm of which she is queen. Let her rule with justice, meekness and quietness'.[10] Thus duty here is gendered and a woman's knowledge is clearly articulated as having value and meaning for herself, her household and for the wider society. The publication of so many guidance volumes, intended for both British and colonial markets, is surely an indicator of social anxieties and of the value placed on success.

To assist the mistress of the house in this complex undertaking she had a corresponding richness of material goods and, until the turn of the century and under normal conditions, a ready supply of relatively able and willing servants. Indeed so significant were servants as a mark of rank that it is scarcely an exaggeration to say that their presence was rated almost as highly as the actual work they performed. As *The Servant's Practical Guide* put it, 'without the constant co-operation of well-trained servants, domestic machinery is completely thrown out of gear, and the best bred of hostesses placed at a disadvantage'.[11] All too often, in the opinion of the employers, these servants proved to be broken cogs, positively intent on disrupting the domestic machinery. Criticisms of their employees and accounts of their supposed shortcomings were published every bit as frequently, if not more often, as assertions that they simply could not do without them. As will be seen in the ensuing discussion, dissatisfaction with servants took on a whole new dimension when they were called upon to set high standards in challenging circumstances empire-wide.

As the middle classes grew and a greater number of households could afford more complex material possessions there was a perceived need amongst employers that the servants should also be a more complex commodity and possess more sophisticated skills. For example, by mid-century onwards one sees an increasing popularity in dining *à la russe* in which the diners are served individually, rather than serving themselves from communal dishes, a presentation style which necessitated having a number of well-trained staff. In reality, however, specialisation was really only found in a very small number of those in service, and they were employed by the upper echelons of society. For the majority of households their female servants were maids of all work, as indicated by the 1871 census which recorded that of the 1.2 million women working as servants nearly two-thirds were categorised as 'general'.[12] All the more important therefore that the mistress should have a firm grasp of household affairs and be in a position to impart her knowledge to her all-purpose servant(s). As Jewry asserted, 'we should have fewer bad servants if they were all under the firm and patient training of an employer who understood what their duties really were, and required the best fulfilment of them, compatible with the frailty of human nature'.[13]

Attention to detail was held to be a cornerstone of household management, and this was exemplified by the keeping of household accounts. By the mid-nineteenth century it was common for girls to be taught some elements of accounting along with basic numeracy, and by the end of the century it was assumed that all literate girls should be equal to the task of balancing the books. Advice manuals provided models and detailed guidance as to how to go about this key task.[14] All household expenditure was duly entered into an account book, be it a volume commercially produced for the purpose or, in more modest households, merely a hand-lined notebook. Foodstuffs were recorded of course, but so too were all costs involving the running and maintenance of the home. Thus household repairs, servants' wages, gas and coal bills, clothing, laundry and medical accounts were all recorded. By such means could the mistress of the house minimise waste, monitor spending and thereby, in theory, control her realm.

Such then was the cultural capital which the woman was required to take to her new home, knowledge shared, understood and valued by her peers. It was to be a key element in mediating her new surroundings and thereby re-establishing her cultural authority in her colonial setting. When faced with the realities of the dislocation of migration – shocking in the otherness she encountered – there was a strong imperative to impose a sense and appearance of control and order over the supposed chaos of the alien surroundings. Food and its management were to prove critical in the success or failure of her enterprise to establish the new home.

'Before the kitchen was built I very often cooked my bread by moonlight, to avoid the great heat of the day':[15] *making meaningful food in colonial homes*

Food, in all its multifarious forms can be a powerful social force. When prepared and presented in ways with which the diner is long familiar it can proclaim Home – soothing or joyous as the occasions demands. When eaten communally it is infinitely reassuring for 'people eating similar food are trustworthy, good, familiar and safe'.[16] The dishes brought to the household table therefore mean so much more than mere nourishment; they signify an entire cultural landscape, and one which the diners travel through on a daily basis. For those moving to new locations the absence of recognisable forms of food can trigger a keen sense of deprivation, indeed loss. Marie Rousselet's memories of making bread by moonlight tell as much of a desire to be a homemaker and provider as of the rigours of the climate in North Queensland. Thus food has critical agency in the process of establishing oneself in a new home.

Running concurrently with a desire for customary food and long-established dining habits was the reality of the sheer impossibility of replicating the practices of the former home. Lack of the usual ingredients, be it because of access or climate, technological difficulties, such as limited cooking equipment, and servants who either were in short supply or were deficient in skills, all these and more posed serious challenges to the smooth running of provisioning the household. Overcoming the difficulties was the responsibility of the mistress of the house, a formidable and never-ending task. In the face of challenges, which of course varied in detail and scale across both sites and time, the woman had to develop strategies for maintaining some degree of elegance under trying circumstances. She had to make decisions regarding substitutions and compromises; sampling of the new and the unfamiliar might convey to all around her that her resources were constrained, but, if she was able to do it with sufficient éclat she could carry the day. When she was able to present a well-stocked and elegant table considerable power would accrue to her. If the food brought forth was 'good', in that specific sense of being culturally acceptable, not only would the physical health of the household benefit, but so too would the psychological health, and hence would show themselves to be successful colonisers.

It will be argued that there was a definite hierarchy to food practices, with that which created the right 'look' being held to be of supreme importance. Gentility was essentially performative in nature and therefore to be genteel one had to be seen to be genteel, with all aspects of presentation, from the table settings to the well-drilled servants, accorded the highest priority. Here servants are discussed in some depth as in many locations this vital 'commodity' was in worryingly short supply. Lack of specialist staff was of particular concern for the women who relied on a smooth and supposedly effortless performance. Although servants have been present in earlier chapters in relation to their other domestic duties, it is in relation to food practices that the mistress-servant dynamic comes into the foreground.

The next stage in food practice hierarchy was the menu, then the main dishes – in which it will be shown that for the diners meat generally took precedence over other foods – and finally fruit, vegetables and other supporting ingredients. In many colonies each stage in the foodway process was subject to challenge, and it is in their various responses to these challenges that the women can be seen negotiating their circumstances through the agency of food.

'Even he says we must have a dinner service, instead of a few willow pattern plates and dishes':[17] the importance of presentation

Elegant presentation was accorded the highest priority and therefore the women sought to establish it as rapidly as possible, and the challenges to which they were subjected and the strategies developed in response lie at the heart of this discussion. There were three main groups of people who loomed large in the woman's world and to whom she made a decisive statement by cultivating a high tone of presentation. To the family it was of course immediately recognisable, signifying a reassuring nurturing continuity and a controlled and stable environment. To her social peers and others of European heritage, immaculate food presentation was a display of both goods and knowledge which denoted rank and status and hence power. It was the basis on which she would be judged as a ladylike hostess.[18] It set the tone and an expectation for both repetition and reciprocity, denoting insider status. Thus in new colonies, or those subject to rapid change – as for example during mining booms in Australia – she solidified an alarmingly fluid social situation, or at least she created the illusion of stability.

By employing in the colony the familiar British genteel conventions – or at least acceptable variations of the model – she sustained the group on its course for a projection of gentility. Rapid establishment of the 'right look' had a bolstering effect, all-important in colonial societies where gentility faced even more challenges than it had in Britain, as many of the reassuring social markers were absent and it was so much harder to tell who 'really mattered'. The third group sharply differentiated by the performance of stylised presentation was the household servants. The display of alien material items and associated practices served to emphasise and reinforce the cultural divide between those designated 'other', be it for reasons of race or rank, and any potential for a 'pollutant' presence was distanced. The woman's household presentation proclaimed her status and her superiority, both social and racial.

Members of all three groups, family, guests and servants, were present in the dining room when the woman acted as hostess. The centrepiece for this performance was the dining table, wherever possible made of highly polished substantial timber, be it of local or British manufacture, as a symbol of 'the family's honour as ritualists and hosts'.[19] Equally, the dining table can be read as a female space because the items she elected to display had both individual and collective meaning for the woman, and because everything contributed to this aspect of her enactment of self as the civiliser of the domestic space and giver of hospitality. Arranging and decorating the table in an aesthetically pleasing manner seems to have been of universal importance, a subject of intense discussion and the vagaries of fashion. British publications of the day provided regular advice on how to create an attractive table. The periodical *The House* included articles on 'Serviette Folding' and 'The Table Tasteful' in every issue from 1897 to 1900 (see Figure 5.1).

Mrs Beeton gave precise instruction of all aspects of table settings, directives which were evidently valued by at least some readers, as witness Mrs Russell in Gambia – see below. The *Gardener's Magazine* also ran regular articles on the use of foliage for table decorations.[20] Use of floral arrangements to feminise domestic interiors has also been discussed in Chapter 3 in relation to living rooms.

By the mid-nineteenth century it was customary to cover the table with a smooth starched white cloth, ideally Irish linen or damask. Attention to the detail of laundering and pressing of table linen equates with the care devoted to the maintenance of dress, as discussed in Chapter 2. Such cloths would be transported overseas and great care devoted to preserving them from the damage wreaked on textiles in hot climates by mould and insects.[21] Table cloths were often part of a woman's trousseau, sometimes handed on from generation to generation, emblematic of the women's knowledge. Sylvia Leith-Ross commented on the lengths to which women went to transport their possessions to African colonies: 'I wonder how many of my sister-in-law's tablecloths, sliding off a pack camel's back, still lie at the bottom of Lake Chad'.[22]

The care typically taken with table arrangement is shown by Emma Rutherfoord's description from Cape Town in the 1850s when, whilst acting as mistress of the house, she arranged a 'tea-party for seventeen people served at seven thirty in the dining-room'. Note how she lingers over the detail of the display: 'In the centre was a trifle, two very elegant dishes of fruit, peaches and grapes, the grapes hanging over the sides, my classical arrangement, cakes etc, a tart and a blancmange and then four pretty little glass dishes of preserves. These are the sort of things I pride myself in displaying good taste'.[23] Rutherfoord clearly places as much store by the 'look' of the table as by the comestibles thereon. Note particularly how each item is described in order to flag up its place in the genteel performance. Katie Hume offers us a similar description of her latest tableware: 'We have a new dinner service – 120 pieces. I thought we should have to build a new room to put it away in! It is green – nothing choice, but we have put up with odds and ends, which

THE TABLE TASTEFUL.

A FLOWER OF THE MONTH: THE CARNATION.

It is by no means an uncommon thing to see dinner tables loaded with rare and beautiful flowers, whose very abundance and lack of taste in arrangement militate seriously—considered from an artistic point of view—against the success of the schemes which they constitute. A few flowers, daintily disposed, are far to be preferred before huge masses of blossom and foliage, and among those who devote that attention to the subject that it deserves, a desire for greater simplicity is becoming more and more apparent. The

From the simple ferns and wild grasses, now so abundant, to the rarest species, it is difficult to make a choice, but, on the other hand, what results may be obtained by their aid! Most of those mentioned last month are still easily obtainable, and it is therefore unnecessary to give a fresh list.

In the accompanying scheme it will be seen that two hearts, composed of blossoms and foliage, form the centrepiece, and who shall say that an arrangement of this kind might not turn the conversation in the direction desired by some modern Daphnis trying to screw up his courage to the crucial point, and lead to the happiest issue. With some apt quotation, revealing at once an erudite "poetic soul" and a longing for something higher than the products of the kitchen, the ball would be set rolling, and Cupid might be left to do the rest.

rare taste of our Princess of Wales finds expression in the embellishment of the domestic dinner table in a bunch of lilies of the valley, when in season, placed in an unpretentious vase; and that is an example which may well be borne in mind by those whose fancy is in the direction of overloading the festive board. This warning is particularly needed just at this time of the year, when Nature is so prodigal of her gifts, and lovely flowers in almost endless profusion seem almost to be crying out: "We are here for your delight: use us all!"

But we must descend from the domain of Venus to that of Flora, to give a few practical hints regarding this design. Our suggestion is that mixed carnations—Napoleon's favourite flower—with croton leaves and asparagus fern should be employed, dark and light blossoms alternating, the two hearts being bound together by broad silk ribbon. The swags or festoons of flowers supported by the lamps and vases would add greatly to the appearance of this centrepiece.

5.1 Guidance on table-setting from the periodical *The House*, London, 1897.

Walter calls "sordid"'.[24] The quantity of crockery purchased is of note. At that time the Humes had not yet had any children, so the implication is that they intended to do some fairly ambitious entertaining, and to that end were working to create a refined performance, though it was but little more than eighteen months since they had arrived in the colony. Isabella Russell's description from Gambia, West Africa is equally revealing:

> I laid the table myself to show 'the boys', folded the table napkins in quite a fashionable manner thanks to studying 'Mrs. Beeton's Household Cookery' and dressed the table in blush pink silk and dishes of crystallised fruits and fancy biscuits ... I flatter myself the table was quite dainty; on the pink silk I had the wrought iron and copper lamp in the centre, four dishes and silver spoons and two pretty little silver castors the Hogarths gave me, so it looked quite bright. We came out without any sherry glasses or sherry decanter so I had to borrow them from Mrs. Pierce! Also having no dessert set, I used the white Coalport breakfast service plates, but they did very well. Our dinner set of grey white and gold Wedgwood that Dr and Mrs. Jim Russell gave us looked very nice.[25]

Despite a certain amount of compromise Mrs Russell pronounced this, their first formal dinner party, 'a great success'. The detailed and precise description and lively use of language not only bear witness to the high value accorded to 'table art' but also suggest that she took an additional pride and pleasure in her achievement made in adverse circumstances.

Arguably, Russell was quite consciously self-fashioning in a manner distinctly different from her performance in Britain. Chattopadhyay notes that the number and quality of dinner services and tableware were key material indicators in Anglo-Indian households. It seems reasonable to assume that in the young colony of the Gambia at the turn of the century, where Isabella Russell was one of just a handful of European women, the material culture of genteel society was obliged to be more flexible.[26] Equally, that Mrs Pierce was willing to lend her sherry glasses and decanter can be read as a sign of a communal concern to present a refined image to these important visitors from beyond the colony, and if the necessary material items had to be spread thin then so be it. Georgina Bowen, writing in 1864 from New Zealand to her sister in Britain, seems not to have hesitated in explaining that when they had a large party to dinner at two o'clock 'We had to have another table in the Diningroom [sic] and to borrow knives and forks from Milford'.[27] Anecdotes such as these lead one to wonder if all the items so proudly displayed at the wedding breakfast, see Figure 5.2, were in fact the property of more than one household. These examples, and

5.2 Table set for wedding feast, possibly for the marriage of Catherine Foley and Thomas Young, Tasmania, c.1891.

the way they are described by the women concerned, lend credence to the argument that shared genteel presentation was sometimes prioritised over ownership. Better to reinforce the genteel insider group, with all the associated messages that sent out to outsiders, than to let standards slip. Such examples of co-operation in the essentially competitive world of gentility are another indication of adaptation and the emergence of a distinctly different interpretation of what constituted refinement. It suggests that far from there being a predetermined set of rules which must be adhered to, which would imply that gentility was fixed and predetermined, rather was gentility a responsive form of knowledge which was in a constant state of flux.

It can be argued that as the complexities of genteel society served to distance the woman from the site of food production, namely the kitchen, so it became ever more important to cultivate this 'table art'. Attar identifies changes in the presentation styles of these formal meals during the Victorian period, with an increased emphasis on dainty and aesthetically complex presentation, providing a mechanism for making modest quantities of food look like grand spreads. Thus aspiring households could still present a genteel table even if the budget was stretched.[28] So the number of items placed on the table increased, though they did not necessarily have a utilitarian purpose. Although Attar is speaking about the British model it seems possible that this trend may have proved useful in colonial settings when limited foodstuffs were available, or indeed where a limited *range* of foods was available, and hence it was harder to differentiate social difference through the actual dishes served.

Such may well have been the case in remote sites in North Queensland where the climate and difficulties of communications constrained access to foodstuffs and related commodities. It seems very probable then that there may have been a gap between this splendidly articulated advice on the 'Ladies Page' of the *North Queensland Register* in 1884 and actual practice:

> To be fashionable now a dinner party must not count more than 12 guests at the utmost, however large the dining-room may be. Flowers are still grouped around but no longer scattered on the tablecloth, which fashion has become disagreeable after a while. Old family plate is to remain on the sideboards; this takes away some of the brilliancy of the table, but the mellow colours of the porcelain have a great softness and charm of their own. The invasion of plated silver, and the cheapness of it, has most likely been the cause of this new decoration for the tables of the rich.[29]

That such advice was published indicates that social anxieties found expression in the new colony in northern Australia in relation to food just as they did elsewhere. It suggests a concern for all aspects of the presentation of the meal, and an assumption that the meanings of any changes to that performance would be understood by the truly discerning amongst their readers, including those social aspirers who sought instruction. This in turn implies a network of well-developed social interactions, though possibly taking place within a society where the hierarchies were not yet fixed and were open to challenge, and where therefore social insecurities would trigger ever more nuanced behaviour.

One must be cautious, however, about assuming that those keeping house in the outback always adhered to such proscriptive advice. The demands of life were such that formal entertaining had to give way to 'bush hospitality'. It was common practice, particularly during the first decades of white colonisation, to maintain an open-door policy to other European settlers and travellers; not least to supply refuge from the extremes of the weather and the possibility of encounters with increasingly angry and desperate indigenous peoples that could quite literally mean the difference between life and death.[30] Callaway comments that

FOOD AND HOUSEHOLD MANAGEMENT

5.3 Dining with some style amidst the cockatoos, Queensland, 1907–9.

what she describes as the 'fictive kinship of European travellers in an alien environment' also prevailed in Nigeria during the early stages of white colonisation.[31] Such spontaneous social interactions naturally prevail against elaborate and formal meals. A homemaker who could, at short notice, transform a meal for the family into good fare for a much larger group was surely more likely to be highly regarded than one who knew that flowers should now be bunched, not scattered. Equally the use of the verandah as both dining and living room (see also the chapter on living rooms) would foster a more informal style of food practice, as indicated by Lucy Gray's description of a visit to a house in Reedy Lake, North Queensland, in 1868: 'The verandah (the chief part of a Queensland house), is very wide. There is a long table where the evening meal takes place, here in the dry season, immediately the sun goes down[,] people lounging about in their white clothes'.[32] Similarly a contemporary photograph of women dining on a verandah – Figure 5.3 – reveals that although the niceties are being duly observed, in terms of the napkin-rings, the crisp white tablecloth and the tableware, the paraphernalia of outdoor living is scattered around and there is an air of informality not normally associated with dining in more temperate climes. See also Figure 2.4, where, to those unaccustomed to such a style of hospitality, the dainty tea-table may seem somewhat at odds

[199]

with the canvas water cooler hanging from the verandah roof and the bare floorboards.

This discussion of presentation has demonstrated, with the aid of illustrations from Gambia, New Zealand, North Queensland and South Africa that practice varied as it responded to challenges across both time and place but always remained a critical aspect of gentility. For those women of genteel persuasion, creating the right 'look' was a precondition of being genteel, and hence an integral part of their performance. There was one commodity that they deemed essential in all households across the Empire, without which the women could not conceive of achieving and maintaining the supposedly effortless 'finish' to their foodways presentation, and it is to that component of the process that the discussion turns next.

'Chose to get a beau and left me at ten minutes notice':[33] *servants, the most troubling of commodities*

In commencing this exploration of the contribution of the servant to the genteel household it is important to stress again the point made throughout this work that performance is not in any way to be understood as artifice – it is the enactment of identity. It follows therefore that even in relation to food, presentation is in fact self-presentation. Bourdieu's assertion that for different classes 'the investment of time, effort, sacrifice and care which they actually put into [presentation is] proportionate to the chances of material or symbolic profit they can reasonably expect from it' was cited in the chapter on dress. It is equally applicable here.[34] As has been stated, the aim of the genteel woman was to establish and maintain her cultural authority and social position, and therefore control of her environment was paramount. The 'profit' was her very identity; the 'effort' she made entirely commensurate with such a goal. Without that most essential of commodities, a good supply of biddable and efficient servants, the genteel performance would be subject to one of its greatest challenges. It follows therefore that in this discussion of the mistress-servant dynamic, the defining analysis of the relationship will be that the servant was just that, first and last, a commodity. Not only is this an appropriate stance for this enquiry, but it was the way in which contemporary advice manuals and indeed personal writings handled the subject.

In focusing on this functional nature of the presence of servants there is clearly a risk that complex relations between people sharing domestic space, sometimes for extended periods of time and under testing circumstances, will be grossly oversimplified. It is not the intention to be reductive or deny such complexities, but rather to explore just one aspect of the servant's presence – how and to what extent they contributed to, and impacted upon, their employer's performance.[35]

Factors influencing whether the woman could get good service from her servants were their availability, gender, race, the languages they spoke, geographical location of the household, and the actual layout of the house. Of course categorising the factors in this fashion is to make somewhat artificial distinctions, for inevitably there were links and overlaps between them. Equally the list is not exhaustive, and omits such significant aspects of the dynamic as the age, life experience and personality of both the mistress of the house and the servant. Nonetheless in order to consider the process of adaptation in various sites this discussion will concentrate on strategies some women developed to overcome challenges to the smooth running of their households. For the purposes of analysing food practices the positions of cook and attendant staff are of course of most consequence, but references are also made to other servants in order to provide appropriate contextual information. In smaller households, or in areas where the commodity was scarce, there was not the same demarcation of duties as was customary in larger households or in sites with an abundance of servants. So in some sites it is not really possible to speak specifically of kitchen and serving staff, unless they are actually described as cooks, and even then they often seem to have had other duties, whereas in other locations, notably in India and West Africa, distinctions and demarcations were integral to the employment of household staff.

When and where possible homemakers seem to have favoured the employment of Europeans as servants, an approach that must have seemed logical; the physical similarities would perhaps be reassuring and, in theory at least, such labour was more likely to be familiar with the domestic customs of European homes. Unsurprisingly employing people principally on the basis of the colour of their skin often proved less than satisfactory. In New Zealand in 1850 Charlotte Godley described how some of her neighbours in Wellington, 'the *greatest* people here', despite having five children, only had 'three house servants; two maids, girls who are nurses and housemaids, and a discharged soldier with long black hair, a light shooting jacket (always) and dirty hands, who is everything else', and how that experience 'goes to prove strongly the impossibility of getting anything like decent servants here'. In consequence the mistress of the house was 'sometime in the kitchen every day'. Godley is careful to explain that although there is a roughness to some aspects of the household there is an 'abundance of good things'. Clearly she considered Mrs Petrie had risen to the challenge of cultural adjustment.[36] Similarly when, some twenty years later, Sarah Courage spoke of her difficulties in securing good servants to work in the home on their Canterbury sheep station she was at pains to explain how she had to instruct her Irish maid on the 'art and mystery' of answering the door and how, prior to those lessons, Courage and her friend 'had a good laugh over Mary's blunders'.[37] The anecdote not only serves to demonstrate that Courage knew how to establish genteel performance in an uncivilised setting – it also flags up that such standards were adhered to from the early days of settlement.

A different form of local challenge was experienced amongst the early settlers of southern Tasmania, where the government policy of supplying prisoners to work as servants seems to have prompted a decidedly mixed response, with inevitable concerns about their acceptability and respectability. Mrs Allport's first impression was that 'our assigned convict servant came – a scotch woman and remarkably clean', but within less than two months Marion had been sent back because of drunkenness and been replaced by another 'old Scotch woman'.[38] Mrs Meredith was characteristically forthright, declaring 'Prisoner women servants are generally of a lower grade than the men ... my first prisoner nurse-girl ... dirty beyond all imagining! She drank rum, smoked tobacco, swore awfully, and was in all respects the lowest specimen of womanhood I ever had the sorrow to behold'.[39] Even non-convict servants of British stock were unreliable, according to Martha Axford, who recorded that her neighbour 'expected a new servant up on Saturday to the Green Ponds, Kempton per Coach, so hired a cart at 15 shillings – and sent for her – could not find her all over the place – sent again on Sunday, another 15 shillings – found her at a public house. Coach hire to pay, expenses at the Inn and now she cannot cook not even a mutton chop'.[40]

Perhaps it is no surprise then that more 'respectable' servants were keenly sought, and certainly after the abolition of transportation in 1853 the numbers of advertisements in Tasmanian newspapers suggest that demand outstripped supply. An edition of the *Mercury* in January 1867 itemises fourteen posts available for laundress, nurses, nursemaid, manservant, general servants, plain cooks and kitchen maids.[41] This suggests that at this date there was an expectation amongst employers that servants should be specialists. It seems though that retaining staff was a common difficulty, and evidently there was a gap between the employer's expectations and realities. Higman's work on domestic service in Australia reports that during the period 1856–57 Tasmanian resident Mrs Arthur Davenport engaged no fewer than twenty-five individuals to fill the posts of gardener, laundress and cook. The women stayed on average twenty-two weeks and the men sixteen.[42] Of course it may be that the servants did indeed prove unsatisfactory, but a more likely interpretation is that the servants themselves were able to be selective in their choice of posts. In 1868 Hobart resident James Reid Scott's household accounts record that in six months the outlay for paying servants was £24 6s 8d. The family employed a cook, housemaid, assistant housemaid and charwoman. (The nurse's wages are not included, being itemised separately along with other nursery expenses.) Although the Reid Scotts evidently were a family of some status the payment of domestic servants does appear to have formed a sizable percentage of their monthly expenditure, which may also suggest that good staff were at a premium.[43] By the 1880s and beyond, when the state was suffering an economic depression, the advertisements in the press indicate that there were more people seeking posts as servants than there were posts to be filled.[44] Thus it can be seen that in Tasmania, as was the case in New Zealand and North Queensland, the supply of servants and the dynamic of employer-servant relations changed dramatically over the period 1840–1910.

Along with accusations, justified or otherwise, of drunkenness, lack of skill and general dirtiness, the other bugbear amongst employers was that their servants were alarmingly lacking in due deference. By mid-century it had become all too apparent that the idealised unfailingly respectful servant was gone, and instead defiance and individuality were often uncomfortably evident. Indeed it may be that such independence of spirit lay behind Mrs Davenport's staffing difficulties, as cited above. Trollope witnessed this shift in the social balance in southern Australia, saying 'The maidservant in Victoria has the pertness, the independence, the mode of asserting by her manner that though she brings you up your hot water, she is as good as you [she] does not shake in her shoes before you because you have £10,000 a year'.[45] If the servant did not show respect then how was the genteel woman to maintain the illusion that she was indeed culturally superior to her employee? This fear of erosion of difference, of no longer being differentially positioned in relation to her servants, lay at the heart of her anxieties; it was a profound source of disquiet for genteel women in many sites and cannot be entirely separated from other complexities of difference.

Elizabeth Ann Anning handles the subject with gentle irony; she had travelled south to Melbourne from the north of Queensland during the 1870s for the birth of her first child, advertising prior to her return 'for a respectable woman to accompany a lady to Queensland'. She received over forty applicants and described how 'one was very concerned to know whether I really was a lady as she had always served ladies. I told her I was afraid I would not suit *her*!'[46] Lewis and Foy comment that 'English servants could be found in South Africa, in ever decreasing numbers admittedly, throughout the nineteenth century [but] they presented problems in a country where social distinctions were drawn by colour rather than by class'. They cite by way of illustration Mrs Heckford, who in the 1880s stated:

> It is certainly demoralising for English servants to come out to this country. They may begin fairly; but even serving under one whom they acknowledge as undeniably their social superior, their ideas of master and man are liable to become confused after a time ... It is not easy to keep up the proper distance between master and servant when the very people one is called upon to bring coffee to whilst they sit on a visit to this master ... are ready to drop into familiar conversation with him the next moment.[47]

Mrs Heckford's remarks surely highlight that social distinctions were drawn by class *in addition to* race, and therein lay the difficulty for would-be elites.

In the absence of servants of European heritage, the mistress of the house was compelled to employ those of other nationalities. The homemakers of northern Australia drew from a particularly complex pool of resources, employing indigenous peoples, migrants from China or, prior to 1891, migrants from the Pacific Islands. In their personal writings the women in the north often prefixed their remarks about their servants by identifying their race. Thus the quality or lack thereof in the servant was attributed to some supposedly inherent racial characteristics. The consequence of this was that one 'group' of servants could then be compared with another – thus the servant was both commodified and racialised. Mina Rawson, for example, was said to have preferred Pacific Islander women to Europeans to help her around the house as she found the former to be more reliable. In the north the majority of the Chinese migrants were single men who had travelled to Australia to work in the goldfields, but in the face of increasing anti-Chinese sentiment many had been driven to seek employment elsewhere, as shepherds or stockmen, as gardeners or as cooks. In the latter capacity they seem to have been highly regarded, with Jane Bardsley declaring that following problems with a cook from New Caledonia she and her husband vowed 'that until we can get a Chinaman we shall not bother with any cook'.[48]

The Pacific Islanders were usually referred to as kanakas (frequently without capitalisation), a Hawaiian word often defined as one who (merely) works in the fields. Thus the term itself was both marginalising and denigrating. Despite this they were usually compared favourably with the indigenous people. Note how Lucy Gray describes the two groups:

The South Sea Islanders take so much interest in everything, they want to know the meaning and use of all they see, and gaze with open eyes and mouths at a sewing machine, harmonium, or whatever is new to them. While the native blacks, until they have become partly civilised do not seem to have the bump of wonder and look with indifference on whatever they are not accustomed to see. The wild ones have only part of their faculties in use.[49]

On 1 January 1891 legislation came into operation which prohibited the import or employment of any new labour from the Pacific Islands. There was also an actively pursued policy of expelling existing migrants and compelling them to return to their place of origin. After they ceased to be part of the labour pool they were often spoken of rather wistfully. Robert Gray went so far as to suggest a supply of 'good coloured servants' could be the determining factor for permanent white settlement.[50] His use of the term 'coloured' is taken to mean Polynesians rather than indigenous Australians, and if that is the case then evidently even by the turn of the century he did not consider indigenous workers to be acceptable domestic employees. Gray's reservations were by no means atypical of European attitudes, despite which the employment of indigenous people as house servants became increasingly more common.[51]

One means of obtaining house servants was to take indigenous children from their families and teach them European ways. Presumably it was considered that the young had not yet become 'hardened savages' and they could be 'civilised'. Lucy Gray describes how her husband 'returned from Townsville lately bringing with him a little "gin" and a black boy. Mournful looking creatures they were, when first they came. The girl, who was about twelve, was for me to train to be a servant'.[52] Stealing children to suit their needs must of course have been a significant contributory factor in the conflict between the two races, and hence increased white anxieties. This would surely reduce the effectiveness of the system as a means of obtaining satisfactory labour, though as most references of racial violence were excluded from their personal writings it is difficult to quantify.

Given the vast cultural gulf across which the Europeans and indigenous peoples faced one another, it is scarcely surprising that relations were less than ideal. The colonists constructed the indigenous peoples as barbaric, and this image was of course regularly reinforced until late in the century by the accounts of cattle raids – which stressed and scattered the stock even if not many were actually killed – and of attacks on isolated and vulnerable settlers.[53] Whilst these stories were based on actual events, there can be little doubt that they were magnified in the telling, which doubtless also strained servant-employer relations, and reduced the servant's usefulness in supporting the household structures.

On the face of it, supply should have been the one problem which the mistress did not encounter in India. However, the intricacies of the caste system necessitated finer divisions of tasks than was customary in households in other sites with servants of other races and religions. By the European mistress's standards this made the servants inefficient, and it was often claimed that was why they were employed in such large numbers, though in truth the size of the household staff was ever a marker of distinction and rank. Buettner speaks of ten to twenty servants in the homes of upper-ranking civil servants, and Chattopadhyay of ten to sixteen for the wife of a civil servant.[54] Personal writings also reveal a tendency to lump together differences of caste, race and religion, and such lack of awareness typifies the cultural misunderstandings which abounded between the British residents and the indigenous peoples. Such misunderstandings were exacerbated if not actually caused by the mistress's inability to speak, or lack of fluency in, their employees' languages.

Unless and until the mistress could communicate with her staff she could not effectively control her kingdom. It was for such reasons that Flora Steele's guidance manual for memsahibs strongly advocated that Anglo-Indians learn Hindustani, as 'the first duty of the mistress is of course to be able to give intelligible orders to her servants'.[55] Such advice does seem to have been followed by many, though with varying degrees of commitment and success, as indicated by Sheila Warwick's remark that her grandmother 'spoke proper Hindustani, not just kitchen Hindustani'.[56] Clementina Benthall recorded that she and her sister 'manage to make our wishes known to our domestics, and they are very quick in grasping our meaning, and in speaking by signs, with the help of a pocket guide I contrive to give all needful orders when Edward is absent, but it is frequently very puzzling to express my meaning when more than a command is requisite, I cannot often comprehend the answer to any questions'.[57] Eustace Kenyon related that his wife and servant overcame the difficulty of communication when they discovered they had an unexpected common language: 'It is most amusing to hear Ethel talking to our old khitmajor; you know the servants here do not speak English as a rule, and he is no exception, but he does talk French! And rather well, and he and Ethel converse like anything. He is a fatherly old gentleman too, and takes great interest in E, doing his best to tempt her to eat well and so on'.[58]

Inevitably the British homemakers in West Africa experienced similar concerns as to how to communicate with their house staff. Mrs Melville in Sierra Leone makes her frustrations decidedly clear:

FOOD AND HOUSEHOLD MANAGEMENT

'Then all my perplexities in endeavouring to make myself understood by the native servants! Not a single sentence that they utter can I comprehend, and they seem as confused by my mode of speech. I ... am told that until I too can talk "country fashion" there's no chance of the household being conducted with regularity or comfort'.[59] Larymore's insistence that her Nigerian servants adopt a lingua franca by speaking Hausa which was not necessarily their first language can be understood as another example of a controlling tactic.[60]

Wages were generally low. Of pay in India, Macmillan notes: 'In the 1890s even the most expensive, a butler for example, cost only 20 rupees a month and a sweeper half of that'. By way of illustration she cites Annette Beveridge who had thirty-nine servants at a cost of 250 rupees per month – her husband's salary was 1,800 per month.[61] Constance Larymore in Nigeria in 1902 gives an itemised list of wages including 'Cook £2 – if an Accra boy £3 or £3 10s', and Decima Moore in Accra in 1908 comments: 'They received absurdly high wages, cooks getting as much as £4.00 a month'. Even Sylvia Leith Ross's more measured words record of their Nigerian cook that 'His salary of £3 a month and 2 shillings a week chop money was considered high'.[62] On the one hand then the servant was a highly valued commodity without whom their employer's lifestyle would collapse for they were the ultimate marker of rank and distinction, but on the other it was resented that they could command such a high price for their services. It could be argued that the high wages served to provide an uncomfortable reminder that the power in the relationship was not all on the side of the mistress. When Lucy Gray's employee Nungita sought to be additionally rewarded for some newly acquired skills, Gray recorded in her journal 'Nungita was a great loss to me. He valued his services very highly, and said he would stop for £1 a week if one of the others would stay. Hitherto they thought themselves rich with 12 shillings a month'.[63]

The grouches about the wages they had to pay epitomise a whole range of comments and complaints the women made about their servants. They suggest a reading of an attempt to objectify and indeed malign the characters of their servants to strip them of their individuality and reduce them to their material function. Thus Larymore again: 'the genus "houseboy" is a light-hearted, easy going, tractable sort of creature', or acidly 'one spends a rough £100 a year, for the services of seven people, all lazy and stupid, mostly untruthful, and frequently dishonest, ignorant of the first principles of order and cleanliness, considering missus rather a bore when she insists on trying to inculcate those'. Even when describing a satisfactory servant Larymore elects to flag up the least attractive aspect of his appearance and personality: 'I began to study the art of Nigerian housekeeping, and forthwith engaged a cook, a most unprepossessing looking individual, a Kru-boy, rejoicing in the name of Jim Dow; he proved an excellent cook, as they go in West Africa, but a frail vessel where intoxicants were concerned, nevertheless, he did us good service for three years in many places, was untiring on the march, and, in the main, sober'.[64] Mrs Melville in Sierra Leone doubts the efficiency of her workers saying 'the domestics here are all men, and they appear to be very indolent, so that you require eight or nine household servants, where in a similar establishment in England four or five would be found sufficient'.[65] Similarly, Decima Moore, also in West Africa, always spoke of her servants as 'boys' irrespective of their age.[66] Boase noted: 'My parents became very attached to their African servants – indeed my mother never really resigned herself to those of a lighter complexion – and their shortcomings and peccadilloes were regarded much as are those of a mischievous but endearing child'.[67] Such attitudes support Macdonald's assertion that 'the colonial relationship was one which took expression through the hierarchy and protectionism of parent-child interaction'.[68] In addition one can also identify within such behaviours that by casting doubts on their moral stature they could be reduced to being 'less than men', and by negating their manhood could generate a sense of safety, for surely such half-men would be more biddable and efficient.

Whilst these attitudes will strike the modern reader as distasteful, indeed shocking, their use is to be understood contextually. As discussed in the early section of this chapter the mistress of the house emerged from a society in which servants were frequently subject to censure; an inclination to criticise this commodity was part of her cultural background. Furthermore the mistress was rarely effectively prepared for life in her new home. She was often guilty, wittingly or otherwise, of absorbing prejudices regarding the indigenous peoples of the lands the British sought to colonise, and also came under pressure to participate in local hierarchies and occupy her appropriate place. Moreover, given the general lack of experience of the new arrival and her alarm at the alien scene, her attitudes though abhorrent start to be understandable. If in addition we recall that for many women their servants were not only their sole point of contact with the indigenous peoples, but in some cases their only companions beyond their menfolk then our readings of their words must also allow for a range of fears and insecurities, and indeed loneliness.

In relation to experiences of homemakers of British colonies in West Africa it must be borne in mind that for the period under investigation colonisation was in its infancy. So, we understand their practices as being both site and time specific. At this date, the women often saw themselves engaged on first-stage pioneering work, as witness

FOOD AND HOUSEHOLD MANAGEMENT

Constance Larymore's attitude that training her servants was a moral responsibility with far-reaching consequences:

> I only hope that every English woman who spends even a few months in Nigeria will leave behind her two or three servants inoculated with habits of scrupulous cleanliness, thoughtfulness and common sense, to lighten the load of some lonely man who now feels uncomfortably that in his mother's house at home the table-cloth is *not* hideously grubby and crooked, the milk and jam served in messy tins, the glasses cloudy, and the forks and spoons more than doubtful, but vaguely supposes all this is necessary in West Africa – *it isn't!*[69]

To set beside the admittedly bleak interpretation of human motivations discussed here, Calloway's views should be noted. She argues 'the evidence confronts one of the received ideas about colonial wives that they bickered continually with their servants. Most of these women grew up in households with servants and were used to the paternalistic (rather than merely contractual) relations that were closer to indigenous custom. On their part, servants felt they were moving up in the world, learning new skills and earning steady wages'.[70] Of course it is important not to overstate the case or construct elite Europeans as always and ever 'in opposition to'. It seems possible that in remote settings good relations may well have developed between the mistress and her servants, not least because of lack of alternative company. Equally Lady Nora Scott spoke generously – or at least fairly sensitively – of her employees: 'Butlers here in Bombay are often Goanese and consequently Christian. They are not forbidden therefore by their religion to touch our food, and I think we can hardly expect these men who have the control and purchasing of the food never to take any for themselves or their families. At least it is expecting a great deal for 20 or 25 rupees a month'.[71] Noordegraaf and Pouw have argued that for Europeans living in relative isolation in small enclaves their servants came to constitute a form of family.[72] This seems to be an overstatement, but does serve to highlight the complexity of the mistress-servant relationship, in which whatever the precise circumstances of the site servants were first and last a commodity, but one whose human form would forever challenge and contest such categorisation. Figure 2.4 is of interest in this regard. It shows a small group of European men and women taking tea on a verandah in North Queensland. A young Aborigine girl dressed in European dress is seated on the floor; her presence arguably ambiguous and troubling, creating space for reading of, at best, benign paternalism.

This analysis has argued that tests and tensions around and within the mistress-servant dynamic were not only a recurrent but indeed a central characteristic for many of those leading genteel lifestyles. In sites where there was a reliable supply of servants they were viewed as a staple, but in situations where the commodity was scarce they had the disconcerting habit of becoming an unexpectedly luxury item. Food practices, with their repetitive tasks, labour-intensive nature and endless complexities were utterly and irrevocably tied to the concept of servitude. Goody has argued that making claims concerning the relational aspect of food, in the fashion so beloved by structuralists, is of limited value unless set against other factors supported by empirical evidence.[73] This examination of mistress-servants relations has conducted just such an exercise, thereby validating the claim that performance, not just as a reflection but as a creator of reality, was constrained and inhibited without a satisfactory supply of this most critical of commodities.

This exploration of the meanings and values of the servant in colonial homes could not however conclude without a brief consideration of women who undertook the physical activities of food preparation themselves, but without suffering a loss of caste. The ostentatious use of domestic staff which is such a distinctive feature of descriptions of colonial life in Africa and India is largely absent from accounts produced in North Queensland and New Zealand, an absence which cannot be fully explained on the basis of lack of supply, for as has been shown in most locations there were various sources of labour available. Doubtless on occasion women had no choice but to take on the responsibilities of cooking, as when Eva Gray explains 'Our cook (a Chinaman), was run by one of the boys and left the same day – (before the flood) so I have plenty of opportunity for cooking, making yeast and bread, and soup and cakes and puddings and boiled beef etc'.[74] Listing the breadth and variety of her work serves to demonstrate her competences; she is more than equal to the task, a thoroughly capable coloniser. Equally Gray remained genteel, for true gentility was a question of sensibilities, and was entirely compatible with hard work. A lady should know how to instruct and supervise the servants, but if the situation called for one to take on the tasks oneself then there was no shame in that, and the only vulgarity would be in doing it badly, or with poor grace. Hence it may be argued that although genteel food practice must on occasion have been sorely tried, in North Queensland it rose to the challenge, and took on distinct site-specific forms.

The situation in the north of Australia can usefully be compared with that of New Zealand where there had been a shortage of servants from the onset of colonisation and where, as the population grew, so proportionately the number of servants fell. Macdonald's analysis constitutes servants at 15% of inhabitants of 12,812 private dwellings in 1858, a figure that had fallen to 9.4% of inhabitants of 57,182 private dwellings by 1871.⁷⁵ This called forth a variety of responses and strategies. The mistress of the house had two courses of action open to her – either to work harder at maintaining the status quo, by finding and keeping acceptable servants, or, more radically, undertaking more of the household tasks herself.

Adela Stewart gives us a representation of a proud and independent settler who did the work herself without losing face. She described her house on a farm in the North Island of New Zealand in the 1880s: 'the new kitchen had an earth floor so Lou [her lady companion] and I busied ourselves grubbing with our hands in the ploughed land for shells to strew thereon . . . It took us 4 days to lightly cover the small kitchen floor'.⁷⁶ This early example of her initiative in participating in the actual construction of the kitchen sets the tone for Stewart's text, and she relates how over the years she painted the kitchen dresser and mastered the notoriously difficult camp-oven. She also describes how despite the peaches ripening at the hottest time of the year she 'made 407 lbs of jam of them. I did the same with small lots of preserved tomatoes and pumpkins, making a grand total of 760 lbs. Thus I was prepared for a siege and stood it'. Thus, as with Eva Gray, Stewart presents her industry as heroic, celebrating her responses to the challenges of her new setting and declaring that in 'New Zealand when you want a thing done you do it yourself'.⁷⁷ Macdonald sees responses such as Stewart's as a redefining of what constituted work for these genteel women and concludes that 'what evolved was a strong practical and cultural tradition of independent housekeeping in which the household's ability to sustain itself was highly valued'.⁷⁸ In the previous chapters we saw how women engaged in a great variety of physical tasks in relation to their apparel, living rooms and gardens. Here we see again how some women positively embraced the opportunity to take on such responsibilities, and how their genteel practice was reformed in response to the challenges of the situation.

'A smoky little hut at the far side of the back compound':⁷⁹ the kitchen, critical but troubling space

In hot climates it was not uncommon for the kitchen to be sited in a separate building from the main house. There were, of course, practical advantages to such an arrangement. It kept the heat, smoke, cooking smells and noise at a distance, and was much safer in the event of fire. It also contributed to the performance of genteel living because the discordant elements – the messiness of food preparation and the people undertaking these physical tasks – were distanced, hidden away. However, another consequence of this physical removal was that for some the kitchen space came to symbolise the 'otherness' of their servants, for the servants' contact with the household food spelt intimacy, an intimacy with which some Europeans felt ill at ease.

Arguably this is why contemporary publications give so much commentary and management advice about kitchens. Guidance manuals produced for British homemakers in India and for those in African colonies, and personal writings by 'memsahibs', indicate an almost obsessional preoccupation with contemporary not to say culturally-specific notions of British cleanliness. Steele asserted that 'Inspection should begin immediately after breakfast, or as near ten o'clock as circumstances permit. The cook should be waiting – in clean raiment – with a pile of plates, and his viands for the day'.[80] Rumer and Jon Godden's account of their mother's daily kitchen inspection does resemble Steele's model, though the final qualifying phrase is rather telling: 'She looked at the table and the floor, lifted some of the dekchis from their papered shelf, tested their cleanliness with a finger, inspected the little mate's hands and nails, gave one or two admonitions and left'.[81] There seems to have been recognition that there was going to be a gap between theoretical standards and actual practice, that the realities of their location might necessitate adaptations and modifications beyond the outlines of some published advice. Indeed at least one work published at the end of the period examined acknowledged this disparity saying: 'Native ways of cooking are not by any means nice, in fact very often extremely nasty; therefore do not seek to know too much'.[82] Mrs Waterfield, in describing her life in the Sholapur District of India, reveals a pragmatic approach to the challenge of the alien kitchen:

> I go into the kitchen fairly frequently, paying spot visits when I have the courage to brace myself for what I may see ... I'm afraid I'm coming to the conclusion that to some extent it *is* bliss to be ignorant concerning these matters. After all, one *must* eat *something* and experience has shown me already how much food we can digest without ill results, which *cannot* have been prepared with the cleanliness that was next to Godliness.[83]

Mrs Melville in Sierra Leone seems to have been somewhat reluctant to have anything to do with the place, limiting herself to: 'Kitchens are almost always detached buildings, and in some instances mere grass sheds. I have only once had a peep into ours, the sole furniture of which seems to consist of an enormous grate of the rudest construction'.[84] By the turn of the century Constance Larymore, in seeking to prepare European women for homemaking duties, adopts a firm approach and urges the utmost attention to detail in relation to kitchen management: 'the Nigerian kitchen is arranged on the Indian plan – apart from the house, and just as much inspection and supervision will have to be exercised ... the kitchen table must be scrubbed with soap and water daily, the pans and utensils scoured, and the walls occasionally white-washed'.[85] So there are tensions to be identified here between the psychological need to feel at ease in one's own home – that which Miller terms an 'authentic locality', and the genteel requirement to distance pollutants, but simultaneously the desire to be understood as colonists, embracing and improving the indigenous peoples.[86]

'Monsignor was so delighted to find the menu written in French':[87] menus and recipes

During the week of 17 February 1900 the newly appointed Roman Catholic Bishop of Senegambia paid a visit to Bathurst, Gambia. Isabella Russell reported that he was 'received with band and flags etc and feted [sic] everywhere'. She evidently felt it to be a great honour for herself and her husband to provide a formal dinner for the bishop and four other local dignitaries.

She reported in a letter to her sister in Britain that the conversation was 'all in French, of a kind!!' and that 'Monsignor was so delighted to find the menu written in French, which I did for his benefit, on one of the pretty menu cards Mother sent me'.[88] By producing a permanent record of the meal, demonstrating her knowledge of at least culinary French and her understanding of how to construct a dainty bill of fare, Isabella is speaking of her grasp of and ease with genteel practice. Producing written menus was a common feature of elegant dining, understood and valued by contemporaries as a representation of women's foodway knowledge.[89] Note the central role Ada Slatter accords to the menu in her account of the dinner party for nine she held in her east African home: 'Colonel Rooseveldt [sic] took the menu card away with him, which was in front of him, as I had painted a flag with stars and stripes and stuck it in the corner of the menu supported by a "fairy hair pin!"'.[90] Wyvern, in his *Culinary Jottings for Madras*, acknowledges their significance and nicely conflates the two meanings when advocating a straightforward choice of dishes: 'Let the little card be clothed in the white garb of simplicity and completeness, and I am prepared to declare that *all* our lady guests, and a majority of the men we entertain, will rejoice at the result'.[91]

The menu, be it written object or simply following an accustomed pattern, reflected and extended the ritual of the meal, the meaning of its shape and the way in which the dishes were served in an orderly procession. This shaping of the meal, presented on the exquisitely prepared table, would be infinitely reassuring for the diners. Each course would remind the diners of the one which had preceded it and, by association, prepare them for what was to follow. Douglas argues that not only does each course recall the whole but so too does each meal recall other meals – the whole being termed a 'meal system'- and this system serves to communicate to all involved the permanence and the status of the event. Any deviation from the established format would seem not only absurdly inappropriate but indeed troubling. However, by focusing exclusively on the meal, Douglas neglects surrounding practice which is not merely supportive but is itself an integral part of the performance, all of which contributes to the articulation of taste and thereby social positioning.[92] Barthes, in speaking of a system of a food-centred means of communication, makes greater allowance for overall foodways than that permitted by a 'meal system'. Analysis of this grid of food practice, within which the meal is sited, reveals not only a variety of practice but also, it can be argued, the arbitrariness and inappropriateness of declaring particular elements British or 'other'.

Consider the example of Georgina Bowen, migrant to New Zealand in 1862, who, horrified to find eggs costing 2s 9d a dozen, was prompted to write to her sister in England: 'any receipt for pudding or anything in the way of 2nd course would be most valuable that could be made without eggs. Most of Mamma's receipts contain more than four'.[93] This raises the question of how many ingredients can be substituted and the recipe be said to remain the same? Surely, it is the meaning and value attributed to the dish which designates it as the recognisable – in this instance British – pudding. When consumed in remote New Zealand with commodities scarce it could be said to have quite different meanings to the supposedly same item when eaten amidst the plentiful supplies of Britain. What is seen here is less an erosion of authenticity, rather a redefining of what was deemed to be authentic.

By the same token the British 'out in the Empire' adopted and adapted so many of the local dishes that they ceased to be viewed as exotic and came to be seen as entirely acceptable for British tastes – of which perhaps 'curries of India' are the most striking example. Note for example Clementina Benthall's remark: 'to Curry in European fashion I always had a strong dislike, but the first tasted here altered my opinion of the dish and every day we have a change in the composition, but each is most excellent'.[94] So accustomed did the British become to such foods that Constance Larymore's advice to women setting up home in Nigeria, published in 1911, included the reassuring comment that 'once one has taught the cook how to make real curries – as they are made in India – a fair variety can easily be had'.[95]

In examining notions of the exotic within food habits it is equally important to avoid oversimplification of what was viewed within

Britain as acceptable fare during the period examined. The high value accorded to the 'roast beef of old England' and the annual urge to make and consume plum pudding are not to be understood as representative of the overall diet in colonial settings, any more indeed than that they were constant fare in England. By the mid-nineteenth century cookery books published in Britain indicate that an array of influences had already impacted upon at least some sections of the national diet. Thus Soyer's *Shilling Cookery Book* of 1855 suggests the substitution of Indian meal for rice and gives a recipe for 'Tame Rabbits Curried', the *Handy Dictionary* of 1886 has a curry recipe which includes coconut milk and recommends the use of a branded item – 'Captain White's Curry Paste', and Wyvern's work for Anglo-Indian exiles published in 1891 urges whilst 'at home' to seek out the 'Oriental Depot' in Leicester Square to procure 'Barrie's Madras Curry Powder and Paste'.[96] As cookery books invariably formalise existing culinary practices, the works cited would indicate that whereas Panayi suggests that it was 'by 1910 [that] Indian food, or curry as understood and constructed by former colonial officials, had become part of the British diet' it may actually have been established somewhat earlier. Critically though, Panayi also identifies such take up and development of Indian food in Britain as exemplar of 'the invention of tradition ... perfectly symbolising the artificiality of giving food a nationality'.[97]

In addition to such influences from the sub-continent, Phyllis Browne, a most prolific author of cookery books, wrote of dishes as varied as a Danish recipe for 'Red Rice' and one for 'Kromskies', which is nominally at least of Russian origin, and as early as 1813 Maria Rundell included in her volume of domestic guidance recipes for 'cooking mutton cutlets in the Portuguese way' and for 'China chilo'.[98] By 1866 Mrs Beeton included 'Australian Meat' in her cold collations, and as meat to be served as 'cold cuts' was readily available in Britain it implies that additional cachet was gained through the meat having been tinned and imported.[99] With examples such as these in mind, comments like that of an anonymous lady from Cape Town – 'if you don't object to the colonial dishes, I consider the cooking to be a great deal better than plain roast or boiled of which I am heartily tired' – are less surprising.[100] When speaking of the drive to establish familiar food in colonial settings it must be borne in mind that the familiar itself was both varied and a variable, and became increasingly so throughout the century. This change, generally attributed to the expansion of international trade, must also surely have received added stimulus as a result of the migrations of women within the British Empire.

In organising the menus and selecting the recipes women naturally drew on their earlier experiences in Britain or other colonial sites, and often display great facility and pleasure in their use of this aspect of their cultural knowledge to negotiate their new circumstances. See how Isabella Russell continues her discussion of her dinner party for the visiting bishop:

> The menu was as per enclosed. It may interest you to know what West Africa can produce – when we have tinned things and no ice or such luxuries.
> *Menu*
> Potage d'arrachides [sic] (groundnuts)
> Mayonnaise (lettuce from our garden and pickles)
> Gigot de Mouton (boiled mutton. Too poor to roast here)
> Pigeon rotis aux petit pois (tinned)
> Oeufs a la neige [sic]
> Blanc Mange
> Pailles de Fromage
> *Fruits*
> Marrons (tinned) Almonds and Raisons [sic] (bottled)
> Oranges from the Verde Islands
> *Legumes*
> Choux de Bruxelles
> Pomme de terre [sic]
> *Vins*
> Sherry, Vin Blanc, Vin rouge, Champagne, Cognac.

Of interest here is the additional annotation she makes to the menu, itemising that they ate local produce – the groundnuts in particular, but also the exotic Verde Islands oranges. The eggs, if not produced by their own chickens, were of course local, and there is evidently satisfaction in mentioning that the lettuce was home-grown. The inclusion of bottled and tinned produce does not merit an apology; rather was there kudos and sophistication in being able to access such goods. The lengths Russell goes to in describing her dinner party to her sister in England not only indicates her personal pleasure in her achievement but also suggests an awareness of a distinct form of colonial living arising out of that precise location. There is nothing rueful in her description of her dinner or its component parts; she clearly saw it as an elegant and refined meal, and offers it up, possibly with a certain amount of relief, as proof of gentility attained, colonial West African-style.

This example of the process of changing food practice is a perfect illustration of what Bourdieu identifies as preference becoming taste. Indeed, he takes it further when speaking of how necessity becomes virtue. Bourdieu's discussion of 'taste' is surely even more apposite when applied to gentility: taste when associated with nineteenth-century gentility had an undertow of moral standards arguably not

FOOD AND HOUSEHOLD MANAGEMENT

as relevant in Bourdieu's study group of the middle classes in late twentieth-century France.

'The fatter the possum the better he tasted':[101] *meat matters*

Wherever in the colonies the eating habits of British homemakers are analysed, the bulk of the evidence suggests that meat was always the 'primary element' in the meal.[102] The cultural precedence of meat has sometimes been accounted for by claims that humans recognise it as nutritionally valuable, as that which is now known as first-class protein. For the purposes of this discussion it is more pertinent to consider its historical status as a food which was eaten by those in positions of power. In British diets, meat dishes were therefore always given pride of place, with carbohydrate staples and fruit and vegetables being 'secondary elements'.[103] It appears then that the genteel household would perceive serving substantial dishes of meat as crucial to their lifestyle. To change this fundamental aspect of their diet would be a high risk, for without it there would be a real sense of cultural deprivation. Equally, once the centrepiece of the meal was in place then other possibly less familiar vegetables could be accommodated. If at all possible, familiar sources of meat were obtained, sometimes at considerable trouble. European settlers of the 1870s in Okaihau, North Island, New Zealand, ate meat imported from Australia until such time as they were able to raise their own stock. The carcasses were taken up the coast from Auckland to Russell and then loaded on to a small vessel and taken on to Waitangi. Bullock drays then transported the load up to Okaihau, taking at least two days for the return journey.[104] That the migrants saw such slow and doubtless costly freighting as warranted gives a clear indication of the cultural value accorded to the flesh of specific types of animal.

Of course, the critical point about meat is that it is always cooked prior to being eaten. It was by cooking it that the woman was able to supply added value, turning it from being merely bodily nourishment into cultural nourishment, and its centrality at her table conveyed a range of moral values involving family and peer group and reinforcement of insider and outsider groupings.[105] If the option of familiar meats did not exist then the woman of the house faced the challenge of rendering acceptable the flesh of the indigenous fauna. Sometimes methods of preparation could transform even alien beasts. South Africa cookery book author Hildagonda J. Duckitt recommends a method for air-curing meat, in which strips of raw meat are sprinkled with salt, pepper, ground coriander and vinegar prior to being hung to dry – a technique which would presumably render springbok or eland every bit as acceptable as the more familiar beef.[106] Similar approaches are employed in Mina (Mrs Lance) Rawson's six cookery books which she published in Queensland between 1878 and 1890 and which included recipes for wallaby soup and baked bandicoot.[107] That there was a keen market for such publications suggests that the incomers to both outback Australia and South Africa sought practical help and indeed reassurance that 'bush meats' could be made fit for genteel households. Eva Gray noted in her journal in 1881 that she went out shooting near her home in North Queensland, bringing back a wallaby and 'white cockatoe [sic] one of those lemon crested ones. Those dear little birds make excellent soup'.[108] Eva Gray included illustrations in her journal of her fishing and shooting activities, see Figures 5.4 and 5.5.

Similarly Mrs Morton Allport noted in her journal in Van Diemen's Land in 1832 how she 'dressed some kangaroo fry for dinner, which everybody pronounced excellent' and how, following a successful hunting trip, she 'stuffed the porcupine with sage and onions, and

5.4 Watercolour sketch of Eva Gray fishing near her home in Queensland c.1881, taken from the journal she later gave to her young son.

FOOD AND HOUSEHOLD MANAGEMENT

5.5 Watercolour sketch of Eva Gray shooting game to supplement the family's diet, c.1881.

roasted it – it tasted very like suckling-pig but looked like a large toad'.[109] Even allowing for the 'gloss' of genteel construction, such anecdotes suggest that in the early days of colonisation when options were severely constrained bush meats were eaten with more than good grace. Although personal writings by women in Africa do not speak directly of eating bush meats it seems highly likely that they would have been obliged to do so, and therefore when the lady in Cape Town declared 'babootie [sic] and fricadel are a great improvement on the minced meats of England', it raises the question of what species of meat was employed for these stew-type dishes.[110] Such practices can also be understood as a growing acceptance of and even intimacy with the environment. (See below for elaboration of this point.) Consuming such meats was not then a negation of gentility but rather a reconfiguration of what constituted gentility.

As pastoral farming became established in Australia and New Zealand, so familiar meats became readily available to a wider proportion of the populace, with large quantities of meat being consumed on

[219]

a daily basis in the majority of households. Twopenny declared that 'of course meat is the staple of the Australian way of life' and claimed that he had once heard a dinner guest say '"I don't like your nasty little English slices of meat, we want something we can put our teeth into"'.[111] Thus meat developed an added meaning in those British colonies. Not only did it denote prosperity, as it always had in Britain; for these colonies it can also be understood as a symbol of national vigour and positive difference. In being able to serve large quantities of meat the woman of the house was therefore making a valued contribution to the energy and growth of the colony. Equally, however, as its increasing availability eroded away its standing as a socially high-status food, the genteel woman had to find ways of presenting the meat in attractive ways. The other, non-meat items presented at the meal therefore had cultural as well as nutritional value.

'With the thermometer indicating 90 degrees or thereabouts, plain animal food is not only distasteful to many, but absolutely unwholesome':[112] the vital fruit and vegetables

Inevitably the dishes served to accompany meats varied widely across the Empire. Douglas argues that these 'secondary elements', such as fruit and vegetables, were subordinate to the primary dishes and therefore substitution was less problematic. 'Secondary' is a less than helpful term in this context, as that inevitably carries implications of 'subordinate to' and of 'less consequence than'; equally, as stated above, Douglas's concentration on 'the meal' singularly fails to take into account the parts which make up that whole. Here it will be shown that for the woman the processes of sourcing, preparing and coordinating the other elements of the meal were rich with possibilities. Of more use therefore in this regard is Barthes's view that food 'is a system of communication, a body of images, a protocol of usages, situations and behaviour'.[113]

It is clear that materialistic factors were often critical; for example, ease of access to supplies, which itself was determined by the site of the settlement and/or climatic factors. Another means of ensuring the household had a supply of familiar species of vegetables was to grow their own, but of course that depended both on obtaining the relevant seeds and on having suitable climatic conditions for their cultivation. Laura Wright's diary in Tasmania made constant references to cooking her own peas, beans, onions, asparagus, cabbages, cherries and peaches, because the relatively benign temperate climate favoured their cultivation.[114] Alice Massey, whose home was in Rawalpindi, referred to peas, cauliflowers and lettuces as 'cold-weather-vegetables' and notes that the vegetable garden is also 'giving bindi, bringal, tomatoes, vegetable marrow, several I do not know the names of'. Interestingly she comments of her husband that 'Francis always enjoys his breakfast and dinner more when he gets plenty of vegetables', a remark which, when taken with the Wyvern quotation cited above, challenges the received wisdom that the prosperous Victorian was a reluctant vegetable eater, and seems to be indicative of another change in food practice prompted by local circumstances.[115]

Inevitably there were occasions when the vegetable garden failed completely, and in cases of geographical isolation this could compel the settlers to forage locally, as described by Charles Eden in North Queensland who wrote of himself and his wife eating fat-hen, which presumably grew on the banks of the creek, and also that he 'knew few things better than a salmon and pigweed salad with plenty of cream and eggs'.[116] Clearly the Edens showed great ingenuity in sourcing their foodstuffs, as presumably all the ingredients for that dish were either home produce or gleaned locally. This particular example of practice echoes that cited above of Eva Gray going shooting to provide variety to the family's diet, and similar though possibly less urgent practice is noted by Georgina Bowen in New Zealand: 'Mushrooms are very plentiful this year and it is great fun gathering them as it makes an object for one's walk and as we have no potatoes or any vegetable but beetroot they are very acceptable for dinner'.[117] Drawing on the natural surroundings in this fashion would tend to thrust the women into a more intimate relationship with their surroundings than they had hitherto experienced. Thus this theme of engagement with the natural environment, which is explored in the previous chapter in relation to their gardens, is seen again in another aspect of the women's practice. Such changes in attitudes and behaviour therefore reposition subjectivity.

Engagement with the local environment sometimes took another form through the sharing of commodities – as discussed in the previous chapter on gardening – and is exemplified by the lady who described how when her household moved to Craddock, South Africa they were overwhelmed by the gifts of 'butter, milk, eggs, beautiful grapes, pepper, dried fruit, quinces, potatoes, besides many other things they are sending in continually and, besides presents, loans of crockery and all sorts of things'.[118] Of significance here is not only that she is commenting on the veritable cornucopia of delights available in the locale, but also that it is other members of the 1,500-strong British population who are showering them in this way, making them part of the community through the agency of the foodstuffs. Such behaviour certainly argues that a high social value was placed on the giving of even seemingly quite modest items of food.

Another area in which expertise was adapted and developed was in the field of bottling, preserving and pickling. Of course there were long-established traditions of such culinary skills in Europe, but in some colonial locations they took on additional meaning, proving a means of enlivening a tedious diet, and also giving the mistress of the house the opportunity to give added value to basic items, and thereby ensure further refined elements at her table. For example, in North Queensland the extremes of the wet and dry seasons meant there was a need not only to preserve in times of plenty to cover periods of want, but also to preserve quickly to prevent 'spoiling' and 'taints'. *Aunt May's Preserves and Pickles* includes recipes for cultivated tropical fruits, such as banana jam and preserved green ginger, but also, significantly, for bush fruits, such as guava jelly, vi apple jelly, paw-paw chutney and choko mustard pickle.[119] Thus by making such an imaginative use of a limited range of ingredients at her disposal, the mistress was able to make important contributions to the table, contributions with so much more value than the merely nutritional. Similar meaning was possibly attached to the Cape resident's remark that in her garden was a 'pretty little species of red tomato growing here, which is not much bigger than a pigeon's egg and which makes a most delicious preserve'.[120]

Whilst a high percentage of the personal writings examined make reference to pickling, preserving and bottling practice, there is a case to be made for suggesting there was not always the same urgency about their endeavours as characterised the industry of the women in remote areas or during the early phases of colonisation when commodities were in short supply, or indeed when financial strictures strained genteel performance. Sarah Terry, homemaking in Bombay in the 1880s itemised a number of cost-cutting measures she was obliged to adopt, so her description of making her own pickles of mango, ginger and peppers may have been a case in point.[121] Conversely in locations where there were no appreciable shortages, of either servants or cash, and where in consequence the women did very little hands-on food work, serving pickles and preserves imported from the metropolis was probably more highly valued. Isabella Russell's use of bottled raisins at her dinner party, discussed above, illustrates this.

The complexity of practice outlined here in relation to 'other ingredients' makes nonsense of any claim that they be termed 'secondary' to the meat dish. Indeed it could possibly be argued that for the mistress of the house the other features of the meal actually had greater import, as it was in relation to other items that she was able to draw on her cultural background and bring it into play in the fresh context, experimenting with local elements and incorporating them into her practice. Experimentation has rarely been associated with the image of these women of genteel sensibility, but such a reading is certainly suggested by much of the primary evidence discussed here. Such innovative approaches throughout food practice would doubtless have increased the woman's sense of involvement in her new setting. No longer would her new home be defined only in terms of the absence or lack of culinary items; rather would it be associated with the presence and presentation of the newly discovered and hence developed in a manner deemed to be compatible with new forms of gentility.

'Fanny very busy with her household accounts':[122] *quantifying housekeeping*

Food practice has emerged as inordinately complex. In her capacity as household manager the woman had to monitor its many and varied elements. By recording the detail of the household's financial life she garnered together a distinct form of knowledge of all material items involved, which could then be quantified and thereby give the household exchequer equivalence to any other business.[123] Keeping household accounts was as common a practice in colonial homes as it was in Britain. Steele and Gardiner, in their advice to homemakers in India assert, 'men are apt to say ... that a young girl entering on life can have no experience in such matters. True; therefore the sooner she buckles to the task the better, and with a very little help at first, and the usual monthly audit and consultation, there is small chance of failure'.[124] By maintaining such accounts the woman would have at least the illusion of control over her world and hence, in theory, confidence in her managerial abilities. That Fanny was so *'very'* busy with her accounts is measure of their value; she kept accounts because they were held to be culturally important, and by so doing she created and furthered their meaning.

In addition every entry in the accounts speaks of the practices in which it is embedded. In the light of the preceding discussion it is useful therefore to deconstruct a set of household accounts and a particular sort of 'shopping list'. At first glance Mrs Betts's 'Housekeeping Book, 1902–4' does not seem very promising material – a simple notebook, of the type often seen as school exercise books, which has a rubbed and worn red cover and only a few pages completed; but its modest appearance belies its importance.[125] The archivist has added a note that Mrs Betts's husband, Cecil Couttes Betts, 'initially worked for an optical firm and later became a jute merchant through his own initiative, building factories and opening agencies in Chanpur, Akhpura and Chatalpar'.

As was outlined earlier in this chapter, by mid-century the keeping of accounts was becoming understood as central to the efficient running of the home. Not only did enumerating things give a sense of control, the more valuable in the disturbing and unfamiliar surroundings of the colonies, it also gave the seemingly mundane an added value. 'Things' and their related practices acquired meaning, gained in status. Simply having the items, with all that they signified to a genteel household, was not enough; they had to be quantified and monitored. Carrying out tight accounting required categorisation, with decisions having to be made as to how, and indeed if, to include items. Thus some items may have been 'counted in' and some 'counted out'. This gave the woman the opportunity to privilege some items or practices over others. In effect if it was not recorded it ceased to exist, it was denied, and this too could be reassuring in the uncertain circumstances in which many of the women found themselves. For the purposes of analysis of course it must be remembered that these accounts will offer only a very partial view of Mrs Betts's life, but nonetheless it can be argued that they are indicative of the subject as embedded in her surroundings, approaching her managerial tasks with an appreciation of their gravitas, and therefore the accounts can be understood as fragments of her identity in her specific location.

The listing of the commodities purchased provides further insight into the way in which the 'local' became the 'familiar' and was incorporated into her household practice. Thus roti, dhal, masala, ghee, mango and goapowder gain new meaning when itemised alongside cloth, 'lining for my blouse', plate brush, 'umbrela [sic]' and mutton. By association the local, initially alien items have been given added value – the mistress has entered and literally 'accounted' for them, they are part of her life and her performance is structured by their presence and use.

Another striking feature of these accounts is the extent to which the household and the business were entwined. The quantities of alcohol bought and the number of presents given every month suggest that the Betts did a lot of entertaining, presumably to 'oil the wheels' of their business. This certainly does support Chattopadhyay's argument that Anglo-Indians did not adhere to the separate spheres lifestyle they had followed whilst in Britain, but instead started from a less clearly defined separateness, with more overlap.[126]

Also of note is the extent of Mrs Betts's responsibilities beyond the immediate house. To her fell supervision for running the garden and compound, and she records the purchase of cauliflower seed, a trap for a

FOOD AND HOUSEHOLD MANAGEMENT

wild cat, and regular supplies of pigin [sic], fowl and dog food as well as paying the mali 'for garden tools etc'. Thus her experiences echo those of Clementina Benthall as discussed in the earlier chapter on gardens. Her interactions with her servants seem to have been complex as not only does she pay the wages for the cook, household staff, 'Johnny Sahib's servant' and the ayah for her son Harold, she also pays for 'Essie's sari' and 'Essie's bracelets'.

Although there remains just a fragment of Mrs Betts's accounts their cumulative meaning is such that they can usefully be compared with those of an order for supplies sent by Mrs Bell, from her outback station in North Queensland, to 'Betzels Stores' in Townsville in 1894.[127] As the distances were great, the roads liable to flooding during the wet season and the cost of haulage correspondingly high, supplies were delivered only twice a year, which constrained housekeeping and necessitated highly efficient storekeeping and ordering. Singularly absent from the list is anything which could be considered exotic or a luxury, and as there is nothing to indicate that the Bell family were struggling financially it suggests that only a very limited range of goods was available. Inevitably there are no fresh foods on the list, and taking those factors together it is hard to imagine how social distinction could be made with the basic commodities available. This suggests a different configuration of creative food practice and supports earlier remarks about the consequences of geographical isolation during the early decades of colonisation.

There are however some similarities with Mrs Betts's life. The large quantities ordered indicate that the mistress of the house had responsibilities beyond that of her immediate family. Forty pounds of dried fruit and one ton of flour rather suggest she was also ordering supplies for the station hands, items which she would distribute and subsequently charge for and enter in the Station Accounts. Such practices demonstrate that in this setting, as in the example from India, separate spheres of activity had a very different meaning to the British model, and that whilst the roles were highly gendered there could be no doubt of the contribution the women were making to the household and the business, and hence the colony as a whole.

This analysis has sought to give another insight into the force and power held by the household's material culture, which constantly emerges with meanings and values quite beyond its 'face value'. These accounts are therefore an ideal example of what Lemire describes as 'quantitative narration', a means of chronicling the household, which further structured the managerial role of the mistress of the house.[128] In the light of the findings of this chapter it is hard to accept Chattopadhyay's assertion, made in relation to the Indian context but presumably intended to have a broader application, that 'Arcane methods of accounting were not only to keep at bay the desire for proliferating material possessions, but the mistresses were to derive consolation from such a mundane task because it cultivated a rational, progressive colonial mindset – requirements for managing empire'.[129] This analysis rejects that view, arguing that when understood in the context of complete food practice there can be no reading of the accounts as a compensatory or consolatory device. In the accounts, as with all their food practices, one does not gain the impression that the women were in any way outsiders in their own lives. Rather they were employing particular ways of using their cultural expertise to establish their authority in new settings and hence become significant markers in the colonial cultural landscape.

'All you want for two small loaves is twelve chittaks of flour . . . it can then be baked in an ordinary degchie':[130] in conclusion

At all stages of its production and consumption food is enmeshed in social activities and has the potential to wield huge power within the community. Food as a social force has therefore attracted some scholarship, but the individual's relationship with it has received less attention – certainly none in a colonial context. This chapter has explored the genteel women's part in the practices associated with food sourcing, preparation and presentation and thereby the meanings food had for that group of homemakers. It has been demonstrated that the women had a distinctive relationship with food. It is evident they drew on expertise acquired in their previous home whether in Britain or by remove in another country, and that knowledge, valuable as it was before, took on further and different meaning in new and alien settings. The sheer complexity of their practices around food, their repetitive nature and the need for daily re-enactment meant they provided the women with an almost instantaneous means of asserting their cultural authority and position and thereby occupying their domestic space within the household.

The case has also been made for saying that far from their sole aim being to replicate British modes of eating, as has often been assumed, behaviours were modified to suit situational factors, and thereby contributed to the development of site-specific subjectivities. Because of its material properties food provided a means of 'testing out the local' in as provisional and tentative a manner as the incomers felt ready so to do. No other feature of their world had quite the same qualities of sensitivity to the surroundings, or permitted such nuanced performance. So,

FOOD AND HOUSEHOLD MANAGEMENT

when speaking of material culture as expressive of and representative of identity in flux, food is in a category of its own.

This discussion has also allocated space for the acknowledgement of individual personalities and preferences. It has shown that for some women sourcing and preparing their food gave them great pleasure, even adventure – consider Eva Gray's hunting and Adela Stewart's prodigious bottling and preserving activities. Similarly Alice Massey's letter to her father, quoted at the beginning of this section, is certainly a gentle boast about her bread-making skills, but it is also clear she was having fun. Fun and adventure are not usually allowed to feature in versions of the lives of colonial married women; only single women have tended to be considered in such a way. For married women everything has been subsumed within notions of duty, and that involves denial. Such explanations effectively deny the woman as agent in her own life, and this discussion of food practice has surely amply shown how inappropriate are such accounts.

Food practices not only served to anchor the woman of the house in time and space, they also provided her with the means of playing a pivotal role in stabilising attachment to the site for other members of the household, and for her genteel peers. In her capacity as food manager the woman determined the form and function that food was to take in the new society. Sharing food is both a very basic and equally a complex human activity. Food therefore has huge agency in such interactions, and through food practice the mistress of the house acted as mediator between the individuals and wider society.

Furthermore the women had critical function in controlling the ways in which memories of food past was structured within food present. This discussion has highlighted the place of food practice memories in the colonising process. Recollections of former homes are often tied up with food, and in turn the sights, smells and tastes of food are evocative of other times, people and places. In food practice – as indeed it has been argued was the case with their design and use of their living rooms and gardens, and the image of their dressed selves – the women stood at the intersection of old mores and new. Food can thus be seen as a force working in opposing ways; as a rapid agent for change, but also resistant to alteration because food habits acquired in youth are adhered to so strongly. In some ways therefore the women's food management directly engaged with, made visible and formalised one of the most problematic topics for all the incomers over whom she had influence, that negotiation of the old ways and the new.

This chapter has made considerable use of micro-analysis of localised behaviours, but equally has set those within wider frameworks of gender roles and expectations in colonising endeavours. By so doing it can now be said that it was the intimate relationship the genteel women had with food that made it such a powerful social force in colonial settings. Food practices as cultural markers acquired such a convincing aura precisely because of the form and manner of the women's performance. The moral space occupied by food in genteel circles can be directly attributed to the tone set by the presiding women; by which they asserted their household's difference, for which read racial and social superiority.

This work has been concerned with examining aspects of material culture and associated practices to cast light on the life of the genteel woman, and how in turn those material aspects of her life affected her contribution to colonial society. In relation to food we see that her performance impacted on the lives of others with a particular immediacy and intensity. No part of her work of migrancy was ever more acutely needed than that of food, where, although the detail varied enormously across time and place, her performance always had the ability to confirm and consolidate her and her household's genteel standing.

Notes

1 Mrs I. Beeton, *Beeton's Household Management* (London, Ward, Lock & Tyler, 1869), p. 91.
2 R. Barthes, 'Towards a Psychosociology of Contemporary Food Consumption' in R. Forster & O. Ranum (eds.), *Food and Drink in History* (Baltimore, Johns Hopkins University Press, 1979).
3 See for example *Colonial Food and Drink: 1788-1901* (Sydney, Historic Houses Trust, 1985).
4 P. Bourdieu, *Distinction: A Social Critique of the Judgement of Taste* (Cambridge, University of Massachusetts, 1984); M. Douglas, *Purity and Danger: An Analysis of the Concepts of Pollution and Taboo* (London, Routledge, 1966); Douglas, 'Deciphering the Meal', *Daedalus* Winter 1972, pp. 61–81; A. Murcott 'Cooking and the Cooked: a Note on the Domestic Preparation of Meals' in A. Murcott (ed.), *The Sociology of Food and Eating: Essays on the Sociological Significance of Food* (Aldershot, Gower, 1984).
5 S. Mennell, *All Manner of Food: Eating and Taste in England and France from the Middle Ages to the Present* (Oxford, Basil Blackwell, 1985); J. Goody, *Cooking, Cuisine and Class* (Cambridge, Cambridge University Press, 1982).
6 Douglas, 'Deciphering the Meal', 1972.
7 Beeton, *Beeton's Household Management*, p. 1.
8 See for example, Mrs J. E. Panton, *From Kitchen to Garret: Hints for Young Householders* (London, Ward & Downey, 1889).
9 Beeton, *Beeton's Household Management*, p. 1.
10 M. Jewry (ed. and compiler), *Warne's Everyday Cookery* (London, Frederick Warne, 1891), p. 9.
11 *The Servant's Practical Guide* 1880 cited P. Horn, *The Rise and Fall of the Victorian Servant* (Stroud, Sutton Publishing, 1990), p. 17.
12 Horn, *Victorian Servant*, p. 19.
13 Jewry, *Warne's Everyday Cookery*, p. 9.
14 See for example Panton, *From Kitchen to Garret*, p. 24.
15 Marie Rousselet, Daintree, North Queensland, 1880s cited by L. E. Dyson, *How to*

FOOD AND HOUSEHOLD MANAGEMENT

Cook a Galah: Celebrating Australia's Culinary Heritage with Recipes for Today's Cooks (Melbourne, Lothian, 2002), p. 191.

16 P. Scholliers, *Meals, Food Narratives, and Sentiments of Belonging in Past and Present*, cited by P. Panayi, *Spicing up Britain: The Multicultural History of British Food* (London, Reaktion Books, 2008), p. 40.
17 J. R. Godley (ed.), *Letters from Early New Zealand by Charlotte Godley, 1850–1853* (Christchurch, Whitcombe & Tombs, 1951), p. 70.
18 S. Crane, *The Performance of Self: Ritual, Clothing and Identity* (Philadelphia, University of Pennsylvania, 2002).
19 L. Young, '"Extensive, Economical and Elegant": The Habitus of Gentility in Early Nineteenth Century Sydney', *Australian Historical Studies* No. 124, 2004, pp. 201–20.
20 Although it has not yet been possible to find evidence that these particular magazines were transported overseas, a journal with a similar readership, the *Englishwoman's Domestic Magazine* (London, Ward Lock & Tyler), ran regular articles, advertisements, and letters from readers all aimed at women in India, America and Australia. Copies of Vols. 8–11, 1871, which were purchased locally, are to be found in a private collection, Hobart. See specifically 1879 issues, examples of which are held at the Central Public Library, Leeds. Examples of *The House* are held at the Museum of Domestic Design and Architecture and the *Gardener's Magazine* at the Lindley Library. Beeton, *Beeton's Household Management*, 1869.
21 Damask, a reversible fabric, usually made of linen and/or silk with a pattern woven into the design. These patterns became increasingly more complex and varied as the manufacture of commodities proliferated. Such items were expensive and highly regarded.
22 S. Leith-Ross, *Stepping Stones: Memoirs of Colonial Africa 1907–1962* (London, Peter Owen, 1983), p. 48.
23 J. Murray (ed.), *In Mid-Victorian Cape Town: Letters from Miss Rutherfoord* (Cape Town, A. A. Balkema, 1953), p. 70.
24 N. Bonnin (ed.), *Katie Hume on the Darling Downs: A Colonial Marriage* (Toowoomba, Darling Downs Institute Press, 1985), p. 141.
25 Isabella Russell, Letters from the Gambia, 1900, British Empire and Commonwealth Museum, henceforth BECM.
26 S. Chattopadhyay, 'Goods, Chattels and Sundry Items: Constructing Nineteenth Century Anglo-Indian Domestic Life', *Journal of Material Culture* Vol. 7 (3), pp. 243–71.
27 C. Macdonald (ed.), *Women Writing Home 1700–1920: Female Correspondence Across the British Empire. Vol. 5 New Zealand* (London, Pickering & Chatto, 2006), p. 348, Georgina Bowen, May 1864.
28 D. Attar, 'Keeping up Appearances: The Genteel Art of Dining in Middle-class Victorian Britain' in C. A. Wilson (ed.), *Food and Society: The Appetite and the Eye. Visual Aspects of Food and its Presentation within the Historic Context* (Edinburgh, Edinburgh University Press, 1991).
29 *North Queensland Register*, 1884.
30 Loos suggests that during the years 1861–97 indigenous peoples were involved in the deaths of at least 470 settlers, both European and non-European. N. Loos, *Invasion and Resistance: Aboriginal-European Relations on the North Queensland Frontier, 1861–1897* (Canberra, Australian National University Press, 1982), Appendix B, pp. 189–247.
31 H. Callaway, *Gender, Culture and Empire* (London, Macmillan, 1987), p. 178.
32 A. Allingham, 'Victorian Frontierswomen: The Australian Diaries and Journals of Lucy and Eva Gray, 1868–1872 and 1881–1892', MA Thesis, James Cook University, 1987. Lucy Gray, September 1868.
33 A. Drummond (ed.), *Married and Gone to New Zealand* (Hamilton and Auckland, Paul's Book Arcade, 1960), p. 61, Jessie Campbell, Wanganui, New Zealand, 1842.
34 Bourdieu, *Distinction*, 1984, p. 202.
35 For further discussion of the complexities of relationships between servants

and their colonial employers see N. de Klerk, 'Home Away From Home' in K. L. Ishizuka and P. R. Zimmerman (eds.), *Mining the Home Movie: Excavations in Histories and the Movies* (Berkeley, University of California Press, 2008), pp. 148–62.
36. Godley, *Letters from Early New Zealand*, p. 72.
37. S. A. Courage, *Light and Shadows of Colonial Life: Twenty Six Years in Canterbury, New Zealand*, 2nd edn (Christchurch, Whitcoulls, 1976), p. 27, first published c.1896.
38. J. Richardson, 'An Annotated Edition of the Journals of Mary Morton Allport', Ph.D. Thesis, University of Tasmania, 2006. 6 October and 2 December 1832.
39. L. A. Meredith, *My Home in Tasmania: During a Residence of Nine Years* (Adelaide, Griffin Press, 1932), original edition 1853, p. 63.
40. Martha Axford Diary, Bothwell, Tasmania, 14 July 1847. Private Collection of Jillian and John Bignell. My thanks to Mr and Mrs Bignell for permission to reference this document.
41. *Mercury*, 8 January 1867; K. Webber, 'Romancing the Machine: the Enchantment of Domestic Technology in the Australian Home 1850–1914' Ph.D. Thesis, University of Sydney, 1996, p. 11, asserts 'that even with the burgeoning population in the second half of the century there was no shortage of servants'. Such a sweeping generalisation clearly does not stand up outside the big urban centres on the mainland.
42. B. W. Higman, *Domestic Service in Australia* (Melbourne, Melbourne University Press, 2002), p. 122. The Davenports lived in Richmond, a few miles from Hobart.
43. James Reid Scott, Household Accounts, 1868, NS52/1/1, Tasmanian State Archives.
44. See issues of the *Mercury*.
45. A. Trollope, *Australia and New Zealand* (London, Dawsons, 1968), pp. 475–6, originally published 1873.
46. Anning Family Papers, AFRS/MEM/1, Special Collections, Library, James Cook University, Queensland. Date of this incident is not given, but Elizabeth Anning had married in 1874.
47. R. Lewis and Y. Foy, *The British in Africa* (London, Weidenfeld & Nicolson, 1971), p. 163.
48. S. Addison & J. Mackay, *A Good Plain Cook: An Edible History of Queensland* (Brisbane, Boolarong Publication, 1985), p. 2; J. Young (ed.), *Jane Bardsley's Outback Letter Book: Across the Years 1896–1936, Pioneer Life in Australia's Tropic North* (North Ryde, NSW, Angus & Robertson, 1987), p. 119.
49. Allingham, 'Victorian Frontierswomen', Lucy Gray Journal Chapter XV.
50. Gray, *Reminiscences of India and North Queensland* (London, Constable & Co., 1912), p. 254.
51. Allingham notes that Eva Gray had both Aboriginal housemaids and a children's nurse, although on her initial journey to Queensland with her first child she records in her journal that when passing through Sydney they engaged an English nurse to take north with them, 'Victorian Frontierswomen', 29 April 1881.
52. Allingham, 'Victorian Frontierswomen'. 'Gin', female indigenous Australian. Now archaic and considered a highly offensive term.
53. Allingham notes that the 'end of 1866 saw 18 human fatalities', 'Victorian Frontierswomen', p. 64. For further discussion of relations between indigenous and European peoples see N. J. Hennington, '"Perhaps if there had been more women in the north, the story would have been different": Gender and the History of White Settlement in North Queensland, 1840–1930', Ph.D. Thesis, University of Melbourne, 1999.
54. E. Buettner, *Empire Families: Britons and Late Imperial India* (Oxford, Oxford University Press, 2004), p. 37; Chattopadhyay, 'Goods, Chattels and Sundry Items'.
55. F. A. Steele, *The Duties of the Mistress* (London, Heinemann, 1889), p. 12.
56. Sheila Warwick, born Uttar Pradesh, India, 1914. Audio tape 405, BECM.
57. Mrs Clementina Benthall, Diary, 1842, Centre of South Asian Studies, University of Cambridge, henceforth CSAS.

58 Eustace Kenyon, Letters from Calcutta, May 1896, CSAS.
59 Mrs E. H. Melville, *A Residence at Sierra Leone by a Lady* (London, John Murray, 1849), p. 13.
60 C. Larymore, *A Resident's Wife in Nigeria* (London, Routledge, 1911), p. 207.
61 M. Macmillan, *Women of the Raj* (New York, Thames & Hudson, 1988), p. 146.
62 Larymore, *Resident's Wife*, p. 206; D. Moore, *Two in West Africa* (London, Heinemann, 1909), p. 59; Leith-Ross, *Stepping Stones*, p. 47. Leith-Ross seeks to provide some context and justification by adding 'to justify these wages it must be remembered that a man could live on 1d per day and that a tenth of a penny could buy a meal for a child'.
63 Allingham, 'Victorian Frontierswomen', Lucy Gray Journal Chapter XXVI, and VII, 18 October, 18–91 (Allingham notes the last number is a page reference, not a year.)
64 Larymore, *Resident's Wife*, p. 207, p. 7.
65 Melville, *Residence at Sierra Leone*, p. 13.
66 Moore, *We Two in West Africa*, p. 60.
67 M. Knowlden (ed.), A. M. Boase and M. Hannah, *When the Sun Never Set: A Family's Life in the British Empire* (London, Radcliffe Press, 2005), p. 10. The family lived in Blantyre, Nyasaland, British Central Africa.
68 Macdonald, *Women Writing Home. Vol. 5*, p. 379, endnote 5.
69 Larymore, *Resident's Wife*, pp. 214–15.
70 Callaway, *Gender, Culture and Empire*, p. 178.
71 Lady Nora Scott, Journal, March 1884, CSAS.
72 J. J. Noordegraaf and E. Pouw, 'Extended Family Films: Home-movies in the State-sponsored Archive' *Moving Image* Vol. 9 (1), Spring 2009, pp. 83–103.
73 Goody, *Cooking, Cuisine and Class*, p. 60.
74 Allingham, 'Victorian Frontierswomen', Eva Gray Journal, 22 March 1882.
75 C. Macdonald, 'Stranger at the Hearth: The Eclipse of Domestic Service in New Zealand Homes' in B. Brookes (ed.), *At Home in New Zealand: Houses, History, People* (Wellington, Bridget Williams Books, 2000), p. 42.
76 A. B. Stewart, *My Simple Life in New Zealand* (London, Robert Banks & Co., 1908), p. 25.
77 Stewart, *My Simple Life in New Zealand*, pp. 47, 62.
78 Macdonald, 'Stranger at the Hearth', p. 44.
79 Knowlden, *When the Sun Never Set*, p. 9.
80 Steele, *The Duties of the Mistress*, p. 17.
81 J. and R. Godden, *Two Under the Indian Sun* (London, Macmillan, 1966), p. 59.
82 Mrs C. Lang, *The English Bride in India: Being Hints on Indian Housekeeping* (London, Madras, 1909), p. 69 cited by Macmillan, *Women of the Raj*, p. 143.
83 Mrs W. G. Waterfield, Journal Sholapur District 1906, CSAS.
84 Melville, *A Residence at Sierra Leone*, p. 26.
85 Larymore, *Resident's Wife*, p. 208.
86 D. Miller, *Why Some Things Matter* (London, University College, 1998).
87 Isabella Russell, BECM.
88 Isabella Russell, BECM.
89 For further examples of menus see 'Miss Pilkington's Commonplace Book', CSAS.
90 S. Strickrodt (ed.), *Women Writing Home 1700–1920: Female Correspondence Across the British Empire. Vol. 1 Africa* (London, Pickering & Chatto, 2006), p 231, Ada Slatter, British East Africa Protectorate, 1909.
91 'Wyvern', *Culinary Jottings for Madras* (Madras, Higginbotham & Co., 1891), p. 4.
92 M. Douglas, *Implicit Meanings: Essays in Anthropology* (London, Routledge & Kegan Paul, 1975).
93 Macdonald, *Women Writing Home. Vol. 5*, p. 307, Georgina Bowen, 15 February 1862.
94 Clementina Benthall, Diary, 1842, p. 37, CSAS.
95 Larymore, *Resident's Wife*, p. 212.
96 A. Soyer, *A Shilling Cookery for the People* (London, Routledge, 1855);

M. A. Everard, *The Handy Dictionary of Cookery* (London, James Nisbet, 1886); 'Wyvern', *Culinary Jottings*, p. 302.
97 Panayi, *Spicing up Britain*, p. 27.
98 P. Browne, *A Year's Cookery* (London, Cassell, Petter, Galpin & Co., 1898); M. Rundell, *Domestic Economy* (London, John Murray, 1813).
99 *Mrs Beeton's Book of Household Management* 1866. Note the 'meat' of which Mrs Beeton speaks was mutton, sold in four pound tins, and in 1871 some 10,000 tons was exported from Australia, much of it destined for Britain.
100 Anon., *Life at the Cape One Hundred Years Ago, by a Lady* (Cape Town, C. Struik, 1963), p. 11.
101 R. L. Atkinson 'The Long Trail', fol. 16r, unpub. MS, Special Collections, Library, James Cook University, Queensland.
102 Douglas, 'Deciphering the Meal'.
103 Douglas, 'Deciphering the Meal'.
104 K. Boase, *Tides of History* (Kawakawa, NZ, Bay of Islands Council, 1977), p. 198.
105 Murcott, *Sociology of Food and Eating*.
106 H. J. Duckitt, *Hilda's Diary of a Cape Household: Being a Chronicle of Daily Events and Monthly Work in a Cape Household* (London, Chapman & Hall, 1902).
107 M. Rawson, *Cookery Book and Household Hints* (Rockhampton, 1878) cited M. Symons, *One Continuous Picnic: A History of Eating in Australia* (Adelaide, Duck Press, 1982), p. 53.
108 Allingham, 'Victorian Frontierswomen', Eva Gray Journal, 9 December 1881.
109 Richardson, 'Allport Journals', 3 September 1832.
110 Anon., *Life at the Cape*, p. 30. Note 'bobotie' is the more common spelling.
111 R. Twopenny, *Town Life in Australia* (London, E. Stock, 1883), cited Symons, *One Continuous Picnic*, p. 65.
112 'Wyvern', *Culinary Jottings*, p. 138.
113 Barthes, 'Towards a Psychosociology of Contemporary Food', p. 167.
114 L. P. Wright, *Laura's Brookville Diaries: 1819–1894* (Launceston, Greenhill, 2003).
115 K. Stierstorfer (ed.), *Women Writing Home 1700–1920: Female Correspondence Across the British Empire. Vol. 4 India* (London, Pickering & Chatto, 2006), pp. 65–6, Alice Massey, 17 September 1875. Bindi – okra; bringal – aubergine.
116 C. H. Eden, *My Wife and I in Queensland: An Eight Year Experience in the Above Colony, With Some Account of Polynesian Labour* (London, Longmans, Green & Co., 1872), p. 120.
117 Macdonald, *Women Writing Home. Vol. 5*, p. 323, Georgina Bowen, May 1863.
118 A. F. Hattersley (ed.), *A Victorian Lady at the Cape, 1849–51* (Cape Town, Maskew Miller, [194?]), p. 48.
119 M. Smith (ed.), *Aunt May's Preserves and Pickles: A Pioneer's Recipes from Tropical North Queensland* (Epping North, NSW, Merrol Media, 2003).
120 Hattersley, *A Victorian Lady at the Cape*, p. 24.
121 Letters of Sarah and Sydney Terry 1844–47, India Office Library, cited P. Barr, *The Memsahibs: The Women of Victorian India* (London, Secker & Warburg, 1976), p. 82.
122 Charlotte Mary Wortley Corbett, Diary, 12 April 1862, Ormsby Papers, CSAS.
123 B. Lemire, *The Business of Everyday Life: Gender, Practice and Social Politics in England c.1600–1900* (Manchester, Manchester University Press, 2005).
124 F. A. Steele and G. Gardiner, *The Complete Indian Housekeeper and Cook*, 7th edn (London, William Heinemann, 1909), p. 19.
125 Mrs Betts Housekeeping Book, 1902–4, Bishop Papers, CSAS.
126 Chattopadhyay, 'Goods, Chattels and Sundry Items'.
127 Bell Family Papers, fol. 341r, Special Collections, Library, James Cook University, Queensland.
128 Lemire, *The Business of Everyday Life*, p. 215.
129 Chattopadhyay, 'Goods, Chattels and Sundry Items'.
130 Stierstorfer, *Women Writing Home. Vol. 4*, Bread recipe, Alice Massey, Rawalpindi, August 1875.

6

Conclusion: the work of migrancy

This study, which has examined the lives of a sample of women ranged in sites across the British Empire, has stepped aside from the oft-employed concepts of gender and class, challenging the notion that a study of subjectivity can reduce the actors to such bald categories. Instead it has scrutinised gentility, a realm of cultural knowledge which, for the women who form the subject of this work, was central to their sense of 'selfhood' and is therefore to be understood as constituting valuable evidence in its own right. Gentility – its ideology and expression – proved to be responsive and adaptable to the environmental changes it encountered, and is therefore a singularly appropriate concept with which to analyse colonial societies. The subtleties of the ways in which women of genteel persuasion arranged their world, and the energies devoted to that end, argue forcibly that the concept of female gentility retained force and relevance in British societies empire-wide. It has become evident that there was a deal of fertile ground in which gentility could and did flourish, for one of the defining characteristics of these societies was their aspirational nature, and in consequence it has been relatively straightforward to identify numbers of seemingly disparate women who yet had in common that they all sought some degree of refinement. A phenomenon which wielded such social and political power, even in seemingly unpromising locations, demands close inspection and the results have proved illuminating.

The women examined lived in highly gendered societies; their role in their new location was to support their menfolk. To that end it has been shown that they brought to bear a whole range of cultural competences as developed in their previous home or homes in order to re-establish a 'sense of self' in their new location. In the light of the findings it is clear that to settle themselves and their household *in situ* and become 'hefted' to a site necessitated any number of effortful and time-consuming activities. These processes are understood to constitute a form of work, the work of migrancy. Both material and social means were employed as both material and moral values had to find expression. All aspects of the self were involved, for the process had to be – both literally and philosophically – all-consuming. To succeed as a migrant one must anchor oneself to the surroundings at many points. If the individual lacks the means, either psychologically or because of environmental constraints, then the anchorage is weakened. Major repositioning of self has to occur, and such was clearly the case for women of genteel persuasion. Their performance was essential for their psychological well-being and any erosion of their gentility would render them adrift in landscapes socially as well as geographically alien.

The concentration in this work on the place and value of the subject's material culture has provided a means of reading not only the processes of the construction of this newly situated identity, but also the very mechanisms by which subjectivity found expression. Critics of material culture studies may assert that there are limitations to such an approach, on the grounds that it is never possible to examine all the belongings of any one individual. It is indeed inevitable that some items have been lost or worn away and equally that there were some objects and practices which their owners did not consider merited recording. In addition some of the meanings of any given object may elude us entirely, lost in the cultural shifts of time. Such gaps as must therefore exist in the data have been overcome by using a range of methods to analyse a variety of objects in the interconnected areas in the lives of a goodly number of women. This has shown that the material culture of each category had power and agency not found elsewhere, providing knowledge of the intricate workings of those individuals' lives which could not have been garnered by any other form of enquiry.

Another criticism levied against object-based work is that some authors are inclined to overstate their case and attribute articulacy to the inanimate. Recovering the life story of an object demands that its biographer site it amidst the relevant associated practices, which in turn compels consideration of a range of personal, developmental and structural factors. Such has been the approach taken here, and it has served to heighten awareness that objects are ever sited within a broad field, often including features of society which at first glance may not appear to be in the arena of value. It has also made explicit that, in addition to understanding such wider contextual meanings, sensitivity to the materiality of the domestic and personal object is a necessary prerequisite to reading its values and thereby gaining an appreciation of its narrative position within the life of the user.

The foregrounding of material culture has also served to cast light on ways in which it was instrumental in containing and controlling

CONCLUSION: THE WORK OF MIGRANCY

memory. There was a danger that these women, whose entire cultural underpinning laid such store by their possessions and who had curatorial and managerial responsibility for their family traditions, could all too easily become swamped by nostalgic longings. The migrant had to develop a means of being comfortable with the past if she were to be securely established in the present. Readings of migrants' possessions from their former homes have tended to focus only on their powers of evocation; here it has been shown that the women used their belongings to manage and control memory as much as to call it forth. In the introduction to this work it was suggested that a fruitful approach to examining how the migrants handled the seductive but potentially heartbreaking matter of recollections of the past was to see memory as a malleable force subject to adjustment as needs dictated. Readings of the material aspects of the women's performance make it apparent that the boundaries between their past lives and the new were more porous than 'the tyranny of distance' may lead one to imagine,[1] thereby challenging the notion of a dichotomy between 'home' and 'away', mobility versus fixedness.

The insistence that material practices can be read as expressions of gradations of gentility, or ambitions thereof, may draw concerns of *a priori* formulations; that instances and modes of behaviour have been deemed genteel in order to satisfy the over-arching rationale. Yet how else to explain the stylised performances witnessed here, the adherence to, and/or adoption of, mores and practices that to modern eyes seem so odd amidst bush, plain and veldt? How else indeed, other than appreciating it as expressive of subjectivity; a desire to express distinction, improve or maintain one's status and accrue or express social power.

We have seen that that is precisely what resulted from genteel behaviour, as witnessed here in individuals as geographically apart as Bathurst, Sierra Leone, the Gulf Country of the far north of Australia, the cities and cantons of India, and the farms and towns of New Zealand. The myriad of engrossing detail involved in the deceptively simple activities of the genteel performance provided the crucial means of making oneself feel 'at home' even if for some that was never to be quite the same as 'at Home'. Conflict within regarding where one's affiliations lay – colony or metropolis – may have been more problematic for sojourners than settlers, for first generation migrants than for their children, but we hear little of that in their personal writings. This further supports the argument that the enactment of their performance was the very mechanism by which they controlled their past and secured their space in the new location.

It is also apparent that the genteel woman and her values proved a resource – literally and psychologically – for wider society. For her peers her determination to adhere to certain modes of behaviour was welcomed with enthusiasm. Hers was the voice of cultural authority and her performance encouraged and stimulated the establishment of like-minded groups, which became powerbases for local society. Such groups generated their own ideas and modes of behaviour on the basis of site-specific circumstances, incorporating them into the broader philosophies of their British heritage. This helped to foster stability in any number of socially uncertain situations, strengthening local confidence, which in turn meant the colony or settlement no longer sought confirmation from the metropolis.

It has been shown that notions of moral superiority and heightened sensitivity to circumstance and setting, deemed to be integral to gentility, took on particular importance in challenging colonial settings. The woman's refined performance was a model for others to emulate, for if she could withstand the trials and tribulations of her lot, then 'lesser beings' should be inspired to strive to follow her example. It seems probable that some of those not of the same social rank may well have been openly dismissive of a genteel lifestyle, and yet still kept a weather eye out on the habits of the elites against which they could then judge their own progress. Even in Australasia, where there was much protestation regarding the egalitarian nature of society, other Europeans seem to have acknowledged the role of the genteel woman and her household. In 1896 Lord Lamington, the Governor of Queensland, bemoaned 'the absence of that substantial and numerous middle-class which exists in Britain', suggesting he saw this as leading to a lack of aspiration in the north.[2] Clearly this was an image residents sought to overcome and in turn this gave vitality to notions of refinement, which some may otherwise have seen as lacking in relevance. Thus the woman's genteel performance had a ripple effect throughout the wider community and was a major component of social ordering, which helps to explain why it was established with such alacrity, in such unpromising places, and also therefore why it evolved into so many healthy and vigorous forms.

Attention has been paid throughout to the ways in which genteel performance varied from site to site, rather than following the well-trodden ground of drawing out similarities. Behaviours which did not accord with the orthodoxy of the 'colonial woman' have hitherto often been dismissed as atypical anomalies. In this study, however, the concentration has been on practices *in situ* and hence an appreciation that context plays a significant role in structuring meaning. Obviously, seeking to quantify the significance of female gentility in one site over another is fruitless, for can those individuals who planted the flag – consider Constance Larymore's endeavours in Nigeria – be valued any more or less than the larger numbers who stimulated economic growth

CONCLUSION: THE WORK OF MIGRANCY

and social consolidation in southern Africa? Equally surely one would be unwise to give greater weight to the genteel woman in the so-called 'white settlements' than to those who worked so hard to hold their ground amidst the hierarchical complexities of Anglo-Indian society, simply on the basis that the former European societies prospered whilst the latter stuttered to an end.

It is critical of course that in all sites of the Empire these women were not only members of social elites, they were members of racial elites. The woman's refined persona, with its reliance on control of person and space alike, ensured her prominence in the colonial landscape. She and her carefully constructed home acted as a metaphor for European notions of civilising alien territories. Her impact was twofold: reducing the strangeness of the foreign terrain for other whites, whilst simultaneously reinforcing the distancing of the indigenous peoples. Her performance made visually and socially explicit the status and significance of white people, for 'taming the wilderness' is not only to be understood as meaning bush clearance and road building, it also applied racially and socially, and her performance was indicative of a 'whitening' of space. Her mannered performance was explicitly designed to convey the message that no matter what other political or military events were taking place – and the situation in India pre and post 1857 is a case in point – her high profile whiteness was the constant and her very presence emblematic of the full might of white empire.

Focusing on the woman's personal and domestic management has also drawn attention to her considerable influence as a prime consumer. Indeed, the intricate connections identified here between genteel performance and the proliferation of material culture has highlighted the contribution made by social elites to the establishment and expansion of both local and international markets. Vickery, in relation to her work on women of comparable standing in eighteenth-century Britain, makes the case for an analysis of consumption as a means of understanding one of women's important historical roles, that of household manager.[3] The critical factor for this enquiry has been that such tasks of management and the associated consumption were undertaken by migrants. It has thereby been possible to articulate some of the ways in which the work of migrancy and the processes of consumption are inextricably linked. It has also become clear that what may appear to be 'only' domestic actually had a much wider economic significance, and this in turn suggests that the individual household unit must be accounted for when considering wider economic structures within the imperial project.

This study of personal and domestic practices and processes has cast light on how genteel women articulated, and indeed manipulated, social difference and affiliation. Their spaces, objects and associated practices have emerged as material communicators, with astonishing agency in the processes of relocation. This has led to numerous revelations regarding the ways in which their users were individually and collectively dynamic in the value systems of their various locations. Interplay of individual practices and collective behaviour must ever be a critical component of studies of migrant groups, always such a significant feature of the British Empire. The genteel woman was an element of many a colonial landscape and foregrounding the workings of her life has provided a better understanding of the wider landscape of empire, and why it evolved and developed as it did. The genteel woman has been a much maligned figure, often portrayed as a constraining device on progress within burgeoning societies. In this reappraisal she has emerged as having agency for continuity and change for herself and the wider community alike. For good or for ill she did much to further the propagation of the ideology that migration across the British Empire would create coherent and harmonious societies.

Notes

1 G. Blainey, *The Tyranny of Distance: How Distance Shaped Australia's History* (Melbourne, Sun Books, 1966).
2 R. Fitzgerald, *From the Dreaming to 1915: A History of Queensland* (St Lucia, University of Queensland, 1982), p. 54.
3 A. Vickery, *The Gentleman's Daughter: Women's Lives in Georgian England* (London, Yale University Press, 2003).

SELECT BIBLIOGRAPHY

Primary sources

Manuscripts located in Australia

Allport Collection, State Library of Tasmania (SLT)
Paintings by Mary Morton Allport, 'Book of Treasures', 1840

W. L. Crowther Library, State Library of Tasmania
Handwritten Recipe Book, Ivy May Chilvers, post 1894, Ephemera Collection
Red Recipe Book: Curzon Allport's personal recipe book, completed by hand in a commercially bound notebook, made Auckland, [188?]

Special Collections (North Queensland Collection), Library, James Cook University, Queensland
Anning Family Papers, AFRS/MEM/1
Atkinson Family Papers, including R. L Atkinson MS 'The Long Trail'
Bell Family Papers
Hann Family Papers, fol. 122r
Thomas Merrin & Son, Grocer's Ledger, 1908–14, TMC/L/1
Watercolour album, 1888–92 (provenance unknown)

Tasmaniana Collection, State Library of Tasmania
Diary Matilda Hale, 1875

Tasmanian State Archives (TSA)
Accounts to be settled sent to Mrs John Meredith from a variety of merchants, 1857–85. Also a list of tasks undertaken by gardener August 1895–March 1896, NS123/81
Diary Miss Hally Bayley, 1905, NS1619/1/21
Diary Mrs R.V. Bayley, 1904, NS1619/1/20
Diary Mrs B. Butler, 1878, NS2089
Household Accounts, James Reid Scott, 1868, NS52/1/1
Inventory of Goods of deceased Maria Meredith, 1831, NS123/192
Last Will and Testament of Mary Morton Allport, 1896, AE763/1/1862
Letters received by Mrs Meredith from Elizabeth Grueber and Caroline Mitchell, NS123/192
Mrs Meredith Housekeeping and Account Book, NS123/192
Pocket Book of Household Expenditure, Maria Meredith, 1854–64, NS123/81
Scrapbook: Articles and Illustrations from British Gardening Magazines, 1890s, AB831

Manuscripts located in Britain

British Empire and Commonwealth Museum (BECM)
Letters from the Gambia, Isabella Russell, 1899–1903. Ref.: 2002/179/1

SELECT BIBLIOGRAPHY

Letters from India, Andrew Morrison, 1895. Ref. 1994/018/11
Letters from India, Col. Rawden E. D. Reilly, 1900

Centre of South Asian Studies, University of Cambridge (CSAS)
Diary Charlotte Mary Wortley Corbett, 1862–64, Ormsby Papers
Diary Mrs Clementina Benthall, Benthall Papers
Holman Papers
Housekeeping Book Mrs Betts, 1902–4, Bishop Papers
Journal Evelyn Beeton, 1912, Beeton Papers
Journal Lady Nora Scott, 1882–86
Journal Mrs W. G. Waterfield, Sholapur District, 1906
Letters from Calcutta, Eustace Kenyon, 1896–98, A. Kenyon Papers
Memoirs Charlotte Stamper, 1860–1936 Cawnpore, S. Laughton Papers
Memoirs Constance Maude, b.1888 Bangalore, Maude Papers
Miss Pilkington's Commonplace Book, Pilkington/Phelps Collection

Cumbrian County Archive Service, Carlisle
'Equipment for a Lady going to India', D/KEN/3/27, Kennedy Papers
Letter from Captain Malloy, Australia, 1887, D/KEN/3/28–9, Kennedy Papers

Unilever Archives and Record Management, Port Sunlight
Accounts of F. Swanzy, UAC/2/33/AG/2/1/1, Swanzy Collection
Letter from F. Swanzy, UAC/2/33/AG/1/2/1, Swanzy Collection

Newspapers and periodicals in Australia
Private Collection, A. Melrose, Tasmania
Englishwoman's Domestic Magazine 1871

Research Library, Powerhouse Museum, Sydney
Draper's Record 1887

Special Collections, Library, James Cook University, Queensland
North Queensland Register 1884, 1894, 1905
Queenslander 1886
Townsville Daily Bulletin 1887, 1888, 1889
Townsville Herald 1876, 1877, 1887
Tasmanian State Archives
Mercury 1856, 1857, 1867, 1877, 1887, 1907, 1910
Tasmanian Mail 1877, 1893

Periodicals in Britain
Central Public Library, Leeds
Englishwoman's Domestic Magazine 1879

Royal Horticultural Society, Lindley Library (LL)
Gardener's Magazine
Villa Gardener 1872–75

Museum of Domestic Design and Architecture, Middlesex
Embroidery 1908–9

SELECT BIBLIOGRAPHY

Private Collection, M. Moatt, Cumbria
English Illustrated Magazine 1885

Trade, auction and exhibition catalogues in Australia
D. Bunce: *Seeds & Plants Catalogue*, Hobart, 1836
W. L. Crowther Library, State Library of Tasmania
Hobart Horticultural Society, *Show Catalogue*, Hobart, 1887
Sonntag & Co. Seed Merchants, San Francisco, 1874–75
William Bros, *Complete House Furnishers and Retailers*, Hobart, 1909
William Coogan, *Furniture Manufacturers and Retailers*, Hobart, 1913
Wunderlich Ltd, *Abridged General Catalogue of Metal Ceilings, Wall Linings and Stamped Metal for Exterior and Interior Decoration*, Sydney, 1912

Tasmaniana Collection, State Library of Tasmania
Official Catalogue of the Exhibits of the Tasmanian Juvenile and Industrial Exhibition, 16th April, 1883. Ref.: TCP607.34

Tasmanian State Archives
Catalogue of Superior Household Furniture and Effects to be sold by order of Mrs Morton Allport, 19 March 1888, NS1885/45(a)

Caroline Simpson Library and Research Collection, Sydney
Foy & Gibson Stores, Melbourne, 1911–12
Anthony Hordern & Sons Stores, Sydney, 1894, 1911
Junior Army & Navy Stores, Inscribed: R. Darling, Murray Street, Hobart Agent, 1892
Alfred Peats, Wallpaper Suppliers, Chicago, 1902
Shepherd and Co., *Garden Suppliers*, Sydney, 1892, 1893, 1894
H. L. Vosz, Wallpaper Suppliers, Adelaide, 1901
Waring & Gillows, Furniture & Household Effects, London, 1910

Local History Collection, Townsville Public Library Service, Queensland
Souvenir Programme of the Jubilee Carnival Held to Commemorate the 50th Anniversaryof the Foundation of Townsville, Townsville, 1913

Trade catalogues in Britain
Royal Horticultural Society, Lindley Library (LL)
H. Cannells and Sons, *Nursery Catalogues*, Swanley, Kent, TS 1882, 1883, 1888, 1895
Duncan & Davies, New Plymouth 1917
Howden & Moncrieff, Dunedin 1911
Howies Spring Catalogue, Johannesburg 1912–13
Nimmo & Blair, Dunedin
Thomas Rivers Catalogues, Sawbridgeworth, Herts. 1897, 1898
Robert Seth & Co., Calcutta 1919–20
Smith Bros Catalogue, Uitenhage 1896–97

SELECT BIBLIOGRAPHY

Walker Catalogue, Launceston 1915
Yates Annual Catalogue, Sydney 1914

Photographic archives in Australia
North Queensland Historic Photographic Collection, James Cook University, Queensland
Photographic Resources, National Library of Australia
Local History Collection, Townsville Public Library Service, Queensland

Photographic archives in Britain
Centre of South Asian Studies, University of Cambridge
Royal Commonwealth Society Collection, University of Cambridge

Photographic archives in New Zealand
Alexander Turnbull Library, National Library

Oral interviews
British Empire and Commonwealth Museum
Sheila Warwick, b.1914, Tape 405 'Voices and Echoes: Oral History Holdings'
Margery Wood, b.1905, Tape 599 'Voices and Echoes: Oral History Holdings'

Conducted by Dianne Lawrence
Mary Coulson, b.1958 Zimbabwe, married to grandson of 1890s settlers. July 2007.
Mrs Lyndsay Bradfer-Lawrence, b. Scotland 1919, granddaughter of 'box-wallah' in India. 2006–7.

Published primary sources: books

Adams D. (ed.), *The Letters of Rachel Henning* (Harmondsworth, Penguin, 1969).
Anderson C. (ed.), *Violet Jacob: Letters and Diaries from India 1895–1900* (Edinburgh, Canongate, 1990).
Aldine's History of Queensland (Sydney, Aldine Publishers, 1888).
Anon., *The Australasian Cookery Book: Specially Compiled for the Requirements of Australian and New Zealand Homes* (Melbourne, Ward Lock, 1913).
Anon., *Flowers from an Indian Garden* (Dusseldorf, Arnz & Co., [187?]).
Anon., *Handbook of Garden and Greenhouse Culture in Tasmania* (Hobart, Walsh Brothers Birchall, 1884).
Anon., *How to Dress as a Lady on £15 a Year by a Lady* (London, Warne & Co., 1873).
Anon., *The Language and Poetry of Flowers* (London, Ward, Lock & Tyler, 1877).
Anon., *Language of the Flowers of Australia, Tasmania and New Zealand*, 4th edn (Hobart, J. Walch, 1877).

SELECT BIBLIOGRAPHY

Anon., *Language of the Native Flowers of Tasmania* (Launceston, Harris & Just, [n.d.]).
Anon., *Life at the Cape One Hundred Years Ago, by a Lady* (Cape Town, C. Struik, 1963).
Beeton Mrs I., *Beeton's Household Management* (London, Ward, Lock & Tyler, 1869).
Bird Y. (ed.), *A Quaker Family in India and Zanzibar, 1863–1865: Letters from Elizabeth and Henry Jacobs* (York, William Sessions, 2000).
Boldrewood Mrs R., *The Flower Garden in Australia: A Book for Ladies and Amateurs* (Melbourne, Melville, Mullen & Slade, 1893).
Bonnin N. (ed.), *Katie Hume on the Darling Downs: A Colonial Marriage* (Toowoomba, Darling Downs Institute Press, 1985).
Browne P., *A Year's Cookery* (London, Cassell & Co., 1898).
Bunce D., *Manual of Practical Gardening Adapted to the Climate of Van Diemen's Land* (Hobart, William Gore Elliston, 1838).
Campbell Lady C., *The Etiquette of Good Society* (London, Cassell, 1912).
Carton-Brookes E., *Another England: Life, Living, Homes and Homemakers in Victoria* (Melbourne, Robertson, 1869).
Cook E. A., *Gardens of England* (London, A. & C. Black, 1908).
Courage S. A., *Light and Shadows of Colonial Life: Twenty Six Years in Canterbury, New Zealand*, 2nd edn (Christchurch, Whitcoulls, 1976; 1st published c.1896).
Deans J., *Letters to My Grandchildren* (Christchurch, Cadsonbury Publications, 1995).
Dickinson J., *The Wreath: Gardener's Manual Arranged for the Climate of Tasmania* (Hobart, Colonial Times Office, 1855).
Diver M., *The English Woman in India* (Edinburgh, William Blackwood, 1909).
Duckitt H. J., *Hilda's Diary of a Cape Household: Being a Chronicle of Daily Events and Monthly Work in a Cape Household* (London, Chapman & Hall, 1902).
Eastlake C. L., *Household Hints in Furniture, Upholstery and Other Details* (London, Longmans, Green & Co., 1878).
Eden C. H., *My Wife and I in Queensland: An Eight Year Experience in the Above Colony, With Some Account of Polynesian Labour* (London, Longmans, Green & Co, 1872).
Eden E., *Up the Country: Letters Written to her Sister from the Upper Provinces of India by Emily Eden* (Oxford, Oxford University Press, 1930).
Godden J. and R., *Two Under the Indian Sun* (London, Macmillan, 1966).
Godley J. R. (ed.), *Letters from Early New Zealand by Charlotte Godley, 1850–1853* (Christchurch, Whitcombe & Tombs, 1951).
Gray R., *Reminiscences of India and North Queensland* (London, Constable & Co., 1912).
Greenaway K., *The Language of Flowers* (London, G. Routledge & Sons, 1884).
Greville Lady V., *The Gentlewoman in Society* (London, Henry & Co., 1892).
Hale Mrs Sarah, *The New Household Receipt Book* (London, Nelson & Sons, 1854).

SELECT BIBLIOGRAPHY

Hattersley A. F. (ed.), *A Victorian Lady at the Cape, 1849–51* (Cape Town, Maskew Miller, [194?]).
Hawies Mrs H. R., *The Art of Beauty* (London, Chatto & Windus, 1878).
Hewitt E., *Looking Back, or Personal Reminiscences* (Auckland, Auckland Bible House, 1928).
Jackson H. St John, *Firminger's Manual of Gardening for Bengal and Upper India* (Calcutta, Thacker, Spink & Co., 1890).
James Mrs E., *Our Servants, Their Duties to Us and Ours to Them* (London, Ward Lock & Co., 1883).
Jewry M. (ed. and compiler), *Warne's Everyday Cookery* (London, Frederick Warne, [c.1891]).
Johnstone W. W., *Gardening: A Guide for Amateurs in India* (Mussoorie, India, Himalaya Seed Stores, 1903).
Larymore C., *A Resident's Wife in Nigeria* (London, Routledge, 1911).
Leith-Ross S., *Stepping Stones: Memoirs of Colonial Africa, 1907–1962* (London, Peter Owen, 1983)
Lord E. E., *Your New Home Garden: Its Design, Construction and Planting* (Melbourne, Lothian, 1858).
Loudon Jane, *Gardening for Ladies* (London, Murray, 1841).
Loudon John, *A Manual of Cottage Gardening, Husbandry and Architecture* (London, 1830).
Lowndes, E. E. K., *Everyday Life in South Africa* (London, S.W. Partridge & Co., 1900).
Maclurcan Mrs., *Mrs. Maclurcan's Cookery Book: A Collection of Practical Recipes Specially Suited to Australia* (Townsville, T. Willmett & Co., 1898).
Maclurcan Mrs, *Mrs. Maclurcan's Cookery Book: A Collection of Recipes Specially Suitable for Tasmania* (Hobart, Walch & Sons, 1920).
Maling E. A., *Flowers for Ornament and Decoration and How to Arrange Them* (London, Smith, Elder & Co.. 1862).
Melville Mrs E. H., *A Residence at Sierra Leone by a Lady* (London, John Murray, 1849).
Meredith L. A., *My Home in Tasmania: During a Residence of Nine Years* (Adelaide, Griffin Press, 1932; 1st published 1853).
Moore D., *We Two in West Africa* (London, Heinemann, 1909).
Murray J. (ed.), *In Mid-Victorian Cape Town: Letters from Miss Rutherfoord* (Cape Town, A. A. Balkema, 1953).
Orrinsmith Mrs. L., *The Drawing-room: Its Decoration and Furniture* (London, Macmillan & Co., 1878).
Panton Mrs J. E., *From Kitchen to Garret: Hints for Young Householders* (London, Ward & Downey, 1889).
Post-Office Directory (Hobart, 1890).
Pugh's Queensland Almanac and Directory (Brisbane, Pugh, 1900).
Roberts E., *The East India Voyager* (London, J. Madden & Co., 1839).
Southgate H., *Things a Lady Would Like to Know* (London, William P. Nimmo, 1874).
Soyer A., *A Shilling Cookery for the People* (London, Routledge, 1855).

SELECT BIBLIOGRAPHY

Staffe Baronne (trans. *Lady Colin Campbell*), *My Lady's Dressing Room* (London, Cassell, 1892).
Steele F. A. and Gardiner G., *The Complete Indian Housekeeper and Cook*, 7th edn (London, William Heinemann, 1909).
Stewart A. B., *My Simple Life in New Zealand* (London, Robert Banks & Co., 1908).
Temple-Wright Mrs R., *Flowers and Gardens in India: A Manual for Beginners*, 5th edn (Calcutta, Thacker, Spink & Co, 1902).
Temple-Wright Mrs R., *Baker and Cook* (Calcutta, Thacker, Spink & Co., 1894).
Treloar H., *Cottage Gardening in Queensland*, 4th edn (Townsville, T. Willmett & Sons, 1915).
Tremlett Mrs H., *With the Tin Gods* (London, Bodley Head, 1915).
Twopenny R., *Townlife in Australia* (London, E. Stock, 1883).
Willmett's North Queensland Alamanac: Miners, Settlers and Sugar Planters Companion (Townsville, T. Willmett, 1877).
Willmett's North Queensland Almanac: Miners, Settlers and Sugar Planters Companion (Townsville, T. Willmett, 1888).
Wright L. P., *Laura's Brookville Diaries: 1819–1894* (Launceston, Greenhill, 2003).
'Wyvern', *Culinary Jottings for Madras* (Madras, Higginbotham & Co., 1891).
Young J. (ed.), *Jane Bardsley's Outback Letter Book: Across the Years 1896–1936, Pioneer Life in Australia's Tropic North* (North Ryde, NSW, Angus & Robertson, 1987).

Secondary sources

Books

Ardener S. (ed.), *Women and Space: Ground Rules and Social Maps* (London, Croom Helm, 1981).
Arnold D. (ed.), *Cultural Identities and the Aesthetics of Britishness* (Manchester, Manchester University Press, 2004).
Attar D., *Cookery and Household Books Published in Britain 1800–1914* (London, Prospect Books, 1987).
Attfield J., *Wild Things: The Material Culture of Everyday Life* (Oxford, Berg, 2000).
Banham J., Macdonald S., and Porter J., *Victorian Design* (London, Cassell, 1991).
Bannerman C., *Acquired Tastes: Celebrating Australia's Culinary History* (Canberra, National Library of Australia, 1998).
Barnes R. and Eichner J. B. (eds.), *Dress and Gender: Making and Meaning* (Oxford, Berg, 1992).
Barr P., *The Memsahibs: The Women of Victorian India* (London, Secker & Warburg, 1976).
Barr P. and Desmond R., *Simla: A Hill Station in British India* (London, Scolar Press, 1975).

SELECT BIBLIOGRAPHY

Barthes R., *Camera Lucida: Reflections on Photography* (New York, Hill & Wong, 1981).
Barthes R., *The Fashion System* (London, Jonathan Cape, 1985).
Barthes R., *The Language of Fashion* (Oxford, Berg, 2004).
Beardshaw A. and Keil T., *Sociology on the Menu: An Invitation to the Study of Food and Society* (London, Routledge, 1997).
Black J., *North Queensland Pioneers* (Charters Towers, Country Women's Association, 1931).
Blackes M. R., *Flora Domestica: A History of Flower Arranging 1500–1930* (London, National Trust, 2000).
Bligh B., *Cherish the Earth: The Story of Gardening in Australia* (Sydney, Ure Smith, 1973).
Bolton G., *A Thousand Miles Away: A History of North Queensland to 1920* (Canberra, Australian National University, 1972).
Bourdieu P., *Distinction: A Social Critique of the Judgement of Taste* (Cambridge, University of Massachusetts, 1984).
Bourdieu P., *Outline of a Theory of Practice* (Cambridge, Cambridge University Press, 1977).
Branca P., *Silent Sisterhood: Middle-Class Women in the Victorian Home* (London, Croom-Helm, 1975).
Brett G., *Dinner is Served: A History of Dining in England 1400–1900* (London, Rupert Hart-Davis, 1968).
Broadbent J., Rickard S. and Steven M., *India, China and Australia; Trade and Society, 1788–1850* (Glebe, NSW, Historic Houses Trust of New South Wales, 2003).
Brookes B. (ed.), *At Home in New Zealand: Houses, History, People* (Wellington, Bridget Williams Books, 2000).
Bryden I. and Floyd J. (eds.), *Domestic Space: Reading the Nineteenth Century Interior* (Manchester, Manchester University Press, 1999).
Buckley C. and Fawcett H., *Fashioning the Feminine: Representation and Women's Fashion from the Fin de Siècle to the Present* (London, Tauris Publishers, 2002).
Buettner E., *Empire Families: Britons and Late Imperial India* (Oxford, Oxford University Press, 2004).
Bush J., *Edwardian Ladies and Imperial Power* (Leicester, Leicester University Press, 2000).
Calder J., *The Victorian Home* (London, Batsford, 1977).
Callaway H., *Gender, Culture and Empire* (London, Macmillan, 1987).
Cannadine D., *Ornamentalism: How the British Saw Their Empire* (London, Allen Lane, 2001).
Cannon M. (ed.), *Our Beautiful Homes, NSW. 1905: Australia's Upper Middle-Class in the Edwardian Age* (Melbourne, Today's Heritage, 1977).
Carlton C. and C., *The Significance of Gardening in British India* (Lewiston, N.Y., Edwin Mellen Press, 2004).
Cieraad I. (ed.), *At Home: An Anthropology of Domestic Space* (Syracuse, Syracuse University Press, 1999).

SELECT BIBLIOGRAPHY

Clarke P. and Spender D., *Life Lines: Australian Women's Letters and Diaries, 1788–1840* (St Leonards, Allen & Unwin, 1992).
Collingham L., *Curry: A Biography* (London, Chatto & Windus, 2005).
Crittenden V., *The Front Garden: The Story of the Cottage Garden in Australia* (Canberra, Mulini Press, 1979).
Dalley B. and Labrum B. (eds.), *Fragments: New Zealand Social and Cultural History* (Auckland, Auckland University Press, 2000).
Dalton B. J., and Gibson-Wilde D., *Townsville 1888* (Townsville, Department of History, James Cook University, 1990).
Darien-Smith K. and Hamilton P. (eds.), *Memory and History in Twentieth Century Australia* (Oxford, Oxford University Press, 1994).
Daunton-Fear R. and Vigar P., *Australian Colonial Cookery* (Adelaide, Rigby, 1977).
Davidoff L., *The Best Circles: Social Etiquette and the Season* (London, Croom Helm, 1973).
Davidoff L. and Hall C., *Family Fortunes* (London, Hutchinson, 1987).
De Grazia V. and Furlough E. (eds.), *The Sex of Things: Gender and Consumption in Historical Perspective* (Berkeley, University of California, 1996).
De la Haye A. and Wilson E. (eds.), *Defining Dress: Dress as Object, Meaning and Identity* (Manchester, Manchester University Press, 1999).
Ditmar H., *The Social Psychology of Material Possessions: To Have is to Be* (Hemel Hempstead, Harvester Wheatsheaf, 1992).
Dixon Hunt J. (ed.), *Garden History: Issues, Approaches and Methods* (Washington, D.C., Dumbarton Oaks Research Library, 1992).
Donald M. and Hurcombe L. (eds.), *Gender and Material Culture in Historical Perspective* (Basingstoke, Macmillan, 2000).
Douglas M., *Implicit Meanings: Essays in Anthropology* (London, Routledge & Kegan Paul, 1975).
Douglas M., *Purity and Danger: An Analysis of the Concepts of Pollution and Taboo* (London, Routledge, 1966).
Douglas M., *Rules and Meanings: The Anthropology of Everyday Knowledge* (Harmondsworth, Penguin, 1973).
Drummond A. (ed.), *Married and Gone to New Zealand* (Hamilton and Auckland, Paul's Book Arcade, 1960).
Drummond A. and L. R., *At Home in New Zealand: An Illustrated History of Everyday Things Before 1865* (Auckland, B. & J. Paul, 1967).
Dyson L. E., *How to Cook a Galah: Celebrating Australia's Culinary Heritage with Recipes for Today's Cooks* (Melbourne, Lothian, 2002).
Eldred-Grigg S., *A Southern Gentry: New Zealanders who Inherited the Earth* (Wellington, Reed, 1980).
Entwisle E. A., *Wallpapers of the Victorian Era* (F. Lewis, Leigh-on-Sea, 1964).
Entwistle J., *The Fashioned Body: Fashion, Dress and Modern Social Theory* (Cambridge, Polity Press, 2000).
Entwistle J. and Wilson E. (eds.), *Body Dressing* (Oxford, Berg, 2001).
Finkelstein J., *Dining Out: A Sociology of Modern Manners* (Cambridge, Polity Press, 1989).

SELECT BIBLIOGRAPHY

Finkelstein J., *The Fashioned Self* (Cambridge, Polity Press, 1991).
Flanders J., *The Victorian House* (London, HarperCollins, 2003).
Flower C., *Clothes in Australia: A Pictorial History, 1788–1980s* (Kenthurst, NSW, Kangaroo Press, 1984).
Forsyth H. K., *Remembered Gardens: Eight Women and Their Visions of an Australian Landscape* (Carlton, Victoria, Miegunyah Press, 2006).
Fortier A. M., *Migrant Belongings: Memory, Space Identity* (Oxford, Berg, 2000).
Francis M. and Hester R.T. jun., *The Meaning of Gardens* (Cambridge, Mass., MIT Press, 1990).
Gernsheim A., *Victorian and Edwardian Fashions: A Photographic Survey* (New York, Dover Publications, 1983).
Gibbs-Smith C. H., *The Fashionable Lady in the 19th Century* (London, Her Majesty's Stationary Office, 1960).
Gilchrist R., *Gender and Material Culture: The Archaeology of Religious Women* (London, Routledge, 1994).
Goody J., *Cooking, Cuisine and Class* (Cambridge, Cambridge University Press, 1982).
Gregson N. and Crewe L., *Second-Hand Cultures* (Oxford, Berg, 2003).
Guy A., Green E. and Banim M. (eds.), *Through the Wardrobe: Women's Relationships With Their Clothes* (Oxford, Berg, 2001).
Hallam E. and Hockey J., *Death, Memory and Material Culture* (Oxford, Berg, 2001).
Hammerton A. J., *Emigrant Gentlewomen* (London, Croom-Helm, 1979).
Hammerton A. J. and Thomson A., *Ten Pound Pom: Australia's Invisible Migrants* (Manchester, Manchester University Press, 2005).
Harper M. and Constantine S., *Migration and Empire* (Oxford, Oxford University Press, 2010).
Hemphill Dallett C., *Bowing to Necessities: A History of Manners in America 1620–1860* (New York, Oxford University Press, 1999).
Higman B. W., *Domestic Service in Australia* (Melbourne, Melbourne University Press, 2002).
Historic Houses Trust, *Colonial Food and Drink: 1788–1901* (Sydney, Historic Houses Trust, 1985).
Historic Houses Trust, *The Decorated Wall: Eighty Years of Wallpaper in Australia c.1850–1930* (Sydney, Historic Houses Trust, 1981).
Holcombe L., *Victorian Ladies at Home: Middle-Class Women in England and Wales, 1850–1914* (Newton Abbot, David & Charles, 1973).
Horn P., *The Rise and Fall of the Victorian Servant* (Stroud, Sutton Publishing, 1990).
Isaacs J., *The Gentle Arts: Two Hundred Years of Australian Women's Domestic and Decorative Arts* (Sydney, Lansdowne Press, 1987).
Jocic L., *Australia Made: One Hundred Years of Fashion* (Melbourne, National Gallery of Victoria, 2010).
Johnson K. P. and Lennon S. J. (eds.), *Appearance and Power* (Oxford, Berg, 1999).

SELECT BIBLIOGRAPHY

Jones R. D., *Interiors of Empire: Objects, Space and Identity within the Indian Subcontinent, c.1800–1947* (Manchester, Manchester University Press, 2007).

Keenan W. J. F. (ed.), *Dressed to Impress: Looking the Part* (Oxford, Berg, 2001).

Kellaway D. (ed.), *The Virago Book of Women Gardeners* (London, Virago Press, 1995).

Kerr J. (ed.), *Heritage: The National Women's Art Book* (Sydney, G & B Arts International, 1995).

Kincaid D., *British Social Life in India 1608–1937* (London, Routledge, 1938).

King A. D., *Colonial Urban Development* (London, Routledge Kegan Paul, 1976).

Kiple K. and Ornelas K. (eds.), *The Cambridge World History of Food, Vol. 2* (Cambridge, Cambridge University Press 2000).

Kirkham P., *Furnishing the World: The East London Furniture Trade* (London, Journeyman, 1987).

Kirkham P. (ed.), *The Gendered Object* (Manchester, Manchester University Press, 1996).

Knowlden M. (ed.), Boase A. M. and Hannah M., *When the Sun Never Set: A Family's Life in the British Empire* (London, Radcliffe Press, 2005).

Korsmeyer C., *Making Sense of Taste: Food and Philosophy* (Ithaca, Cornell University Press, 1999).

Kranidis R. S. (ed.), *Imperial Objects: Essays on Victorian Women's Emigration and the Unauthorized Imperial Experience* (New York, Twayne, 1998).

Lane T. and Searle J., *Australians at Home: A Documentary History of Australian Domestic Interiors from 1788–1914* (Melbourne, Oxford University Press, 1990).

Leach H. M., *Cultivating Myths: Fiction, Fact and Fashion in Garden History* (Auckland, Godwit, 2000).

Lech M., *Wallpaper* (Sydney, Historic Houses Trust, 2010).

Ledward D., *The Victorian Garden Catalogue* (London, Studio Editions, 1995).

Lemire B., *The Business of Everyday Life: Gender, Practice and Social Politics in England c.1600–1900* (Manchester, Manchester University Press, 2005).

Lewis R. and Foy Y., *The British in Africa* (London, Weidenfeld & Nicolson, 1971).

Lloyd J. M., *Rhodesia's Pioneer Women, 1858–1896* (Bulawayo, Rhodesian Pioneers and Settlers Society, 1974).

Logan T., *The Victorian Parlour: A Cultural Study* (Cambridge, Cambridge University Press, 2001).

Lupton D., *Food, the Body and the Self* (London, Sage, 1996).

Lyman B., *A Psychology of Food: More than a Matter of Taste* (New York, Van Nostrand Rheinhold, 1989).

Mackenzie J. M., *The Scots in South Africa: Ethnicity, Identity, Gender and Race, 1772–1914* (Manchester, Manchester University Press, 2007).

McCracken D., *Gardens of Empire: Botanical Institutions of the Victorian British Empire* (London, Leicester University Press, 2007).

SELECT BIBLIOGRAPHY

McGee D., *Writing the Meal: Dinner in the Fiction of Early Twentieth Century Women Writers* (Toronto, University of Toronto 2001).

Massey D., *Space, Place and Gender* (Cambridge, Polity Press, 1994).

Maynard M., *Dress and Globalisation* (Manchester, Manchester University Press, 2004).

Maynard M., *Fashioned from Penury: Dress as Cultural Practice in Colonial Australia* (Cambridge, Cambridge University Press, 1994).

Mennell S., *All Manner of Food: Eating and Taste in England and France from the Middle Ages to the Present* (Oxford, Basil Blackwell, 1985).

Miller D., *Why Some Things Matter* (London, University College, 1998).

Miller D. (ed.), *Home Possessions: Material Culture Behind Closed Doors* (Oxford, Berg, 2001).

Miller D., Jackson P. and Rowlands M., *Shopping, Place and Identity* (London, Routledge, 1998).

Montana A., *The Art Movement in Australia: Design, Taste and Society, 1875–1900* (Carlton, Victoria, Miegunyah Press, 2000).

Murphy P., *Historic Wallpapers in Australia: 1850–1920* (Castlemaine, Victoria, Castlemaine Art Gallery and Museum, 1996).

Panayi P., *Spicing up Britain: The Multicultural History of British Food* (London, Reaktion Books, 2008).

Paston-Williams S., *The Art of Dining: A History of Cooking and Eating* (London, National Trust, 1993).

Pownall E., *Mary of Maranoa: Tales of Australian Pioneer Women* (Sydney, F. H. Johnston, 1959).

Probyn E., *Carnal Appetites: Sex Food Identities* (London, Routledge, 2000).

Procida M. A., *Married to the Empire: Gender Politics and Imperialism in India, 1883–1947* (Manchester, Manchester University Press, 2002).

Reekie G., *On the Edge: Women's Experiences of Queensland* (St Lucia, University of Queensland Press, 1994).

Rendell J., Penner B. and Borden I. (eds.), *Gender, Space Architecture: An Interdisciplinary Introduction* (London, Routledge, 2000).

Ribeiro A., *Dress and Morality* (London, Batsford, 1986).

Riggins S. (ed.), *The Socialness of Things: Essays on the Socio-Semantics of Objects* (Berlin, Mouton de Gruyter, 1994).

Rose G., *Visual Methodologies* (London, Sage Publications, 2001)

Russell P., *A Wish of Distinction: Colonial Gentility and Femininity* (Melbourne, Melbourne University Press, 1994).

Saini B. and Joyce R., *The Australian House: Homes of the Tropical North* (Sydney, Lansdowne Press, 1982).

Samuel R. and Thompson P. (eds.), *The Myths We Live By* (London, Routledge, 1990).

Schaffer K., *Women and the Bush: Forces of Desire in the Australian Cultural Tradition* (Cambridge, Cambridge University Press, 1998).

Scourse N., *The Victorians and their Flowers* (London, Croom Helm, 1983).

Scripps L., *The Industrial Heritage of Hobart, Vol. 1 Historical Study* (Hobart, Hobart City Council, 1997).

SELECT BIBLIOGRAPHY

Seddon G., *Landprints: Reflections on Place and Landscape* (Cambridge, Cambridge University Press, 1997).

Shennan M., *Out in the Mid-day Sun: The British in Malaya 1880–1960* (London, John Murray, 2000).

Simpson H. M., *The Women of New Zealand* (Wellington, Department of Internal Affairs, 1940).

Smith M., *Aunt May's Preserves and Pickles: A Pioneer's Recipes from Tropical North Queensland* (Epping North, NSW, Merrol Media, 2003).

Spain D., *Gendered Spaces* (Chapel Hill, University of North Carolina Press, 1992).

Stanford J. K., *Ladies in the Sun: The Memsahib's India, 1760–1860* (London, Galley Press, 1962).

Stapleton M., *Historic Interiors: A Collection of Papers* (Sydney, Sydney College of Arts, 1983).

Steele V., *The Corset: A Cultural History* (New Haven, Yale University Press, 2001).

Stierstorfer K. (ed.), *Women Writing Home 1700–1920: Female Correspondence Across the British Empire* (6 vols., London, Pickering & Chatto, 2006).

Sturken M. and Cartright L., *Practices of Looking: An Introduction to Visual Culture* (Oxford, Oxford University Press, 2001).

Sutton D. E., *Remembrances of Repasts: Anthropology of Food and Memory* (Oxford, Berg, 2001).

Symons M., *One Continuous Picnic: A History of Eating in Australia* (Adelaide, Duck Press, 1982).

Tarlo E., *Clothing Matters: Dress and Identity in India* (London, Hurst & Co., 1996).

Taylor L., *The Study of Dress History* (Manchester, Manchester University Press, 2002).

Telfer E., *Food for Thought: Philosophy and Food* (London, Routledge, 1996).

Vickery A., *The Gentleman's Daughter: Women's Lives in Georgian England* (London, Yale University Press, 2003).

Vincent S. J., *The Anatomy of Fashion: Dressing the Body from the Renaissance to Today* (Oxford, Berg, 2009).

Visser M., *The Rituals of Dinner: The Origins, Evolution, Eccentricities and Meaning of Table Manners* (London, Viking, 1992).

Walkley C. and Foster V., *Crinolines and Crimping Irons: Victorian Clothes, How They Were Cleaned and Cared For* (London, Peter Owen, 1978).

Watts P., *Historic Gardens of Victoria: A Reconnaissance* (Melbourne, Oxford University Press, 1983).

Webster S., *British Wallpaper in Australia: 1870–1940* (Sydney, Historic Houses Trust, 1996).

Wetherall L., *Consumer Behaviour and Material Culture in Britain 1660–1760* (London, Routledge, 1988).

Young L., *Middle-Class Culture in the Nineteenth Century: America, Australia and Britain* (Basingstoke, Palgrave Macmillan, 2003).

SELECT BIBLIOGRAPHY

Chapters in edited collections

Ash J., 'Memory and Objects' in P. Kirkham (ed.), *The Gendered Object* (Manchester, Manchester University Press, 1996).

Archibald D. C., 'Angel in the Bush: Exporting Domesticity through Female Emigration' in R. S. Kranidis (ed.), *Imperial Objects: Essays on Victorian Women's Emigration and the Unauthorized Imperial Experience* (New York, Twayne, 1998).

Attar D., 'Keeping up Appearances: The Genteel Art of Dining in Middle-Class Victorian Britain' in C. A. Wilson (ed.), *Food and Society: The Appetite and the Eye. Visual Aspects of Food and its Presentation within the Historic Context* (Edinburgh, Edinburgh University Press, 1991).

Barthes R., 'Towards a Psychosociology of Contemporary Food Consumption' in R. Forster and O. Ranum (eds.), *Food and Drink in History* (Baltimore, Johns Hopkins University Press, 1979).

Capon J., 'The Development of Decorative Wall and Ceiling Ornament in the Colonial Period' in M. Stapleton (ed.), *Historic Interiors: A Collection of Papers* (Sydney, Sydney College of Arts, 1983).

Entwistle J., 'The Dressed Body' in J. Entwistle and E. Wilson (eds.), *Body Dressing* (Oxford, Berg, 2001).

Floyd E., 'Without Artificial Constraint: Gentility and British Gentlewomen in Rural Australia' in R. S. Kranidis (ed.), *Imperial Objects: Essays on Victorian Women's Emigration and the Unauthorized Imperial Experience* (New York, Twayne, 1998).

Innes S. A., '"An Act of Severe Duty": Emigration and Class Ideology in Susanna Moodie's Roughing it in the Bush' in R. S. Kranidis (ed.), *Imperial Objects: Essays on Victorian Women's Emigration and the Unauthorized Imperial Experience* (New York, Twayne, 1998).

Kinchin J., 'Interiors: Nineteenth Century Essays on the "Masculine" and the "Feminine" Room' in P. Kirkham (ed.), *The Gendered Object* (Manchester, Manchester University Press, 1996).

Klerk N de, 'Home Away from Home' in K. L. Ishizuka and P. R. Zimmerman (eds.), *Mining the Home Movie: Excavations in Histories and the Movies* (Berkeley, University of California Press, 2008).

Leach H.M., 'The European House and Garden in New Zealand: A Case of Parallel Develoopment' in B. Brookes (ed.), *At Home in New Zealand: Houses, History, People* (Wellington, Bridget Williams Books, 2000).

Maynard M. '"A Great Deal Too Good for the Bush": Women and the Experience of Dress in Queensland', in G. Reekie (ed.), *On the Edge: Women's Experiences of Queensland* (St Lucia, University of Queensland Press, 1994).

McPherson B., 'The Verandah as Feminine Site in the Australian Memory' in J. Horn (ed.), *Strange Women: Essays in Art and Gender* (Melbourne, Melbourne University Press, 1994).

Murcott A., 'Cooking and the Cooked: A Note on the Domestic Preparation of Meals' in A. Murcott (ed.), *The Sociology of Food and Eating: Essays on the Sociological Significance of Food* (Aldershot, Gower, 1984).

SELECT BIBLIOGRAPHY

Petridou E., 'The Taste of Home' in D. Miller (ed.), *Home Possessions: Material Culture Behind Closed Doors* (Oxford, Berg, 2001).

Taylor L., 'Women, Cloth and Gender: The Use of Woollen Cloth in Women's Dress in Britain 1865–1885' in A. de la Haye and E. Wilson (eds.), *Defining Dress: Dress as Object, Meaning and Identity* (Manchester, Manchester University Press, 1999).

Thane P., 'Late Victorian Women' in T. R. Gourvish and A. O'Day (eds.), *Late Victorian Britain, 1867–1900* (Baskingstoke, Macmillan Education, 1988).

Journal articles, conference papers and lectures

Allingham A., 'Pioneer Squatting in the Kennedy District', *Lectures on North Queensland History*, Department of History, James Cook University, 1975, pp. 77–96.

Avery T., 'Furniture Design and Colonialism: Negotiating Relationships between Britain and Australia 1880–1901', Home Cultures Vol. 4 (1), 2007, pp. 69–92.

Blum D. E., 'Englishwomen's Dress in Eighteenth Century India: The Margaret Fowke Correspondence 1776–1786', *Costume: The Journal of the Costume Society* No. 17, 1983, pp. 47–8.

Cahir P., 'Women in North Queensland', *Lectures on North Queensland History*, Department of History, James Cook University, 1975, pp. 97–117.

Chattopadhyay S., 'Goods, Chattels and Sundry Items: Constructing Nineteenth Century Anglo-Indian Domestic Life', *Journal of Material Culture* Vol. 7 (3), 2002, pp. 243–71.

Douglas M., 'Deciphering the Meal', *Daedalus* Winter 1972, pp. 61–81.

George M. R., 'Home in the Empire, Empires in the Home', *Cultural Critique* No. 26, Winter 1993–94, pp. 95–127.

Ginsburg M., 'Rags to Riches: The Second-hand Clothes Trade: 1700–1978', *Costume: The Journal of the Costume Society* No. 14, 1980, pp. 121–35.

Hawkins J., 'The 1839 Gillows Commission to Furnish "Woolmers" in Van Diemen's Land for Thomas and Susannah Archer', *Australiana* Vol. 24 (1), February 2002.

Hubbard T., 'Cultivating the Maidenhair and the Maiden Fair: The Social Role of the Late Nineteenth Century Conservatory', *Australian Garden History Society* Vol. 21 (3), January–March 2010, pp. 10–15.

Jasanoff M., 'Collections of Empire: Objects, Conquests and Imperial Self-fashioning', *Past and Present* No. 184, August 2004, pp. 109–36.

Lockren P., 'Why Were Women of the 1900s Slow to Take Up the New, More Economical Ready-made Clothing?' Pasold/Chord Conference Paper, University of Wolverhampton, 2010.

Lupton D., 'Food Memory and Meaning', *Sociological Review* 42 (4), 1994, pp. 664–85.

McGowan A. S., '"All that is Rare, Characteristic or Beautiful": Design and Defence of Tradition in Colonial India, 1851–1903', *Journal of Material Culture* Vol. 10 (3), 2005, pp. 263–87.

SELECT BIBLIOGRAPHY

Marcoux J. S., 'The "Caisser-Maison" Ritual: Constructing the Self by Emptying the Home', *Journal of Material Culture* Vol. 6 (2), 2001, pp. 213–35.

Parkin D., 'Mementoes as Transitional Objects in Human Displacement', *Journal of Material Culture* Vol. 4 (3), 1999, pp. 303–20.

Shrimpton J., 'Dressing for a Tropical Climate: The Role of Native Fabrics in Fashionable Dress in Early Colonial India', *Textile History* Vol. 23, 1992, pp. 55–70.

Simmons P., 'The Genesis of Tasmanian Gardens', Proceedings of the First Garden History Conference, National Trust of Australia (Victoria), 1980, pp. 59–62.

Sumner R., 'Pioneer Homesteads of North Queensland', *Lectures on North Queensland History*, Department of History, James Cook University, 1975, pp. 47–63.

Tarrant N. E. A., 'A Maternity Dress of about 1845–1850', *Costume: The Journal of the Costume Society* No. 14, 1980, pp. 117–20.

Toynbee C., 'Class and Social Structure in Nineteenth Century New Zealand', *New Zealand Journal of History* Vol.13 (1), 1979, pp. 65–80.

Tyrell I., 'Environment, Landscape and History: Gardening in Australia', *Australian Historical Studies* No. 130, October 2007, pp. 389–97.

Woodward I., 'Domestic Objects and the Taste Epiphany: a Resource for Consumption Methodology', *Journal of Material Culture* Vol. 6 (2), 2001, pp. 115–36.

Young L., '"Extensive, Economical and Elegant": The Habitus of Gentility in Early Nineteenth Century Sydney', *Australian Historical Studies* No. 124, 2004, pp. 201–20.

Unpublished theses

Allingham A., 'Victorian Frontierswomen: The Australian Diaries and Journals of Lucy and Eva Gray, 1868–1872 and 1881–1892', MA Thesis, James Cook University, 1987.

Hennington N. J., '"Perhaps if there had been more women in the north, the story would have been different": Gender and the History of White Settlement in North Queensland, 1840–1930', Ph.D. Thesis, University of Melbourne, 1999.

McBriar M., 'The Use of Australian Plants in Gardens of Federation and Other Edwardian houses in Melbourne 1890–1914', Thesis for Graduate Diploma in Landscape Design, Royal Melbourne Institute of Technology, 1980.

McGufficke C. M., 'Parlours in North Queensland Houses 1861–1920', MA Thesis, James Cook University, 1992.

Richardson J., 'An Annotated Edition of the Journals of Mary Morton Allport', Ph.D. Thesis, University of Tasmania, 2006.

Scripps L., 'The Domestic Life of Middle-Class Women in Tasmania during the First Half of the Nineteenth Century', BA Essay, University of Tasmania, year unknown.

SELECT BIBLIOGRAPHY

Webber K., 'Romancing the Machine: The Enchantment of Domestic Technology in the Australian Home 1850–1914', Ph.D. Thesis, University of Sydney, 1996.

Exhibitions and exhibition catalogues

'Converting the Wilderness: the Art of Gardening in Colonial Australia', Brisbane City Art Gallery and Museum, 1979.

'Tasmanian Lace-making: Miss Ada Grey-Wilson's Lace Collection' A. Melrose, Tasmanian Museum and Art Gallery, 1990.

'Furnishing the Colonial Bungalow', Historic Houses Trust of New South Wales, 2008.

Brochures

The Townsville House (Townsville, Townsville City Council, Heritage Unit, 2000).

Websites

www.dunedin.govt.nz Otago Settlers Museum, Aotearoa/New Zealand
http://search.archives.tas.gov.au Archives in Tasmania, Australia
www.hht.net.au/ Historic Houses Trust, New South Wales, Australia
www.immigration.museum.vic.gov.au National Museum of Immigration, Australia
www.leics.govt.uk/museums Leicestershire Museums Services
www.moda.mdx.ac.uk Museum of Design and Architecture, University of Middlesex
www.aucklandmuseum.com Auckland Museum, Aotearoa/New Zealand
www.ngv.gov.au National Gallery of Victoria, Melbourne, Australia
www.pictureaustralia.natlib.govt.aus Photographic Resources, National Library of Australia
www.powerhousemuseum.com Powerhouse Museum, Sydney, Australia
www.qm.qld.gov.au State Museum of Queensland, Brisbane, Australia
www.tepapa.govt.nz Te Papa Museum, Wellington, Aotearoa/New Zealand
www.timeframes.natlib.govt.nz Alexander Turnbull Library, National Library, New Zealand

INDEX

Note: 'n' after a page number indicates a note on that page.

adaptation 1, 10
  dress 28, 44, 46, 47, 64
  food 197, 201, 212
  garden 145, 157
  living room 76, 90, 127
added-value 137, 163, 164, 171, 173, 217, 222, 224
advice manuals 74, 78, 99, 100, 162, 171, 191, 200
  see also guidance manuals
affiliations 7, 8, 12, 65, 76, 80
agency of dress 14, 18, 19, 27, 35, 36, 64, 65
  food 187, 188, 191, 192, 193, 221, 227
  garden 137, 160, 179
  living room 75, 114
  material culture 6, 10, 36, 75, 127, 234
alien environment 82, 186, 187
alien territory 10, 17, 137, 237
Allport, M. Mrs, *Van Diemen's Land*
  dress 29, 31, 34–5, 36, 37, 44, 45, 46, 52
  food 202, 218–19
  garden 165, 173
  living room 102, 115
anchorage 74, 161
ant-bed floors 92, 94
anxiety 139
anxieties 16, 17, 63, 100, 118, 139, 190, 198, 203, 205
Aotearoa *see* New Zealand
Ardener S. *et al* 9, 75, 82, 175
Arts and Crafts Movement 83n29, 103, 118
attachment to place 18, 179
attachment to site 178, 179, 227
Australia 1
  dress 20–1, 24, 38, 41, 43–4, 50, 54, 55, 63
  food 193, 203, 204, 217, 219–20
  garden 137, 146, 147–8, 151–2, 157, 158, 159, 163, 171–2, 179
  living room 74, 97, 100, 102–3, 118
Australian 6, 74, 148
Australasia 74, 82, 90–2, 169

Bardsley, J. Mrs, *North Queensland* 25–6, 57, 94, 96, 107
Beeton, I. Mrs, 78, 189–90, 194, 215
Benthall, C. Mrs, *India* 4
  dress 39, 41, 47
  food 206, 214
  garden 160, 165, 166, 173
  living room 88, 109

body 3, 12, 14, 43, 44, 63, 65, 120
boundary 165, 177
boundaries 178, 235
Bourdieu P. 8, 9, 19, 26, 164, 188, 189, 200, 216–17
Bowen, G. Mrs, *New Zealand*
  dress 26, 30, 34, 58
  food 196, 214, 221,
  garden 144–5, 148–9, 152
  living room 91, 95, 113
Britishness 42, 63
'Britishness' 9, 188
Buettner E 6, 164, 206
Butler, B. Mrs, *Tasmania* 29, 33

calls 173
callers 174
calling 78, 80, 146
calling cards 146
  see also carte de visite
Cape Town
  dress 27, 28, 32, 34, 41, 43, 46–7, 51
  food 194, 219, 222
  garden 146, 156, 161, 162, 173, 176–7
  living room 80, 115, 116, 125
carpets 86, 87, 88, 89, 90, 91, 94, 151
carte de visite 20, 59–62
  see also calling cards
caste 10, 151, 167, 210
challenge 18, 154, 171, 198, 202, 212, 217
challenges 8, 10, 14, 20, 35, 75, 80, 81, 103, 106, 114, 117, 141, 148, 169, 170, 178, 192, 193, 200, 201, 211
Chattopadhyay, S. 75, 81, 109, 196, 206, 224, 225–6
Chinese migrants 107, 168, 204–6
  see also labour
'civilise' 104
civilised 76, 140
civilisation 140
civilising 2, 83, 125, 137
class 4, 5, 204, 233
cleanliness 35, 36, 212
climate 13, 24, 104, 115, 122, 127, 141, 146, 159, 169, 191, 198
climates 1, 2, 14, 17–28, 81, 86, 122, 127, 148, 174, 211
commodity
  dress 63
  food 198, 214

[257]

INDEX

commodity (cont.)
  living room 86, 91, 100, 103, 109
  servants as 200, 207, 208
  see also labour
commodities
  dress 16, 17, 29, 30, 31, 32, 42, 43, 55
  food 200, 210, 221, 222, 224
  living room 79, 86, 91, 93, 96, 107
  see also supply/supplies
competitive 43, 51, 159, 197
consumption 3, 4, 12, 50, 75, 77, 91, 95, 187, 188, 226, 237
control 2, 3, 18, 25, 35, 37, 65, 86, 124, 140–1, 187, 191, 200, 223, 237
cook 201, 202, 203, 204, 207, 212, 225
cookery books 187, 215, 217, 218
Corbett, C. *India* 47, 109, 117
corsets 23, 25–6
Courage, S. Mrs, *New Zealand* 145, 152–3, 201–2
crinolines 26, 58
cultural authority 186, 191, 200, 226, 236
cultural capital 5, 79, 187, 191
cultural expertise 142, 144, 226
  see also expertise
cultural landscape 2, 17, 191, 226
cultural value 115, 151, 217
  values 64, 65
Curzon, M. Lady, *India* 21–3, 99n70

dainty 197, 199, 213
'dainty' 125
diet 215, 217, 222
diets 171, 217
diners 190, 191, 192, 213, 214
dining 190,191, 193, 199, 213
dinner party 196, 216, 222
dirzees (sic) 47, 48, 51
  see also tailors
display food 193, 194
  garden 139, 148, 149, 162, 163, 165, 175, 180
  living room 73, 80, 124, 127, 128
distinction 10, 31, 104, 127, 158, 204, 206, 207 225, 235
Douglas M. 19, 188, 214, 220
drapers 16, 49, 55
  drapery 26, 48
dress 10, 12–72
  assembling the look 52–62
  in Britain 15–17
  caring for 27, 35–8
  in colonies 17–20
  devising new 45–52
  for all weathers 20–8
  re-cycling/modifying 29–35
  sourcing textiles 38–44
dressmakers 45, 46, 47, 49, 51, 58
duty 15, 17, 190, 212, 227

Eden, C., *North Queensland* 26, 92, 96, 104, 107, 221
Eden, E. Miss, *India* 18, 26–7, 56–7, 105
egalitarianism 74, 159, 236
elite 18, 19, 80, 117, 167, 168, 209
elites 9, 16, 18, 27, 30, 35, 44, 48, 88, 128, 204, 236, 237
elitist 136
  see also superiority
Englishwoman's Domestic Magazine 29, 30–1, 32, 51, 53, 151
etiquette 50, 78
  see also calling
expertise in dress 12, 14, 31, 35, 38, 47
  food 189, 222, 226
  garden 137, 139, 141, 157, 167, 168, 173
  living room 80, 91, 118, 125, 128
  see also cultural expertise

fabrics 13, 28, 31, 32, 38, 39, 43, 44, 50, 88
  see also textiles
fashion
  dress 13–14, 26, 51, 52, 53, 54, 56, 58
  food 194
  living room 76, 99, 118, 125
fashionable garden 148, 157, 163
feminine
  dress 28, 45, 142
  garden 142
  living room 77, 78, 85, 120, 127
'feminine' garden 138
feminise food 194
feminised living room 105, 124
femininity
  dress 15, 18, 65
  living room 83, 86, 124, 125
Floyd E. 6, 50
food/household management 10, 186–232
  in Britain 189–91
  in colonies 191–3
  fruit and vegetables 220–3
  kitchen 211–13
  meat 217–20
  menus/recipes 213–17
  presentation 193–200
  quantifying housekeeping 223–6
  servants 200–11
  see also garden; kitchen foodstuffs 169, 191, 198, 221
frock 18, 19
  see also garment
furniture 75, 83–4, 88, 105–13, 118, 124

Gambia 23, 28, 43, 169, 196, 213
garden 10, 64, 135–85
  in Britain 138–40
  in colonies *intro*, 140–5
  flower 137, 139, 145, 150–64, 165
  front 137, 145–9

[258]

INDEX

kitchen 137, 145, 164–74
   see also food, fruit and vegetables, menus/recipes
  on verandah 137, 174–7
gardeners (employees) 138, 165, 168, 170, 202
   see also labour
garment 28, 31, 33, 38, 39, 45–6, 53, 58
garments 13, 14, 15, 27, 28, 29, 31, 32, 33, 50, 52, 53
   see also frock
gaze 18, 19, 165, 177
'gaze' 66
gifts 55–7, 84, 173
   see also requests
Godden, R. and J., *India* 25, 47–8, 92–3, 125, 175, 212
Godley, C. Mrs, *New Zealand*
  dress 53, 56
  garden 154, 156, 159–60, 201
  living room 90–1, 114
Gold Coast, West Africa 64, 83–4, 161, 107–8, 208
grass-matting 93–5
Gray, E. Mrs, *North Queensland* on
  dress 34–8, 51
  food 210, 218, 221, 227
  garden 171
Gray, L. Mrs, *North Queensland*
  on Cape Town 27
  food 199, 204–5, 207
  garden 146, 167–8, 170, 179
  living room 81, 104, 107
Gray, R., *North Queensland* 37, 160, 205
Greenwood, S. Mrs, *New Zealand* 29, 57, 82
guidance manuals 16, 74, 85, 189, 190, 206, 212
   see also advice manuals

habitus 78, 135, 178
harmonium 115, 117, 124
hats 27, 31, 33–4
Henning, R., *North Queensland* 27, 45–6, 65, 103
hierarchies of practice 189, 198
home 8, 84, 91, 160, 191, 224
home-grown 145, 169, 216
homemaker 77, 83, 191
homemakers
  food 201, 212, 217, 226
  garden 137, 141
  living room 75, 77, 78, 96, 98, 99, 100, 102, 104, 107, 108, 118
homes 3, 4, 75, 81, 96, 98, 135, 148
hostess 46, 78, 140, 171, 193
household 4
  dress 10, 34, 49
  food 187, 188, 190, 191, 192, 201, 206, 217, 225, 226

  garden 137, 141, 146, 149, 165, 166, 167, 174, 180
  living room 80, 88, 91, 105, 114, 117, 123, 128
household manager 189, 223
households
  dress 10, 46, 65
  food 190, 196, 198, 201, 220
  garden 138, 145
  living room 73, 83, 100, 103, 116, 127
household accounts 29, 189, 191, 203, 223–6

identity 3, 5, 7, 10, 234
  dress 14, 19, 35, 63, 64, 65
  food 186, 200, 224, 227
  garden 135, 154, 178, 180
  living room 73, 74, 75, 84, 95, 113, 118, 127, 128
identities 1, 5, 7, 14
ideological 6, 14, 76, 140
ideology 4, 5, 9, 36, 233, 238
ideologies 54, 73, 86
image 12, 65, 74, 138, 196, 223, 227, 236
imperial cause 128, 136, 140, 180
imperial enterprise 7, 74
imperial project 64, 65, 237
India 1, 2, 3, 6, 41, 42
  dress 21, 23, 25, 26–7, 28, 32, 34, 36, 37, 39, 41, 47, 48, 51, 54, 56–7, 63
  food 212, 213, 214, 220–1, 223, 225, 227
  food and servants 201, 206, 209
  garden 137, 142–3, 146, 147, 151, 152–3, 155, 156, 159, 160, 161–2, 164, 165, 166, 169, 170–1, 172, 173
  living room 79, 80, 81, 82, 84, 85, 88, 90, 92–3, 95, 97, 99, 105, 108, 109, 113, 123, 124
  verandah 174, 175, 177
indigenous fauna 21, 217
   see also mats
indigenous flora 142, 155, 156–7, 157, 158
indigenous peoples 35, 82, 177, 178, 213
Indigenous peoples, Australia 204, 205–6
   see also labour
indigenous species 125, 158, 178
ingredients 189, 214, 221, 222
insecurities 63, 77, 100, 198
insider 8, 193, 197
interiority 10, 23 75, 79, 81, 96, 109, 114, 127, 128, 140, 154

Jacob, V. Mrs, *India* 81, 124, 125, 147, 166, 177
Jewry, M. 190, 191
Jones, R. D. 75, 85, 109–10, 113, 124
journals 15, 161
   see also periodicals

Kenyon, E., *India* 28, 79, 90, 113, 162, 172, 206
kitchen 165, 173, 197, 201, 211–13

INDEX

labour 36, 88, 90, 96, 141, 147, 148, 163, 168, 170, 178, 189, 201, 205, 210
language of flowers 120, 125, 137, 142
Larymore, C., Mrs, *Nigeria*
 dress 23, 24, 38
 food 212–13, 207–8, 209
 garden 140, 147, 153, 154, 157, 159, 161, 169, 173, 175, 179
 living room 94–5, 96, 105, 108
laundering 36, 48, 194
laundress 36, 202
laundry 27, 191
 see also cleanliness
Leach, M. H. 136, 146, 148, 151, 163, 164
Leith-Ross, S., Mrs, *Nigeria* 84–5, 94, 146, 194
living room 10, 24, 39, 64, 66, 73–134, 140, 150–1,
 in Britain 76–9
 for changing lives 79–85
 floors 85–95
 ceilings 75, 95–8
 furniture 105–13
 needle and craft 118–24
 piano 75, 88, 114–18
 plant material 124–7
 see also table art
local circumstances 1, 2, 13, 20, 44, 45, 52, 55, 57, 58, 113, 126, 157, 221
Loudon, Jane 138, 151
Loudon, John 138, 150–1, 162

mail-order 15, 47, 49, 53, 55, 58, 64, 113
Malloy, G. Mrs, *Western Australia* 1
 dress 44, 46, 52, 56
 garden 151, 155–6, 157, 171
 language of flowers 142
 piano 114–15
 see also harmonium
man of the house 4, 150, 152, 162
Massey, A. Mrs, *India* 125
 food 220–1, 227
 garden 166–7, 172, 177
mats 86, 92, 94
 see also carpets, grass-matting and rugs
Maynard, M. 13, 18, 21, 24, 46, 50, 55, 63
meals 188, 189, 197, 199, 213, 214, 217, 220
meat 19, 192, 198, 215, 217–20
Melville, E. H., Mrs, *Sierra Leone* 46, 81, 105, 116, 206–7, 208, 212
memories 84, 127, 128, 153, 164, 227
 see also nostalga/nostalgic
memory 7, 84, 106, 127, 128, 235
menfolk 3, 4, 5, 57, 63, 74, 79, 123, 140, 160, 162, 179, 233
menus 189, 192, 213–17
 see also recipe/recipes
Meredith, M., Mrs, *Tasmania* 36, 49
 food 202
 garden 156, 160, 168–70, 176
 language of flowers 142
 living room 106, 108–9, 115, 118, 119
migrancy 228, 233–8
migrant 2, 8, 10, 78, 84, 127, 180, 234, 235, 238
migrants 1, 2, 3, 6, 7, 8, 53, 56, 57, 63, 84, 95, 154, 157, 205, 217, 235, 237
migration 1, 5, 8, 9, 17, 191, 238
Miller D *et al* 6, 9, 14, 75, 213
mistress of the house 73, 82, 106, 109, 124, 137, 141, 150, 162, 166, 171, 175, 187, 192, 201, 208, 222, 225, 227
 in Britain 190, 191
mistress-servant dynamic 192, 200, 201–11
modification 1, 10, 26, 34, 35, 44, 57, 64, 76, 127
modifications 31, 212
Moore, D., Mrs, *Gold Coast, West Africa* 83–4, 107–8, 161, 208
moral worth 5, 15, 138
museum 13, 75
museums 13, 136

needlework 38, 45, 46, 48, 75, 78
 see also living room, needle and craft
negotiation of circumstances 19, 106, 127, 193
newspapers 15, 20, 32, 36, 54, 58, 94, 97, 101, 103, 116, 158–9, 202
New Zealand 1
 dress, 20, 26, 29, 30, 34, 43–4, 52–3, 56, 58, 63
 food, 196, 210, 211, 214, 217, 219–20, 227
 and servants 201–2, 203, 210
 garden 137, 140, 141, 144–5, 146, 147, 148, 149, 151, 152, 154–5, 156–7, 159–60, 161, 162, 163, 164, 166, 167, 170, 173, 174
 living room 82, 90, 91, 95, 97, 105, 106, 113, 114, 122
Nigeria
 dress 19, 23, 38, 64
 food 194, 207–8, 212–13, 214, 222
 garden 137, 140, 146, 147, 153, 154, 157, 159, 169, 175, 179
 living room 94–5, 96, 105, 108
North Queensland 2
 dress 17, 20, 25, 26, 30, 32, 33, 37, 38, 41, 44, 45, 49, 50, 51, 54, 55, 57, 58, 65
 food 191, 198, 199, 218, 221, 222, 225, 227
 and servants 203, 204–5, 207, 210
 garden 141, 144, 151, 160–1, 163, 167, 170, 173, 174, 175, 177, 179
 living room 79, 80, 81, 82, 92, 93, 94, 96, 97, 103–4, 105, 107, 108, 110–11, 115–16, 122, 123, 124
nostalga 145, 172, 187
nostalgic 152, 157, 235

INDEX

off-the-peg 32, 43, 45, 47, 50
   see also ready made
Orrinsmith, L. Mrs, 39–40, 86, 87–8, 99
'other' 18, 43, 48, 65, 97, 177, 178, 179, 193
'otherness' 13, 18, 35
outsider 8, 65, 128, 197, 226

Pacific Islanders 37, 168, 204–6
   see also labour
paper patterns 51, 54
performance 3, 4, 6, 9, 10, 235
   dress, 17, 27, 29, 30, 31, 33, 35, 38, 39, 42, 47, 52, 56, 58, 66
   dress in Britain 12, 16
   food 186, 187, 192, 193, 194, 196, 198, 200, 211, 214, 222, 226, 228
   food servants 200, 201, 202, 21
   garden 135, 136, 137, 139, 148, 150, 151, 159, 162, 164, 165, 174, 180
   living room 73, 78, 83, 93, 117, 124, 127, 128
performative 3, 9, 12, 74, 192
periodicals 15, 53, 54, 58, 139, 155, 163, 194
photographs 15, 20, 24, 26
photography 20, 85
photographic 20, 85, 125
physical effort 152, 165
physical work 56, 178, 166, 167, 168
preparation food 10, 187, 189, 210, 211, 226
presentation dress 18, 38
   food 10, 187, 190, 192, 193, 197, 198, 200, 223, 226
   garden 146, 149

Queensland
   dress 21, 26, 45, 46, 56, 57–8,
   food 194
   garden 153, 161, 167, 170, 171, 173, 179
   living room 80

racial 10, 18, 193, 204, 228
racial elite 18
racialised 18, 82, 204
racist 168
rank 10, 176, 155, 193, 206, 207, 236
ranking 162
ready-to-wear 45, 51, 53
   see also off-the-peg
recipe 214, 215
recipes, 213–15, 218, 222
refashioning 1, 9, 128
refinement 3, 4, 31, 44, 73, 78, 90, 96, 100, 102, 114, 145, 157, 197
Reid Scott, J., Tasmania 29, 49, 203
Reilly R., India 41, 42, 79
relocate 1, 2, 8
relocating 4
relocation 1, 2, 7, 9, 10, 16, 17, 238
requests 55–7, 172
   see also gifts

resettlement 1, 8, 10
rugs 91, 92, 93, 95
   see also carpets/mats
Russell, I., Mrs, Gambia dress 23–4, 28, 43,
   food 196, 213, 222
   garden 169
Russell, P. 3, 4–5, 6, 74
Rutherfoord, E., Miss, Cape Town dress 34, 46–7, 48, 51
   food 194
   garden 156, 161, 176–7
   piano 116

Scott, N., Lady, India 84, 88, 209
second-hand
   dress 29–31
   furniture 109–10, 113
self 9, 10, 12, 15, 19, 37, 64, 65, 194, 233
Selwyn, S. Mrs, New Zealand 52–3, 105, 106
servant and dress 97, 146, 147
servants and dress 24, 30, 36–8, 64
   food 189, 190, 191, 192, 193, 200–11, 222
   garden 146, 147, 152, 162, 167, 168, 169, 178
   living room 82, 91, 102, 106
   see also labour
settlement 2, 30, 32, 46, 50, 56, 63, 103, 160, 161, 202, 205, 220
settler 2, 211, 235
settlers 20, 29, 30, 43, 103, 108, 140, 154, 163, 170, 198, 202, 205, 217, 221
sewing 45, 46, 47
sewing machines 51, 54, 118
Sierra Leone 46, 81, 95, 96, 105, 116, 206–7, 208, 212
site-specific identity 84, 135
site-specific subjectivities 73, 226
social cohesion 128, 188
social force 66, 180, 191, 226, 228, 233
social hierarchy 8, 75, 76, 82, 162, 173
social inferiors 16, 44, 179
social positioning 4, 214
social power 76, 158, 235
social standing 12, 117, 146, 168
social value 99, 222
sojourners 2, 140, 235
sourcing 10
   dress 29, 38, 41, 44
   food 220, 221, 226, 227
   for garden 154, 155, 156, 159, 171
   for living room 91, 95
South Africa
   dress 17, 28
   food 217–18
   garden 137, 142, 152, 154, 159, 161, 177
   servants 203–4
space 9
   dress 18, 19, 20
   food 194, 200, 212, 226

INDEX

space (cont.)
   garden 135, 137, 139, 140, 148, 166, 178, 180
   living room 73, 80, 81, 82, 83, 85, 86, 96, 105
   psychological space 161, 179
   verandah 174, 175, 177
Stamper, C., Mrs, *India* 81, 179
status 4, 5, 8, 10, 235
   dress 16, 17, 36, 52
   food 193, 203, 214, 217, 224
   garden 138, 145, 166, 167, 176
   living room 76, 82, 93, 115
Stewart, A., Mrs, *New Zealand*
   food 211, 217
   garden 145, 146, 149, 154–5, 156, 157, 161
   living room 122
strategies 10, 14, 20, 29, 30, 44, 75, 79, 84, 106, 115, 163, 178, 192, 193, 201
style
   dress 13–14, 15, 16, 18, 31–2, 49, 50, 51, 52–61
   food 190, 197
   living room 77, 81
subject 3, 12, 14, 23, 74, 106, 224
subjective 15, 78
subjectivities 10, 73, 135, 180, 226
subjectivity 3, 9, 12, 17, 19, 64, 79, 114, 128, 187, 221, 234, 235
superiority 3, 9, 18, 88, 180, 193, 228
supplies
   dress 14, 29, 50, 56, 66
   food 214, 220, 225
   garden 141, 172
   living room 90, 103, 108, 112–13, 116
   see also commodity/commodities
supply
   dress 30, 32
   garden 137, 155, 158, 170, 171, 172
   living room 90, 103, 108, 112–13, 116

table 107, 139, 193, 194, 196, 198, 199, 213
'table art' 196, 197
table cloths 194, 199
tableware 189, 194, 196, 199
tailors 45, 48
   see also dirzees/dressmaker/s
Tasmania 2
   dress 20–1, 29, 36, 49, 51, 54, 55, 58,
   food 220
   and servants 202, 203
   garden 141, 142, 148, 151, 153, 155, 156, 158–9, 160, 168–70, 173, 174, 176

living room 36, 88, 79, 91, 93, 97, 100–2, 103, 106–7, 108–9, 110, 115, 119, 120–1, 123
taste 8, 13, 52, 54, 73, 76, 79, 87, 127, 142, 158, 189, 214, 216–17
tasteful 85, 135
Taylor, L. 28, 53
tea table 199
technological developments 15, 28, 51, 77, 98, 141, 146, 158
Temple-Wright, R., Mrs, 146, 147, 151, 152, 166
Terry, S., Mrs, *India* 4, 39, 222
textiles
   dress 10, 13, 14, 16, 20, 28, 29, 30, 31–2, 33, 35–44, 50
   living room 77, 96, 97, 104, 106–7, 123
   moral meaning 39, 53
   table-cloth 194
Tremlett, H. Mrs, *Nigeria* 19, 64

Van Diemen's Land
   dress 29, 31, 33, 34–5, 36, 37, 44, 45, 46, 52
   food 218
   garden 154, 155, 156, 158–9, 165, 173
   living room 95, 115
verandah 20, 24,
   dining 199, 200
   garden 136, 137, 146, 163, 164, 174–7

wages of servants 191, 203, 207, 209, 225
wallcoverings 77, 99–105, 106
West Africa 1, 2
   dress 24, 41, 43, 64
   food 206–7, 208, 209
   and servants 201
   garden 140, 141, 147, 161, 169, 173, 174
   and verandah 174, 177
   living room 83, 107–8
Western Australia 1
   dress 44, 46, 52, 56
   garden 151, 155–6, 157, 171
   language of flowers 142
   piano 114–15
wilderness 19, 83, 125, 146, 237
wildlife 170, 174, 177, 178
Williams, J., Mrs, *India and Tasmania* 34, 156
Wright, L., Mrs, *Tasmania* dress 30, 49
   food 220
   garden 170, 173
   language of flowers 142
   living room 102, 119

Young, L. 5, 6, 74, 82

EU authorised representative for GPSR:
Easy Access System Europe, Mustamäe tee 50,
10621 Tallinn, Estonia
gpsr.requests@easproject.com

www.ingramcontent.com/pod-product-compliance
Lightning Source LLC
Chambersburg PA
CBHW030119240426
43673CB00041B/1337